D1272820

DATE DUE

Louisiana in the
Age of Jackson

LOUISIANA IN THE AGE OF JACKSON

A Clash of Cultures and Personalities

JOSEPH G. TREGLE, JR.

Louisiana State University Press   *Baton Rouge*

Designer: Michele Myatt Quinn
Typeface: Goudy Old Style
Typesetter: Wilsted & Taylor Publishing Services
Printer and binder: Edwards Brothers, Inc.

Portions of Chapter II first appeared as "Early New Orleans Society: A Reappraisal," *Journal of Southern History*, XVIII (1952), 20–36, and are reprinted by permission. Portions of Chapter IV first appeared as "The Political Apprenticeship of John Slidell," *Journal of Southern History*, XXVI (1960), 57–70, and are reprinted by permission. Portions of Chapter IX first appeared as "Andrew Jackson and the Continuing Battle of New Orleans," *Journal of the Early Republic*, I (1981), 373–94, and are reprinted by permission.

Library of Congress Cataloging-in-Publication Data

Tregle, Joseph George, 1919–
    Louisiana in the age of Jackson : a clash of cultures and
personalities / Joseph G. Tregle, Jr.
        p. cm.
    Revision of the author's thesis (Ph.D.)—University of
Pennsylvania, 1954.
    Includes bibliographical references and index.
    ISBN 0-8071-2292-0 (cloth : alk. paper)
    1. Louisiana—Politics and government—1803–1865. 2. Louisiana—
Ethnic relations. 3. United States—Politics and
government—1829–1837. 4. Jackson, Andrew, 1767–1845. I. Title.
F374.T74 1999
976.3'05—dc21   98-24708
                                                    CIP

Contents

Preface   ix

Abbreviations Used in Notes   xi

I
Hesperides on the Nile   1

II
The Ethnic Imperative   23

III
Frontier on the Mississippi   42

IV
Skeleton of Iron   54

V
Both Their Houses   79

VI
The Transcendent Ego   98

VII
Birth of a Cause   131

VIII
The Spirit of '98   174

IX
Democracy Triumphant   208

X
Democracy Regnant   229

XI
Democracy Discordant   265

XII
Valedictory   296

Epilogue   333

Appendix: On the Term *Creole*   337

Bibliography   345

Index   361

Illustrations

following page 200

Andrew Jackson

Pro-Jackson campaign broadside

Henry Clay

Edward Livingston

Alexander Porter

Caricature of Etienne Mazureau

John Slidell

John Randolph Grymes

Jacques Villeré

Bernard Marigny

Jean B. Plauché

Edward Douglass White

Preface

This study of Louisiana in the early part of the nineteenth century is a revised and updated version of a doctoral dissertation presented at the University of Pennsylvania in 1954. Primarily a political essay, the work takes up the affairs of the state around 1820, at a time when the transition from territorial status had matured enough to allow the emergence of some adaptation of the techniques of American politics on both local and federal levels.

The special relationship of Andrew Jackson and Henry Clay to Louisiana in the early decades of the century provided a decided stimulus to the state's interest in national affairs, while the local struggle between the French and Anglo-American populations for ethnic supremacy continued to rack the community in a completely different parochial political contest which confused even those most familiar with its patterns. Behind these battles for favorites and factions lay the geographic, social, and cultural forces which gave shape to the loyalties and action of the people, and the introductory chapters of the work attempt therefore to sketch those basic features of Louisiana life in the 1820s and 1830s which would find reflection in its political experience.

No other state seems to have been so seriously affected by ethnic cleavage as Louisiana in the early nineteenth century, and the chapters which follow seek to explain how this issue produced the two strands of national and local politics in the community, each spun from diverse threads which only occasionally came together by chance or skillful planning. The relationship of the state to the concept of "Jacksonian Democracy" is also examined, for continuing debate over the nature and significance of the Jacksonian era must indeed turn upon findings drawn from disparate and distinctive component parts of the Union. No national expression is likely to be determined simply from the vantage point of the Potomac, the Hudson, or the Harvard Yard.

The passage of years has provided access to many sources unavailable in 1954, allowing amplification and extension of several aspects of the original manuscript. The work retains, however, what some might call the old-fashioned narrative style of historical writing, though, as noted, I have tried to provide a comprehensive analysis of the social, cultural, and demographic milieu in which political events developed. Findings from newer techniques employing quantitative analysis of data bases may eventually add to our understanding of the issues and topics considered here, but as shown in a 1970s effort to apply the new approach to Jacksonian Louisiana, to date, the paucity of reliable statistics has not allowed the methodology to add much substance to the account. That new dimension waits, accordingly, upon the work of others.

My greatest debt in 1954, as it is now, was to my mentor and dear friend, the late professor Roy F. Nichols, whose belief in the value of local and regional studies provided the inspiration for this work. Acknowledgment of the help and guidance of others who made the project possible may be found in the original dissertation manuscript, and it is my profound regret that so few of them are still among us to receive my renewed gratitude. For their more recent assistance in bringing the work to publication I am equally indebted to Sylvia Frank, Catherine Kadair, and John Easterly of the Louisiana State University Press; Sarah Doerries, for her invaluable editing skills; and James Sefcik and Shannon Glasheen of the Louisiana State Museum, and Jon Kukla and Sally Stassi of the Historic New Orleans Collection.

Abbreviations Used in Notes

FRC   Federal Records Center, Fort Worth, Texas

GRDS General Records of the Department of State

GRDT General Records of the Department of the Treasury

HU   Houghton Library, Harvard University

HSP   Historical Society of Pennsylvania

JSH   *Journal of Southern History*

LC   Library of Congress

LH   *Louisiana History*

LHQ   *Louisiana Historical Quarterly*

LSM   Louisiana State Museum

LSU   Hill Memorial Library, Louisiana State University

MHS   Massachusetts Historical Society

MSA   Mississippi State Department of History and Archives

MVHR *Mississippi Valley Historical Review*

NA   National Archives

NYHS New-York Historical Society

NOPL   New Orleans Public Library, Louisiana Collection

NYPL   New York Public Library

PLHS   *Publications of the Louisiana Historical Society*

PU   Firestone Library, Princeton University

RG   Record Group

THS   Tennessee Historical Society

TU   Howard-Tilton Memorial Library, Tulane University

UNC   Southern Historical Collection, University of North Carolina

Louisiana in the Age of Jackson

· I ·

HESPERIDES ON THE NILE

No spot on earth was more desolate and lonely than the Balize in the early part of the nineteenth century. Here where the great floods of the Mississippi rushed to wash themselves in the clearer depths of the Gulf, only a small cluster of shacks huddled about the base of the lighthouse which marked the southeast pass of the river revealed that even in this dreary expanse of mire man had set his outposts. For miles without visible end there stretched away on all sides a yet unformed mass, suspended between liquid and solid state, empty of verdure or signs of life. Only the river seemed to live, unchanging and untiring in its search for the sea, unceasing in its creation of this emptiness from the fullness of its waters.

Few persons indeed looked out upon this morass unmoved by a sense of the "full sublimity of desolation," but fewer yet lost themselves for long in pondering upon the vagaries of nature. For in truth this was a land of hope, not of despair. To those who caught sight of its flickering lamp for the first time, the Balize appeared as a beacon standing at the entrance to a new world, guiding the way to the riches of Louisiana. Up the course of the great river lay lands of fabulous fertility, ready to burgeon with cotton and cane. Smaller streams and bayous ramified through the state like a great web, carrying the same gift of fecundity into prairies and rolling uplands. And on the crescent bend of the Mississippi itself stood New Orleans, a crossroad of the world, bustling and charming, dirty and delightful, disease-ridden and joyous, and, above all, growing and prospering. Greatest export city of the United States, financial and trading capital for the whole Mississippi valley, New Orleans in the early 1800s rejoiced in the certainty of her destiny. Others found themselves captured by it as well and came streaming into her cramped quarters—clerks, merchants, physicians, Irish laborers, German butchers, lawyers and gamblers, all anxious to share in the startling growth of the metropolis of the West.

To these vast acres of land unrivaled in fertility, to the noisy marts of a city which controlled the trade of the greatest river on the continent: to all this did the Balize stand as invitation. And the invited came.

Three major routes led into early Louisiana. One of these was by sea, past the Balize and up the river to the settled parts of the state. The going-up provided an experience not soon forgotten. Quiet and mysterious, the naked shores stretched interminably, uninhabited save for large white birds staring impassively at the moving ships amidst countless alligators dozing on logs lodged against the trembling borders of the river.[1] Mile after mile, nothing changed. Silence and empty distances enfolded everything in this empire of mud. Then, twelve leagues upstream from the Gulf, the marsh finally congealed into land solid enough to hold Forts Jackson and St. Philip,[2] but not until the traveler had come to within twenty or thirty miles of New Orleans did the first signs of regular human habitation and industry begin to make their appearance.[3] Great earthen embankments rose up on either side to protect the lands from the overflow of the Mississippi, and beyond their summits could be seen fields of sugarcane, corn, and rice surrounding a typical raised plantation dwelling of the area. This generally sat back some two hundred yards from the levee, approached along a graveled walk which ran from the embankment through a large gateway into gardens of fabulous tropical growth and splendor, where oranges, pomegranates, figs, and lemons dangled from the shade trees as they formed a canopy over the path to the central building. In the Lower Coast country, as the delta lands below New Orleans were called, most "big houses" sat upon

1. J. E. Alexander, *Transatlantic Sketches* (2 vols.; London, 1833), II, 1–12; Basil Hall, *Travels in North America in the Years 1827–1828* (2 vols.; Philadelphia, 1829), II, 289.

2. Forts Jackson and St. Philip were forty-three miles above the mouth of the Mississippi and some sixty miles below New Orleans. W. Bullock, "Sketch of a Journey through the Western States of North America," in *Early Western Travels*, ed. R. G. Thwaites (32 vols.; Cleveland, 1904–1907), III, 121.

3. [Joseph H. Ingraham], *The Southwest. By a Yankee* (2 vols.; New York, 1835), I, 74.

great brick columns which allowed air to circulate freely beneath the living quarters and kept a safe distance between floor and earth, testimony to the unceasing war against heat and water. The dwellings themselves, almost always of wood, gleamed white in the sunshine. Slender pillars on all sides looked in on wide verandahs protected by louvered blinds and lattices and strung with hammocks for restful enjoyment of the river breezes.[4]

Beyond the main house lay the service buildings and slave quarters, usually neat and orderly rows of huts towered over by the great plantation bell and generally crowded with every conceivable mixture of young and old, in close companionship with the inevitable throng of dogs, pigs, and chickens which provided at least some sense of ownership to the black bondsmen. Fields ran back from the levee for one or two miles, until the swamps reasserted their claim and once more held sway. The cultivatable areas yielded bountiful crops of corn, rice, tobacco, indigo, and sugar, but generally proved too fertile and lush for cotton. Though it grew along this Lower Coast, the white-bud plant was happiest in the higher upland country.[5]

Topping the levee in front of the estates ran the road to New Orleans, through more and more densely populated countryside, where roses grew in a luxuriance and color seen in few parts of the world. On the river, the ships grew more and more numerous the closer one came to the city, until finally those which had made the slow ascent up from the Balize found themselves vying for space with smaller rafts and great steamboats from the north, all maneuvering for position along the crowded levee fronting the metropolis.[6]

These vessels from above had followed the second major route into Louisiana, down the many rivers and streams which emptied into the Mississippi, and down the great Mississippi itself, floating with the current or

4. *Ibid.*, 80.

5. David B. Warden, *A Statistical, Political, and Historical Account of the United States of North America* (3 vols.; Edinburgh, 1819), II, 493. Other interesting accounts of this Lower Coast area may be found in Frances Trollope, *Domestic Manners of the Americans* (2 vols.; New York, 1894), I, 2; Thomas Hamilton, *Men and Manners in America* (2 vols.; Philadelphia, 1833), II, 119; Charles Daubeny, *Journal of a Tour Through the United States and in Canada, Made During the Years 1837–1838* (Oxford, 1843), 137; Harriet Martineau, *Retrospect of Western Travel* (3 vols.; London, 1838), II, 155; Louis F. Tasistro, *Random Shots and Southern Breezes* (2 vols.; New York, 1842), II, 10 ff.

6. Martineau, *Retrospect*, II, 155; [Ingraham], *The Southwest*, I, 84; James Stuart, *Three Years in North America* (3 vols.; Edinburgh, 1833), II, 255 ff.

pushed along by churning paddle-wheels. They first met the state some three hundred miles north of New Orleans, where the river still formed a boundary separating Mississippi from the Louisiana parish of Concordia to the west. There rolling bluff lands followed the sweep of the Mississippi southward in a long attenuated stretch, until the river finally reached its juncture with the Red, which had coursed down from the northwest for the union. Then the great currents of the mingled rivers left both Concordia and Mississippi behind to push into the heart of antebellum Louisiana. Southward from the mouth of the Red, beginning with Pointe Coupee Parish on the west and West Feliciana on the east, the shores of the Mississippi bounded a much more highly cultivated agrarian region than anything found in the still sparsely settled Concordia area to the north. From this point began that rich belt along both sides of the river known as the Mississippi Coast, extending some 150 miles down to New Orleans and continuing past that city as the Lower Coast for approximately 20 or 30 miles more. Within this area just above New Orleans lay subdivisions famed as the German and Acadian Coasts, the first including the parishes of St. Charles and St. John the Baptist, the second embracing St. James and Ascension, and each indicating by name the character of its first settlers.[7]

In Pointe Coupee, where the levees began their stand against the river, cotton and sugar flourished together, sustaining an area noted for lovely orange groves and clumps of great oaks. Directly across the river in West Feliciana the lands ran in high bluffs, stretching back into rolling hills where abundant laurel and oak gave unerring sign of luxuriant soil and led inland to similar richness in the companion parish of East Feliciana. To its inhabitants the region seemed one of "almost fairy beauty," abounding in fertile valleys pierced by rock-filled streams, with placid lakes and a profusion of wild flowers and birds. At the crest of a long ridge overlooking the river sat the principal town of St. Francisville, thriving center of an area containing some of the most affluent planters in the state. From miles around during the picking season there came a steady stream of cotton bales hauled to this town on the ridge and then carted down the bluff to the little port of Bayou

7. Benjamin Moore Norman, *Norman's New Orleans and Environs* (New Orleans, 1845), 31 ff.; Timothy Flint, *Recollections of the Last Ten Years* (Boston, 1826), 297; Warden, *Statistical Account*, II, 491–93; Estwick Evans, "A Pedestrious Tour of Four Thousand Miles Through the Western States and Territories During the Winter and Spring of 1818," in *Early Western Travels*, ed. Thwaites, VIII, 325.

Sara on the batture below, where steamboats waited to carry the cargo to New Orleans.[8]

Almost halfway past the Felicianas the Mississippi took a sharp turn to the east and then moved on again in a southerly direction toward the parish of East Baton Rouge, where the bluffs finally evened out into level ground just beyond the town of Baton Rouge, a sleepy little village beginning to awaken to the possibilities of its position in this rich farm section. From this point southward the coast extended as a continuous flat plain, two miles deep from the levees on either side—supporting an unending succession of plantations following regularly one after the other to form what comprised probably the richest and most highly developed stretch of cultivated land in the world. Here sugar ruled as king, the beauty of its domain somewhat diminished by a monotony of terrain not completely overcome by the brilliant flares of waste burning in the fields or the curling white smoke issuing from working sugar mills. Everything here reflected commitment to an order of proper place and balance, Negro quarters neat and compact, cane stretching away in solid banks to the swamps in the rear, fences straight and unbroken, the whole dominated by the plantation manses, some of which had already deserted the plain indigenous style still common in the Lower Coast for the newer, more pretentious forms of the Greek revival.[9]

This approach to New Orleans from the north culminated in dramatic and striking effect. For miles as the traveler moved southward, the coast slipped by with almost dulling regularity of contour. Little changed until the vessel passed the outer posts of the port. Then, as one rounded a great turn in the river, the city was suddenly there, sprawled out along its half moon, crouched behind its unbroken barricades of earth, the teeming and vibrant center of this new and enticing frontier.[10]

There remained yet another water approach to the great metropolis, the

8. Warden, *Statistical Account*, II, 490; Flint, *Recollections*, 296–98; Louise Butler, "West Feliciana: A Glimpse of Its History," *LHQ*, VII (1924), 97; *Norman's New Orleans*, 32; Timothy Flint, *The History and Geography of the Mississippi Valley* (2 vols.; Philadelphia, 1832), I, 236.

9. *Norman's New Orleans*, 31; Warden, *Statistical Account*, II, 491; Evans, "Pedestrious Tour," in *Western Travels*, ed. Thwaites, VIII, 330; Flint, *Recollections*, 299; Stuart, *Three Years*, II, 260.

10. *Louisiana Advertiser* (New Orleans), December 13, 1828.

terminus of the third main path into the state. A short distance behind the city Lake Pontchartrain connected to Lake Borgne and thus to the free waters of the Gulf. Not far from the streets of New Orleans ran a twisting little tributary of the lake called Bayou St. John, linked to the city by a canal built during the days of the Spanish control of Louisiana. This Canal Carondelet edged right to the ancient limits of what had been the walled town of New Orleans, where a basin provided facilities for the receiving and unloading of small cargo ships. These vessels plied a profitable trade in transporting to the metropolis the goods of the Louisiana parishes across the lake, lugging such valuable items as bricks and lumber to meet the ever growing demands of the expanding city. From the Gulf ports, too, in Mississippi and Alabama, came vessels loaded with cotton. This route to the city had the great advantage of bypassing the long, tortuous pull up the Mississippi, where sailing craft were at the mercy of inconstant winds or the none too reliable services of steam tows. After 1831 the canal became overshadowed completely by the Pontchartrain Railroad, which ran from the city to Milneburg on the lake, where extensive wharves allowed ships to unload directly into waiting railroad cars for a swift fifteen-minute run back to New Orleans through dank and smelly swampland. The city's merchants welcomed the speed of the new line's services, as did hordes of travelers weary from the frequent buffetings experienced in the run from Mobile, point of departure for most of those landing at the Pontchartrain terminus. Despite its attractions, however, at no time did the volume of this lake traffic into New Orleans even approach in magnitude that which bustled along the river banks.[11]

Anyone coming into Louisiana by one of these usual paths had seen, obviously, only a fraction of the complex structure of the state: the coast, New Orleans, Lake Pontchartrain. In the hinterland other areas of storied richness and fabled opportunity awaited the newcomer. Some sixty miles upstream from New Orleans on the west bank of the river, the town of Donaldsonville looked out not only upon the Mississippi but also upon the waters of Bayou Lafourche, which darted out from the river like a feeler reaching for the Gulf, impatient with the greater artery's twisting south-

11. David B. Morgan to Josiah S. Johnston, January 5, 1827, in Josiah Stoddard Johnston Papers, HSP; *Louisiana Gazette* (New Orleans), March 29, 1826; Flint, *Recollections*, 317; Henry Wikoff, *Reminiscences of an Idler* (New York, 1880), 80; Daubeny, *Journal of a Tour*, 140.

easterly course to the sea. Cutting behind the belt of land along the coast, the bayou built up its own rich alluvial deposits to create acres as productive of cane as any in the state, with its principal town of Thibodaux generally considered the heart of Louisiana's sugar bowl. But the large plantations behind the bayou levees never managed to monopolize the Lafourche area as they had the coast, and many *petit fermiers* always persisted in this center of the Acadian region of Louisiana, as much a vital part of the life along the bayou as the masters of the larger estates patterned after the imposing demesnes lining the Mississippi. The plantations generally clustered along the upper reaches of the bayou, for as the Lafourche came closer and closer to the Gulf, its land borders began a slow compromise with the sea, growing progressively more and more spongy and treacherous until only native trappers and fishermen, born to the pirogue, proved willing or able to maintain life in the trackless miles of its coastland marsh.[12]

West of the Bayou Lafourche area the whole nature of the land changed. The rank undergrowth of the river and bayou bottoms suddenly gave way to almost immeasurable plains of grass stretching in unbroken distances westward from the Atchafalaya to the Calcasieu and running inland from the Gulf until they lost themselves in the pine hills, canebrakes, and swamp which bordered the Red River lands to the north. Somewhat arbitrary distinction divided this whole vast area into two separate prairies, Attakapas being to the east and watered by the Atchafalaya, Bayou Teche, and Vermilion River, with Opelousas lying to the west and northward and along the Teche in the area above the Vermilion.

There was no more beautiful section in all of Louisiana. Frequent breezes from the Gulf swept across the plain, ruffling and agitating the tall grass and moving through the occasional patches of timber which arose here and there in such regular and symmetrical circles, squares, and triangles as to defy belief that they had not been placed there as part of some ancient, long-forgotten purpose. Great moss-draped oaks lined the slow and gentle Teche as it meandered southward through the prairie, unmenacing and unfeared, with no levees or embankments poised along its flow. Rising in easy slopes from the stream, the land extended back for a mile on either side in a rich belt of arable soil ideally adaptable to sugarcane and studded with stands of orange and magnolia trees surrounding ancient whitewashed

12. *Norman's New Orleans*, 33; Warden, *Statistical Account*, II, 494–95.

adobe huts or new and more imposing mansions reflecting the growing prosperity of the area.[13]

Out in the fields clumsy breaking-up plows might be seen dragged behind four great horn-yoked oxen, and from a distance an indescribable shrieking and screeching often heralded the approach of a venerable cart trundling along on its all-wooden wheels and axle tree. Beyond the tilled acres, off in the rolling waves of grass, roamed the thousands of cattle and horses which prospered and multiplied in these perfect grazing lands unattended by any extended or solicitous care. Small and wiry, they presented no great show of four-footed beauty, but they provided a comfortable mainstay to planters always interested in ready food for slaves and strong motive power for sugar mills. Opelousas especially, with its grass lands running almost as far west as the Sabine River, profited from this far-flung industry of the prairies.[14]

The rich lands along the Atchafalaya suffered considerably from the too-frequent floodings of the river, but along the Vermilion deep borders of fertile soil produced bountifully in cotton, corn, tobacco, rice, and cane, almost as sought after as those crops on the Teche. Opelousas fared particularly well in this generally favored region. Cotton and cane sprouted from its soil with a vigor to equal almost anything in Attakapas, and the sicknesses which tormented so much of Louisiana came as less frequent scourges here than elsewhere: in the midst of plenty, her people could be doubly thankful that fortune had also placed them in the healthiest part of the state.

Essentially rural, like all of Louisiana outside New Orleans, the prairielands nonetheless possessed several small towns of notable charm and distinction—New Iberia, Franklin, and St. Martinville on the Teche; Vermilionville, later to be rechristened in honor of the well-loved Lafayette; and the village of Opelousas itself, which shared its name with the western part of the prairie region. Small they might have been, but each in its own way mirrored the same optimism and ambition which so galvanized the great metropolis of New Orleans.[15]

North of the prairies, the grassy plains began to merge with undulating

13. *Norman's New Orleans*, 30–35, 37–41; Warden, *Statistical Account*, II, 494–95.

14. F. D. Richardson, "The Teche Country Fifty Years Ago," *Southern Bivouac*, n.s., I (1885), 593.

15. *Norman's New Orleans*, 33; Warden, *Statistical Account*, II, 493.

pine hills, low marsh ground, and the rich canebrake bordering the bayous which ran close to Red River or emptied themselves into its waters. The usual approach to the Red River region came not through the prairies, however, but via the Mississippi. A broad stretch of rusty iron-tinted water, swarming with alligators at low season, marked where the Red emptied itself into the greater river. Not far above its mouth, and only a little beyond the point at which it received the Black from the north, the Red roiled in a series of rapids, dangerous and treacherous when not deeply covered. Few houses could be seen along its shore until one reached Avoyelles, where an extensive prairie pushed back from the stream to provide excellent cotton and grazing lands. Above this point the banks began to rise, dotted with scattered plantations leading to Alexandria in Rapides Parish, some one hundred twisting miles up from the Mississippi. A town of white houses shaded by china trees, the settlement sat on a smooth plain surrounded by a magnificent forest of great moss-covered oaks, which soon dropped off to a swamp fifteen to twenty miles across, crawling with alligators and snakes. For a third of the year a constant roar from the ten-foot rapids in the river engulfed the town, audible warning of the constant menace threatening smaller craft which dared push past even at low water mark.[16] Infinitely more propitious, the rich soil along the Red and its many tributaries, such as Bayou Rapides, Bayou Boeuf, and Bayou Robert, produced with a readiness which made Alexandria the center of a region renowned as a "cotton planter's paradise."

Sixty miles farther up the Red, Natchitoches prided itself as the oldest settlement in Louisiana and flourished as the "jumping off place" to New Spain, with which it carried on a bustling trade for Mexican and Indian furs and horses while the surrounding countryside busied itself with cotton, cattle, and the largest and best tobacco crop in the state. North and east of Alexandria and Natchitoches, rolling pine hills provided little development of any importance until the barrens stopped short at the alluvial lands of the Ouachita, third largest river of the state, which rose in distant mountains between the Red and the Arkansas, came into Louisiana through Ouachita and Catahoula Parishes, and finally emptied into the Red. Broad and deep, the stream coursed through fertile cotton country and afforded

16. *Norman's New Orleans*, 34; Warden, *Statistical Account*, II, 496–97; Flint, *Recollections*, 321–24.

excellent steam navigation into the Red-Mississippi system. Beyond, to the east, stretched the even more productive cotton acres of Concordia.[17]

East of the Mississippi lay a part of the state generally outside the itinerary of the average traveler. By the Treaty of 1762 transferring Louisiana to Spain, the part of the colony east of the river known as the Isle of Orleans had been given a northern boundary running roughly from the mouth of Bayou Manchac, some fifteen miles below Baton Rouge on the Mississippi, eastward through the lakes north of New Orleans. The lands above this line were integrated with British West Florida, and after much shifting of sovereignty, finally became part of Louisiana shortly after her creation as a state: they were known forever after as the Florida parishes. They ran from the Mississippi to the Pearl and from the old Isle of Orleans north to the Mississippi border, embracing a region rich in contrasts of almost infinite variety. Those parishes close to the Mississippi, such as the Felicianas and East Baton Rouge, shared the munificence of the fruitful lands along the coast. But the interior north of the lakes knew no such golden haze as that which settled over great plantation fields and treasured money crops of more favored regions. St. Helena, St. Tammany, Washington, and Livingston Parishes did produce some cotton, but as late as 1840 their combined crop equaled only one-fifteenth the massive output of West Feliciana alone. These east Florida parishes consisted largely of a mixture of low grass prairies, extensive piney woods, and swampland ranged along river margins thick with cypress and live oak. No better than second rate, the soil had no possibility of sustaining a plantation economy like that flourishing in the great alluvial or upland regions of the state, supporting instead a population made up largely of yeomen engaged in the production of lumber, tar, charcoal, and bricks. They frequently diversified their subsistence farming with modest plantings of rice and oats, supplemented by considerable holdings of poultry and pigs. The tall grass between the ubiquitous pines afforded excellent grazing land for cattle as well, and report had it that one measured the wealth of a nubile Floridian by the number of her cows. In contrast to the planter class which dominated so much of the state, these small farmers and graziers seemed to many to be poor indeed, and Florida "bogues" or "resin heels" often found themselves charged with indolence

---

17. *Washita Gazette* (Monroe), May 21, 1825; *Norman's New Orleans*, 54; Warden, *Statistical Account*, II, 497.

and lack of enterprise. But by and large they managed fairly well. The pine woods generally provided a healthy environment, a sufficiency of food, and what many considered a special blessing: salvation from the many financial worries which dogged those tied to the price vagaries of the great money crops. Nabobs they might not be; neither were they a people dispossessed.[18]

These then composed the integral parts of Louisiana: the coast, with its rich belt of unsurpassed cotton and sugar lands; the Lafourche area, following its bayou through Assumption, Lafourche, and Terrebonne Parishes, sustaining its plantations and *petit fermiers*, its trappers and fishermen; Attakapas and Opelousas, beautiful plains of waving grass, of cane and cotton and ugly cattle; Red River, with its fertile Rapides river bottoms and its distant Natchitoches, center of a flourishing Mexican trade and a sturdy cotton and tobacco culture; Ouachita, bountiful alluvial lands in the midst of pine hills; and the Floridas, where magnificence and simplicity shared the land. Diverse as the sections of the state might have been, one thing remained always clear—cotton and sugar provided the substance of agrarian Louisiana, the unmythical golden gift of this newfound Hesperides.

And withal, there was still New Orleans.

Each Saturday evening as dusk began to gather around the Place d'Armes, the bells from the cathedral overlooking the square tolled a melancholy reminder, that those who heard might bless themselves and wish well for the soul of Don Almonester y Roxas.[19] Many of course would not heed, much too intent upon getting to the political meeting at Bishop's Hotel or hastening to catch the railroad car for a cool ride through the suburbs with dinner waiting at the splendid new hotel in Carrollton. There would be some to whom the bells bespoke only the passing of time as they planned the precise correctness of the next day's Sabbath with their New England neighbors. And there would be others, crowding perhaps into the Camp Street Theatre or the gaming chambers of Davis's Ball Room, who knew little of Don Almonester and cared less about the repose of his soul.

18. Flint, *Recollections*, 317–19; Warden, *Statistical Account*, II, 490; *Compendium of the Enumeration of the Inhabitants and Statistics of the United States* [Sixth Census, 1840] (Washington, D.C., 1841).

19. *Gibson's Guide and Directory* (New Orleans, 1838). A wealthy Spanish philanthropist, Don Almonester contributed greatly to the rebuilding of New Orleans after the disastrous fire of 1788 and is remembered especially as the patron of the cabildo and the cathedral.

For the past and the present lived side by side in New Orleans, each distinct in its own way, separated by worlds as well as years, and yet fused into a vibrant identity which pursued the future almost with a frenzy. It was the city of the old colonial French and Spanish customs and peoples; the city of the Anglo-Saxon purchaser with new language and new ways; the city of all these together, conscious of its growing size and wealth, determined to realize the vision which had come to possess the whole community—that one day, and not far off, New Orleans would become the greatest and most prosperous city the world had ever known.

It was already a remarkable place. That became apparent the moment one set foot on the levee from one of those ships or steamboats which crowded so thick in the harbor. Noise and confusion ruled everywhere. An indescribable variety of cargo, dominated by endless rows of cotton bales, lined the area behind the great earthen embankment, to be stumbled over by the continuous line of pedestrians shoving their way in all directions. Huge Negro and Irish draymen added to the hurlyburly with torrents of curses as they careened their vehicles through the crowds, careless of danger to themselves or to those too slow to leap to safety. Along the levee as far as one could see, lines of hucksters competed for the custom of the turbulent throng, some from stalls or tables but most with their wares simply spread on the ground or arrayed on canvas and palmetto leaves, all shouting the excellence of their goods at full voice in a jumble of probably all the tongues known to man. Hardware, shoes, clothes, dry goods, food, trinkets, jewelry—everything was pushed at prospective buyers with an insistence frequently bordering on aggression. Shouts and oaths, jeers and laughter marked the many brawls and battles which such confusion inevitably produced. All in all, there could have been no better introduction to New Orleans, for it captured so much of the essence of this vibrant city: a bewildering variety of men and goods; a polyglot mixture of races and nationalities; and the intensity of that compelling drive which activated all who lived or paused here, the passionate pursuit of wealth.[20]

In reality, three distinct cities actually existed under the rubric "New

20. B. H. Latrobe, *The Journal of Latrobe* (New York, 1905), 161–64; Henry Didimus [Edward Durrell], *New Orleans as I Found It* (New York, 1845), 16, 36; Joseph Conder, ed., *The Modern Traveler* (30 vols.; London, 1830), XXIV, 214; Edward H. Barton, *Introductory Lecture on the Climate and Salubrity of New Orleans* (New Orleans, 1835), 5.

Orleans": the original settlement, the Faubourg Marigny, and the "American section." Primacy belonged to what had been the old colonial town, known in the 1820s and 1830s simply as "the City" and preserved to us today as the Vieux Carré, or French Quarter. It followed the great curve of the river from Canal Street to Esplanade, some eleven squares, and ran back six blocks from the levee to Rampart Street, where palisades had once walled in the original site. Its straight but narrow streets intersected at right angles and read like a roll call of Gallic nobility and Catholic sainthood—Chartres, Burgundy, Royale, Conti, Condé, St. Pierre, Ste. Ann. There could be no doubt that this was a French town. In the center of the plot, opening to the river, the Place d'Armes, or city square, fronted on the imposing mass of the cathedral, flanked by the Cabildo (city hall) on one side and the Presbytere (courthouse) on the other. The whole life of the city more or less converged here. Hard by, abutting the central quadrangle along the levee to the front, the old market swarmed with bedizened slaves out for the day's purchasing, haggling with the equally black overseers of stalls loaded with meat, fish, fowl, and vegetables of the neighborhood. Ranged along either side of the square, cramped and murky dry-goods stores shared the view of the parade grounds with even more numerous grog shops and tippling places, for then even more than now the city bulged with centers of cheer. To the front, jostling in the market, pushing along the levee and the bustling Levee Street which ran with it parallel to the river, crisscrossed the life of New Orleans. Solemn Indians surveyed the scene in near-naked silence, hawking their own wares, while Italians vied with mulatto, Asian, and indefinable pitchmen in competition for the favor of the crowd.[21]

A somewhat more decorous atmosphere prevailed along Chartres Street, which stretched toward Canal from where the Cabildo looked out upon the Place d'Armes. The Broadway of New Orleans, with luxury shops displaying finery from all quarters of the globe, it served as the major avenue for both the proper New Orleans belle and the promenading quadroon of somewhat easier virtue. Close to the square, in the confectioneries, millineries, and perfumeries, French influence ruled supreme, but as one

21. [Ingraham], *The Southwest*, I, 91, 102; James S. Buckingham, *The Slave States of America* (2 vols.; London, 1842), II, 299; New Orleans *Mercantile Advertiser*, March 11, 1825; Alexander, *Transatlantic Sketches*, II, 14.

moved nearer Canal, Anglo-American jewelers, booksellers, and dry goods merchants predominated, ever increasing symbols of the rising power of the newer segment of the city's population.[22]

Even this infiltration of the American had little effect on the Latin atmosphere of the old city. Its buildings, almost universally of French or Spanish design, reflected the climatic demands which had shaped life in the community since early colonial days, with cool patios, high ceilings, breeze-catching balconies, and shaded walks providing appreciated comfort in even the most commercial part of the town. Beyond Royal toward Rampart Street almost all the houses were one-story affairs, picturesque structures with high roofs covered with tile or shingles and with eaves projecting over the *banquette*, or sidewalk, to furnish both dweller and passerby with welcomed protection against sun and rain. Uniformity of color had obviously no appeal here, and the pink and white of plaster, the red of exposed brick, and the drabness of unpainted wood gave a mottled and dappled appearance to the City which added still more to its seductive charms.[23]

Downriver from the original town, below its lower boundary at the Esplanade, there sprawled an extensive and relatively backward suburb bearing the name Faubourg Marigny in honor of its most noted and certainly its richest inhabitant, Bernard Marigny, scion of the famed colonial family, the de Mandevilles. In many respects the suburb constituted a feudal domain, its population largely made up of the poorer Spanish, Portuguese, and Mexican element of the city, leftovers from the colonial regime or refugees from the scattered violence of Europe and the Caribbean in the late eighteenth and early nineteenth centuries. Unkempt and sluggish, the section lagged behind the rest of the city in almost every respect, nurturing a frustrated pride which fed on resentment against the newer Anglo-American precinct, more and more clearly destined to be the wealthiest and most dominant segment of the community.[24]

A general consensus has developed over the years to the effect that the American section of early New Orleans identified entirely with the suburb

22. [Ingraham], *The Southwest*, I, 91, 93; Herbert A. Keller, ed., "A Journey through the South in 1836: Diary of James D. Davidson," *JSH*, I (1935), 358.

23. Latrobe, *Journal*, 209; [Ingraham], *The Southwest*, I, 159.

24. [Ingraham], *The Southwest*, I, 90; *Louisiana Gazette*, December 24, 1821; New Orleans *Argus*, November 25, 1829.

called the Faubourg Ste. Marie. In this scenario, "aristocratic" and "cultivated" creoles, contemptuous of the vulgarity and boorishness of the Anglo-Saxon newcomers, closed them off from residence in the City, thus forcing them into the still largely undeveloped suburb beyond Canal Street, the upriver boundary of the original town. Unabashed by this rejection, the growing hordes of new arrivals supposedly went on to develop the raw Faubourg Ste. Marie into the rich and powerful dominion destined to be called the American section of the city. Adding dramatic color to the story, Canal Street would win fame as the "neutral ground" separating the two bitterly antagonistic ethnic groups in the society.[25]

Like so much else in the history of New Orleans, this representation wraps a kernel of truth in a bundle of myth and fantasy. Actually, the first American immigrants to New Orleans after the Louisiana Purchase settled primarily in the upper reaches of the City, quickly establishing themselves as the dominant element in the squares from Conti to Canal Streets. Only when their numbers had clearly outgrown the cramped confines of the old town did they spill over into the Faubourg Ste. Marie, and Canal Street never really divided the populations at all, the American presence always remaining dominant in the upper reaches of the City. To early New Orleanians the term *American section* became interchangeable with *commercial section*, the area in which banks, insurance companies, specialty retail shops, factors, commodity brokers, wholesalers, and commission merchants proliferated, which meant, in short, the portion of the city from Conti Street in the Old Quarter to the upper limits of St. Mary. The utterly Gallic Bernard Marigny in 1822 maintained that American control extended into the City as far as St. Louis Street. The center of that control, however, clearly rested in the area of the Faubourg Ste. Marie, and it became a matter of convenience simply to identify that influence with the geographic entity.

In the 1820s the section entered upon a period of remarkable growth and expansion, to the amazement, chagrin, and despair of the more placid Latin New Orleanians. More and more the burgeoning river trade concentrated in the upper faubourg, and as the great warehouses and cotton presses continued to rise along the river front, as Magazine and Camp

25. The Faubourg Ste. Marie took its name from Marie Josephe Deslondes Gravier, who had inherited the great tract from her husband. Francis P. Burns, "The Graviers and the Faubourg Ste. Marie," *LHQ*, XXII (1939), 385 ff.

Streets began to fill with flourishing commission and wholesale houses, more and more did New Orleans take on, in this area at least, the air of an American city. In energy, cleanliness, ambition, capacity, and sheer vitality, the American suburb fast left the City and Faubourg Marigny far behind, but it, for its own part, lacked that mellowness of age and charm of the bizarre which set old New Orleans apart. In appearance St. Mary seemed not unlike many other cities of the United States, the red-brick façades of her dwelling places reminding the critical Latrobe of nothing so much as the "dull, dingy character of Market Street in Philadelphia."[26]

Divided in so many ways, these disparate parts of the city nonetheless found much that bound them together. It was to the Mississippi that the whole city clung, safe but wary behind its great levees. Literally hundreds of craft from all parts of the world nuzzled against these thick embankments: the rough and vulgar backwoods flatboats and long crocodilelike rafts parked highest up the river, loaded with a confused array of hams, ears of corn, apples, barrels of whiskey, and other outpourings of the vast western interior; next came the somewhat more pretentious keel boats, piled high with cotton, furs, liquor and flour; then the steamboats, crammed with a profusion of cotton bales and other heavy cargo; and finally the seagoing ships, their masts a dense forest of shafts as they crowded sometimes six deep along the wharves. Before the very heart of the city, looking up to the cathedral, a tangle of nondescript rafts, pirogues, canoes, and skiffs overflowed with provisions for the bustling markets of the town. This rich mix of the city's waterfront never failed to amaze those who looked upon it, acclaimed by some as the most striking panorama of shipping to be seen in all the ports of the world.[27]

It was largely this booming river trade which made the whole city by 1830 acutely aware of the promise of its economic future. As the western country began to fill up and the Mississippi received the growing volume of

26. Latrobe, *Journal*, 187; Bernard Marigny, *Memoire of Bernard Marigny, Addressed to His Fellow Citizens of New Orleans* (New Orleans, 1822), 8–10; [Joseph Rodriguez], *Défense Fulminante contre le Violation des Droits du Peuples* (New Orleans, 1827), 35; *Louisiana Advertiser*, October 5, 1831. For a fuller discussion of the ethnic composition of the various sections of the city, see Joseph G. Tregle, Jr., "Creoles and Americans," in *Creole New Orleans*, ed. Arnold Hirsch and Joseph Logsdon (Baton Rouge, 1992), 154–55.

27. [Durrell], *New Orleans as I Found It*, 7; S. A. Ferrall, *A Ramble of Six Thousand Miles Through the United States of America* (London, 1832), 190; Buckingham, *Slave States*, II, 326; *Louisiana Advertiser*, December 13, 1828.

its produce, the position of New Orleans as the terminus of this great inland commerce took on ever increasing importance. By 1836 she surpassed New York as the chief export center of the United States and boasted a population of at least sixty thousand, a remarkable spurt from the meager eight thousand of 1803.[28] Despite competition from the Erie Canal, the Pennsylvania canal and rail systems, and the Baltimore and Ohio Line, downriver traffic on the Mississippi would grow from $22,065,518 in 1830 to $49,763,825 in 1840.[29] Removal of Indian tribes in the Southwest opened large new cotton areas in Alabama and Mississippi, which with the already producing acres of Louisiana and Tennessee became by far the chief source of the crop received in the Crescent City.[30] St. Louis, with no rail connections to the East, sent practically all its exports down to New Orleans, where they frequently unloaded next to the tobacco from the rich acres around Nashville.[31] The variety of goods funneling into the city from great upstream marts and small backwoods plots throughout the great valley literally defies cataloging and frequently found other passage than on the dominant steamboats. Even as late as 1840, for example, the jumbled cargo carried by flatboats, barges, and keels made up one-fifth of the traffic on the lower Mississippi.[32]

Trade with Mexico also played a vital role in the city's commercial life. By 1836 nearly a dozen vessels plied regularly between New Orleans and Mexico, reaching to the Tampico, Matamoras, Brazoria, Tuxpan, and Galveston Bay areas. Although almost always small vessels transshipping cargo originally from Britain, these ships funneled into New Orleans large sums of Mexican silver bullion, an invaluable item in the rapidly expanding financial exchanges of the city.[33]

To her great disadvantage, New Orleans never managed to match her export prowess with a comparable strength in the import trade, her upriver

28. James E. Winston, "Notes on the Economic History of New Orleans, 1803–1836," *MVHR*, XI (1924), 200–203. In 1835 the relative export totals of the two ports were New York, $30,345,264; New Orleans, $36,270,823. New Orleans *Bee*, September 26, 1836.

29. R. B. Way, "The Commerce of the Lower Mississippi in the Period 1830–1860," *Mississippi Valley Historical Association Proceedings*, X (1918), 60.

30. *Ibid.*; *Hunt's Merchants' Magazine*, V (1841), 475.

31. Way, "Commerce of the Lower Mississippi," 61.

32. Winston, "Notes on the Economic History of New Orleans," 205.

33. *Ibid.*, 208. New Orleans also supported a thriving trade in grain with many parts of Latin America. See Alfred T. Wellborn, "The Relations Between New Orleans and Latin America, 1810–1824," *LHQ*, XXII (1939), 774.

business in its best year measuring only one-half that of the downriver traffic. Except for occasional handling of heavy machinery or space-consuming cargoes like coffee and sugar, most of the upriver shipments went no farther than the nearby plantations of Louisiana and Mississippi.[34] Equally disabling, without any shipping lines of her own the city depended upon New York and other eastern ports for transport services, a weakness in her economic system of constant concern to many of her shrewdest financial leaders.[35] But the great flood of downriver cargo kept the drays racing precariously through the streets; the cotton presses never ceased reducing bale after bale to proper seagoing size; warehouses bulged, wharves piled high with cargo; and the city regularly rejoiced in the human wave of upcountry traders, roistering seamen, and the riffraff of the world which engulfed her in the busy parts of the year. River trade brought them all, together with additional ranks of clerks, salesmen, lawyers, artisans, and adventurers seeking the alluring fortunes to be made in this bazaar of the western world.

Its position as the great export mart of the Mississippi valley made the city the financial center of the western states as well. The New Orleans branch of the Second Bank of the United States served as a great clearinghouse for the commercial paper of the whole valley, providing credit and discounting functions critical to the financing and crop marketing so vital to the plantation economy. By the 1830s state banking had been tied to an almost frenetic rush into civic improvements, including the building of the Pontchartrain and Carrollton Railroads, the New Basin Canal, the St. Charles and St. Louis Hotels, and the city's gaslight and water companies. These and other comparable enterprises mushroomed the city's banking capital from the $5,665,986 of 1830 to the $39,943,832 of 1837.[36]

No wonder, then, that New Orleans in the early 1800s should have been wide-eyed at her own good fortune and supremely confident of the future.

34. Henry A. Mitchell, "The Development of New Orleans as a Wholesale Trading Center," *LHQ*, XXVII (1944), 941.

35. Winston, "Notes on the Economic History of New Orleans," 211–12; New Orleans *Bee*, September 17, November 5, 1834.

36. New Orleans *Bee*, February 13, March 14, April 23, 1836; S. A. Trufant, "Review of Banking in New Orleans, 1830–1840," *PLHS*, IX (1917), 32; T. P. Abernethy, "The Early Development of Commerce and Banking in Tennessee," *MVHR*, XIV (1927), 317. The cited figures represent actual capitalization; the nominal capital of New Orleans banks in 1837 reached $55,032,000.

One city newspaper in 1826 assured its readers that canals across the Rockies would soon tie the city to the rising population centers of the Pacific slope, bringing her into control of the trade to China and India. Who could doubt, then, the city's progress toward "the maximum of all human grandeur." Nothing could "prevent her taking the very first stand amongst the celebrated cities of the world, whether for population or wealth," her citizens were told, with promises that they would yet "see their city without a parallel both in the old and new worlds."[37] To those who knew how far this bustling metropolis had come since the sleepy days of 1803, such assurances seemed to state no more than the obvious.[38]

But in this city of hopes an excess of optimism about the future oft times ignored the realities of the present. In many ways it certainly could not have been a pleasant place to live. The slack season from May to October brought ever recurring tension and terror, spent either in dreadful battle against yellow fever or in the almost equally wracking trial of waiting for the scourge to strike. Heat proved an even more dependable visitor, the city sweltering in summer under a sun which dried up the streets and turned them into swirling avenues of dust. Nor could one find any escape from the torture of the mosquito except into the folds of the netting which might give some release, at least for sleep.[39]

The very smells of the town could be overpowering. To lay suffocating street dust, city workers sprayed the thoroughfares at noon with water from the gutters, slops and all, leaving behind as the surface dried a stench better imagined than experienced. Streets and empty lots provided dumping ground for garbage, the contents of chamber pots, bodies of dead animals, crabs, oysters, and turtle shells, and palmetto leaves loaded with catfish heads and entrails. Even by day they served the populace as public conveniences as well. Nine-tenths of the city's yards and lots, by one report, constantly festered with solid or semifluid matter in decomposition.[40]

37. New Orleans *Mercantile Advertiser*, as quoted in *Louisiana Messenger* (Alexandria), December 15, 1826.

38. *Louisiana Gazette*, May 1, 1823; New Orleans *Bee*, April 17, 1835; Margaret Hall, *The Aristocratic Journey* (New York, 1931), 254; Tyrone Power, *Impressions of America* (2 vols.; Philadelphia, 1836), II, 143.

39. Martineau, *Retrospect*, II, 124, 128; Alexander, *Transatlantic Sketches*, II, 13–16.

40. New Orleans *Mercantile Advertiser*, June 8, 1825; *Louisiana Advertiser*, May 12, 1826, July 7, 1832, January 31, February 6, 1834.

Not even the winds helped clear the air. Western and northern breezes frequently wafted the stench of decaying swamp filth into the streets, sometimes mixed with the horrible odor which seeped from none-too-well-sealed tombs in the cemeteries on the outskirts of town. Even the drafts from the river carried the smell of waste dumped along the levee and of excrement which citizens carelessly emptied into the stream, which clung close to shore and contaminated the city's water supply.[41] The rains brought surcease only of a sort. For then the city more often than not became a quagmire, with mud so thick and deep in the streets that drays were necessary to carry pedestrians from one side to the other.

But even these vicissitudes of life could not quench the fire of the city's spirit. The very danger in which her people lived, the sharpness of her odors and the constant awareness of the physical which seemed to pervade her atmosphere, all these mingled with the bubbling rush for money, the excitement of the wharves and the counting houses, the confusion of the polyglot people teeming in her streets, to give the city an earthy and sensuous nature which made it unique in the American scene. There was little that was stable or fixed in New Orleans. With traditions so mixed, interests so fluid, and a society still so much in process of being formed, no hard crystalization of mores or set tenor of ways had yet appeared to discourage the individuality and unbridled pursuit of one's own ends which dominated the great mass of the population. Thinking in terms of social or community responsibility seldom occupied much time here, and few felt inclined to worry about the hindmost.

Small wonder then that violence, rowdiness, and what many saw as gross immorality figured prominently in the city's life. Probably no community in the world revolved so much around its grog shops, cabarets, gambling dens, circus pits, and theaters as did this mistress of the Mississippi. Outlets for drink crowded its streets in such numbers as to defy any strict count, ranging from the shadowy holes where slaves and free persons of color mingled in defiance of the law, through the rowdy and violent dives frequented by the riverboatmen in the waterfront sections of the American quarter, and on to the more genteel and respectable establishments euphe-

41. *L'Ami des Lois* (New Orleans), April 24, 1823; *Louisiana Courier* (New Orleans), July 21, 1824; Michel Halphen, *Mémoire sur le Cholera-morbus qui a Regne à la Nouvelle-Orléans en 1832* (Paris, 1833), 28.

mistically known as "coffee houses."[42] These last provided fashionable gathering places for the great mass of the male population, to such an extent that the most famous of them, such as Hewlett's Exchange, Davis's Ball Room, Maspero's, and Bishop's, seemed to many to be the city itself. Spacious and brilliantly lighted, they served as barroom, meeting hall, reading room, restaurant, and general recreation center, and, typical of the city, usually featured splendid engravings and paintings of such licentious character that one visiting Yankee observed that had they been so openly displayed in Boston's Merchant's Hall they would have been "instantly defaced by the populace."[43]

Drink took an appalling toll, especially among those who found that it offered the only solace while waiting expectantly for the fortune so slow in coming. One eminent medical man reached the startling conclusion in 1837 that a third of the city's death rate could be laid at the door of drunkenness, but this should perhaps be discounted somewhat in the light of the physician's confessed desire to relieve New Orleans of its reputation as the "wet grave" of yellow fever victims. If one behaved himself, some maintained, the area provided chances for a long life better than those to be found in most parts of the world.[44]

There could be little dispute, however, about the ravages of another New Orleans disease. Gambling seems to have been endemic to the soil since colonials in the days of the Le Moynes wagered on the arrival of the first flight of ducks over the ramparts of the town, and by the 1830s those with the money and the inclination could flock to Davis's Ball Room on Orleans Street behind the cathedral to try their luck at keno, twenty-one, craps, chuck-a-luck, faro, monte, or roulette. In the 1830s almost every street corner in the city provided much the same facilities as Davis's, even if with somewhat less glitter and opulence. Rich and poor alike crowded into these gaming centers, for they offered yet another way to court quick wealth, the pursuit of which all New Orleans could understand and appre-

42. New Orleans *Mercantile Advertiser*, March 11, 1825; *Louisiana Gazette*, June 7, 1822; Henry B. Fearon, *A Narrative of a Journey of Five-Thousand Miles Through the Eastern and Western States of America* (London, 1819), 278; Buckingham, *Slave States*, II, 299.

43. [Ingraham], *The Southwest*, I, 113; Alexander, *Transatlantic Sketches*, II, 16; Keller, "Diary of James D. Davidson," 358.

44. Edward H. Barton, *A Discourse on Temperance* (New Orleans, 1837), 26.

ciate. No one thought it strange, therefore, that gentlemen bought and sold stock in gaming banks all over the city, in much the same way they might have handled the securities of the Citizens Bank. Charitable institutions and even churches participated gladly and enthusiastically in lotteries for worthy causes, every issue of the newspapers proffering several of these beguiling opportunities to a receptive public. But, then as now, not everyone could win, either at Davis's or in a church lottery, though a disproportionately large part of the community must have had some illusions of the sort. No family was secure against the inroads of this destructive obsession, and the wreckage of lives and fortunes which it so often produced introduced another note of tragedy and uncertainty into the affairs of an always turbulent and captivating city.[45]

45. [Ingraham], *The Southwest*, I, 127; Thomas J. Spear, *Ancient and Modern New Orleans* (New Orleans, 1879), 32; *Louisiana Gazette*, January 27, 1823.

· II ·

THE ETHNIC IMPERATIVE

More than disease, cupidity, heat, and ambition contributed to the ebullient instability of the antebellum state. The very population itself fragmented into a variety of groups and shadings of groups, whose suspicions and hatreds fed on the isolation from each other occasioned by differences of language and tradition and battened on the resentments bred by inevitable competition for political and economic power.

The largest single group in the community, the *ancienne population* traced its roots back to the original settlers of the French and Spanish colonial era. Protagonists of much of the historical literature of the state, they have in reality been ill served by those presuming to memorialize them. Imaginative folklore, filial pride, and uncritical if effusive writings have hidden these people behind a romantic fog which even today it is socially dangerous to try to penetrate. Few things in Louisiana survive so tenaciously or summon up such vehement explication as the myth of the "creole," the term almost universally employed to identify those included in the ancienne population community. That legend affirms an almost religious dogma that all those who bore the name were white Louisianians born to descendants of the French and Spanish, and that they comprised an almost uniformly genteel and cultured aristocracy immune to vulgar concerns about wealth, disdainful of physical labor, and too sensitive to indulge in the dirty business of political and monetary struggle with the "crude Americans" who descended upon them after the Louisiana Purchase, although dominant enough to engulf the barbarism of the latter and give social and artistic tone to the community.

Nothing so infuriates the apostles of the creole myth as the widespread belief in some outland quarters that the term implies a mixture of white and black blood. But the proscription extends much farther. Even the descendants of the Acadian migrants from Canada are ruled out of this select society—they may be Cajuns, but never creoles, for who has ever heard of a lowly creole? On only one point is there any compromise, and that is in the willingness of the elect to admit that *creole* may be legitimately used as an adjective to identify any number of things as native to the state, so that one might speak correctly of a slave as a "creole negro," for example, if never simply as a "creole." Some latitudinarians will even concede a place to those such as the scions of the German settlers who came into Louisiana under John Law, or to post-Purchase French migrants, since all these eventually became identified with the Gallic culture of the community. But the more frequent insistence is on the narrower definition.

It must be admitted that these creoles of fancy are a charming and thoroughly delightful people. After all, they possessed physical and moral qualities, if we are to believe the tradition, which place them among the favored of Providence. Models of beauty and feminine virtue, their young women moved through life sheltered from its crudities by a rigid and impenetrable family supervision, the very epitome of those social graces and accomplishments which make for the delight of men. Deferential to their mates, wives and mothers nonetheless ruled as arbiters of style and behavior, presiding with elegance and charm over gracious households. And who would not recognize the young creole males, dark and lithe hotspurs, handsome, gallant, and recklessly brave, educated in France or select American colleges, all charged with an electric pride which sparked at the slightest affront and led inevitably to numberless duels, generally of the gentlemanly kind involving slender swords and as little common gore as possible. Lords of this domain, the older, dignified, and chivalrous seigneurs ruled with pride and gentility, wise in the ways of the world, urbane and courtly, the very soul of honor and hospitality.

Their great accomplishment, we are told, was to know how to live. Not for them the rush and greed of the grasping American, who worshiped the dollar and had little time for social amenities which gave fullness and richness to existence. Good breeding, never money, counted with the creole of tradition, and family pride made it impossible for him even to consider an economic pursuit which required the removal of his jacket or the laborious use of his hands. He could be a banker, of course, an eminently respectable calling, a professional man, a planter, or even a merchant, if on a large enough scale. But it should occasion no surprise that he fell farther and farther behind in the economic race with the Yankee—no man of his sensibilities could be expected to care enough for mere money to chase it with the almost frightening intensity of a John McDonogh, or to allow the bothersome details of business to interfere with the important things of life such as the theater, the opera, the ball, or the hunt. One could not be expected always to have an eye on the Americans. Thus life for the traditional creole had few sharp edges—he moved in the circles of his society with seductive grace and an awareness of all the subtleties of good living which derived naturally from his noble lineage. Paragon of style, judge of good wine and fine food, connoisseur of spirited horses and handsome women, he was to the manner born.

The only serious fault with this hallowed doctrine of the creole lies in its demonstrable violence to historical truth. The contemporary record makes it undeniably clear that in the 1820s and 1830s Louisianians used the term *creole* to designate any person native to the state, whether white, black, or colored, French, Spanish, or Anglo-American, rich or poor, eminent or lowly, and used it not as an adjective but as a noun. *Creole* and *native*, in effect, meant the same thing, and only the phrase *ancienne population* correctly identified Latin Louisianians who could trace their ties to the soil back to colonial days. Since Anglo-American creoles had hardly become numerous enough or old enough in the 1820s and early 1830s to necessitate a more precise usage in any discussion of public concerns, convenience dictated acceptance of the phrase "the creoles" in place of the more cumbersome *ancienne population* if one wished to reference that group, though that in no way ever displaced the right of any native-born individual to classification as a creole. Clearly, with nonwhites relegated to a purely extracommunity status, no one could conceive of their being included in that sort of allusion. Recognizing, moreover, that origin in the soil might be used as a principal claim to precedence in political and cultural contest with the Americans, the ancienne population could hardly deny creole identity to anyone native born, regardless of ethnic considerations. Given the absolute distinctions between white and black in the society, that such a connection between birth and rights might attach as well to black creoles sim-ply fell outside the bounds of reason. Nor did any question as to Cajun inclusion within creole ranks ever arise, as abundant evidence in the news-papers and correspondence of the period clearly demonstrates.

In summary, out of this confusing and multifaceted social order, antebel-lum Louisianians managed to establish a functional usage clearly under-stood by the entire community: the term *creole* in its singular form attached to anyone native to the state, whatever his ethnicity, color, or status; the plural *creoles*, used in such expressions as "creoles are generally resistant to yellow fever," also applied universally to the native born; but the phrase "the creoles" generally implied reference to members of the ancienne pop-ulation.[1]

It was as a native Louisianian that the Latin creole primarily thought of himself, for he saw in that powerful and mystical bond which ties most men to the soil of their birth the principal justification for his determination not to become a forgotten man in his own land. The danger of that eventuality coming to pass could not be taken lightly in the 1820s and 1830s. Two other major groups in New Orleans and throughout the state had gradually come to dominate the affairs of the community to the growing exclusion of all others: the Anglo-Americans and the so-called foreign French.

The Americans were of all kinds and from all places. They had come down into Louisiana principally after the Purchase, to seek their fortunes in the rich acres of the new territory and in its markets, banks, courts, and thriving trading centers. There had been other Americans in New Orleans before them, to be sure, and they had generally been of a breed difficult to forget. Rough, violent, profane, and brawling, the floating adventurers, the river bullies, and the backwoods denizens come to market had made the American and Kentuckian names things to be feared and often detested among the citizens of the great port, who welcomed the trade but regretted the traders. One did not need the pride of the creole of tradition to decide that he would have little to do with men such as these. But Louisiana folk-lore has too greatly stressed this vulgarity and barbarism of the early Ameri-cans in Louisiana, and a part of the creole myth would have it that for many decades the creoles held aloof from the newcomers, conscious of their own evident superiority, keeping alive the social, artistic, and cultural traditions

---

1. For a fuller discussion of the meaning of *creole*, see the appendix of this volume; details of the clash among these ethnic factions for political control may be found in Chapter V.

of the community while the Yankee changed money in the temple. Nothing could be farther from the truth, for it misrepresents both the Latin creole and Anglo-American types.

Stripped of the romantic trappings attached to them by worshipful descendants, the members of the ancienne population actually had little resemblance to the people met with so delightfully in the creole myth. The charm of their society can hardly be denied, but its attraction sprang from an innate simplicity, from a natural sensate joy in life, and from the easily aroused and mercurial emotionalism of their temperaments, rather than from any claims to high culture or accomplishment. Many of them unquestionably possessed the courtliness of manner passed down from the days of the greatness of France and Spain, but the form had long outlived the substance of any aristocratic heritage. Illiteracy among them was appalling, for example, and spread through all ranks of their society. Members of their own group frequently commented on the limited education of both Jacques Villeré, the state's first creole governor, and Bernard Marigny, perhaps its wealthiest citizen, though each had spent time in France and unquestionably belonged to the creole elite. Some accounts, originating in Latin creole, not American, sources, charged that neither man had any facility in speaking or writing his native tongue.[2] As for elegance, one observer, perhaps maliciously, reported that Marigny, the so-called Creole of Creoles, frequently enjoyed eating with his fingers instead of the more customary knife and fork.[3]

Educational facilities had been severely neglected in the colony before 1803, and with rare exception Louisianians did little studying anywhere, France included, until well after the Purchase. Their status as colonials had allowed them no opportunity to develop any of the faculties which might have permitted them to compete on an even footing with those who moved into their midst after 1803. They had known no banks under France

2. *L'Ami des Lois*, January 20, March 3, 1824; *Louisiana Gazette*, April 3, June 28, 29, 1824; New Orleans *Argus*, January 22, 1828; *Louisiana Courier*, June 28, 29, 30, 1824. The roots of this problem are indicated in Daniel Clark to James Madison, September 8, 1803, in Clarence Carter, ed., *The Territory of Orleans* (Washington, D.C., 1948), 38, Vol. IX of Carter, *The Territorial Papers of the United States* (26 vols.; Washington, D.C., 1934–1962); Martin Luther Riley, "The Development of Education in Louisiana Prior to Statehood," *LHQ*, XIX (1936), 625; Stuart G. Noble, "Governor Claiborne and the Public School System of the Territorial Government of Louisiana," *LHQ*, XI (1928), 536; and Amos Stoddard, *Sketches, Historical and Descriptive, of Louisiana* (Philadelphia, 1812), 308.

3. John S. Whitaker, *Sketches of Life and Character in Louisiana* (New Orleans, 1847), 83.

and Spain, had produced no commercial princes or political leaders of their own, and by and large remained a people with little initiative and only a limited awareness of the facts of nineteenth-century life. Provincial in outlook, style, and taste, the typical Latin creole was complaisant, unlettered, and unskilled, content to occupy his days with the affairs of his estate or the demands of his job, for it should be obvious that he possessed no more wealth than the average man anywhere, and worked where work might be had. He lived in sensation rather than reflection, enjoying the balls and dances, betting heavily at the table or perhaps at the cock pit, endlessly smoking his inevitable cigar, whiling away hours over his beloved dominoes, busying himself with the many demands of his close-knit family life.[4] Seldom a fashion plate, he generally favored a costume of blue cottonade pantaloons, coarse and ungainly in appearance and separated from misshapen shoes by a considerable visible stretch of blue-striped yarn stockings. A hat of no standard style and an ill-fitting coat with long narrow collars and skirts usually completed the attire. The women, fortunately, displayed greater selectivity in their dress, but inclined to an ornateness more appreciated by Gallic than American taste.[5] It must be stated regrettably, as well, that the creole belle did not sweep all before her. To many she was beautiful, to be sure, with clear classic features and magnificent black hair,[6] but others preferred the charms of her American sister,[7] and even her

4. [Ingraham], The Southwest, I, 114; New Orleans Argus, December 18, 22, 23, 1826, January 17, February 2, 1827. It was not until the 1820s that the first native Louisianian entered medical practice in the state. See Cyprien Dufour, "Local Sketches," LHQ, XIV (1931), 222. For a review of contemporary evidence on creole society as it existed under Spain, see Minter Wood, "Life in New Orleans in the Spanish Period," LHQ, XXII (1939), 642–709. A similar impression of the simplicity and backwardness of Louisiana around the turn of the century can be found in various chapters of Berquin-Duvallon, Vue de la Colonie Espagnole du Mississippi (Paris, 1803); the anonymously written Mémoires sur la Louisiane et la Nouvelle-Orléans (Paris, 1804); Jean B. Bossu, Nouveaux Voyages aux Indes Occidentales (Paris, 1802); H. M. Brackenridge, Views of Louisiana (Pittsburgh, 1814); Philip Pittman, The Present State of the European Settlements on the Mississippi (Cleveland, 1906); and C. C. Robin, Voyages dans l'Intérieur de la Louisiane (3 vols.; Paris, 1807).

5. [Ingraham], The Southwest, I, 188.

6. Bernard Saxe-Weimar Eisenach [Duke of Saxe-Weimar], Travels Through North America During the Years 1825 and 1826 (2 vols.; Philadelphia, 1828), II, 72; Charles A. Murray, Travels in North America During the Years 1834, 1835, and 1836 (2 vols.; London, 1839), II, 188.

7. Buckingham, Slave States, II, 345.

admirers admitted that she generally ran to plumpness too early in life.[8] As to her manners, some found them an interesting and gay mixture of small talk and flirtation, while others saw only shallowness and superficiality in young girls and matrons whose entire education consisted frequently of some small instruction in dancing and music.[9]

Even the romanticizers of the Latin creole have seldom presented him as an intellectual; literature, art, and scientific knowledge had little appeal to the ancienne population. Every library begun in New Orleans from 1806 to 1833 seems to have been the product of Anglo-American rather than Latin planning.[10] An observant Prince Murat remarked that New Orleans in 1832 presented "a striking contrast to all the other large cities" visited on his tour, intellectual conversation being met with but rarely. The entire city supported only three libraries, he noted, "while the bookstores contain works of the worst description of French literature." Having seen all of New Orleans, however, the prince hastened to point out that as against the lack of stimulating conversation, "ample means are afforded for eating, playing, dancing, and making love."[11]

It was as a patron of the theater that the Latin creole supposedly demonstrated the most exquisite taste and refinement, but here again the historical record fails to substantiate any claim to Gallic superiority. For all their love of the famed Théâtre d'Orléans, the native population gave it such anemic support in 1824 that manager John Davis announced reluctantly that he would shortly be forced to close his doors, and such crises arose frequently in the next decade.[12] By the early 1830s the enterprising English entrepreneur James Caldwell had so advanced the American theater in the city that even such rabidly French papers as the *Bee* had more or less come to slight the older but backward Orléans.[13] In quality of presentation and performance, the French theater differed but little from the American in a

---

8. Duke of Saxe-Weimar, *Travels Through North America*, II, 72; Murray, *Travels in North America*, II, 188.

9. Duke of Saxe-Weimar, *Travels Through North America*, II, 72; New Orleans *Argus*, December 18, 1826, January 17, 1827.

10. Robert P. McCutcheon, "Libraries in New Orleans, 1771–1833," *LHQ*, XX (1937), 152–158.

11. Achille Murat, *America and the Americans* (New York, 1849), 247.

12. *Louisiana Advertiser*, May 19, 1824.

13. New Orleans *Bee*, February 21, 1831, May 13, 1835.

community which could accommodate not only Shakespeare and Molière but favorites of decidedly lesser quality as well. If the Americans rejoiced in the exhausting antics of *Tom and Jerry*, the Latin creoles had their *Jocko or the Monkey of Brazil*.[14] Nor did supposed American influence lag behind that of the Latin sector in more rarified levels of musical performance. The Englishman Caldwell, rather than a French or native impresario, launched the first real season of grand opera in New Orleans.[15]

On yet another point, tradition notwithstanding, the creole exhibited no greater delicacy in money matters than did his American counterpart. The acquisition of wealth preoccupied the major portion of the citizenry, and if the creoles generally lacked experience in devising new ways of growing rich, those among them not immobilized by the inertia of colonial habits or the burden of educational neglect could and did pursue the known ways with a passion which yielded nothing to that of the Yankees. In frank emulation of the American newcomers, the energetic among them, however limited, engaged with equal gusto in deception, trickery, political exploitation, and even outright fraud to gain advantage in business and trade. And like the Americans, they as frequently fell prey to the law. It happened to Major Bartholomew Grima, for example. One of the best known sons of a prominent old family, a dealer in crockery and glassware, the major late in 1835 forged the name of former mayor Nicholas Girod to $120,000 worth of notes, gathered his considerable if ill-gotten gain, and quickly fled the place of his birth.[16] Romance to the contrary, "breeding" and "gentility" felt the universal pull of the dollar.

And so we must take the Latin creole as he actually was, rather than as some would give him to us: a provincial whose narrow experience and even narrower education left him painfully unprepared to compete for leadership with the Americans and foreign French. He could surpass them in nothing but numbers. Generally illiterate, almost always politically naïve, genuinely uninterested in intellectual or artistic concerns, and not unduly fastidious in his theatrical taste, the typical creole could best be described as a simple man averse to change. He was no more an aristocrat than he was an Ottoman Turk.

14. See, for example, the New Orleans *Argus* for March and April, 1827.

15. New Orleans *Bee*, March 6, 1836.

16. Alexander Porter to Josiah S. Johnston, December 23, 1825, Nathaniel Cox to Johnston, December 23, 1825, in Johnston Papers, HSP.

But he was human, and he could not help but resent the Americans and the foreign French, because they represented in many ways everything that the Latin creole community as a whole found beyond its reach. Most of the Americans who settled in the state after 1803 had little resemblance to the ignorant roustabouts and backwoodsmen who, though they might continue to plague the city during the busy season, as transients played no part in the continuous life of the community. More often than not, those who came to stay possessed considerable ability and even greater ambition. Recognizing the opportunities opened in the newly acquired territory of the Union, they had flocked there to take advantage of them: young lawyers with their eyes on the many administrative jobs in the new territorial government, or very much aware of the demand for legal talent in the booming commercial and maritime concerns of the region; merchants anxious to share in the prosperity guaranteed to the trade center of the Mississippi valley; thousands of junior clerks with dreams of serving out an apprenticeship under those already established and then going on to enterprises of their own; physicians anxious to grapple with the notorious "plagues of the wet grave"; divines equally inspired to bring salvation to the people of this new Sodom; and planters to whom the rich soil of the state held out hopes for all those things which had not been forthcoming in older settlements now left behind. The very fact of their migration gave testimony to their initiative and independence; in a very real sense they represented a select strain of the American stock. Nothing in this suggests that they necessarily possessed any greater refinement of spirit or higher measure of morality than did those among whom they came to settle. No more aristocrats than were the Latin creoles, they responded even more enthusiastically to the lure of wealth and power. Moreover, they knew what they wanted and as a rule had superior means to get it. Better educated, more sophisticated politically, economically, and even culturally, the Anglo-American generally possessed an energy and resourcefulness which the native Louisianian usually found beyond his ability to match.[17]

Inevitably, the Latin creole rapidly reacted toward these newcomers with feelings of envy, jealousy, and an overwhelming sense of inferiority. He naturally resented their assumption that creole backwardness made it impossible for those of that community to understand the nature of repub-

17. *L'Ami des Lois*, January 14, 1823.

lican government; he bridled when they made English the legal language of the state; and he fumed at the staid New England piety which consigned him to hell because he managed to enjoy himself on Sundays. He knew full well his limitations in this struggle for supremacy, and finally in desperation he sought help from those closer to him in blood, language, and heritage, the foreign French, though these too he hated and feared for their supercilious and patronizing manner. Little else was left him, however. Creoles held few positions of leadership at the bar, and fewer still had the training and experience to fill the important editorial chairs which so influenced public opinion—for such important leadership the natives had no recourse but to depend on foreign talent.[18]

The foreign French had no reluctance to take up the task. Like the Americans, they generally possessed at least some education and training, with initiative enough to have triumphed over disaster or misfortune in their original homes and with stamina sufficient to have brought them to this new world for the fashioning of new careers. Frequently skilled in the intricacies of political competition, often deeply versed in the law or experienced in editorial duties, some of their leaders could have made their mark probably in any community of the world. They included men like Etienne Mazureau, the brilliant attorney and orator; Louis Moreau Lislet, the profound student of civil law; Nicholas Girod and Joseph Roffignac, longtime mayors of New Orleans; Pierre Derbigny, state governor in the late 1820s; François-Xavier Martin, the eminent chief justice of the Louisiana Supreme Court; and Pierre Soulé, the fiery political spellbinder.[19]

They had been coming into Louisiana ever since the early days of the French Revolution, fugitives from the Reign of Terror, victims of Napoleonic oppression, emigrés from the conservative strictures of the Bourbon Restoration, escapees from the nightmare of slave insurrection in St. Domingue. In Louisiana they found not only a safe refuge but a society with which they had much in common, including language, religion, mores, and law, and from the very beginning they formed a major force in their new home.[20] But they had clearly failed to endear themselves to the Louisian-

18. Everett S. Brown, "Letters from Louisiana, 1813–1814," *MVHR*, XI (1924), 571 ff.; Dunbar Rowland, ed., *The Official Letter Books of W. C. C. Claiborne, 1801–1816* (6 vols.; Jackson, Miss., 1917), III, 299; New Orleans *Argus*, May 15, 1827.

19. *Louisiana Gazette*, October 3, 1825, January 3, 1826.

20. New Orleans *Argus*, January 18, 1827.

ians. Conscious of their general superiority, they lacked the sensitivity to hide their disdain of creole provincialism, allowing themselves free rein to indulge in open criticism of local styles and native backwardness. Never blind to their own advantage, most of them readily accepted United States citizenship with loud avowals of loyalty,[21] and yet they had more cause even than the creole to hate the new Anglo-American settlers. For not only did these latter threaten a disruption of those Gallic forms and ways of life which the refugee had good reason to cherish—they also made up the major competition for that mastery of the affairs of the state which the foreign French had determined to enjoy themselves. It was a prize worth fighting for, and the Anglo-Americans soon felt the effectiveness of this leadership against them. These French stalwarts, not the creoles, presented the greatest obstacle to American supremacy, and as much as the Americans might detest this foreign faction, they did it the honor never to underestimate its skill or prowess.[22]

The other major foreign elements in the city's population, such as the numerous Irish and Germans, lacked the cohesion and leadership which made the foreign French so powerful. At first they settled primarily in the Faubourg Lafayette beyond the American section and in the less desirable parts of the City and Faubourg St. Mary. By 1850 the sheer explosion of their numbers gave New Orleans a population 49 percent foreign born, with a majority of the white residents of even the old so-called American section and City made up of members of this group. But much of that flood had come in the 1840s, indicating a substantially lesser impact during the decades of the 1820s and 1830s.[23] With little to build on except their own brawn, the Irish turned to the boisterous life of draymen, canal diggers, or street laborers, some to suffer the indignity of expending themselves in competition with convicts or slaves, others to enjoy the free man's privilege of dying in droves to push the New Basin Canal through pestilential swamps to the lake behind the city.[24] Many fell prey to the ravages of the

21. G. W. Pierson, "Alexis de Tocqueville in New Orleans," *Franco-American Review*, I (1936), 34.

22. *Louisiana Gazette*, April 14, 1824, October 3, 1825.

23. Tregle, "Creoles and Americans," in *Creole New Orleans*, ed. Hirsch and Logsdon, 165–66; *Louisiana Advertiser*, February 26, 1828.

24. [Durrell], *New Orleans as I Found It*, 16; Alexander, *Transatlantic Sketches*, II, 29; *Louisiana Gazette*, October 23, 1823; New Orleans *Bee*, February 24, 1834.

whiskey which at least helped make such a life livable. The more stolid and phlegmatic Germans contented themselves generally with less exciting and demanding tasks as butchers, hired hands, and mechanics.[25] Some, however, found place in the police detail of the city, the New Orleans Guard, a notorious force of heavily armed gendarmes equipped with swords, pistols, muskets, and bayonets, whose frequent drunken and riotous violence made them as much a menace as a protection to public safety. The greatest part of the Guard, however, seems to have been recruited from that section of the city's population which remained least integrated into the normal pursuits of the community, the Spanish and Mexican residents of the Faubourg Marigny.[26] There in their retreat below the Quarter, apparently divorced from the interests of the rest of the city, these dark and silent people remained wrapped in their own concerns, difficult to discover from the forbidding and dangerous-looking men who lounged endlessly along the levee, enfolded in their great cloaks of foreign design, with no seeming occupation except that of leisure.[27]

A very large part of the city's population, giving their own character and vitality to the community, Negro slaves and free persons of color numbered twenty thousand and fifteen thousand respectively in the overall sixty thousand permanent residents of New Orleans in 1835.[28] Despite the city's ever-present preoccupation with the possibility of racial insurrection, this nonwhite segment of the community enjoyed an unbelievably free and un-disciplined existence. Seemingly masters of their own time in a great number of instances, slaves often managed to come and go where and how they pleased. Hiring themselves out as draymen, laborers, and mechanics, they frequently lived under no obligation except that of bringing to their masters a fixed portion of their incomes, beyond which they were free to establish themselves in separate dwellings in various parts of the city, to roam the streets at will, or to frequent their own gambling dens and public houses.[29]

25. *Louisiana Advertiser*, February 26, 1828; Duke of Saxe-Weimar, *Travels Through North America*, II, 84.

26. New Orleans *Mercantile Advertiser*, June 25, 1831, February 17, 1834; *Louisiana Advertiser*, February 14, 1834.

27. [Ingraham], *The Southwest*, I, 90.

28. New Orleans *Bee*, September 30, 1835.

29. New Orleans *Mercantile Advertiser*, January 20, 1825; *Louisiana Gazette*, August 7, 8, 1823; *Louisiana Advertiser*, October 23, 1823.

They made a picturesque sight, especially on Sundays, when they openly defied the law which confined their gatherings to Congo Square and congregated in various parts of the city. Hearty and fat, fitted out handsomely in the best of broadcloth and the finest of hats, they might be seen headed for balls and carousals, raising their voices in joyous and carefree song to a reigning favorite, "Rose, Rose, Coal Black Rose."[30] They loved to hire carriages for themselves on a Sabbath afternoon, and on the gala occasion when the Pontchartrain Railroad made its first run in 1831, slaves in hacks crowded around the road and even added to the congestion before the city hall.[31] One disgruntled white man indignantly protested in 1836 against the nuisance of having to dodge the smoke from slaves puffing cigars in the streets, but little seems to have come from his complaint.[32]

The overall behavior of the blacks showed little of the deference to whites which might have been expected in a slave community. They regularly gathered on street corners at night, for example, where they challenged whites to attempt to pass, hurled taunts at white women, and kept whole neighborhoods disturbed by shouts and curses. Prudence discouraged interference with them, for many went armed with knives and pistols in flagrant challenge to all the precautions of the Black Code. Much of this independence almost certainly stemmed from the clandestine familiarity which prevailed to a great extent between black and white in almost every part of town. On Tchoupitoulas, Camp, Julia, and New Levee Streets, for example, innumerable houses provided facilities in which both races, bound and free, caroused together in what could only be called intimacy.[33]

Equally unrestrained, the free persons of color enjoyed a status in Louisiana unequaled in any other part of the South.[34] They frequently owned and operated cabarets and gaming houses where slaves and free Negroes might consort without interference from the authorities, even after the curfew gun.[35] Many became so prosperous as barbers, stone masons, tailors, and artisans in a variety of specialties that they acquired large holdings of real

---

30. New Orleans *Bee*, June 13, 1833.

31. New Orleans *Mercantile Advertiser*, April 26, 1831.

32. New Orleans *Bee*, July 2, 1836.

33. *Louisiana Gazette*, November 6, 1823; New Orleans *Mercantile Advertiser*, October 29, November 4, 1825; New Orleans *Argus*, August 13, 1829; *Louisiana Courier*, July 30, 1833.

34. Annie Stahl, "The Free Negro in Ante-bellum Louisiana," *LHQ*, XXV (1942), 376.

35. New Orleans *Mercantile Advertiser*, October 29, 1835.

property throughout the city. Objections to the presence of Negro dwellings in the midst of a white neighborhood, interestingly enough, arose not from any protest against the Negroes themselves but against their frequent inability or refusal to keep their buildings in the proper state of repair.[36]

It was the free women of color who proved themselves the most enterprising. Many, burdened by age, ugliness, or a sense of righteousness, contented themselves with modest shops or presided over oyster, gumbo, and coffee stalls along the levee.[37] But a large if undetermined number monopolized the task of accommodating the licentiousness of the male part of New Orleans, no mean ambition when it is remembered that perhaps half of the city's men lived as bachelors in rooming houses or as husbands whose wives remained in the North. Those of the women favored by nature set themselves up in bordellos all over the city, even in the most respectable neighborhoods, or roamed the streets in open pursuit of trade.[38]

The most famous of these colored women, the quadroons, have been translated into another of the almost sanctified myths of New Orleans. Tradition notwithstanding, no evidence exists to suggest that these most handsome of the colored population, "Heaven's last, worst gift to white men," as one irate New Orleans housewife called them,[39] belonged to a kind of academy for the provision of highly cultivated and well mannered mistresses of white men. Any fairly light negress, as a matter of fact, might pass as a "quarteroon," and the activities of the class as a whole are not nearly so shrouded in mystery as has so often been reported. Newspapers openly engaged in frequently heated discussion of these people, and the facts are there for anyone to read.[40]

In the New Orleans custom known as *plaçage*, white men did, unquestionably, frequently establish so-called *ménages* in which to place the most favored of the quadroons as their paramours, usually in the picturesque row of low white houses which lined Rampart Street to the rear of the Quarter.[41] But most quadroons never won such favor, nor did white men usually

36. New Orleans *Bee*, May 13, 1836.

37. *Ibid.*, September 24, 1831.

38. New Orleans *Mercantile Advertiser*, September 29, October 6, 1825; New Orleans *Argus*, August 1, 1829.

39. *Niles' Register* (Baltimore), November 5, 1825.

40. New Orleans *Mercantile Advertiser*, January 18, September 29, 1825; *Louisiana Advertiser*, January 27, February 10, 1826.

41. Martineau, *Retrospect*, II, 127.

provide such caring attention. The famed "quadroon balls," those functions which tradition describes as gatherings of exemplary propriety where the tawny girls supposedly received the courtly invitations of the young bloods of the city, generally figured in newspaper and police reports as disreputable and usually violent assemblies deserving nothing so much as the proper title of interracial orgies.[42] At the St. Philip Street Theatre or the Washington Ball Room, quadroon prostitutes frequently delighted the crowd by parading in their night clothes,[43] often partnered by white women who attended out of curiosity "if not other motives," as the *Bee* reported in nicely turned phrase.[44]

Rigorously excluded from these affairs and tormented by the additional psychological confusion which set them apart as persons intermediate between slave and white, free men of color reacted in often bitter and contentious reaction to their estate. Easily provoked to assault whites in the streets, on several occasions they rioted in cabarets and railroad coaches, proclaiming their equality with white men and refusing to accept what they considered persecution from the ruling caste. Like the more unsupervised slaves, many lived within the system but refused to cower before it.[45]

The rural population outside New Orleans presented an almost equally varied composition. Surrounding the city, in Jefferson, Plaquemines, and St. Bernard Parishes, Latin creoles made up a clear majority. Along the Lower Coast the more well-to-do of their group presided over some of the state's richest sugar plantations, among a growing number of Americans attracted by the fabled productivity of the region. But the larger part of the population lived on a more modest scale, tending the many dairy farms and vegetable plots which made Jefferson Parish a chief provider of the city's

42. New Orleans *Mercantile Advertiser*, January 18, 1825; *Louisiana Advertiser*, February 10, 1826; Jabez W. Heustis, *Physical Observations and Medical Tracts and Researches on the Topography and Diseases of Louisiana* (New York, 1817), 26–27; Pierson, "Alexis de Tocqueville in New Orleans," 16. The immorality of the quadroon balls considerably shocked de Tocqueville, who found sensuality to be the "single tie" which brought the races together.

43. Keller, ed., "Diary of James D. Davidson," 362. There is no evidence that the quadroon balls were ever held at the Orleans Ball Room, despite tradition to that effect.

44. *Ibid.*; New Orleans *Bee*, November 21, 28, 30, 1835.

45. *Niles' Register*, August 24, 1833; New Orleans *Mercantile Advertiser*, November 24, 1825; New Orleans *Bee*, August 24, 1830, September 30, 1835, July 2, 1836; *Louisiana Courier*, July 30, 1833.

food,[46] toiling in flooded rice fields, or buried in the anonymity of those who hunted and fished in the teeming acres and waters of the deep delta country. Most isolated of all, a group called the Isleños traced their ancestry back to early Iberian settlers who had established New World homes in the Terre aux Boeufs, or "Ox Land," of St. Bernard, clustered along the bayou of the same bucolic name as it cut through the coastal marshland headed for Breton Sound. Few concerns of the rest of mankind filtered into this old-world fastness, where men lived much as their forebears had before them, crooning old Spanish songs as they watched over oxen or repaired their traps and nets. Removed from close neighbors almost as much as from the streets of the city, they kept to their own affairs in a paternalistic society whose patriarchs ruled practically as kings.[47]

Creoles predominated in the Upper Coast regions above New Orleans as well, though here, too, the rich lands and the promise of quick fortune had brought increasing American settlement to establish a demographic pattern replicated in the southwest along Bayou Lafourche and in the beautiful prairielands of Attakapas and Opelousas. But the southwestern parishes and segments of the coast also nourished a particularly distinctive Louisiana subculture, that of the Acadians, or Cajuns. Victims of one of the dramatic tragedies of western history, which had expelled their forebears from ancestral Canadian homes in the mid–eighteenth century, they allowed no rancor or bitterness to mar the natural good humor and contentment of their lives. That equable adjustment to fate certainly sprang from no enjoyment of a plentitude of material goods. They occasionally could be found settled on modest plots separating great plantations along Bayou Lafourche or even in the rich alluvial bottoms of the coast, but usually their domain was the poorer acres of the prairie region or the trackless miles of swamp and marsh which supplied so much of their sustenance. Rude frame houses provided their shelter, simple structures of wood, packed mud, and moss, sometimes covered by whitewash applied in sporadic bursts of energy and almost always backed by pig pens and hen roosts to add to the larder primarily filled by fishing and hunting.

As individuals, they generally possessed little in the way of physical attractiveness, the men gnarled and weather-beaten, the women unkempt

46. *Compendium of Inhabitants and Statistics of the United States* [Sixth Census, 1840].

47. Walter Prichard, ed., "Some Interesting Glimpses of Louisiana a Century Ago," *LHQ*, XXIV (1941), 46; Stoddard, *Sketches of Louisiana*, 167.

and poorly dressed, all running rapidly through the cycle of life to a premature old age. They purchased practically nothing except a little gunpowder, shot, and flour, and showed no envy of those with more of the world's goods. Generous in their friendship (so long as those who received it did not attempt to trick or deceive them), they related to other groups with kindness and respect, generally with less hostility to the American than that frequently exhibited by other creoles. Not overfond of work, at least they asked support from no one else, extended their hospitality to all, and accepted life as a pleasant journey cushioned by the joys of a warm family intimacy. Hardly distinguishable from them, a smaller group of Spanish creoles in the same area joined their numbers to make up the majority of the population along the Lafourche and around Donaldsonville. Generally small farmers, as illiterate and isolated as the Cajuns, they showed no more inclination than the latter to expand the narrow limits of their lives.[48]

Much the same population mixture prevailed, in effect, through this whole southwest area below the Red River, with the creoles in major preponderance, those of greater substance and social position dominating the river coast and some stretches of the rich bayou lands in the interior, while the more numerous and lowly Cajuns and Spanish held fast to those points not yet appropriated by wealth. Scattered through the whole, Americans who had purchased their way into this Latin domain held place generally in the upper class on the better lands.

But the principal stronghold of the Americans west of the Mississippi lay in the valley of the Red River and along the canebrake bayous which emptied into it. The Americans knew cotton better than they did sugar, and Red River cotton lands produced with a munificence sufficient to fulfill the dreams of any man. The area attracted not only the wealthy and industrious but the less endowed and energetic as well, those without capital or excess ambition recognizing that the pine acres north of the Red afforded healthy ground for leisurely and undemanding agrarian pursuits, a combination irresistible to many of the American newcomers.[49] Goodly numbers of French and Spanish creoles had settled there too, but the American clearly gave leadership and command to this community. The same held

48. W. H. Sparks, *The Memories of Fifty Years* (Philadelphia, 1870), 372–83; Nicholas P. Trist to Thomas M. Randolph, September 12, 1822, in Nicholas P. Trist Papers, LC; Richardson, "The Teche Country Fifty Years Ago," 593.

49. Flint, *Recollections*, 329.

true for the rich cotton lands along the Ouachita, and to some extent for the distant Natchitoches settlement, but in that latter outpost, with roots deep in the colonial past and with so many ties to Mexico, the French and Spanish could not be so easily overshadowed.

By and large, rural creoles and Anglo-Americans related to each other with much less friction and conflict than their counterparts experienced in New Orleans. On the whole an easygoing sort, profligate and reckless with money, and like his city cousin a man whose humors had created him more for the senses than for the intellect, the creole planter felt less threatened by the American presence than did those in the Gallic community of the metropolis. Very often unable to read or write, he claimed particular expertise in anything relating to horseflesh and would forego almost any pleasure to witness a race or hold a wager in one. He could and did consume vast quantities of claret, but even when sober had such uncertain control of his emotions as to be easily convulsed into explosive anger or moved to demonstrative expressions of good-fellowship. Beside him the American remained more reserved and taciturn, less outgoing in his behavior, but equally prone to that violence which cursed the Louisiana countryside. Though they frequently found it difficult to understand each other, rural distances did much to keep down friction, and on one thing they could agree—nothing in the world surpassed the importance of cotton, sugar, and dollars.[50]

Nowhere in Louisiana did the Americans dominate so completely as in the Florida parishes. For here they had status not as newly arrived migrants invading an old Latin stronghold but as men at home in a region which had known the English and American since the land first passed to British rule in 1763. That English control had been short-lived, to be sure, the Floridas going back to Spain in 1783, but it had been extended enough to establish a dominant Anglo-Saxon character to the section strengthened by steady reinforcements which moved in from Mississippi and the other American states. Many of the Floridians prided themselves on their descent from what they called the "blue bloods" of English, Scotch, and Irish nobility, especially in West Feliciana where the generous cotton lands sustained an affluent planter class as prosperous as any in the state.[51] But powerful and

50. *Ibid.*, 334–37.
51. Butler, "West Feliciana," 103.

influential as the cotton nabobs might have been, they represented but a small fraction of the total Florida population. The great mass of the people consisted of small farmers, artisans, or professional men, drawn from distant New England towns or from the closer southern countryside. Those who occupied the piney woods of St. Helena, Washington, and St. Tammany had no claim to superiority over the most backward Cajun or Latin creole, possessed no more of this world's goods, and remained content with an existence reliant on marginal farming and stock grazing. A little labor being sufficient to supply their needs, they labored only that little, comfortable in their "indolence, health, and poverty." But as has already been pointed out, this paucity seldom approached a truly desperate level, and by and large the "resin heels" fared quite well.[52]

Blacks composed a major portion of the rural population throughout the state, generally outnumbering the whites several times over in the great sugar and cotton plantation areas. The relatively few free persons of color outside New Orleans and Jefferson resided in older towns like Natchitoches, St. Martinville, and Alexandria, almost always creoles with ties back to the colonial period.[53] Information on the treatment accorded them and rural slaves in this early period remains rather sketchy, but some evidence suggests a control over their activities frequently as slack as that exercised in New Orleans. Slaves kept charge accounts with various publicans in Baton Rouge and could apparently roam the streets at will in search of balls, their favorite card games, and whatever else might catch their fancy,[54] while in St. Francisville whites lodged frequent protests against the presence of drunken Negroes who filled that village's streets almost every Sunday afternoon.[55] But these might well have been exceptions to a general rule.

Who could say, then, with any degree of completeness, what Louisiana was, this mixture of men and tongues, of conflicting ambitions, traditions, fears, and hopes? But as to what it was to become, its expectant public agreed that all signs seemed to point to a greatness unparalleled in the history of the young republic.

52. Flint, *Recollections*, 317, 329; Sparks, *Memories of Fifty Years*, 393 ff.; Baton Rouge *Gazette*, September 13, 1828.

53. *Compendium of Inhabitants and Statistics of the United States* [Sixth Census, 1840].

54. Baton Rouge *Gazette*, March 27, 1830.

55. *Louisiana Journal* (St. Francisville), May 19, 1825.

· III ·

FRONTIER ON THE MISSISSIPPI

With so much demanding attention in the bustling marts of the city, the broad fields of cane and cotton, the busy courts of law, and the Byzantine political arena, post-Purchase Louisiana had little time for introspection.

Querulous complaints occasionally appeared in the press bemoaning the intellectual and cultural sterility of the community, and some of the more serious-minded citizenry attempted to detail how that condition impoverished the spirit of the state. But these keen flashes of insight generally aroused only passing interest, proof in large measure of the basic accuracy of the analyses. Louisiana shrugged off examination of her failings with impatience, eager to get on with the pursuit which essentially defined the society as a whole—the business of acquiring wealth.[1] So thoroughly did this theme dominate the life of the community that it made of Louisiana a frontier settlement in as real a sense as if the area were still a battleground between white man and savage.

The same ruthlessness, unrestrained individualism, and hidden desperation which had so often been part of the pioneer push into the American West moved with relentless determination through the ranks of those who saw in Louisiana's fields or counting houses the promise of a golden ava-

1. For contemporary comments on this aspect of Louisiana, see Barton, *Introductory Lecture on New Orleans*, 5; Fearon, *Narrative of a Journey*, 278; Latrobe, *Journal*, 170; Conder, *Modern Traveler*, XXIV, 214; Daubeny, *Journal of a Tour*, 138.

lanche. This grasping for wealth almost brutalized the people, cutting great inroads into personal and public honesty, draining the society of those energies and visions which might have contributed to the fashioning of a life better suited to moral and rational beings, and twisting its leadership into ambitious seekers-after-power, impatiently vying for the right to rule rather than to serve. No other frontier demanded more alertness or guile, more insensitivity to evil, or more resistance to considerations of justice and mercy. These constituted the price of success, if not of mere survival.

Nothing better characterizes this Louisiana scene of the 1820s and 1830s than the inelegant phrase "on the make." Expectation ruled everywhere—it flourished out in the acres of cotton and sugar, where anxious planters watched and calculated for that one crop which would meet their money needs and allow perhaps for more land and slaves; it teemed in the city, where dreams of grandiose financial or mercantile killings found continual rebirth; it burned in the gambling dens, where the next turn of the card, the next roll of the dice must certainly bring fortune. Expectation provided the food on which every man fed, for certainly tomorrow would be his day.

In such an atmosphere little time or care could be allotted to things not directly connected to the exploitation of the region's opportunities or designed to gratify the senses, the urgings of which kept easy pace with the acquisitiveness of the community. Here was the sensate society in full flower.

The enormous educational needs of the state went largely unchallenged, the legislature refusing to do more than parcel out a pitiful sum to the parishes for the schooling of indigent children.[2] Governor Roman in 1832 admitted that even this pittance produced little but wasted time and effort. In one parish with two hundred educables, only ten attended public schools, all of them among the so-called indigents. The others could not afford the tuition charged by these institutions and refused to accept what they called charity.[3] Some wealthier families sent their children north for training, to Georgetown, for example, or to Mount St. Mary's College in Emmitsburgh, Maryland, St. Mary's College in Baltimore, or St. Mary's in Perry County, Missouri, but never in numbers greater than a small fraction

2. *Louisiana Gazette*, June 17, 1822; St. Francisville *Asylum*, November 13, 1824; *Louisiana Courier*, February 15, 1831; New Orleans *Bee*, June 10, 1835.

3. *Louisiana Courier*, February 15, 1831, January 4, 1832.

of the total educables.[4] By the 1830s New Orleans did begin to support a few private academies and had brought some order to its elementary central and primary schools. The Catholic Church, for its part, maintained the famous Ursuline Convent for girls, and St. Louis Cathedral provided some funds for charitable education,[5] but all these together could accommodate only a handful of students, with the inescapable result that the great mass of the youngsters of the state faced growing up without the slightest contact with formal education of any sort.

The evil was at its worst in the country parishes. Few of the Latin population had any appreciation for schooling in the first place, content to raise their sons in the knowledge of crops and horses and seeing little need for learning in the domestic calling of women.[6] The tutors that did offer their services to those of more enlightened views generally proved a disgrace to the profession, intellectual mountebanks with a reputation for drunkenness and dissoluteness exceeded by hardly any other group in the community. Few able men found any attraction in the work, for patrons frequently expected tutors to work out in the fields when the need arose or to fill in at any other chore, no matter how remote from the atmosphere of the classroom.[7] Among the Americans, many justified their neglect with the observation that peculiar cultural factors made it impossible to set up worthwhile schools in Louisiana, coupled with the pronouncement that education could best be obtained by sending children outside the state.[8] But relatively few Louisianians ever enjoyed the luxury of this distant training, especially when the conviction spread that the northern schools had become dens of antislavery propaganda and the academies of Europe the purveyors of monarchical heresy.[9]

No institution of higher learning worthy of the name existed anywhere in the state. The never successful Collège d'Orléans, opened in 1811 as a pathetic symbol of the early community's attempt to refute its supposed cultural poverty, finally came to a disgraceful end in the mid-1820s,

4. New Orleans *Bee*, August 6, 1831.

5. *Louisiana Gazette*, November 3, 1823; New Orleans *Bee*, June 10, 1835.

6. New Orleans *Argus*, January 17, February 2, 1827; St. Francisville *Asylum*, November 20, 1824.

7. New Orleans *Argus*, December 22, 23, 1826.

8. Flint, *Recollections*, 324.

9. New Orleans *Argus*, January 17, 1827.

brought to ruin by the presidency of the French regicide Joseph Lakanal in a tempest of personal scandal and ethnic bitterness. Jefferson College in St. James parish, the College of Louisiana at Jackson in the Floridas, and Lafayette College at St. Martinville never really attained a level above that of secondary schools, high in purpose and woefully low in accomplishment.[10]

Other phenomena equally disturbed those who felt that all was not right with Louisiana. "Literature in general is at its lowest ebb," sighed the editor of the New Orleans Bee in 1835, "and science and the fine arts have not yet dared to make their appearance among us. Not one literary society has yet been organized, there are no literary meetings, no literary parties. There is not a single lyceum or public library of repute for higher classes of intellect." The fledgling Louisiana Historical Society and the Medical Society of New Orleans offered some hope, but even these received but passing support. "Commercial transactions are indeed the prime objects of all our citizens," the editor observed, lamenting that "there is not one law library, not one medical library among us; and we all know too truly that there is not one library of any nature patronized by the professors of law, physics, and divinity." The complaint ended with the somber reflection that "The vacuum of professional leisure is therefore whiled away in idle gossiping or public carousing at balls, hotels, or theaters—and too often and fatally at banking games."[11] Meanwhile, the only literary paper in the state, the New Orleans Recorder, made ready to close its doors. It had gone broke.[12]

But some signs of creative genius flashed even in this realm of hedonists. The bizarre François-Xavier Martin, as famous for his restricted life of seclusion and miserliness as for the keen analytical decisions which he handed down from the state's supreme court, gave tribute to his adopted home with a History of Louisiana in the late 1820s. It remained for a brilliant young native, however, to produce what is still the classic story of the founding and growth of Louisiana down to 1815. Charles E. A. Gayarré, descendant of the colonial Spanish and true son of his own romantic age,

10. Louisiana Advertiser, July 21, October 1, 1823; Louisiana Courier, September 6, 1830; Attakapas Gazette (St. Martinville), May 15, 1830. A joint legislative committee reported in 1824 that with "the exception of some preparatory schools, Louisiana is without any means of education." Louisiana House Journal, 1824, p. 30.

11. New Orleans Bee, June 10, 1835. For a similar charge as late as 1846, see De Bow's Review, II (1846), 349.

12. New Orleans Bee, November 13, 1835.

at first called his work an *Essai Historique*, which he developed into the *Poetry or the Romance of the History of Louisiana*, replete with legend and fancy designed to amuse his readers. As he continued his creative labors, however, the spinner of tales succumbed to the fascination of ungilded fact, and the last volumes of Gayarré's study, joined to the flowery pages of his earlier work to form the *History of Louisiana*, stand as one of the state's major scholarly achievements and place him in the very forefront of the literary historians of his day.

No such excellence marked the excursions into drama made by some few Louisianians in the early 1830s. *The Martyr Patriots*, by T. W. Collens, gave to the St. Charles Theatre's patrons in 1836 a bombastic Greek tragedy version of the 1768 rebellion of Lafrenière and the Louisiana colonials against Spanish authority, a work which made it apparent that restraint did not figure among the literary virtues of the author. Somewhat earlier, John Reese's *Charlotte Temple* had been presented at the Camp Street Theatre, and in 1831 a Mr. Kennicott had fathered the amazing *Irma, or the Prediction*, with wild convolutions of plot and a multiplicity of soldier heroes, Indians, and sorcerers sufficient to bewilder even the most sophisticated.[13] In other fields, John J. Audubon had begun the nature paintings destined to make him world famous, but there was little else. The poetry of Abbé Rouquette, the delicacy of *Les Cenelles*, and the music of the fabulous Louis Moreau Gottschalk belonged to the future.

In the midst of this society wedded to money and pleasure, even the Kingdom of God had its difficulties. Primarily Roman Catholic by affiliation, Louisiana had small claim to any dedication to religious commitment. Internal turmoil had beset the Catholic Church throughout the colonial period, with French and Spanish Capuchins intriguing and plotting against each other and with the whole of that humble order in frequent clashes with the more urbane and accomplished Jesuits. The rationalism of the eighteenth century found receptive ground in Louisiana, and with the French Revolutionary upheavals there flowed into the colony and state

13. *Ibid.*, May 16, April 27, 1836. For Gayarré, see Henry P. Dart, ed., "The Autobiography of Charles Gayarré," *LHQ*, XII (1929), 10–11; John R. Ficklen, "Judge Gayarré's Histories of Louisiana," *PLHS*, III (1905), Pt. IV, 14–20. Nellie Smither, "A History of the English Theatre at New Orleans, 1806–1842," *LHQ*, XXVIII (1945), 87, says that some twelve plays in this period were supposedly authored by New Orleans writers.

many vocal champions of the views of Voltaire and Rousseau, men who attacked the pretensions of Rome at every turn.[14] None of these, however, proved as troublesome and dangerous to the Church as did those who embraced the Gallican view that the religious institution should be subservient to the state and who claimed the right as laymen to dictate the choice of their ecclesiastical leaders. Although centered in New Orleans, the heresy flared up occasionally in widely separated areas of the diocese, and the excitement and fury which howled around the question kept Louisiana Catholicism plunged for most of the first third of the nineteenth century in a storm of theological upheaval which threatened to destroy the religious life of the community.[15]

The quarrel bore characteristics reflective of more secular aspects of Louisiana life. The wardens of the St. Louis Cathedral—the *marguilliers*, as they were called—approached the Church with sentiments natural to their acquisitive fellowship. State charter designated the cathedral as their property, and they determined to manage their fief without interference, even claiming the right to name their own pastor and bishop. As chief exponent of their cause they chose the venerable Père Antoine de Sedella, a Spanish Capuchin once exiled by colonial governor Miro as an agent of the Inquisition, and perhaps the most beloved clergyman ever to serve New Orleans. No thunderings of the hierarchy could budge these stalwarts, no episcopal thrusts against the brown-clad monk could topple him from his place. For the nineteen years before 1820, indeed, no bishop dared set foot in the church of St. Louis and Père Antoine.[16]

The Capuchin's impregnable position rested on a firm and broad base, largely because in the truest sense he epitomized the character of his flock. Unlearned but shrewd, he moved through life with a supreme indifference to the niceties of ecclesiastical form or canon law and a tolerance for the weaknesses of his people which many more stern than he could accept as nothing short of an open invitation to sin. Sin seemed to concern Père Antoine hardly at all. Marriages, baptisms, burials—he performed them all, for

14. See, for example, the articles on religion in the New Orleans *Argus*, January 18, 19, 31, October 20, September 16, 19, 21, 1826, January 17, 1827, and in the *Louisiana Courier*, May 28, 1827.

15. New Orleans *Argus*, January 7, November 17, 1826.

16. Roger Baudier, *The Catholic Church in Louisiana* (New Orleans, 1939), 279.

the pious, the excommunicant, the duelist, the libertine, with a gracious charity which asked no questions and applied no law.[17] But with leniency, not surprisingly, there went indifference, and during the Capuchin's reign the New Orleans Church became little more than a shell. Few men ever went to Mass; confirmations declined almost to extinction, fasting and abstinence had slight or no observance, and during one six-month period including the Easter season, not a single parishioner received Communion in the cathedral.[18]

The rural areas suffered no less difficulty. There, too, secularism, deism, and indifference took their toll, abetted by the great distances which challenged the handful of priests who carried the burden of ministering to widely scattered congregations. Often ill prepared to serve in an American society, unfamiliar as they were with the ideas and mores of this new continent, the priests sometimes found their work further complicated by the resistance of parishioners who conceived them to be foreign agents of hated European states, in a region where the old enmities of Europe still festered.[19] Thus the Catholic Church occupied a position at this time and in this place with very limited power to give much of a moral or spiritual tone to the community. The awesome strength of its voice remained yet muted in Louisiana. Not until 1837, when the Jesuits opened their college at Grand Couteau, was there a successful Catholic school for Louisiana boys in an area which had known the cassock as long as it had known the white man.[20]

Nor did the weakness of Rome add strength to the forces of Geneva. The way of Protestantism in Louisiana had been blocked by almost insuperable obstacles, even after the transfer of the colony to the United States destroyed the exclusive rights granted to Catholicism by the traditional policy of France and Spain. Some Protestant missionaries had probably penetrated into Louisiana before 1803, and though the whole question remains buried in obscurity, some evidence indicates that a mulatto Baptist, Joseph Willis, preached at Vermilionville as early as 1789, while the ubiquitous Lorenzo Dow may well have toured the colony in the course of his

17. *Ibid.*, 275–76; Charles L. Souvay, "DuBourg and the Biblical Society," *St. Louis Catholic Historical Review*, II (1920), 25; *Louisiana Advertiser*, April 22, 1824.

18. Baudier, *Catholic Church in Louisiana*, 276.

19. New Orleans *Argus*, January 17, 1827.

20. Baudier, *Catholic Church in Louisiana*, 323.

journeys.[21] After the Purchase, Mississippi, especially Natchez, became the base of operations from which Protestant ministers began to push down into the territory. Their arrival created little stir in the Floridas, as might have been expected in that dominantly Anglo-Saxon region, but in New Orleans, the Latin southwest, and the deep delta country, the newcomers met with a stony hostility and resentment which rested on more than simple religious antagonism.[22] Protestantism inevitably suggested to Latin residents the shame of Anglo-American invasion, the wickedness of the hated British, and puritanical rigidities abhorrent to their natures.[23] As with the Catholics, Protestant missionary work suffered from a lack of funds and available workers, and even the flood of Americans to the newly acquired area helped little in the discouraging struggle. Resented and rejected by the creoles, the Protestant ministers often received only feeble encouragement from coreligionists absorbed in the business of setting up new careers in a new home.[24] In 1805 Edward Livingston and several associates established the first Episcopal church in New Orleans,[25] but in that same year Elisha Bowman, a Methodist cleric sent out by Bishop Francis Asbury with one hundred dollars as an expense fund, found his labors completely unrewarding in "this ungodly city" which seemed to him the very locus of hell itself. He moved on to Opelousas, only to be shocked again by the mores of the creoles, who told him, perhaps in solemn jest, that their priest swore, danced, and owned several race horses. Then, had he replied, would they all go to hell together. At the year's end, he had added seventeen members to his church; by 1825 the Methodists numbered in the whole state little more than ninety-nine whites and ninety Negroes.[26]

Aside from their firm establishment in the Floridas, the Baptists fared much the same, and only the brilliance of such young preachers as Sylves-

21. John T. Christian, A History of the Baptists of Louisiana (Shreveport, 1923), 33 ff.

22. Walter B. Posey, "The Advance of Methodism into the Lower Southwest," JSH, II (1936), 451.

23. John K. Bettersworth, "Protestant Beginnings in New Orleans," LHQ, XXI (1938), 835; New Orleans Bee, September 24, 1831.

24. Christian, History of the Baptists of Louisiana, 50 ff.; Posey, "Advance of Methodism in the Lower Southwest," 451.

25. Georgia F. Taylor, "The Early History of the Episcopal Church in New Orleans, 1805–1840," LHQ, XXII (1939), 432 ff.

26. Julie Koch, "Origins of New England Protestantism in New Orleans," South Atlantic Quarterly, XXIX (1930), 66; Posey, "Advance of Methodism in the Lower Southwest," 451.

ter Larned and the remarkable Theodore Clapp gave some vigor and prominence to the Presbyterian foundation in New Orleans.[27] By and large, not until the mid-1830s could the Protestant Church be assured of a growing place in the life of Louisiana. The great prosperity and expansion of the port and the opening of new cotton and sugar lands in the state meant eventual reinforcements for the Protestant sects as thousands of psalm-singing yeomen farmers moved into the uplands of the northern parishes and hordes of displaced German Reformed and Lutheran believers poured into New Orleans.[28]

But for most of the 1820s and 1830s, the ecclesiastic establishment could count few triumphs in this community. Particularly in New Orleans, with its extremes of every conceivable kind, there seemed to be pervasive acceptance that life might very well be short and brutal, and so while time remained there was money to be made, oceans of claret and whiskey to be drained, and a full measure of sins to be enjoyed. No Moses marched down into their midst from Sinai and the idols ruled supreme.

Many additional factors conspired to keep Louisiana relatively undeveloped and culturally backward. A peculiar geography cut the interior of the state into several isolated pockets, forcing settlers to forego much of that social and intellectual quickening which thrives upon close contact and exchange with the great communities of the world. The mass of the people lived along the network of rivers, streams, and bayous which twisted and curled through the state like the feelers of some great preternatural insect, and few of these as early as the 1830s had links to any system of navigation which might provide easy and regular interchange of goods and travelers.[29] The journey from New Orleans to the Attakapas, for example, could be one of almost incredible delay and arduousness, as Professor Charles Daubeny of Oxford discovered in 1837 when he went to visit with Alexander Porter at Oak Lawn. Finding entrance to Bayou Plaquemine blocked because of the low water in that stream, Daubeny and Porter abandoned their Mississippi steamboat, traveled the bayou by skiff, and then pushed

27. See Theodore Clapp, *Autobiographical Sketches and Recollections during a Thirty-five Years' Residence in New Orleans* (Boston, 1857), *passim*.

28. Christian, *History of the Baptists of Louisiana*, 50 ff.

29. *Louisiana Courier*, January 11, 1828; New Orleans *Commercial Bulletin*, June 24, 1836.

on by foot through three miles of swamp before reaching their destination in the Teche country. On the return trip the steamship had to be pulled up Bayou Plaquemine by crew members straining at the end of a hawser, only to run aground in the Mississippi above New Orleans and thus force the outdone Daubeny to trudge another three miles to the city.[30] Even the great Red River, leading to Alexandria and Natchitoches, frequently became unnavigable during low water, passage blocked by the tremendous raft of tangled logs above the latter town, which for many years delayed the growth of the northwestern section.[31]

Travel by land in many areas often proved extremely difficult if not impossible. One or two miles back from the waterways the ground generally fell away into swamp or marshland, trackless, vast, and alive with danger. Except for the roads which ran before the farms and plantations ranged along the rivers and bayous, or the Military Road built by Jackson across the lake from New Orleans through the Floridas to Mississippi, few land arteries of any consequence could be found.[32] Bridges across the larger streams were rare,[33] and what roads and facilities did exist often became impassable as a result of natural decay or the ravages of neglect. No travel overland from Alexandria to the Mississippi, for example, was possible except in late fall or winter, for in spring the road became an "inundated swamp."[34] This lack of easy movement and transportation persisted as one of the greatest constraints on Louisiana's growth and development, few immigrants being drawn to settlement in areas, no matter how rich the land, where they found themselves cut off from the outside world, surrounded by stagnant water, bayous, and marshland navigable only to the snake and the alligator.[35]

30. Daubeny, *Journal of a Tour*, 141–46. See also Walter Prichard *et al.*, eds., "Southern Louisiana and Southern Alabama in 1819: The Journal of James Leander Cathcart," *LHQ*, XXVII (1945), 835.

31. John Sibley to Josiah S. Johnston, October 5, 1825, in Johnston Papers, HSP. J. Fair Hardin, "The First Great Western River Captain," *LHQ*, X (1927), 36 ff.; Caroline S. Pfaff, "Henry Miller Shreve," *LHQ*, X (1927), 224.

32. Julian P. Bretz, "Early Land Communication with the Lower Mississippi Valley," *MVHR*, XIII (1926), 18.

33. New Orleans *Commercial Bulletin*, June 24, 1836.

34. Flint, *Recollections of the Last Ten Years*, 322.

35. New Orleans *Commercial Bulletin*, June 24, 1836.

The isolation suffered by these disparate sections of the state found reinforcement in a mail service which had not yet begun to approach control over distance, natural barriers, the carelessness of federal administrators, and the ineptness of postal agents. Almost from the time of the Purchase, the federal government had made vague promises of a great Washingtonto-New Orleans highway east of the Alleghenies, which would have meant a vast improvement in the communication service to the state. Secretary of the Treasury Albert Gallatin pushed such a measure in 1808—it reappeared in Congress in 1817 and again in 1824—but as late as the 1830s nothing had been done, and economic news basic to merchants, political information vital to the public, and private correspondence of great and small import moved into the state with haphazard irregularity by slow stage from Nashville or perhaps on the leaky and plodding mail boats from Mobile. To be thus served in an era when mail was virtually the only link with distant parts was hardly to be served at all.[36]

These failings intensified tremendously the natural rural tendency to separateness and localism, and the areas of settlement throughout the state consequently bent back in upon themselves in a way which generated both frontier simplicity and violence. A man learned to depend upon his own resources in such a community, with sword canes, dirks, Spanish knives, and pistols ever within easy reach to serve in the explosions of anger and conflict so much a part of the regular experience of the region.[37] Few men had the superb gift for this sort of thing possessed by Jim Bowie, already settling his quarrels in the Alexandria area with the deadly butcher knife which still bears his name, but others with various levels of his deadly skills could be found in every part of the state.[38]

On the lighter side, even such a proud region as the Felicianas could not hide its rough and rustic manners, as seen, for example, in the reports of a German immigrant to his family in 1825. "We celebrated July 4th, our Indepen[den]ce Day," he wrote, "by holding a parade of canoes on the bayou, and firing a salute. . . . At 3 o'clock P.M. we had a splendid dinner at the Stephenson Hotel, and at 4 o'clock most of the citizens of St. Francisville

36. Bretz, "Early Land Communication with the Lower Mississippi Valley," 9–28; *Louisiana Courier*, December 4, 1832, January 5, 1833.

37. *Louisiana Messenger*, December 15, 1826.

38. Samuel L. Wells to Josiah S. Johnston, September 27, 1827, in Johnston Papers, HSP.

were more or less drunk. That practically ended the 4th of July celebration."[39]

But this same Max Nuebling would also write that here in Louisiana he
had found the land of his hopes.[40] The lure of its promise had caught him
as it had so many others, the merchants, planters, clerks, the lawyers and
politicos, the natives and the transplanted. Violent, rough, materialistic,
and grasping it might be, but it was a society which knew and savored the
excitement of life.

39. Max Nuebling to Dietrich Hall, July 24, 1825, in Nuebling Letter Book, LSU.
40. *Ibid.*

· IV ·

Skeleton of Iron

It was said of the creoles, George Washington Cable tells us, that when the tricolor came down in the Place d'Armes in 1803, they wept.[1] Some have read into those tears a sign of despair at the termination of the brief reunion with a beloved France, but the greater likelihood is that they bespoke a different message altogether. There can be no question as to the native Louisianian's emotional attachment to the homeland of his forebears. He spoke its language, shared its loyalties and prejudices, reflected its manners and customs. To be separated from it again meant surely to suffer the pangs of ending a treasured and binding relationship. But nothing in his reaction pointed to a rejection of his new status as citizen of the young and prospering Union to which he had been joined by the Louisiana Purchase. And so he wept and looked forward to a future brightened by the prospect of economic blessings and political empowerment which he had never known as a subject of European monarchy. But the mixed reaction evidenced by his behavior in the square that December morning gave clear signal that both he and his new fellow countrymen had embarked on an experience unique in the expansion of American democracy.

In truth, the assimilation of Louisiana into the United States in 1803 presented a tremendous challenge to all those engaged in the enterprise. With little preparation of any sort, provincial and sheltered Louisianians

---

1. George E. Waring and George W. Cable, *The History and Present Condition of New Orleans* (Washington, D.C., 1881), 32.

plunged into the confusing business of learning to govern themselves while striving at the same time to adjust to the swarm of newcomers who descended into their midst to become partners in the venture. The task weighed heavily upon them. Behind the Virginia of President Jefferson and the territory's new governor, W. C. C. Claiborne, there stretched decades of participation in self-government and even longer centuries of Anglo-Saxon traditions of freedom. Behind the Louisiana of the creoles stretched nothing but the colonial rule of France and Spain, nations themselves destitute of any vital substance of political democracy. The Legislative Assembly of Virginia had been almost one hundred years old, it is well to remember, when Bienville first planted New Orleans on the banks of the Mississippi.

Only twelve years bridged the gap in Louisiana from colony to full statehood in the American union. Political immaturity and the clash of cultures and national groupings were not auspicious stars under which to begin a new life, but they were inescapable. How much, then, could be expected from the Constitution of 1812 under which Louisiana entered into statehood? Cumbersome, conservative, unbalanced, a patchwork of conflicting interests and designs, it remained in effect until 1845. To understand what went into its making is to begin to understand the political milieu of Louisiana's Jacksonian experience.

Sensing that time played to the advantage of the American invader, the native Louisianians in 1812 used their numerical strength to structure a state government favorable to their interests and almost impervious to change. They designed it specifically to freeze legislative power in those areas where they might hope to maintain dominance and then instituted property qualifications for officeholding and a tax-based suffrage system which severely limited political participation by those new to the land.

The constitution divided the state into fourteen senatorial districts, forever indivisible and allocated in a pattern which guaranteed that New Orleans and the sections above Red River where American numbers might grow would always have a voting strength less than that of districts along the coast and in the southern interior where Gallic influence almost certainly would remain paramount.[2] Even the addition of the Florida parishes

2. Article II, Section 10, in Benjamin W. Dart, ed., *Constitutions of the State of Louisiana and Selected Federal Laws* (Indianapolis), 500.

to the state shortly after adoption of the constitution, with a dubiously valid assignment of three extra senate districts to that area, failed to equalize regional representation in the upper house. With their great superiority of population and qualified voters, the Floridas and New Orleans had to content themselves with a senatorial voice no greater than that accorded the combined forces of the four least developed districts in the state. The single vote of the great metropolis counted no more than that of Pointe Coupee, with a fraction of New Orleans' population and voting strength.[3]

Composition of the lower chamber, too, though to a lesser degree, reflected this determination to preserve the status quo. Representation was apportioned among thirteen counties, subdivided into the unique parish units peculiar to Louisiana, to be "forever regulated and ascertained by the number of qualified electors therein," as determined by regular four-year census counts. Total membership of the house of representatives could never exceed fifty, thus placing a limit on the possibility of a significant shift of power by the rapid growth of any one area.[4]

Buttressing this already sturdy design, a series of qualifications limited those who might sit in these bodies or participate in the choice of their membership. In addition to the pro forma requirement that all legislators be free white citizens of the United States, senators had to be at least twenty-seven years of age, resident four years in the state and one year in their district, and possess landed property in that area valued at one thousand dollars or more. Representatives must have reached the age of twenty-one, with residence of two years in the state and one in their county, with a landed property holding of at least five hundred dollars according to the tax list.[5] Suffrage was limited to adult American citizens who had resided at least one year in their county and whose names had been enrolled on the state tax list during the six-month period immediately preceding an election.[6]

The same purpose which shaped these legislative and suffrage patterns also determined the constitution's provisions respecting the state's gover-

3. See, for example, Henry A. Bullard and Thomas Curry, eds., A New Digest of the Statute Laws of the State of Louisiana (New Orleans, 1842), 544, and Louisiana House Journal, 1822, p. 26.

4. Article II, Section 6, in Dart, ed., Constitutions of Louisiana, 500.

5. Article II, Section 12, ibid., 500.

6. Article II, Section 8, ibid., 500.

norship. Election of the chief executive was by joint ballot of the two houses of the assembly, choice being limited to one of the two candidates standing highest in the returns from a general state election. To be eligible, a candidate had to be a citizen of the United States, at least thirty-five years of age, resident six years in the state, and possessed of landed property valued at five thousand dollars or more. Tenure was for four years, with succession in office prohibited. This peculiar indirect electoral process assured the creole faction almost foolproof certainty of control over the choice of governors. Guaranteed a legislative majority by the constitution's apportionment schedules, and equally certain that at least one of the two leading candidates would be of their number, creoles could await the popular returns and then snatch their man to the governor's chair even if he stood second on the poll.[7]

Having assured a creole advantage in the gubernatorial election process, the constitution then placed extraordinary powers in the hands of the executive. In addition to the usual right to enforce the laws and command the state militia, governors received sweeping command of appointments, allowing them to name, with advice and consent of the senate, a secretary of state, all judges, the attorney general, all sheriffs, all justices of the peace, and all other state officers whose method of choice had not been specified.[8] In addition, they might veto proposed legislation, a right not generally accorded executives in most state constitutions of the period. State legislation eventually gave them additional power to name attorneys for the state's judicial districts, all surveyors, notaries, auctioneers, various state bank directors, coroners, regents for the central and primary schools in New Orleans, port wardens and harbormasters—creating, in effect, a vast gubernatorial patronage system.[9] The life terms of judges, surveyors, notaries, coroners, and several other lesser officers added considerably to this structure of aristocracy by tenure. As crowning testimony to their exalted position, Louisiana governors enjoyed a salary of $7,500 a year, higher by $2,500 than the closest similar payment by a sister state.[10] Legislative checks on executive power conformed to the typical American pattern. A

7. Article III, Section 2, *ibid.*, 501.

8. Article III, Section 9, *ibid.*, 502.

9. Bullard and Curry, eds., *New Digest of the Laws of Louisiana*, 26, 30, 36, 37, 373, 464, 537, 796.

10. *Louisiana Gazette*, June 14, 1821.

two-thirds vote of each house might override a gubernatorial veto, and any executive misdemeanor in office could lead to impeachment.

The judicial system reflected much the same conservative temper, capped by a supreme court with appellate jurisdiction in civil cases involving sums over three hundred dollars. Administratively, the court functioned in two distinct districts, the eastern comprising the Isle of Orleans, the Floridas, the coast up to Red River, and the Lafourche area, the western embracing the prairies, Red River country, Ouachita, and Concordia.[11] It met in regular session in New Orleans from November through July, then moved west for sittings at Opelousas and Alexandria during August, September, and October. Despite a usually crushing press of business, its membership remained at the minimum three justices required by the constitution until as late as 1839.[12]

District judges presided over seven inferior judicial districts, hearing most criminal cases and possessing final decision in such matters—no appeal could lie to the high court in other than civil cases. The district court also tried civil disputes brought to it on appeal from the parish courts and justices of the peace, its judgments being final in all litigation involving less than three hundred dollars. Each parish had in addition a parish judge, whose jurisdiction extended to all civil matters in suits under three hundred dollars and to a criminal authority over abuse, assault or battery, and all crimes committed by slaves. Finally, justices of the peace throughout the state served as judges in lesser suits and functioned as general preservers of order in the community.[13]

Legislation established a system of local government based on parish divisions, with police juries in each empowered to regulate slaves, make and repair roads, bridges, dikes, and levees, control movements of cattle, establish ferries, police taverns and public houses, levy taxes for public works, and appoint treasurers and constables for the various units. The same qualifications as those which applied to the lower house of the state assembly governed eligibility in local elections, extending the constitution's conservative limitations down to the most basic level.[14]

11. Article IV, Section 3, in Dart, ed., *Constitutions of Louisiana*, 501.
12. Bullard and Curry, eds., *New Digest of the Laws of Louisiana*, 176, 180.
13. *Ibid.*, 182–83, 208, 528.
14. *Ibid.*, 639, 640, 647.

As the single major urban community in the state, New Orleans enjoyed a considerable degree of self-government and exemption from many of the otherwise universal restraints imposed outside her limits. Executive authority vested in a mayor, required to be at least thirty years old, a resident for four or more years, owner of city property valued at no less than three thousand dollars, and with status as head of a family (a strange requirement with potential of various kinds of trouble). Chaired by an official called the recorder, a city council served as the legislative body of the municipality, its membership made up of aldermen representing wards whose limits and relative delegate strength were fixed by the state legislature. Membership on the council required a two-year residence in the city and a landed property holding of one thousand dollars within its jurisdiction. Any adult citizen with a year's residence in the city and a listing on the state tax rolls might vote in municipal elections.[15]

This city government wielded broad powers of local control. Subject to the mayor's veto, which might be overridden, the council levied taxes on city property, licensed taverns, inns, drays, and carts, regulated building standards and wharfage space, and held complete police power over those within its bounds. A New Orleans parish court exercised concurrent jurisdiction with the state district tribunal over all civil cases arising in Orleans Parish, criminal cases being assigned to a third and completely distinct judicial unit. After 1825 a city court with five judges replaced justices of the peace to hear cases involving minor infractions of the law.[16]

Elections of a complete house of representatives and one-half of the senate took place every two years, with each fourth year given over also to the election of a governor. Constitutional edict scheduled balloting in these contests to begin on the first Monday in July and to last for three days, another sign of the foresight of the native Louisianians in fashioning this organic law. The political strength of the American faction dwindled significantly at that time of the year as many of its numbers fled the state in the sound conviction that the summer months could be a season of death for those not acclimated to its rigorous seasons.

State law made parishes the basic electoral units, combining them in

15. *Ibid.*, 99–102.
16. *Ibid.*, 99–102, 192–93, 208, 213.

senatorial balloting, however, when more than one parish made up a senatorial district. In either case, voting took place in the parish division, presided over by the parish judge, assisted by two justices of the peace chosen by him as commissioners of the election. The various parish commissioners in a multiparish senate district would meet subsequent to the voting and combine their returns, while house members were decided immediately on the parish level. The process worked somewhat in reverse in Orleans, which, although a single parish, made up two senatorial districts, one the city of New Orleans, the other the rest of the parish plus Jefferson. Each parish filed its returns in a gubernatorial race with the state legislature, which then met the following session to make the formal choice from the two highest candidates.[17]

Parish judges and commissioners chose the polling places in elections unless these had been otherwise fixed by special enactment, not uncommon when a parish was subdivided into electoral districts to make the polls more accessible to voters. In such cases respectable citizens served as poll commissioners, their returns subject to final accrediting by the parish judge. Each eligible citizen entered his vote for all candidates on a single ballot, which might be written or printed. At receipt of the ticket the judge called out the name of the voter and confirmed his residence in the district and his registration on the tax list. Absence of one's name from the roll could be rectified by producing a suitable tax receipt or by convincing the judge and commissioners by oath that the required tax had been paid and that the property on which it had been levied had not been received from another party simply to confer the right of suffrage, with the property to revert to the original owner following the campaign.[18]

Maintenance of order at the polls fell to the parish sheriff, subject to the lawful direction of the commissioners. Anyone offering more than one ballot lost his vote, and any attempt by unauthorized persons to read the deposited tickets made them subject to criminal prosecution. Sale of one's vote for any consideration, whether for money, food, or drink, credit or extension of debt, resulted in loss of that ballot and the possibility of fine and imprisonment, a penalty equally applicable to the briber. During the three

17. *Ibid.*, 390–91.
18. *Ibid.*, 389, 395, 386.

days of the poll, the ballot box remained securely fastened by three locks, each commissioner holding a different key.[19]

At the federal level, the counties of Orleans, German Coast, Acadia, and Lafourche made up the state's First Congressional District; Iberville, Pointe Coupee, and Feliciana, the Second; and Attakapas, Opelousas, Rapides, Natchitoches, Ouachita, and Concordia, the Third. Elections for these offices were held in the same manner and at the same time as those for the state assembly.[20] The legislature chose the state's federal senators by joint ballot of both houses on the second Monday of the January preceding expiration of an incumbent's term, with vacancies filled in the same way except when the legislature's being out of session required a gubernatorial appointment, valid until the assembly resumed its meetings.[21]

Consistent with the idea of limited suffrage and centralized power, state law kept the choice of Louisiana's five presidential electors firmly in the hands of the state legislature until after the disputed election of 1824. How change came to be introduced into this single aspect of the voting system of the state may better be told in the later narrative of the beginnings of the Jacksonian movement in Louisiana.[22]

Much of these governmental details depended on legislative enactment. But the great pillars of the edifice—representation and suffrage requirements, legislative and executive powers—rested on foundations cemented into the organic law and designed to keep Louisiana forever French and forever free of control by the American intruder. Having built to their pleasure, the original planners then made it practically impossible to change the design of the structure. Amendment of the constitution required a process so awkward and baffling as to frustrate any attempt at reform. If the legislature during the first twenty days of a regular session passed a measure listing specific changes to be made in the constitution, the proposal was referred to popular vote at the next election of representatives. Popular disapproval killed it, but a favorable reception required the next legislature to vote for a *second* referendum on the same question the following year. Rati-

19. *Ibid.*, 386–93.

20. Louis Moreau Lislet, ed., *A General Digest of the Acts of the Legislature of Louisiana Passed from the Year 1804 to 1827, Inclusive* (2 vols.; New Orleans, 1828), I, 424–26.

21. Bullard and Curry, eds., *New Digest of the Laws of Louisiana*, 378–79.

22. Moreau Lislet, ed., *Digest of the Acts of the Legislature of Louisiana*, I, 449–50.

fication of a proposal by both of these popular votes bound the legislature at its next meeting to call for a constitutional convention to readopt, amend, or recast the fundamental law.[23] Not surprisingly, this first state constitution remained completely unaltered from 1812 to 1845.

The geographic patterns of Louisiana politics in the 1820s might best be compared to an enormous kaleidoscope, whose basic design regularly twisted into new shapes as perspectives and vantage points themselves shifted to reflect the multifaceted workings of a functioning governmental system. At first glance its fundamental composition seemed simple enough, formed naturally by the distinct geographic sections of the state. Almost like feudal domains they stood, each with its own interests, its own leadership and pride: the metropolitan center of New Orleans and its suburb parish of Jefferson; St. Bernard and Plaquemines below the city; then the Upper Coast, stretching along the banks of the Mississippi up to the Florida parishes and Red River; Lafourche, following its spinal bayou down to the sea; Attakapas and Opelousas in the midst of vast prairielands; the Red River country of Avoyelles, Catahoula, Rapides, and Natchitoches, with its productive river bottoms and equally bountiful uplands; Ouachita and Concordia, resting on the rich alluvial gift of their waterways; and finally the Floridas, composite of seignorial plantations and petty farms.

Common interests linked various of these geographic districts together at one political level, only to yield to another set of objectives forging different alliances to compete in a second arena. The predominantly creole communities along the coast and in the southwestern parishes, for example, united in unflagging Gallic antagonism against the equally combative American stronghold in Florida and the north-central districts beyond Red River, a division which consistently dominated sectional disputes over legislative apportionment and gubernatorial choice. But elections to the United States Senate split the state along entirely different eastern and western judicial district lines, each region jealously guarding its claim to one of the posts in the national chamber. Biennial campaigns to fill the three congressional seats generated combinations in yet a third configuration as well, and a final pattern, related to the entire scope of public policy, massed all of the rural sections, divided as they might be in other matters,

23. Article VII, in Dart, ed., *Constitutions of Louisiana*, 506–507.

into one solid bloc against the city of New Orleans. This was the crazy-quilt plain on which political leaders of early Louisiana fought their battles.[24]

Traditional historiography has regrettably gone astray in seeking to define the major issues and motives shaping Louisiana politics in the antebellum period. It centers on an assumption that the Constitution of 1812 and those who directed political life under it aimed primarily at fixing control in the hands of a slaveholding, commercial upper class, with intent to exclude from office holding and voting all those outside that favored group. One such estimate claims flatly that the constitution "never admitted to the polls more than a third of the adult freemen," and "favored planters in the black belt at the expense of white people in New Orleans and on the frontier." Everything in the political activity of the early state is consequently represented as having its root cause in the determination of an undifferentiated "black belt" aristocracy to establish and maintain hegemony over "white belt" common folk.[25]

That such observations contain at least some truth can scarcely be denied. Suffrage requirements under the Constitution of 1812 did give undue influence to the older, rural, slaveholding regions. The state tax program rested primarily on the kind of property an agrarian slaveholder would of necessity own—real estate, slaves, cattle, horses, and mules. Towns and the sole city of New Orleans paid their share too, not only in taxes on real and slave property, but in a variety of other levies charged against merchants, retailers, brokers, auctioneers, taverns, carriages, billiard tables, and corporation stock. But a surprisingly large number of city dwellers, clerks, laborers, draymen, barbers, tailors, mechanics, and even professional men owned no such properties and paid no such taxes, causing them to be politically impotent. Many in the new American migration belonged to this category, and when one considers also that a large part of the rural population, French and American alike, remained landless or settled in fringe areas where clouded land titles, the practice of squatting, and a relatively lower incidence of slaveholding pared down the tax list, it is easy to understand

24. *Louisiana Gazette*, January 12, December 29, 1824.

25. The classic statement of this class conflict interpretation is that of Roger W. Shugg, *Origins of Class Struggle in Louisiana* (Baton Rouge, 1939). For a detailed analysis of the methodological and interpretative failures of this study, see Joseph G. Tregle, Jr., "Another Look at Shugg's Louisiana," *LH*, XVII (1976), 245–81.

how such a system gave undisputed political advantage to the more affluent segments of society.[26]

But the interpretation which sees class conflict as the primary moving force in this political system, pitting a slaveholding aristocracy against a lower class of yeoman farmers and unpropertied workers, stems from a failure to grasp how thoroughly that dynamic was actually energized instead by the ethnic and regional antagonisms described above. Any upper-class aggrandizement flowing from the governmental patterns established by the Constitution of 1812 came as a by-product of the Gallic formula for containing the American threat rather than as the galvanizing purpose of aristocratic policy. The factor of timing also requires attention. A number of state constitutions in 1812 contained restrictive aspects derived from an earlier, less democratic climate. It was Louisiana's fate to embrace these arrangements when the tides of change had already begun to sweep them away in other areas. Once accepted, the peculiar inflexibility of the 1812 document maintained them for decades, secure against any innovation which might upset the delicate political balance in a state torn between the forces of the past and those of the ever growing non-Latin future.[27]

Even given its undoubted restrictive consequences, the Constitution of 1812 never produced the degree of political exclusionism posited in the class-conflict interpretation. Despite an incidence of slaveholding less than that found in the southwestern black belt, for example, the Florida parishes and those north of Red River in 1820 possessed 38.5 percent of the qualified voters of the state, a considerable margin over their 30.5 percent of white male Louisianians over age twenty in that same year. Property qualifications and all other difficulties encountered under the 1812 constitution did not keep the voting eligibility of this area below 58 percent of the adult male population of 1820, a figure not to be guessed from the assertion that the strictures of the organic law never admitted more than a third of Louisiana's freemen to the polls. In the region south of Red River, excluding Orleans and Jefferson Parishes, 59 percent of the white adult males in 1820 had access to the ballot box.

26. Bullard and Curry, eds., *New Digest of the Laws of Louisiana*, 700–701. John Sibley to Josiah S. Johnston, January 3, 1826, in Johnston Papers, HSP; *Louisiana Advertiser*, August 25, 27, 1823. For an examination of the demographics of the antebellum state, see Tregle, "Another Look at Shugg's Louisiana," 245–81.

27. See Fletcher M. Green, "Democracy in the Old South," *JSH*, XII (1946), 11–16.

Despite its 34.5 percent of the state's white male population, the Orleans-Jefferson metropolitan area in 1820 held only 17 percent of Louisiana's eligible electors, and only 23 percent of its adult white inhabitants possessed the right to vote—a dismal record compared with that of any other section of the state. Things improved not at all during the ensuing decade, the metropolitan area sending only 15 percent of its adult white males to the polls in the gubernatorial election of 1830, to cast a meager 15.3 percent of the total state vote. Many factors occasioned this seeming disfranchisement of the great commercial mart. As already noted, the tax requirement for voting proved particularly discriminatory against city dwellers not likely to own the kind of property subject to taxation. But an accurate estimate of the exact degree to which the metropolitan area's white male inhabitants lagged behind those elsewhere in enjoyment of voting rights is impossible to determine. Official lists of certified citizens of the United States simply did not exist in the state at that time, nor did census returns indicate place of birth of residents until the tabulation of 1850. Evidence on all sides, however, clearly indicated that the percentage of foreign-born in the New Orleans population far exceeded that to be found anywhere else in the state, just as experience supported the likelihood that the great proportion of that number had never been naturalized. No one could say, therefore, how many of the free white males of the metropolis were actually citizens, making it consequently impossible to determine precisely how much legitimate inequity is reflected in its paucity of legislative registration and voter strength as compared to its total population numbers. All in all, despite the dismal totals in the metropolitan area, at least 45 percent of adult white Louisianians had the right to vote in 1820, and as many as 34 percent of them did so in the gubernatorial election of 1830, figures which would be considerably higher if one were able to factor out the unquestionably large number of unnaturalized foreigners included in the total white male population count. (For more information on suffrage percentages and qualified electors, see Tables 1 and 2.)[28]

28. These computations are based on the unpublished federal census returns for Louisiana in 1820 and 1830, the census of eligible electors in the state taken in 1821 (*Louisiana House Journal*, 1822, p. 26), and the state election returns for 1830 (*Louisiana House Journal*, 1831, p. 7). These last returns were used instead of the state voter census taken in 1829 because though that survey was reported to the legislature, seemingly no copies were printed, nor are they extant in the archives of the Louisiana secretary of state.

TABLE 1: SUFFRAGE PERCENTAGES, 1830

Parishes	I	II	III	IV	V
Florida and North of Red River					
Ouachita	708		265		531 families, 218 hold slaves
Avoyelles	452		222		
Catahoula	415		176		
Claiborne	389				271 families, 61 hold slaves
Concordia	384		90		
E. Baton Rouge	984		399		
E. Feliciana	871		437		
Natchitoches	1,168		390		
St. Helena	633		366		480 families, 214 hold slaves
Rapides	671		274		404 families, 246 hold slaves
St. Tammany	360		143		
Washington	354		265		278 families, 113 hold slaves
W. Feliciana	710		282		487 families, 297 hold slaves
Totals	7,680	30%	3,315	39.4%	

   I: White Male Population over Twenty-one
  II: Percentage of State Population over Twenty-one
 III: Vote in 1830 Election
 IV: Percentage of Votes Cast in 1830 Election
  V: Slaveholding Incidence

As liberalization of suffrage and representation spread quickly in other states during the so-called Era of Good Feeling, demands for similar democratization of the Louisiana political system became more and more frequent during the 1820s and 1830s. But all such proposals shattered against the rock-hard determination of Gallic political leadership to maintain the advantages given its particular ethnic constituency by the Constitution of 1812. The New Orleans–Jefferson metropolitan area provided this faction its most readily exploited instrument for maintaining a status quo favorable to the Gallic interest. By continuing to link suffrage to tax liability, it kept a cap on any significant increase in American voting strength in the area

Table I, *continued*: Suffrage Percentages, 1830

Parishes	I	II	III	IV	V
South of					
Red River					
Terrebonne	268		85		
St. Landry	1,529		438		
St. John	441		195		196 families, 179 hold slaves
St. James	596		391		445 families, 333 hold slaves
St. Charles	233		94		190 families, 142 hold slaves
St. Bernard	219		157		
Lafayette	697		280		
Plaquemines	433		124		221 families, 140 hold slaves
Pte. Coupee	363		170		
Ascension	468		167		360 families, 150 hold slaves
Assumption	814		334		
Lafourche	751		303		620 families, 232 hold slaves
Iberville	694		265		
St. Mary	600		214		340 families, 252 hold slaves
St. Martin	676		281		545 families, 371 hold slaves
Totals	9,042	35.4%	3,708	44.3%	
Orleans and	8,203		1,241		
Jefferson	616		90		
Totals	8,819	34.5%	1,331	15.3%	

most likely to experience steadily mounting immigration, a policy not nearly as limiting on the original population, possessed as they were of wider vested holdings in taxable property. In the rural parishes along the coast and in the southwest, this tactic had less importance, for in those areas American numbers never presented the same threat as that feared in the city, and there Gallic influence had the additional protection of the considerable preferential status accorded it by the legislative apportionment provisions of the constitution. The permanent division of the state

TABLE 2: RELATIVE ELECTORAL STRENGTH, 1820

Parishes	% of Total Louisiana Adult Population*	% of Total Louisiana Electors	% of Own Population Eligible to Vote
Florida and North of Red River	30.5	38.5	58
South of Red River	34.9	44.4	59
Orleans and Jefferson	34.5	17.0	23

*White male

TABLE 3: REPRESENTATION PERCENTAGES, 1820

Parishes	House	Senate
Florida and North of Red River	38.0	41.1
South of Red River	45.2	47.0
Orleans and Jefferson	16.6	11.7

into unchangeable senatorial districts gave these Latin country parishes 47 percent of the membership of the Louisiana senate. Against the 41.1 percent strength of Florida and the north-central parishes, the Gallic segment could also count upon sufficient support within the 11.7 percent controlled by Orleans and Jefferson Parishes to assure an almost certain majority in the proceedings of the upper chamber, a margin which ensured, in effect, at least veto power over all state legislation. Much the same pattern prevailed in the composition of the lower house, where from 1820 to 1841 the indexes of relative delegate strength remained fixed at 16.6 percent for Orleans and Jefferson, 45.2 percent for the coast and southwestern parishes, and 38 percent for the Floridas and the area north of Red River (see Table 3).[29]

29. For the apportionment laws, see *Louisiana Acts*, March 12, 1822, and April 7, 1826.

Time and time again representatives of American districts tried to breach this wall by proposals to amend the constitution, but just as regularly Gallic legislators from the city and the southwestern parishes combined to stem the attack. Ironically, these efforts frequently drew opposition even from some American rural areas, which would have most benefited from reform—so profoundly did they distrust any measure which might aggrandize the influence of the city. Conversely, many New Orleans legislators shied away from constitutional change which could have significantly improved the status of the metropolitan area, fearing that any such alteration might disrupt the status quo to the advantage of the American interest. Attempts to reform apportionment of the house of representatives met the same fate. Despite direct constitutional mandate directing reallocation of seats every four years on the basis of qualified electors, Gallic champions managed to defeat all new apportionment acts from 1826 to 1841.[30] Despite its limited delegate strength, the city nonetheless held the balance of power between the concentrated Gallic force in the southwest and the American in the Florida and north-central parishes. The sharp-eyed Henry Clay in his 1830 visit called New Orleans the pivot around which Louisiana legislative control revolved (see Table 3).[31]

All of these factors made for a political climate in constant agitation. Despite a clear advantage in the constitutional organization of the state, the French element could never relax, aware of American determination to overcome discrimination and gather strength from ever increasing numbers. They saw the growing influx of small farmers into the northern sections of the state and the constant flood of immigration into New Orleans as harbingers of a political reordering which might alter forever the ethnic and cultural substance of the state. To the Americans, the Gallic foe represented stultifying ignorance and backwardness rooted in European traditions at odds with basic precepts of democracy and progress. In a not overly dramatic sense, the battle which ensued might well be termed a struggle for the soul of Louisiana.

The epic contest which resulted summoned up a variety of political expedients and exploited a full measure of differing folkways, some of them com-

30. *Louisiana House Journal*, 1828, p. 22; 1833, p. 69; 1835, p. 34; *Louisiana Senate Journal*, 1828, p. 62; 1833, p. 11.

31. Henry Clay to Josiah S. Johnston, March 11, 1830, in Johnston Papers, HSP.

monplace throughout the nation, others with the stamp of a unique Louisiana culture. The French camp found its greatest prop in the paternalistic cast of the old population's society, which vested concentrated power in the hands of innumerable patriarchs throughout the state and bestowed upon politically ambitious natives a natural following difficult to minimize in a community so loyal to family ties. "Strong men" like Henry Schuyler Thibodaux in Lafourche, and Charles Olivier, Neuville Declouet, and Agricole Fusilier in the prairie parishes reputedly could marshal hundreds of voters to march to their command,[32] and the influence of Martin Duralde, son-in-law of Henry Clay, spread along family lines into so many parts of the state that his power as a clan chieftain won the begrudging respect and fear of his foes.[33]

The simplicity and cultural isolation of creole life made such deference to respected elders neither craven nor irresponsible, and no election plans or calculations in Louisiana could afford to ignore or minimize these block votes or the men who controlled them.[34] But their threat to American dominance lost much of its impact because of the general political inexperience and naïveté of the ancienne population as a whole. For many years after the Purchase, native Louisianians generally failed to recognize any tie between local and national political affairs,[35] confining their interest to the state because in that arena they clearly perceived the necessity of maintaining French control and everything that went with it—jobs, a way of life, and the sense of being master of their historic turf. Such an attitude made it relatively easy for the Americans to preempt the state's representa-

32. Isaac Baker to Josiah S. Johnston, March 11, June 12, 1823, November 1, 1825, January 16, 1826, Henry A. Bullard to Johnston, April 19, 1824, Alexander Porter to Johnston, August 10, 1827, *ibid.*; *Louisiana Courier*, October 24, 1828, November 2, 1832; *La Fourche Gazette* (Donaldsonville), July 29, 1826.

33. Alexander White to William S. Hamilton, July 22, 1826, in William S. Hamilton Papers, LSU; Isaac L. Baker to Josiah S. Johnston, November 1, 1825, January 16, 1826, Alexander Porter to Johnston, March 10, 1830, in Johnston Papers, HSP; William L. Brent to Henry Clay, September 3, 1824, in Henry Clay Papers, LC.

34. H. B. Trist to Nicholas P. Trist, May 12, 1828, Robert Carter Nicholas to Nicholas P. Trist, October 22, 1831, in Trist Papers, LC; H. B. Trist to Nicholas P. Trist, December 14, 1837, in Nicholas P. Trist Papers, UNC; Alexander White to William S. Hamilton, July 22, 1826, in Hamilton Papers, LSU.

35. Alexander Porter to Josiah S. Johnston, June 21, 1826, April 16, 28, 1828, April 13, 1830, in Johnston Papers, HSP.

tion in national councils, an advantage compounded by their ability to monopolize federal appointments in Louisiana. Those jobs flowed from Washington, where the native Louisianian stood small chance of breaking the
web of relationships and associations which tied the Americans to political
influence in other parts of the nation. This ability to appropriate to themselves offices like those of collector of the customs, naval officer and surveyor at New Orleans, federal judge and district attorney, postmaster, land
surveyor, and collector of public moneys added immeasurably to the American ability to survive the French concentration on state patronage.

Control of state and local positions lay in the hands of the governor and
the mayor of New Orleans. The vast appointive powers of the chief executive gave him control of practically all important state jobs, creating in effect a kind of self-perpetuating circle, since many of these offices managed
the very procedures by which governors were themselves chosen. Especially powerful in this respect, parish judges and sheriffs served as supervisors and police authorities at the polls, with almost unlimited right to decide suffrage eligibility under the tax law, to admit or reject ballots, to cast
deciding votes, and to regulate activity around the polling places.[36] In New
Orleans the police power of the mayor placed at his command a company
of armed men so critical to the concerns of a multitude of owners of grog
shops and coffee houses, to hack and dray drivers, and to countless others
engaged in the complex life of the metropolis that they could generally be
counted on to produce some three or four hundred votes for whatever candidate pleased the city administration.[37]

To be dominant in the city actually meant, moreover, to be custodian of
the nerve center of Louisiana. Not even the peculiar devices which denied
the metropolis a proportionate voice in the suffrage and representation
could alter the natural primacy which New Orleans enjoyed by reason of its
commercial importance, its access to credit and accumulated capital, and
its ability to draw from its numbers political leaders of wide experience and
ability. Despite their vocal and unquestionably sincere antagonism to the
great urban community, rural political leaders seldom launched any exten-

36. Isaac L. Baker to Josiah S. Johnston, September 2, 1823, May 19, 1825, *ibid.*; *Louisiana Journal*, September 7, 1826; Baton Rouge *Gazette*, June 17, 1826; *Louisiana Advertiser*,
June 28, 1834.

37. New Orleans *Argus*, August 29, 1829; New Orleans *Bee*, November 22, 1833, October 17, 1835.

sive plans for political campaigns before laying a firm foundation in the capital and looking to city experts for advice.[38] This held true particularly in the Gallic faction, for much of its leadership and tactics, if not its numbers, depended upon the political skill of the foreign French, primarily city men to whom the patriarchs looked for leadership of a cause which they themselves could best serve by guaranteeing a following. Finally, as the center of government and headquarters of the legislature and chief executive, New Orleans enfolded the state's political life in the atmosphere of its amazingly variegated and seductive milieu. However much they might decry the wickedness of the city, legislators and civil servants flocked to the capital to frolic at balls, patronize theaters and coffee houses, gamble in sporting dens, and succumb to the pleasures of countless bagnios and brothels. Political persuasion could frequently be by other than vocal means.[39]

Try as they might, the Gallic and American factions never managed to realize complete unity of purpose within their own ranks, much of the effectiveness of their many ingenious tactics frequently dissipated by the sheer perverseness of human nature. Despite their realization of the danger of division in the face of the Americans, native Louisianians frequently weakened themselves by internal jealousies and quarrels, some of their number being known to vote against a measure vital to their cause simply to prevent praise being bestowed on a rival creole who had introduced it. Clannishness had drawbacks as well as advantages, only too clearly revealed by frequent family dissensions among the French which spread disorder in their ranks.[40] Internal rivalries plagued their opponents as well, generated especially by the virulent hatred of New England Yankees felt by those of southern stock, a passion which combined with notorious interne-

38. Thomas G. Morgan to Josiah S. Johnston, January 29, 1832, Henry Clay to Johnston, March 11, 1830, in Johnston Papers, HSP; Peter K. Wagner to William S. Hamilton, July 30, 1826, in Hamilton Papers, LSU.

39. Sparks, *Memories of Fifty Years*, 404; New Orleans *Argus*, January 27, February 3, 1827.

40. W. C. C. Claiborne to Henry Clay, May 23, 1830, in Clay Papers, LC; Alexander Porter to Josiah S. Johnston, September 5, 1824, in Johnston Papers, HSP; *Louisiana Gazette*, May 6, 1822; *L'Ami des Lois*, February 1, 1823, January 20, February 13, 1824; *Louisiana Courier*, July 5, 1830.

cine squabbles in the Red River population to make many Americans despair of ever cementing a workable coalition among their followers.[41]

Ethnic and personal antagonisms so flourished in Louisiana that they may well have diminished controversy along other lines. Whatever the reason, dispute over the economic or professional status of those who filled its political leadership seldom occupied much of the state's attention. Throughout the 1820s and 1830s the state legislature consisted largely of planters and lawyers, and though occasionally someone grumbled in the press about the pretensions of this group and demanded a wider representation of the commercial community, such carpings seldom added much to the already bewildering complexities of the political scene.[42]

Not everything in the world of Louisiana politics departed from the national norm. Here as elsewhere in the Union a familiar pattern emerged in the process of nominating men to office and in molding the public opinion necessary to carry them into place, an indication, perhaps, of some essential common denominator in the equation of American democracy. Until the struggles of the Jacksonian period began to impose the additional factor of national group loyalties upon the older ethnic divisions of the state's politics, no formal party organizations figured as such in Louisiana's experience. Before 1830 nominations to all elective offices proceeded from supposedly spontaneous action on the part of interested citizens anxious to put before the public the names of candidates whose ability and integrity fitted them for public service. Just as on the national scene, by the 1820s the term *caucus* had fallen into disrepute, the practice which it identified being so tainted by political professionalism that Louisiana discarded it with little difficulty. Nominations of candidates generally originated in the columns of the local press, another long-standing custom, and since a current fashion seemed to favor the idea that a man should not seek the office, most proposals claimed to be the suggestions of friends and supporters or of anonymous sponsors who frequently pretended to no object other than the

41. Archibald Haralson to William S. Hamilton, July 31, 1830, Peter K. Wagner to Hamilton, July 30, 1826, in Hamilton Papers, LSU; Isaac L. Baker to Josiah S. Johnston, January 16, October 5, 1826, in Johnston Papers, HSP; David C. Ker to Andrew Jackson, November 11, 1828, in Andrew Jackson Papers, LC; *Louisiana Journal*, May 18, 1826.

42. *Louisiana Gazette*, June 21, 1822; *Louisiana Advertiser*, December 22, 1823; New Orleans *Argus*, February 24, 1827.

presentation of a worthy man to the consideration of his fellows. Rivaling these newspaper nominations in importance, widely publicized public meetings might also serve to launch a candidacy.[43]

Politics could hardly be that simple or spontaneous, even in those early days of the republic, and behind these reputedly unplanned proposals generally lurked clear and skillful maneuvering on the part of the office seeker and his supporters. Most commonly, especially in campaigns for important offices, managers engaged in wide canvassing of possible candidates throughout the state long before the day of election. When sufficient agreement had been reached among the principal leaders of a group, the agreed-upon candidate's name would then be offered in the press, usually well in advance of election day. Matters moved slowly in the months immediately following to allow for cautious checking of the reception of the proposal and to avoid any impression of trying to force a choice upon the people. If all went well, the nomination might then be pushed with greater fanfare as the election drew nearer. Not infrequently, peculiar circumstances of a particular campaign might upset such long-range planning and require the drafting of last minute candidates to fill a breach or thwart an opponent's move. Then as now, inevitably, some perennial candidates managed to get their names regularly before the public regardless of support or chances of success.[44]

By the 1830s the primitive beginnings of a convention system for nominations began to appear, made practical at last by the greater crystallization of party lines achieved during the Jacksonian era, but even then the older practices persisted. Indeed, it would take years before the party-meeting plan developed enough to dislodge the older procedures from their place of first importance.[45]

Actual political campaigning swept candidates and backers into a swirl of words and action so spirited and vigorous—and frequently so brutal and lusty—as to make modern techniques seem pallid indeed. Most of it found voice in the columns of what we today would consider an unbelievable number of newspapers (distinction between objective reporting and out-

43. *Louisiana Gazette*, June 21, 26, 1822; *Louisiana Advertiser*, January 19, 20, 1824; *Louisiana Herald* (Alexandria), April 2, 1823; St. Francisville *Asylum*, May 20, 1823.
44. L. S. Hazelton to Josiah S. Johnston, March 30, 1825, in Johnston Papers, HSP.
45. W. L. Robeson to William S. Hamilton, March 21, 1830, in Hamilton Papers, LSU.

right advocacy had few defenders). Several of the New Orleans publications in particular matched in quality and influence anything to be found in other parts of the nation.

The political arena of the Jacksonian era had little place for reticence and even less respect for privacy, truth, or the common sensibilities of those who entered it. Campaign propaganda frequently spilled over from newspapers into widely circulated pamphlets, almost always anonymous and filled with vicious attacks couched in prose designed to vilify and malign to such a degree that their creators seldom dared admit to their authorship.[46] The sheer number of legitimate newspapers made them all vulnerable to financial difficulties, and publishers often found relief from such stringency by simply selling their entire operation to one or another of the political factions eager to possess additional access to public favor, sometimes for remarkably modest sums. The long-established and influential *Louisiana Gazette* (New Orleans) changed owners in 1823 for as little as $2,783, and as late as 1833 a faction of the Jackson party acquired the *Louisiana Advertiser* (New Orleans) for a mere $8,000.[47] Even when an owner resisted pressure to sell, financial constraints might make him an eager partner in political strife. Much of the enthusiasm demonstrated by the press in critical elections could be traced back to judicious "gifts" from interested partisans or to pledges of support when the state legislature or national administration went about the selection of public printers.[48] Having incurred the expense of buying a favorable press, in one fashion or another, political leaders made certain that the papers did not go unread, frequently flooding the state with as many copies as could be afforded, even if this meant padding the mailing list with the names of persons who had never subscribed. This became especially commonplace in the 1830s, when complex national is-

46. Henry A. Bullard to Josiah S. Johnston, November 13, 1821, August 5, 1824, Charles T. Scott to Johnston, November 16, 1821, in Johnston Papers, HSP; John Sibley to S. F. Austin, July 8, 1824, in Eugene C. Barker, ed., *The Austin Papers. Annual Report of the American Historical Association for 1919. Vol. II* (Washington, D.C., 1924), Pt. 1, p. 849; Isaac L. Baker to Andrew Jackson, March 21, 1825, in Jackson Papers, LC.

47. George Eustis to Josiah S. Johnston, October 31, 1827, Alexander Porter to Johnston, April 16, 1828, in Johnston Papers, HSP; *Louisiana Advertiser*, March 2, 1824; New Orleans *Bee*, February 12, 1834.

48. H. B. Trist to Nicholas P. Trist, August 8, 1832, in Trist Papers, LC; *Louisiana Gazette*, July 24, 1823; New Orleans *Mercantile Advertiser*, April 18, 1825.

sues required wide circulation of such sheets as the Washington *Globe* and the *United States Telegraph,* which could be depended upon to speak with the voice of party authority.[49]

Despite the great influence of the press in political campaigning, no wise political leader could afford to ignore the many other outlets for his propaganda message. This prompted sponsorship of great public meetings, and especially lavish dinners, favorite devices for gathering audiences which might respond to florid bursts of oratory and join in the elaborately turned political expressions which accompanied a string of almost endless toasts. Much less formal but perhaps more subtle, nightly gatherings at the New Orleans coffee houses allowed for intense proselytizing from which not even the gaudy paintings distracted.[50]

The voting public demanded more than knowledge of a candidate's ideas, however. They insisted on knowing the man himself. No matter how exhausting and draining of time and money, no candidate could survive without travel through even the most inaccessible parts of the state where he was not familiar, to be seen and heard by those whose support he courted. There could be no evading of the responsibility, and the political correspondence of the period is replete with admonitions on this point.[51] The experienced office seeker could find many opportunities for making a "regular tour" without evidencing an unseemly grasping after office. Militia reviews, the innumerable racing events throughout the state, and especially the sessions of the Louisiana Supreme Court as it moved on circuit through the western district presented natural gathering places where a candidate might well exhibit himself to the public. Beyond this open field of political strife, indispensable as it was, lay other more secret but nonetheless critical battlegrounds. The private letter, the intimate conclave, and the wooing of the political strong men belonged to the weapons of a

49. Hugh Alexander to Francis P. Blair, January 2, 1832, in Blair-Rives Papers, LC; *Louisiana Journal,* September 28, 1826; New Orleans *Emporium,* October 5, 1832.

50. *Louisiana Gazette,* June 26, 1822; *Louisiana Herald,* April 2, 1823; Alexander, *Transatlantic Sketches,* II, 16.

51. Thomas W. Chinn to William S. Hamilton, April 21, 1822, Archibald Haralson to Hamilton, May 13, 1822, Isaac L. Baker to Hamilton, March 29, 1823, in Hamilton Papers, LSU; Baker to Josiah S. Johnston, July 26, 1822, Johnston to Baker, December 24, 1823, Philemon Thomas to Johnston, December 5, 1830, in Johnston Papers, HSP.

struggle generally hidden from public view. Who could say where the victory was really won?[52]

The three days given over to state elections often proved tumultuous and frequently violent, the very length of the voting period itself allowing for the accumulation of desperation as the final polling hours approached. Each faction prepared its own list of the eligible voters in a district, generally broken down into small numbers which became the special responsibility of individual workers. The most affluent and respected of these took up position at the polls to greet arriving voters and solicit their support, while others manned carriages to transport the tardy to the ballot boxes, even the sick and the lame being frequently bundled off to perform their civic duty. When persuasion failed, trickery might easily come into play. This worked on various levels to accommodate the particular astuteness or stupidity of the individual citizen. Some could be gulled by the simple device of putting into their hands counterfeit or rigged printed ballots, which incautious voters might fail to recognize as favoring candidates not actually of their choice. Others too wise to be taken in by such simple deception frequently found themselves at the mercy of hostile election commissioners who might turn away any voter imprudent enough not to have ensured that he had been rightfully entered upon the tax list; it was not uncommon for assessors to delay tax demands against those opposed to their political views and thus fail to register them officially as tax payers. For those of more venal character, whiskey and outright bribes sufficed. Employing one of the most effective techniques of all, Gallic protagonists regularly planted in their newspapers terrifying information of the visitation of yellow fever on the very eve of an election, in the sound expectation that many potential American voters would panic and flee for their lives.[53]

Despite these frequently sordid maneuverings, however, respect for the

52. Archibald Haralson to William S. Hamilton, May 13, 1822, Alexander Barrow to Hamilton, January 28, 1830, in Hamilton Papers, LSU; Isaac L. Baker to Josiah S. Johnston, June 12, September 2, 1823, in Johnston Papers, HSP; *Louisiana Courier*, September 18, 1828.

53. Walter H. Overton to Josiah S. Johnston, July 10, 1824, in Johnston Papers, HSP; Thomas F. Hunt to William S. Hamilton, July 30, 1826, in Hamilton Papers, HSP; *Louisiana Gazette*, July 7, 1820, June 15, 1822, August 1, 1823, July 7, 1824, November 30, December 1, 1825; Baton Rouge *Gazette*, April 10, 1830.

sovereignty of the public will, once expressed, seldom met with any challenge. Some elections were contested, to be sure, but only infrequently and rarely in any instance of importance. As high as political hatreds might run, no faction ever dared to attempt bypassing the popular choice for governor when the legislature met to exercise its constitutional right to select either of the two candidates who stood highest on the official ballot. American democracy had become at least this real in its newfound domain of Louisiana.

· V ·

Both Their Houses

Long before national parties or issues attained any degree of importance in Louisiana, the deep and divisive antagonisms pitting creole versus American overwhelmingly preoccupied the concerns of its citizens and provided the principal issues around which the political life of the state would take shape. That fact complicated tremendously the emergence of a Louisiana counterpart to the common national political party dichotomy familiar in other sections of the country, the state's peculiar local loyalties having no relevance to national issues or candidates. Who could vote for a French president? And of what use were traditional parochial prejudices and divisions in any evaluation of the tariff or the Second Bank of the United States? Nonetheless, despite her newness to the Union, Louisiana had no intention of avoiding her responsibilities or losing her rights in the national political arena.[1]

The rise of the Jacksonian movement, or perhaps one should say the intensification of national politics in the late 1820s, developed in Louisiana as a foreign addition to an already existent order with totally different dynamics and orientations. National political allegiances could not be superimposed on the older local factions, to rest as a separate structure on an earlier foundation. Instead it was necessary to immerse them in the turbulent waters of Louisiana's prior and continuing conflicts, to mix them with

1. The St. Francisville *Asylum* of February 13, 1823, voiced a conviction common to many Louisianians during the 1820s and 1830s: "To have a firm, upright and impartial Governor, is of more importance to Louisiana, than the choice of President of the United States."

those deeply flowing currents in all the ways perceivable to shrewd political intelligence. As a result, no national party emerged in Louisiana based on one ethnic or geographic faction as against a second organization based on the other; no Jacksonian army of Americans poised against a Whiggery completely French. Rather would there be national parties exploiting each in its own way the traditional divisions in the state and finding with an irritating frequency that national attachments often broke before the demands of older gods. The intensity and persistence of these original rivalries make it necessary, therefore, to understand more clearly their substance.

The triple division of the Louisiana population—creole, foreign French, American—unquestionably presented the most formidable challenge to those attempting to create national party units in the state. The long battle for internal control which these factions had been waging since 1803 had a vigorous life of its own, not possible to suspend so that men might turn their attention to the war between Clay and Jackson. Leaders of the national parties in the state could be satisfied, however, with nothing less than unquestioning allegiance to the party candidate in every campaign, those of a purely local character as well as those which sent their winners to Washington.[2] Clearly, they needed to exploit old issues when profitable and to keep them submerged when they might fragment hard-won unity. That such an assignment proved impossible to accomplish reflects less on the quality of their leadership than on the vitality of Louisiana's traditional hatreds.

No political movement in the state, on whatever level, could ignore, for example, the still smoldering resentments against the United States felt by a large number of the ancienne population. Whatever else might be said of the Louisiana Purchase, it certainly engendered a variety of responses, and the Louisianians never forgave what they considered to be bad faith on the part of the United States in its interpretation of that document. No treaty in all history, their champions charged, had been more clear or more unworthily violated.[3] They had been especially infuriated by the Act of 1804, which broke the new American acquisition into the two territories of Orleans and Louisiana in complete defiance to the native insistence that the

2. See, for example, the *Louisiana Advertiser*, May 18, 1830, which carries a demand for support of the Jacksonian gubernatorial candidate.

3. *L'Ami des Lois*, January 10, 1822.

treaty had guaranteed the integrity of the whole Purchase area and its immediate admission into the Union as a state possessed of all the rights common to the signatories of the Constitution. Persistent claims by Jefferson
and his appointees that Louisianians lacked proper preparation for self-
government struck them as a gross insult, and they generally refused to col-
laborate with a territorial government which they professed to find more
arbitrary and confining than anything they had known under France or
Spain. They added to these general complaints specific protests against the
1804 act forbidding introduction of Negro slaves from abroad and the federal decision that the treaty did not grant unique trading privileges to
France in her onetime colony, measures which the Louisianians denounced
as malicious and punitive disregard for the rights preserved to them in the
1803 compact.

In reality, much more than disagreement over particular provisions of a
treaty created this breach between disaffected partners. Equally productive
of tension, Louisiana suddenly found itself required to submit to a new and
vigorous government, whose edicts could not be trifled with as had been
possible under the inefficient and anemic rule of a Spanish colonial system
already suffering the death pangs of dissolution. Prompt application of
strict revenue laws, for example, and immediate American steps to wipe
out smuggling and piracy in the Gulf introduced Louisianians to a governmental policy so threatening to long-established freedom from supervision
that many saw it as the hand of oppression.[4]

The Americans who flocked to Louisiana after the Purchase brought
with them no soothing balm to ease these injured feelings. Most of these
newcomers seem to have been unbelievably lacking in tact, and with the
brashness perhaps symptomatic of youth and nascent nationalism, they
rushed in to claim as their own the full slate of offices created to govern the
new Territory of Orleans. They dismissed any suggestion that some of these
might go to natives of the area with blunt pronouncements that ex-colo-
nials had no understanding of republican principles and thus lacked any
ability to serve. As late as 1814, one visitor to Louisiana remarked, creoles
were still being advised "not to interfere with Government, as that is a
subject peculiar to ourselves. They have even been told that in purchasing

4. *Ibid.*; J. W. Windship to William Plumer, Jr., November 1, 1813, in Brown, ed., "Letters from Louisiana," 575.

the Country we purchased them also, at no higher price than 50 cts. pr. head."[5]

Conferring of statehood in 1812 did much to ease these early tensions. Marriage into a creole family and genuine charity toward refugees of St. Domingue who settled in Louisiana finally made W. C. C. Claiborne acceptable enough to the old population to win him the first governorship of the new state in 1812, a victory hardly to be predicted during his tempestuous administration of the Territory of Orleans. This apparent relaxation of ethnic tensions signaled a native willingness to support a compromise rotation of the executiveship between the two populations, with the Louisianians looking forward to their turn in the office in 1816. But the wounding behavior of Andrew Jackson during the trying days of the British attack on New Orleans did much to disturb this still uneasy reconciliation. That doughty son of the frontier made no secret of his doubts as to the loyalty of the French-speaking Louisianians and their willingness to defend the city whatever the cost. His fears led him to a rigorous enforcement of martial law, a dissolution of the suspect state legislature, and defiance of the rulings of a federal judge attempting to free a French Louisianian accused of inciting disobedience to his commands. Typically, Jackson made no effort to justify his actions until after danger had passed and he had submitted once again to civil authority, but many Louisianians saw in his behavior yet another confirmation that they still had not been accepted as Americans. Others in the Gallic community, however, acclaimed him as a true and deserving patriot, defender of their soil, and protector of the chastity of their wives and daughters. For the rest of his life the Hero of New Orleans would continue to be loved and hated in the Louisiana which he had saved.[6]

Amelioration of these ethnic antagonisms abated considerably during the term of the state's first creole governor, Jacques Villeré, who succeeded Claiborne as governor in 1816, presumably in implementation of the rotation compromise. This venerable favorite of the old population had little genius or political skill but much innate charity and good will, which he expended liberally in a sincere attempt to dissipate ethnic hostilities in the community.[7]

5. J. W. Windship to William Plumer, Jr., April 2, 1814, in Brown, ed., "Letters from Louisiana," 575.

6. Marquis James, The Life of Andrew Jackson (New York, 1940), 232–33, 250–62.

7. St. Francisville Asylum, July 3, 1824; Marigny, Memoire Addressed to His Fellow Citizens, 36.

But the antagonisms ran too deep to be so readily suppressed. By 1820, stimulated by the growing leadership of the foreign French, many of the Gallic group began to feel more secure in their American citizenship and to yearn for that greater dominance which they felt to be rightfully theirs. Villeré's support of the gubernatorial rotation policy ensured election of a Virginian, Thomas B. Robertson, to the governorship in 1820, but only at the price of rising opposition in his own faction. For their part, the Americans too grew more and more impatient for a trial of strength. To the native Louisianians they held out the invitation to join them in an American fusion, to study under them the lessons of true republicanism, while they put away the seductive blandishments of the foreign French who knew and understood only the repugnant doctrines of European aristocracy and tyranny.[8]

The creoles, however, understood full well that in such a venture they would be junior partners and suspected that by *republicanism* might well be meant the renunciation of their character as a culturally distinct group. These "strangers in the land,"[9] Marigny fumed, "want to take all and share nothing,"[10] and any persistence in Villeré's "extreme kindness and condescension for the new population," he warned, would lead to shameful slavery: "Virginia will exhaust itself before a Louisianian is made governor in his country!"[11] Aware of this deep attachment to a traditional Gallic way of life, the foreign French kept alive creole fear of the Americans, content to forswear the governor's chair for one of their own while they moved behind the seats of power and gave strength and guidance to the battle against the "outsiders." But their own supercilious and scornful dismissal of creoles as crude country bumpkins proved almost as infuriating to native Louisianians, who frequently toyed with the idea that it might be well to wish a curse on both French and American outsiders and thus prevail in their own homeland by steering a course between these two extremes.[12] It was a beguiling thought—but then would come the realization that without their French-speaking ally the old population stood vulnerable indeed to the wiles of the American.

8. *Louisiana Gazette*, April 14, 1824; *Louisiana Advertiser*, April 27, May 7, 1824.

9. Baron de Montlezun, *Voyage Fait dans les Années 1816 et 1817 de New Yorck à la Nouvelle-Orléans* (2 vols.; Paris, 1818), I, 336.

10. Bernard Marigny, "Reflections on the Campaign of General Andrew Jackson in Louisiana in 1814 and '15," *LHQ*, VI (1923), 76.

11. Marigny, *Memoire Addressed to His Fellow Citizens*, 36.

12. New Orleans *Argus*, April 19, 1824.

The election of Robertson in 1820 ushered in a time of troubles, during which ethnic controversy brought the state perilously close to civil war. Dissatisfaction with Villeré's concessions to the Americans burst into flaming anger when Robertson began to employ his wide appointive powers in a fashion which the already aroused French faction accepted as proscription against their part of the community.[13] When the usual early political explorations revealed some Americans already plotting to make yet another Virginian Robertson's successor, the state plunged into a tempest of ethnic conflict.

The storm raged around those divisions which had never been bridged and which now loomed more than ever as symbols of the war between disparate ways of life which refused to be reconciled. Creole attack concentrated against the hated system of the common law which had been brought into their midst by the American lawyers and judges after 1803. They denounced this "monstrous English code . . . this confused mass of edicts handed down by the most ferocious despots"[14] as a devilish device meant to despoil the original settlers of their property and lead them into a slavery like that imposed upon the hapless creoles of Missouri, snatched from their beloved Louisiana by the treacherous Territorial Act of 1804.[15] In their most exaggerated fantasies, they perceived defenders of these barbarous English customs as plotters who hoped one day to subvert American freedom through the courts and return the nation to the bondage of British colonialism.[16] They found especially vile and humiliating what they conceived to be the trickery by which they had been innocently led to accept as part of the Constitution of 1812 a provision making English the legal language of Louisiana, a maneuver which they now discovered made illegal the use of their own tongue in such intimate documents as the *procès verbal* of family meetings or the awards of arbitrators.[17] And where, they demanded, could one find any justice in a system which allowed a Louisianian to be at the mercy of a judge whose language he could not understand and whose judgments derived from traditions and customs alien to his ways and hidden from his knowledge?

13. *Louisiana Gazette,* July 24, 1821, December 17, 1823; *Louisiana Courier,* February 11, 1824.

14. *L'Ami des Lois,* February 8, 1823.

15. *Ibid.,* October 7, 1822.

16. *Ibid.,* February 7, 1823; *Louisiana Gazette,* October 29, 1822.

17. Henry A. Bullard to Josiah S. Johnston, February 2, 1822, in Johnston Papers, HSP.

Jury trials in federal courts they looked upon as rigged to the same pattern of American favoritism and persecution; the federal marshal selected panels at his discretion from larger pools chosen by lot, a procedure which they claimed led to unequal voice being given to the more literate American segment of the community.[18] Not even the advent of changes such as legislation in 1822 which permitted the use of French in most legal business,[19] the congressional measure promoted by Edward Livingston which fixed selection of Louisiana federal juries completely by lot,[20] or the great Louisiana Civil Code of 1825, quieted fears that their legal rights remained forever in jeopardy. Convincing them of the legitimacy of their concerns, American reaction to their plaints consisted generally of accusations that they represented nothing but typical Gallic attempts to subvert justice.[21]

The passage of years did little, moreover, to lessen the creole conviction that the swarm of Americans in their midst had come to despoil their land in search of quick fortunes which might be carried away to support lives of ease in the North at some future date. Each summer's migration by those who feared to tarry in the yellow-fever zone called down from the native population strident denunciation of these "Yankee Buzzards" and "birds of passage."[22] Americans naturally bitterly resented this blanket condemnation and ridicule, not unreasonably, for after more than a decade of tenure in New Orleans in which he had probably given more than he had taken, James Caldwell, for example, still heard himself derided as a bird of passage by one of his more moderate French-speaking rivals.[23]

18. *L'Ami des Lois*, October 14, 1822.

19. Bullard and Curry, eds., *New Digest of the Laws of Louisiana*, 451.

20. *Louisiana Advertiser*, January 20, 1826; George Eustis to Josiah S. Johnston, January 17, 1826 (Alexander Porter file), Letters of Application and Recommendation During the Administration of John Quincy Adams, 1825–1829, in RG 59, GRDS, NA.

21. Eustis to Johnston, January 17, 1826 (Alexander Porter file), *ibid*. Important for any understanding of the confused legal system of Louisiana in this period are Eberhard P. Deutsch, "Jury Trials Under the Federal Rules and the Louisiana Practice," *Louisiana Law Review*, III (1941); Gordon Ireland, "Louisiana's Legal System Reappraised," *Tulane Law Review*, XI (1937); John H. Tucker, Jr., "Source Books of Louisiana Law," *Tulane Law Review*, VI–IX (1931–34); and John H. Wigmore, "Louisiana: The Story of Its Legal System," *Southern Law Quarterly*, I (1916).

22. *Louisiana Gazette*, June 29, 1821, October 30, 31, 1822; *L'Ami des Lois*, February 18, 1823.

23. *Louisiana Advertiser*, April 10, 1834.

Few areas of Louisiana life escaped the corrosive effect of this pervasive ethnic discord. In an almost pathetic plaint, the creoles began to talk of those halcyon days of the past "when neighbor was not required to bespatter his neighbor with dirt, or perhaps blood as the *douceur* for which he was to receive a petty office—when Shylock jurisprudence was unknown" and the frauds of banks and paper money had yet to be born.[24] In short, when the American was still foreign to the land. More and more the American seemed to menace every social and cultural form precious to those of Gallic ancestry. Never a particularly religious people, the native Louisianians reacted with disbelief and repugnance to the puritanical impress upon so much of the American culture to which they were introduced. The endless attempts to establish sabbatarianism in their midst particularly outraged them, threatening as it did their passionate dedication to dances, bear baitings, cockfights, and general patronage of ubiquitous places of good cheer on their favorite day for relaxation, and they winced to see appended to advertisements of a Sunday ball the earnest New England admonition to "Remember the sabbath day to keep it holy!" On their side, American Protestants girded themselves with sincere determination to reform a society which did violence to their every precept of Christian morality, flooding the legislature with petitions to ban desecration of the Sabbath, which they claimed gave "iniquitous advantage over all those who are disposed to keep that day holy."[25] Having little success, they charged persecution of Protestantism,[26] blasted at "priestcraft,"[27] and demanded of those resistant to sainthood, "will it not be more tolerable for Sodom in the day of judgment than for you!"[28] They found particularly reprehensible the *ménages de couleur* in which Gallic New Orleanians set up handsome quadroon women as mistresses of second households,[29] and when the legislature received a request to allow a Louisianian to marry his niece, nothing more remained, said one shaken American, than for the state to be asked to legalize incest. Gallic tradition saw in these attitudes little of honesty and nothing of virtue, frequently making the legitimate point that as much as Protestant divines might decry dalliance with dusky beauties and patron-

24. *Louisiana Gazette*, May 1, 1824.
25. *Louisiana Advertiser*, February 8, 1824.
26. *Ibid.*, December 27, 29, 1823.
27. *Ibid.*, July 24, 1834, March 23, 1835.
28. *Ibid.*, June 12, 1826.
29. *L'Ami des Lois*, January 18, 1823.

age of gaming halls and brothels, they seemed notably unsuccessful in making it unpopular among their own countrymen.[30]

Even matters of considerably less import generated other levels of misunderstanding. Management of public receptions and functions frequently foundered in the face of rival concepts of protocol and places of honor.[31] Americans charged that French ignorance and backwardness continued to blight the educational hopes of the community, only to be answered that American pride and arrogance had caused the death of the Collège d'Orléans.[32] Champions of the rival French and American theaters lashed their opponents with ridicule and often vulgar derision,[33] and differing burial practices and competing cemetery rights came under regular cross fire from both factions.[34]

Furious arguments raged over Napoleon Bonaparte, a hero dear to the French heart and a conqueror in whom the creole found a vicarious pride, one thing at least to which he could cling without fear of being bested by the American. Americans could, however, express disgust at the adulation bestowed on an emperor called "the Man," the "Great Man," or the "Greatest of Mortals,"[35] and then go on to proclaim that perhaps little else could be expected of those who mourned the death of Louis XVIII, amused themselves with bull baiting and cockfighting, visited unmerciful cruelty upon mules and horses,[36] and kept alive the debauchery of the masked balls of New Orleans, that "rotten relict of European degeneracy."[37] In the face of such barbarism, they asked, who could condemn those who felt it necessary to import "our house materials, our workmen, and our society."[38]

30. *Ibid.*, February 4, 1823; New Orleans *Argus*, July 7, 1825; *Louisiana Advertiser*, February 7, 1824; New Orleans *Observer*, February 28, 1835; *Louisiana Courier*, May 28, 1827, December 1, 1830.

31. *Louisiana Courier*, August 15, 1826; *Louisiana Gazette*, August 8, 1826.

32. New Orleans *Argus*, December 18, 22, 23, 1826, January 17, February 2, 1827; *Louisiana Gazette*, April 18, 1826.

33. *Louisiana Gazette*, February 28, 1821, March 24, 1823; *Louisiana Advertiser*, March 28, 1823.

34. *Louisiana Gazette*, November 15, 1822, October 29, 1923; *Louisiana Advertiser*, March 24, 1823.

35. Helen Parkhurst, "Don Pedro Favrot, a Creole Pepys," *LHQ*, XXVIII (1945), 729; *Louisiana Gazette*, November 22, 1822; *Louisiana Courier*, November 5, 8, 1834.

36. *L'Ami des Lois*, January 1, 1824; *Louisiana Gazette*, December 9, 1825.

37. *Louisiana Gazette*, January 7, February 11, 1825.

38. James Pearse, *Narratives of the Life of James Pearse* (Rutland, 1825), 17.

These quarrels ramified throughout the whole state but always flared with greatest intensity in New Orleans, where the three population groups were packed so closely together and responded so quickly to the exhortations of their leaders. Much of the violent dispute also had origins in clashes local to the great metropolis. Gallic leadership always dominated the city, providing the mayor and a majority of the members of the council, an arrangement which worked obviously to the advantage of those parts of the municipality which retained their old population character. As the American section of New Orleans grew in commerce and wealth, fattening on the ever increasing stream of trade down the Mississippi, those who spoke for her interests began to demand fairer representation in the city governing body. Nothing but expansive reform, they insisted, could protect them from neglect and the effects of Gallic inefficiency and corruption.

They pointed to the city's dismal record in such matters as street paving and the erection of wharves and dock space, protesting what they called deliberate attempts to cripple the American section and force trade unnaturally into those precincts where the older population prevailed. Such misguided policy, they warned, would make it impossible for New Orleans to offset growing competition from eastern ports for control of the great western commerce.[39] The extent of such Gallic stupidity, they charged, could be clearly gauged by that faction's support of quarantine regulations drafted and enforced by a French-dominated Board of Health not to protect the city from disease, as they pretended, but to make entry into New Orleans so troublesome and vexing as to cut off the stream of new American settlers into the city.[40] They pointed to waste and favoritism encouraged by the council, saw corruption in city purchases of useless property at exorbitant prices,[41] criticized as incredibly wasteful the tax farming system of collecting city revenue,[42] and decried the carefree manner in which the council released its fa-

39. George Kernion, "Samuel Jarvis Peters, The Man Who Made New Orleans of Today and Became a National Personality," PLHS, VII (1913), 72; Louisiana Advertiser, July 14, October 11, 1823; Louisiana Gazette, February 11, 1823, July 29, August 3, 5, 10, 15, 17, 19, September 9, 1825.

40. L'Ami des Lois, January 31, 1823; Louisiana Advertiser, May 24, June 19, 26, July 8, 1823.

41. L'Ami des Lois, May 24, 30, June 13, 1823; Louisiana Advertiser, May 5, 6, 20, 21, 24, 26, 27, 28, 1823; Louisiana Gazette, May 9, 19, 22, 23, 24, 26, 28, 29, 30, 31, 1823.

42. Louisiana Gazette, February 25, 1823; Louisiana Advertiser, August 9, 1823.

vorites from any monetary obligation when the city treasurer for whom they had given bond absconded with sixty thousand dollars of the city's money.[43] French venality or incompetence even jeopardized their lives and homes, they fumed, on one occasion actually relaxing fire ordinances to allow an old and feeble man to build a forge in a wooden building.[44]

Gallic leadership replied to these charges with complaints of their own, equally fiery and impassioned. What community anywhere, they demanded, would be so fatuous as to improve suburbs while the "bosom of the city" withered and decayed?[45] Control of the council must be retained by the Gallic sections, Marigny warned, or the Faubourg Ste. Marie would turn the old quarter into a colonial appendage, shamed and degraded in the eyes of the world.[46] No better summary of these fears could be found than in the philippic of another champion of the original city, Joseph Rodriguez, who climaxed his prophecy of destruction with the cry, "Such is the grand plan of the Vandals of the West, *delenda est carthago!* And passersby, surveying with pity all this debris and ruin, will read, *hic Troja fuit! Ici exista la Nouvelle-Orléans!*"[47] In such contrasting ways did the citizens of New Orleans fear for their city's safety.

It was in 1823 that this ethnic bitterness came closest to plunging the state into actual armed conflict. For some time the French had realized that the most ominous threat to their control of Louisiana lay in the growing strength of the Florida parishes. They listened in rising anger and fury to continued demands in the legislature that the state capital be removed from New Orleans to the interior, which they understood rightly to mean a shift to the Florida area. The arguments presented in favor of such a change flowed from a strategy designed to exploit the rural conviction, pervasive even in Gallic parishes, that New Orleans had no legitimate claim to the seat of government, being a notorious sinkhole of iniquity where official business went ignored in a riotous round of dissipation and where the excesses of party feeling kept alive hatreds racking the state.[48] In addition, removal of the capital from the city, the argument ran, would end the domi-

43. New Orleans *Argus*, March 23, 1830; New Orleans *Bee*, September 10, 1834.
44. *Louisiana Advertiser*, October 1, 1831.
45. *Louisiana Gazette*, August 3, 10, 1825; New Orleans *Argus*, September 27, 1826.
46. Marigny, *Memoire Addressed to His Fellow Citizens*, 8–9.
47. [Rodriguez], *Défense Fulminante*, 35.
48. *L'Ami des Lois*, June 26, 1822.

nance exercised over state affairs by the foreign power concentrated in its old-world milieu.[49]

New Orleans creoles and foreign French rushed to the defense of the metropolis and pleaded with their country brethren to recognize this attack as but one more of the insidious plans by which the Americans hoped to enslave all those not part of an Anglo-Saxon tradition and to "wrest forever from the Louisianians control over their own affairs."[50] The intensity of their anxiety even generated recriminations among their own number, Marigny lashing at those of his compatriots who had refused to heed his jeremiads in 1812 that to submit to the annexation of the Florida parishes would be to betray the French people of Louisiana.[51]

To frustrate these threats against their capital required not only vigor but skill, and here, as usual, the foreign French stepped in to show the way. Late in January 1823, Louis Moreau Lislet threw the Louisiana senate into confusion with the demand that the Florida members be ousted from their seats for the simple reason that their districts were unknown to the Constitution of 1812 and had never been legally incorporated into the state. The French press of New Orleans overflowed with praise for this move, and L'Ami des Lois expressed amazement "that a question of such great interest to the Louisianians, had not been agitated sooner." "Let honor be given to the Senator faithful to Louisiana," they proclaimed, "to the statesman who is aware that to defend the Constitution, is to defend our liberties, our property, and National Independence!"[52] Recovering from their shock, the Florida delegation soon demanded immediate expunging of all mention of the Florida Bill from the records of the senate, blasting it as an insult to their constituents and a threat to republican government in Louisiana as guaranteed by the Constitution of the United States. Legislative decorum promptly collapsed. A cry went up from Arnaud Beauvais that the motion of the Floridians should be spread upon the records so that all might see the shameful extent to which some men could push party feeling,[53] and for days the New Orleans papers kept the argument going at white heat. Sentinels stood guard, and patrols roamed the city at night to preserve order, while

49. *Louisiana Gazette*, June 25, 1822.
50. *L'Ami des Lois*, October 16, 1822, January 18, 1823.
51. Marigny, *Memoire Addressed to His Fellow Citizens*, 16.
52. Quoted in *Louisiana Gazette*, January 22, 1823.
53. *L'Ami des Lois*, January 24, 1823.

one American editor proposed that "if they were on the watch for *traitors*, we imagine they could sooner catch them, at noonday, in the [Senate] house."[54]

American anger flared through the state, and in the Florida parishes men talked of taking up arms to defend their rights.[55] Even Moreau Lislet began to grow uneasy at the tempest he had blown up; it is clear that he had hoped only to force the Floridians to give up their moves against New Orleans as the price for ending the challenge to their place in the senate.[56] Feeling that his main objective had been won, he steered a conciliatory measure through the upper chamber admitting the senate's lack of power to inquire into the right of the Florida delegation to its seats,[57] and technically the battle was over. But no easing of tension followed, for the Florida Bill had opened the way to a series of enflaming controversies.

The times themselves engendered suspicions, charges, and counterattacks. A conservative temper and the force which most people called the Holy Alliance hovered over Europe, menacing and unpredictable, triggering fear and conjecture in Louisiana to a degree probably unknown in other parts of the Union. Reacting uneasily to the nebulous intentions of the allied European powers, the American faction in the state had no reluctance to question whether creoles and especially the foreign French could be trusted to remain loyal to the United States in the event of foreign invasion. Proclaiming the existence of a "foreign faction" in Louisiana, masterminded by the foreign French but spread through the whole Gallic community in the state, they warned that national security could be guaranteed only by vesting complete political control in the hands of those whose Americanism traced back through long generations. Now the real objective behind the attempt to keep French influence paramount in Louisiana had been made clear, went the American charge, predicting that when the Holy Alliance felt free to move it would find an agent in Louisiana to throw open the door to invasion of the Western Hemisphere. Bred to the traditions of European aristocracy and tyranny, the Americans

54. *Louisiana Gazette*, January 23, 1823.

55. Isaac L. Baker to Josiah S. Johnston, January 21, 1823, Alexander Porter to Johnston, February 16, 1823, in Johnston Papers, HSP.

56. Alexander Porter to Josiah S. Johnston, February 16, 1823, *ibid.*; *L'Ami des Lois*, January 28, 1823.

57. *L'Ami des Lois*, January 31, 1823.

claimed, this foreign faction hoped to incite Louisiana to treason.[58] The French readily agreed that treason indeed stalked the land, but it did so, they proclaimed, not so much in New Orleans as in the Floridas, where Hartford Convention Yankees busily spawned hate against those who loved their homeland, spreading alarums designed to paralyze the state with fear of a foreign faction while they made ready to push the whole Gulf area into the hands of British warlords already grasping at Cuba and the islands of the Caribbean.[59]

How much of all this noise reflected sincere alarm for the safety of Louisiana and how much had no real purpose but to inflict damage on an old foe is difficult to determine. But that it constituted something more than mere political bombast finds ample demonstration in the fierce struggle which ensued for control of the militia companies in New Orleans. Late in 1822 tension began to mount when the Americans made it clear that the Louisiana Legion, largest of the military units in the capital, had become suspect because of the large number of foreign French who held commissions in its ranks without being citizens of the United States. What could present a more alarming danger, they asked, with the nation's safety imperilled by tyranny from abroad, than to have the defensive forces of the state under the command of men who still owed allegiance to the "imbecilic Louis XVIII?" What clearer sign could be found than this to prove the evil purpose of the foreign faction, the American press demanded, once more raising the ghost of supposed French and creole treachery in the desperate days of the Battle of New Orleans. In this hour of threat from France and the Holy Alliance, they asked again, who could trust men who would have surrendered their homes and their women to the depraved seekers after "Booty and Beauty," men who even now insisted that American citizens should submit themselves to the orders of aliens who admitted no loyalty to the state or nation?[60] The necessity of choosing a new major in the Legion in December 1822 brought a stiffening of battle lines, plaguing the city for a while with sporadic brawls between the contending militia factions.[61]

For the American companies, the election of Pierre A. Cuvillier came as an insufferable insult. Major Cuvillier had taken no steps toward natu-

58. *Louisiana Gazette*, July 13, 1822, July 22, 1823; *L'Ami des Lois*, February 7, March 22, 1823; *Louisiana Advertiser*, August 28, 1823.

59. *L'Ami des Lois*, January 27, 1823.

60. *Louisiana Advertiser*, March 8, August 25, 1823.

61. *Louisiana Gazette*, December 10, 1822.

ralization, though a resident of Louisiana for more than five years. He admitted having fought as a mercenary soldier for the British during the American Revolution, and worst of all, he was the law partner of the arch-conspirator Moreau Lislet. What man worthy of the name, bristled the Americans, would take orders from such "vile mercenary wretches?" "Let them manufacture anathemas against the proud sons of America—but let these shameful things be done under the flag, and in the name of Louis XVIII, *their master!*"[62]

Hopes of peaceful reconciliation collapsed on January 8, 1823, when the Louisiana Guards under Captain Edward Fenno refused to obey Cuvillier's command to join the Legion in the Battle of New Orleans celebration[63] and filed demands with the legislature that all alien officers be read out of the Louisiana militia,[64] a move which the French condemned as being intolerant and in violation of the Militia Act of 1815.[65] Prompt steps to court-martial Fenno faltered when proof emerged that the charging officer, Brigadier General Pierre Lacoste, had never taken the oath of office and allegiance required by the state constitution,[66] but Cuvillier then brought separate complaints against the rebellious captain and made ready to dismiss him from his command.

At daybreak on Sunday, August 24, Cuvillier marched his Louisiana Legion through the city streets, arranged them in a hollow square in the Place d'Armes, and read out the order to strip Fenno of his rank. One irate American youth threw himself through the military cordon with drawn poignard, only to be repulsed unharmed. The next day as Fenno and the Guards marched in defiance to the decree, armed rowdies gathered in the public square and only good fortune averted certain bloodshed as bricks hurled from the watching crowd whistled harmlessly past the parading color guard.[67] By this time General Lacoste had taken his proper vows and, fearful that the city might be plunged into factional violence, had countermanded Cuvillier's action against Fenno. The major promptly resigned and tempers relaxed.[68]

62. *Louisiana Advertiser*, August 27, 1823; *L'Ami des Lois*, February 26, 1823.
63. *Louisiana Gazette*, January 10, 11, 1823.
64. *Louisiana Advertiser*, March 3, 1823.
65. *L'Ami des Lois*, March 3, 1823.
66. *Louisiana Advertiser*, March 8, 1823.
67. *Ibid.*, August 27, 1823; *Louisiana Gazette*, May 15, 1824.
68. *Louisiana Advertiser*, August 28, 1823.

The relief from tension proved to be little more than a truce. Near panic seized New Orleans on November 13, when Mayor Joseph Roffignac hastily called out the Legion and the Guard, paraded them in full battle garb past city hall and then shipped them by steamboat four leagues up the coast. Roffignac's absolute refusal to comment upon whatever danger might be threatening the metropolis extended even to keeping Commodore Patterson of the United States Navy in the dark, and wild fears spread over the city. The next day the troops straggled back to New Orleans, exhausted and slimy with the mire of the swamps, obviously having met no enemy.

The American papers exploded with mingled anger and boisterous glee when they finally learned that an anonymous letter reporting a band of one thousand runaway slaves on the outskirts of New Orleans had impelled Roffignac to launch this grandiose and fruitless campaign. They exploited the comic aspects of the march of the "Grand Army" to the fullest, delighting especially in the supposed dejection of Roffignac and the French because of their lost opportunity to strut as lesser Napoleons. Their touchy Gallic targets found nothing at all amusing in the event, and when the *Louisiana Advertiser* published *Nigraud*, a burlesque poem ridiculing the Legionnaires as effeminate city boys, discord burst once again over the city. One section of the *Advertiser's* piece particularly infuriated the Gallic community. It ran:

> Peut on marcher quand on a peur
> J'en appelle aux timides.
> Enfin les voilà nos bourgeois
> A battre la Cyprière
> Dans la boue et l'eau je les vois
> Plongez jusqu'au derrière.

> Can one march when afraid,
> I called out to the timid ones.
> Finally there were our city boys
> Battling the cypress grove
> Plunged in mud and water
> Up to their behinds.

A boisterous crowd at Elkin's Coffee House threatened to mob James Beardslee, editor of the *Advertiser*, and in the city council, Alderman P. A.

Rousseau, up to then rather friendly to the Americans, bellowed that with the help of twenty men like himself he would have marched on the offender's plant and destroyed his presses.[69]

And so it went. Throughout 1824 the quarrel continued, the French complaining of insults against their troops and still grumbling at the refusal of the American companies to rejoin the Legion,[70] the Americans busying themselves with a successful fight to win legislative prohibitions against aliens holding state militia commissions.[71] Then in December of 1824 the legislature elected William L. Robeson as brigadier general of the 1st Brigade to succeed Lacoste, promoted to major general,[72] and the French officers in their turn refused submission to superiors of the rival faction. The visiting Lafayette did everything in his power to restore amity in the midst of these ruffled tempers, but to no avail.[73] The Legion insisted it did not belong to the 1st Brigade and ignored Robeson's orders, whereupon the latter called Major Bartholomew Grima before a court-martial, in ironic reversal of the 1823 Cuvillier-Fenno quarrel. Furious debate raged over the trial proceedings, and although Grima remained under arrest, he received orders from Lacoste to lead the Legion in the July 4 parade. The continuing clash between Grima and Robeson plunged the city and state into another angry affray, with the sharpest intensification of the American charges of a foreign faction yet seen, and with the French employing the full talents of their redoubtable defenders.[74]

R. D. Richardson of the *Louisiana Gazette* took the lead in assailing what he called the vicious intrigue of the faction, and did much to arouse American demands for a division of the city into independent sections based on ethnic groupings.[75] The French gave blow for blow, none so satisfying, perhaps, as the offer by Benjamin Buisson, editor of the *Journal of Commerce* and ex-soldier of Napoleon, to pay five dollars to anyone who contrived to knock out Richardson's brains.[76] A thoroughly outdone Governor Henry

69. *Ibid.*, October 31, November 15, 18, 20, 21, 22, 27, 1823.

70. *Louisiana Gazette*, September 15, 18, November 15, 18, 20, 21, 22, 27, 1823.

71. *Louisiana Advertiser*, February 7, 1824.

72. *Louisiana Gazette*, December 22, 1824.

73. A. Levasseur, *Lafayette en Amérique, en 1824 et 1825* (2 vols.; Paris, 1829), II, 218.

74. *Louisiana Gazette*, July–October, 1825; *Louisiana Courier*, July 20, August 17, 22, 1825.

75. *Louisiana Gazette*, July 29, August 3, 5, 19, 15, 17, 19, September 9, 1825.

76. *Ibid.*, August 3, 1825.

Johnson finally managed to restore some semblance of order by allowing Grima to retain his command upon submission to Robeson. Designation of the Legion in 1826 as a separate regiment of the 1st Brigade under Roffignac as colonel brought eventual equilibrium to the militia question,[77] but the basic antagonisms had by no means disappeared. Chances of actual ethnic warfare grew more remote with the passage of the years, but Jacksonian politics could never escape completely from the shadow of these abiding hatreds.

The clash between New Orleans and the rural parishes proved less enervating but no less real. In part this animosity sprang from the deeply held American conviction that the capital was the Medusa head with which the French party froze into immobility any movement aimed at weakening their hold on the political life of the state. But even traditionally creole parishes shared the general rural resentment aroused by the city's economic hegemony over the agrarian countryside. New Orleans controlled access to capital funds and to the marketing of crops, and no argument that this undisputed fact derived from the immutable nature of the economic system could persuade the planting interests that the city did not exact from them more than it had a right to demand. A major complaint charged New Orleans banks with deliberately frustrating every legislative attempt to make easy credit available through country branches[78] and with engaging in speculation responsible for needless fluctuation in cotton prices.[79] Planter animosity centered as well on the city's many commission houses as an integral part of an insatiable profit-seeking "monied aristocracy" bent on making "overseers of the backbone and sinew of the country."[80]

The stringencies of the economic depression of the early 1820s so severely affected Louisiana that the planting interest moved to attack what seemed to them their most obvious and vulnerable enemy. Attempts to weaken the New Orleans monopoly by removing the capital to the interior received widespread rural approval, only to be blocked not only by skillful city tactics such as Moreau Lislet's assault upon the senators of the Florida

77. *Louisiana Advertiser*, July 3, 1826.

78. Baton Rouge *Gazette*, November 1, 1826.

79. Henry Johnson to Josiah S. Johnston, January 17, 1826, in Johnston Papers, HSP.

80. Baton Rouge *Gazette*, June 14, 1828; *Louisiana Courier*, January 5, 1823; New Orleans *Bee*, October 5, 1833; Alexander Porter to Josiah S. Johnston, February 14, 1832, in Johnston Papers, HSP.

parishes, but just as effectively by failings in the rural ranks as well. Paralyzing rivalries made it impossible for the rural strength to be united behind any one of the many locations competing to replace New Orleans, an immobility intensified by stubborn refusal of some rural legislators to abandon a capital which afforded them the means of caring for their own business affairs while they made laws for the state.[81] Even when success crowned these efforts and the capital moved to Donaldsonville in 1830, the inconvenience and boredom of that small community drove the legislators quickly back to the hateful but alluring precincts of the metropolis.

Some independence from the city's economic hegemony came in 1827 with the creation of the Consolidated Association of Planters of Louisiana, which pioneered the principle of using land for banking collateral, but the fiery demands in 1823 for a usury law to cripple the so-called shaving and extortion practices of the New Orleans money lenders failed to push the measure past the veto of Governor Robertson, who resisted firmly what he considered unconstitutional and harmful limitations on the rights of private property.[82] By the turn of the decade many rural spokesmen saw no hope except in trying to bypass New Orleans altogether. Alexander Porter regularly lectured his friends on the wisdom of selling directly to northern houses,[83] and the whole Attakapas region seriously explored ways by which to exploit its outlets to the Gulf as avenues to direct trade with New York and Philadelphia.[84]

Such animosities no doubt reflected age-old town and country antagonisms, ancient then and persistent even to the present day. Mixed with the bitterness of ethnic rivalries, they made up profound and lasting issues in Louisiana politics. With them would pro- and anti-Jacksonians alike have to contend.

81. John Sibley to Josiah S. Johnston, February 26, 1822, in Johnston Papers, HSP; *Louisiana Gazette*, November 6, 1822; *Louisiana Herald*, April 21, 1824; *La Fourche Gazette*, February 11, 18, 1826.

82. James Brown to Josiah S. Johnston, April 11, 1823, in Johnston Papers, HSP; *L'Ami des Lois*, January 17, March 3, 6, 8, June 12, 1823; *Louisiana Advertiser*, March 18, 1823; St. Francisville *Asylum*, May 13, 1823.

83. Alexander Porter to Josiah S. Johnston, February 14, 1832, in Johnston Papers, HSP.

84. New Orleans *Mercantile Advertiser*, October 16, 1829.

· VI ·

THE TRANSCENDENT EGO

Through this maze of passionate hatred and icy calculation there passed a cadre of political leaders as colorful and variegated as any to be found elsewhere in the Union. In the natural fashion of men, they responded to the geographic, ethnic, and traditional loyalties which were their inheritance, but they shaped these, as is also the wont of men, to their own individual propensities. Neither issues, political philosophies, nor commitments could be really dominant in the climate of aggrandizement which pervaded the Louisiana of the early nineteenth century. Those basic dividing themes already described—ethnic and regional differences—figured largely as vehicles to serve the purposes of individual egos striving for personal ascendancy or as screens behind which to blur the lines of personal ambition. The necessities of politics nonetheless grouped the state's prominent men according to sectional localities. In the prairie region, despite its position as a stronghold of the Gallic interest, strangely few French leaders emerged in the 1820s as major figures in their own right. Most of the patriarchs, such as Neuville Declouet, Agricole Fusilier, Michel Broussard, Louis Guidry, Valery Martin, and Charles Olivier, preferred to remain close to their flocks, following the lead of their more skilled compatriots in New Orleans.

The Americans in the area proved not nearly so self-effacing. Most vocal of them all and American at least by adoption, Alexander Porter could claim prominence both as jurist and politician. Born in County Tyrone, Ireland, in 1786, Porter had come to the United States in 1801 after the

Irish hanged his father as a spy for the British. Following a brief sojourn in Nashville he moved to St. Martinville in 1810, soon to become an active member of the convention which drafted the Constitution of 1812. Settling finally on a handsome estate at Oak Lawn on Bayou Teche, he busied himself with sugar planting and his duties as associate justice of the Louisiana Supreme Court, to which he had been appointed in 1821.

Judicial status did nothing to diminish Porter's love for politics, and probably no man of his generation in Louisiana cast a more searching eye over the activities of his colleagues or reported on their doings with greater charm and obvious delight. Witty and urbane despite a limited schooling, he pretended to no great love for mankind in the mass, though bound to many associates in warm and abiding friendship. Impatient with stupidity or dullness, he could be brusque and curt to those he thought to be wasting his time. Such arrogance seldom extended to his servants, if reports are true, and to his guests he proved the most charming of hosts. Presiding over a table sumptuous even for Louisiana, he delighted in hours spent discussing Shakespeare, Byron, and Scott, his speech tinted by the light brogue which was never to leave him. A firm champion of strong central powers in government and a warm admirer of Henry Clay, one of whose sons studied law in his offices, he looked upon the federal compact as a sacred covenant. Governor Troup's behavior in the Georgia-Creek controversy struck him as so prejudicial to national integrity that he wrote his friend Josiah Johnston that the very name of the Union should be held in the same awe as that which the Jews gave to the word Jehovah. A haughty pride seems to have been his greatest fault, one which led him to almost universal criticism of his colleagues. The French he thought unreliable, stupid, and ignorant of the real meanings of republicanism, while many of his American colleagues he judged to be concerned only with corruption and thievery.[1]

Opposed to him in bitter enmity, his brother-in-law, young Isaac L. Baker of St. Martinville, had an equally developed capacity for critical ap-

1. *Biographical Directory of the American Congress, 1774–1927* (Washington, D.C., 1928); Daubeny, *Journal of a Tour*, 144; Hall, *Aristocratic Journey*, 254; Sparks, *Memories of Fifty Years*, 418; William K. Dart, "The Justices of the Supreme Court," *LHQ*, IV (1921), 115; Alexander Porter to Josiah S. Johnston, November 16, 1825, in Johnston Papers, HSP; Henry Clay, Jr., autobiographical note dated November 27, 1840, in Henry Clay Papers, King Library, University of Kentucky.

praisal of his contemporaries. They shared nothing except a love for politics and a willingness to commit themselves to paper. Baker threw himself into every political fray with an intensity and fervor which shook him as much as the consumptive coughs which spilled blood from his lungs. His ambition yielded place only to his capacity to hate, and his letters overflow with recriminations of one sort or another against most of the leading political figures of the day, as he tried to promote the victory of American candidates lucky enough to escape his list of cravens. "Yankees," anti-Jacksonians, the French—in short, all who disagreed with him—he put down as either "mad or corrupt."[2]

One of those who inspired Baker's special wrath—supposedly for ruining his chances of marriage to a politically desirable creole belle—William Leigh Brent, also of St. Martinville, generated strife seemingly everywhere he went. A native of Maryland, Brent had come to Louisiana in 1809 as attorney for the western district of the Territory of Orleans. Sent to Congress in 1823, he played a peculiar role in the political quarrels of his day. Gigantic in size and a close friend of Henry Clay, he was continually involved in a swirl of controversy, disliked and distrusted even by those who steadfastly supported him. In a strange reversal of the usual attitudes of the time, his strength appeared to lie in his almost habitual absence from the state, for the many shafts of his enemies fell harmlessly to the ground, averted from their target by a wall of public determination to refuse final judgment on a man not present to defend himself.[3]

Farther to the east, in the domain of Bayou Lafourche, political power concentrated almost completely in the person of one man, Henry Schuyler Thibodaux. Hailed by his neighbors as the "Founder of Terrebonne Parish" and *père* of the whole Lafourche community, he defied classification in any of the political categories of the state. Born in Albany, New York, in 1769, he combined in himself both French Canadian and American ancestry, and when he arrived in Louisiana in 1794 after a youth spent in Scotland, he immediately adapted to the cultural pattern of the Spanish colony. The coming of the Americans after 1803 allowed him to exploit his New York

2. Isaac L. Baker to William S. Hamilton, July 25, 1823, in Hamilton Papers, LSU; Alexander Porter to Josiah S. Johnston, December 13, 1826, in Johnston Papers, HSP.

3. *Biographical Directory of the American Congress;* Anne Royall, *Letters from Alabama,* 186; Isaac L. Baker to William S. Hamilton, July 25, 1823, in Hamilton Papers; John H. Johnston to Josiah S. Johnston, June 19, 1824, Alexander Porter to Josiah S. Johnston, November 27, 1826, in Johnston Papers, HSP.

origins as well, and he deliberately sought to hold a middle position in the ethnic wars of the period. When this proved to be not always possible, Thibodaux generally cast his lot with the French. As the *père* of Lafourche, it would have been difficult to do otherwise.[4]

Almost a counterpart of Thibodaux in some ways, Edward Douglass White also chose the Lafourche area as the base for his political career, though his early meanderings found him settled in various parts of the state. Three years after his birth in Nashville in 1795, White came to Louisiana when his father, Dr. James White, a former superintendent of Indian affairs in the government of the Confederation, migrated to the Spanish colony. He began his law practice at Donaldsonville, moved to New Orleans as judge of the city court in 1825, and in 1828 retired to his sugar plantation on Bayou Lafourche to campaign for Congress. Like Thibodaux, he in large measure represented both populations, for while unquestionably an American, his early life in the prairies and along the bayous had made him at home among the Gallic population, and his command of French and Spanish helped win him acceptance by them beyond that generally accorded those of his ethnic identity. Many of his contemporaries, indeed, actually thought him to be a legitimate member of the creole community. Aside from this favored position, his greatest asset seems to have been a tenderness and attractiveness of demeanor sufficient to disarm even his most decided political opponents. An obviously complex and puzzling man, his winsome nature nonetheless had a darker side easily aroused to violence (he once drew a dagger against a critic at a polling booth, shouting "I want to kill him!"). Even his closest friends, like Judge Porter, admitted the eccentricities of his lifestyle, but their wide notoriety seemingly resulted, regrettably, in their not being spelled out for the historical record. Most of his associates obviously thought him slightly mad, but whatever his aberrations, they apparently yielded to his ingratiating charm, for as Duff Green remarked when told of his escape from death in a steamboat explosion, no public official in his memory had "more endeared himself to his numerous friends, than this excellent and amiable man."[5]

4. A. Meynier, Jr., *Louisiana Biographies* (New Orleans, 1882), 11; *La Fourche Gazette*, July 29, 1826.

5. *Biographical Directory of the American Congress*; Diedrich Ramke, "Edward Douglas [sic] White, Sr., Governor of Louisiana, 1835–1839," *LHQ*, XIX (1936), 275–81; Sparks, *Memories of Fifty Years*, 460; Alexander Porter to J. Burton Harrison, March 8, 1835, in J. Burton Harrison Papers, LC; Alexander Porter to Josiah Stoddard Johnston, September 20, 1828, in

The pattern of powerful but not too obtrusive patriarchs characterized the coast as well, though here a spokesman for the Gallic cause, such as Sebastian Hiriart or Arnaud Beauvais, would occasionally make himself heard. Of them all, A. B. Roman of St. James clearly stood preeminent. Son of a wealthy cattleman of Attakapas, as a youth he moved with his family to St. James Parish, settling on a sugar plantation whose profits enabled the boy to study at St. Mary's College in Baltimore. Master of a sugar estate of his own while still in his early twenties, Roman rose rapidly in Louisiana politics, going to the state house of representatives in 1818, where he quickly became speaker of the assembly. Discreet and moderate in address, he possessed a fixity of purpose which often rose "even to obstinacy," his most frequently noted characteristic, joined to a deliberate behavior almost "rigidly formal and conventional in the ordinary affairs of everyday life." Alexander Everett found him totally devoid of conversation and surrounded by a wife and children equally solemn and taciturn, surprisingly lacking in "French vivacity." These were hardly attributes of a sort to arouse any committed or spontaneous following. But young Roman's undoubted talents and almost frightening dedication to purpose made him so clearly the jewel of the creole population that leadership rested on him almost as a natural garment.[6]

Only a short distance from the Roman estate, Willow Island Plantation at Donaldsonville served as the Louisiana base of the widely connected Trist brothers. Nicholas, the older of the two, remained but seldom on his Louisiana holdings, more at home in the Virginia halls of his wife's family, the Randolphs, or the Washington chambers of Andrew Jackson, whom he served for a while as private secretary. His contacts with the state remained close, however, kept alive by a steady flow of letters from his sibling Hore Browse Trist at Willow Island. Browse married into the wealthy Bringier family and maintained a sharp watch on the political currents of his neighborhood. Small and quick of wit, he kept active in the state's Jacksonian

---

Johnston Papers, HSP; Lafayette Saunders to Andrew Jackson, July 18, 1828, in Jackson Papers, LC; *United States Telegraph* (Washington, D.C.), June 12, 1833. Some anecdotal indications of White's idiosyncrasies may be found in George M. Wharton, *New Orleans Sketch Book* (Philadelphia, 1852), 106, and the *Louisiana Courier*, July 1, 1834.

6. Dufour, "Local Sketches," 399; Edward Everett Diary, March 14, 1841, in Edward Everett Papers, MHS; Edward Everett to Lucretia Everett, March 5, 1841, in Alexander Everett Papers, MHS.

faction but never rose to a status of major importance, prizing as he did his own leisure and the competing pleasures of his beloved Greek and Latin library. But the breadth of his associations, through Nicholas, the Bringiers, and Edward Livingston, whose wife was his godmother and in whose home he had been raised, made him always at least someone to consider in Louisiana affairs.[7]

Probably the most successful of the Donaldsonville politicos, Henry Johnson channeled his prodigious energy and ambition into a highly successful progress from a district judgeship to the United States Senate and finally to the governorship of the state. A native Virginian, his life revolved around politics, and he pursued it with a dedication and businesslike efficiency profoundly irritating to many of his less successful competitors. A prodigious letter writer, he kept the Washington mail pouches to Louisiana heavy with correspondence. Industry, indeed, appears to have been his greatest virtue, for he possessed little profundity or imagination and nurtured a professional caution which made Alexander Porter observe that he must have shared the sentiment of a favorite dramatic character that "the world is wicked . . . and the fewer people we praise in it the better." Insistence upon political place, moreover, could become wearisome after a while, and Johnson's insatiable thirst for office frequently proved a disturbing factor in the political planning of the day.[8]

In the Red River parishes, with a population fed by steady migration from other sections of the Union, American leadership easily dominated the political scene. The stubborn temper and determined conviction characteristic of the neighborhood had no better exemplar than General Walter Hampton Overton, a Virginian by birth who had made his way to Louisiana after sojourns in North Carolina and Tennessee. A professional army man, his gallantry as commander of Forts St. Philip and Jackson during the Battle of New Orleans had won him considerable fame, and upon retiring from the service he had settled in Alexandria in Rapides Parish to combine the life of planter and major general in the state militia. The stirrings of the Jacksonian movement aroused him to political activity despite a crippling "inflammatory rheumatism" which often confined him to bed, for he had

7. H. B. Trist to Mrs. Edward Livingston, February 5, 1829, in Trist Papers, LC; H. B. Trist to Nicholas P. Trist, August 17, 1834, in Trist Papers, UNC.

8. *Biographical Directory of the American Congress;* St. Francisville *Asylum,* November 1, 1823; Alexander Porter to Josiah S. Johnston, January 12, 1827, in Johnston Papers, HSP.

long ago determined to crush what appeared to him Yankee conspiracies to bend the great agricultural interests of the state to the will of the "minor forces" of manufacturing. Loud and gruff, he bore little of the conspirator stripe himself. But he clung fast to his principles, always ready to fight.[9]

One of the Yankee plotters Overton so feared, Henry Adams Bullard joined General Jackson at least in convictions of incontestable personal infallibility. A native of Massachusetts, Bullard had attended Groton and Harvard, where only a student row kept him from receiving his master of arts degree. Study of law in Boston and Philadelphia left him so restless that he joined the ill-fated Texas invasion of José Alvarez Toledo in 1813, winding up penniless in Louisiana the following year. Possessed of not even a single book and endowed with nothing, as he said, but "Yankee obstinacy of purpose," he began to practice law in Natchitoches and Alexandria. His success eventually proved so great that he soon concluded that only his love for politics kept him from becoming the highest figure at the Louisiana bar, a happy condition which "I owe all to myself," he confided to his old friend Amos Lawrence. Such brashness did not attract any overwhelming political success, though it did not prevent his eventual rise to Congress. Recurrent attacks of gout frequently propelled his naturally morose temperament into "harsh and . . . petulant" irascibility, confining him to his chambers to curse the cultural sterility of his frontier home and pine for someone who might discourse with him on the beauties of Tasso and Shakespeare. Handsome in person and gifted with a musical voice, he regretted most that he could not be the equal of his great idol, Daniel Webster. Abandoning his first love of politics, he would spend his last years on the bench of the Louisiana Supreme Court.[10]

Perhaps the most able of the Red River leaders, Josiah Stoddard Johnston joined to his many talents an equanimity of character which makes him almost colorless against the backdrop of Bullard and Overton. Also Yankee born, he left his native Connecticut at the age of six for the Ken-

9. *Biographical Directory of the American Congress*; Walter H. Overton to Josiah S. Johnston, December 1, 1825, January 17, 1829, in Johnston Papers, HSP.

10. *Biographical Directory of the American Congress*; W. H. Ivy, "The Late Henry A. Bullard," *De Bow's Review*, XII (1852), 56; "Memoire of the Honorable Henry A. Bullard, LLD," *LHQ*, XIX (1936), 18; Dora Bonquois, "The Career of Henry Adams Bullard, Louisiana Jurist, Legislator, and Educator," *LHQ*, XXIII (1940), 999–1002; Henry A. Bullard to Amos Lawrence, January 29, 1832, in Amos Lawrence Papers, MHS.

tucky frontier, moving on to Louisiana and entering the practice of law in 1805 at Alexandria, which he would represent in the territorial legislature from that year to 1812, when he became a district judge under the new state constitution. Sent to Congress in 1821, after one term he lost his seat to William Leigh Brent in a bitter campaign, but returned to Washington as a senator in 1824 to serve in that capacity until his death ten years later. His soundness of judgment and evenness of temper made him a valuable ally of Henry Clay. Their association transcended that of political captain and lieutenant and grew into a firm personal friendship so close that Johnston acted as one of Clay's seconds in his famous duel with John Randolph. Gifted with an exceptional memory which often made him appear dogmatic, Johnston busied himself especially with economic questions in Congress, his services to Louisiana as defender of her interests in tariff affairs winning him a respect more widespread than that accorded most of his colleagues. An undeviating party loyalist, he nonetheless managed to preserve the reputation of an honest man.[11]

That family politics might exist outside the circle of the Gallic community found striking confirmation in the Morgan clan of Ouachita Parish. Headed by Ferdinand Morgan, they controlled practically every office in their county. The chieftain held rank as brigadier general in the militia and served in the state senate; one brother presided as parish judge; and a second functioned as sheriff. Two brothers-in-law to the Morgans, General John Hughes and Henry Bry, held posts as register and receiver of the Public Land Office, and young Henry Bry, Jr., filled the Monroe postmastership. The tribe used their power ruthlessly, stealing elections by fraud and resorting to violence whenever necessary to keep their enemies, particularly the Morehouse family, in submission.[12]

With a record of factional violence almost equal to that of Ouachita, the Florida parishes provided the political base of many of the most powerful and colorful of the American standard-bearers of the stormy 1820s and 1830s. Grand old man of the region, General Philemon Thomas of Baton Rouge had won his laurels as a hero of the American Revolution and leader of the West Florida rebellion against the Spanish in 1810. He first visited Louisiana as early as 1784, when he steered a flatboat loaded with Ken-

11. *Biographical Directory of the American Congress;* New Orleans *Bee,* September 30, 1830.

12. *Louisiana Advertiser,* January 5, 1831, April 14, 1832.

tucky produce down to New Orleans, a voyage he liked to imagine as having begun that interior trade destined one day to enrich the whole state. Following his permanent move to Baton Rouge in 1805, Thomas gave many years of service to his community as a major general in the militia, as a member of the state's house and senate, and eventually as a national congressman. The one job Thomas wanted most continued to escape him. Ardent champion of the American faction, he launched repeated campaigns for the governorship, his flaming red hair and huge frame becoming one of the most familiar sights in the Louisiana hustings. Sure in his own mind that his years and experience entitled him to that post, he almost childishly failed to see how frequently his enemies used him for no other purpose than to split the vote of the Florida parishes. In some ways he seemed a pathetic remnant of the past, unable to grasp the meaning of events, puzzled by political thrusting and parrying which he thought devious, cowardly, and dishonest. In the untutored spelling and style which characterized his correspondence, the old general finally confessed his bewilderment in a letter to Amos Lawrence as he sat through one indecisive meeting of Congress after another in the spring of 1834: "Little did I eave think to live to se the day I now se—the people mite at least have weighted untill the old farthers had been moved from this world to a nother, where thay might have been at peas. . . . I much fear the suns is more tame than there farthers. . . . It makes my old blood run hot through eavery vain." Nonetheless, his simplicity and sincerity won him the love of most of his fellow citizens, and his long and fruitful service gave him an unchallenged place of honor in the state. But it was never to win him the governorship.[13]

From his estate near St. Francisville, called the Cottage, another Floridian frequently went forth to contest with Thomas for the support of the American voters of the state. A native Pennsylvanian, Thomas Butler moved to the Felicianas in 1811 to become in quick succession an affluent planter, judge of the parish, and representative in Congress from 1818 to 1821. A onetime association with Aaron Burr threatened to curtail his po-

---

13. *Biographical Directory of the American Congress;* M. L. Bonham, "A Conversation with the Granddaughters of General Philemon Thomas," *Proceedings of the Historical Society of East and West Baton Rouge,* I (1917), 48; Francis Robertson, "The Will of General Philemon Thomas," *Proceedings of the Historical Society of East and West Baton Rouge,* II (1917), 27; *Louisiana Gazette,* March 24, 26, 1824; Philemon Thomas to Amos Lawrence, March 3, 1834, in A. A. Lawrence Papers, MHS.

litical advancement, a disability which he countered by frankly admitting the relationship but insisting that like so many others he had thought Burr engaged simply in a campaign against Mexico. Unfortunately, he found it considerably more difficult to dispel a common impression that indolence figured as one of the judge's more pronounced characteristics. But as with Thomas, no campaign of the 1820s or early 1830s proceeded far without some consideration being given to the master of the Cottage.[14]

"Whenever I hear everybody speak well of a man, I set him down as a damn'd rascal," Thomas B. Robertson once shouted in summing up his opinion of a particularly troublesome rival. Vain to a fault, Robertson prided himself upon being descended from the Indian chief Powhatan, and as if this conferred upon him some peculiar nobility, he seemed to feel, as Alexander Porter put it, that other men were not "made *with* him, but *for* him." He had indeed done well in life, progressing steadily from the office of secretary of the Territory of Orleans to a seat in Congress, the state governorship, and finally, in 1824, to the post of United States district judge. In the process he became the owner of two plantations in the Baton Rouge area and the husband of Lelia Skipwith, daughter of Fulwar Skipwith, one of the heroes of the West Florida rebellion.

Success came to Robertson as no surprise, for he considered himself a master politician, gifted with great acumen and a keen logical mind. In truth, he did command a considerable degree of ability and could express himself in a virile and straightforward style of address. But he was his own set of values. Envious, suspicious, emotional, and proud, he remained blind to any but his own point of view, frequently flying into a rage at the slightest opposition. Seldom burdened by any great sense of responsibility, he once allowed charges of negligence to be brought against a parish judge for failure to report election returns to him while governor, coming forward only after the impeachment trial had begun to announce to the astonished legislature that "thanks to God and His prophets," he had by accident finally found the missing returns in the bed of his hound bitch. His faith in his own emotional and intuitive responses extended even into his public attitudes, and he once startled Porter by a violent harangue against a recent Supreme Court decision, which he called the greatest bit of sophistry he

14. *Biographical Directory of the American Congress*; Butler, "West Feliciana," 103; *Louisiana Gazette*, March 18, 29, 1824.

had ever read. He could not point it out, he sputtered, as Porter demanded to know of what the sophistry consisted—he just felt it! For such a man, politics had no mysteries.[15]

One of his closest associates, Henry H. Gurley, a Connecticut Yankee, often found himself accused by enemies of being more Robertson's hireling than friend. Like Brent, Gurley spent most of his time outside the state, serving as congressman from 1823 to 1831. And as with Brent, his role in the disputed presidential election of 1824–1825 would make him for a while a storm center in Louisiana politics.[16]

Considerably younger than any of these men and a bitter foe of Robertson, John Barrow Dawson provided the state a one-man parade of contradictions. Related to the extensive and influential Barrow clan of the Felicianas, though born in Tennessee, he strengthened these family advantages by marriage to Margaret, sister of another prominent figure of the Florida region, Isaac Johnson. A husband at seventeen, young Dawson boasted of his masculine precocity and flaunted his skill with the pistols, offering to sever a hair with his shot or split the ball on a knife blade. Yet in appearance and mannerisms he appeared almost effeminate, garbing himself in dazzling colors which won him a reputation as a "painted butterfly." His letters reveal a mind of unquestionable shallowness hiding a vain and pompous desire to appear learned and philosophical. He filled them with gushy quotation and vaulting apostrophe, and, more disturbing, with pleadings and sentiments which might almost be taken for the cajoleries addressed by a woman to a reluctant swain. These may well have been simple affectations, for no one at the time seems to have questioned his manliness, something which the political mores of the day would have had no hesitation in accepting had it been worthwhile. By his own appraisal, malignant hatred was the worst trait of his character, a judgment supported by his many envenomed attacks upon his enemies. He assailed one rival as being possessed of a "heart of the genuine Yankee clay," composed primarily of "cunning, management, dissimulation, and arrogance," and these antipathies on oc-

15. A. Meynier, Jr., *Louisiana Biographies* (New Orleans, 1882), 10; *Louisiana Gazette*, January 10, 1823; Isaac L. Baker to Josiah S. Johnston, November 11, 1822, Alexander Porter to Johnston, December 23, 1825, February 15, April 4, 21, 1826, in Johnston Papers, HSP; John B. Dawson to William S. Hamilton, April 6, 1825, in Hamilton Papers, LSU.

16. *Biographical Directory of the American Congress*.

casion moved him to actual physical violence. A confirmed agrarian, he found the city always alluring; an aristocrat in taste, he cast himself as the self-proclaimed enemy of aristocracy.[17]

Something of a political and intellectual guardian to Dawson, William S. Hamilton displayed none of the flagrant excesses of his protégé. A graduate of the state university of his native North Carolina, he continued his studies at Princeton before entering a military career which eventually brought him to New Orleans in 1809 as judge advocate of the Army of the Mississippi. He resigned his commission in 1812 to settle in St. Francisville, but war saw him once again in service along the Canadian border, where his skills so impressed James Monroe that he won command of the riflemen dispatched to scatter the Hartford Convention. A strict disciplinarian, he carried his military love for regularity and precision into his private life when he again retired to the Floridas in 1816 to practice law and eventually to establish himself as a planter. Cautious and reserved by comparison to the impetuous and fluttery Dawson, Hamilton's philosophical bent of mind won the admiration and confidence of myriad friends. Eventually he turned seriously to politics, until its treacheries proved too much even for his philosopher's spirit and soldier's stomach.[18]

If French leadership seemed comparatively weak in the country parishes, it commanded truly prodigious strength in the city of New Orleans. Most able of the Gallic spokesmen, Etienne Mazureau accordingly became the most hated and feared by the Americans. Born in France about 1777, he came to New Orleans in his early twenties, married into the prominent creole family of the Grimas, and set about to develop a reputation for great legal attainments and oratorical power, which he proposed to use to make himself the great chieftain of the French cause in Louisiana. Almost constantly in public service as secretary of state, state legislator, or attorney general, Mazureau tried incessantly to identify the interests of the ancienne population with those of the foreign French, succeeding at least to the extent of calling down upon himself the most bitter curses of those Ameri-

17. Ibid.; Elrie Robinson, Early Feliciana Politics (St. Francisville, 1936), 21, 30, 57; St. Francisville Asylum, August 16, 1823; Louisiana Journal, May 18, 1826; Louisiana Advertiser, February 14, 19, 1834; Merchants' Daily News, April 16, 1834; John B. Dawson to William S. Hamilton, June 29, 1824, April 6, 1825, in Hamilton Papers, LSU.

18. Louisiana Advertiser, June 18, 1830.

cans who saw him as the archfiend of the foreign faction trying to subvert Louisiana.

Short and rotund, with jet black hair and quick, dark eyes, Mazureau arrogantly exploited his manifold powers and moved with a constant air of command, delighting in ridiculing the common law and all things Anglo-American. His face reflected his emotions perfectly, cheery and bright when he engaged in the witty and rapid pleasantries of which he was capable, dark and disdainful when he found himself questioned or opposed. Then he could be startlingly violent in speech, his enormous head thrown back, nostrils pinched in contempt, and his deep voice thundering out in endless sound. His vanity knew no bounds, and in the terribly digressive and ornate style which he favored he was forever proclaiming on the countless scholarly and military fields over which he asserted mastery. Gentleness and affection he hoarded for his private life as husband and father.[19]

Second only to Mazureau in the hierarchy of Gallic leadership, Louis Moreau Lislet also belonged to the foreign French community, having come to Louisiana from St. Domingue, where he had been born at Cape Francois in 1767. "Everything [seemed] soft in him," Charles Gayarré recalled in a later day, "even his bones. His flesh [was] tremulous, like blancmange or jelly, and as yielding under the touch." But within that gelatinous hulk dwelled a mind of adamantine genius. He was an "index to all legal learning," said one of his contemporaries, "a walking library, containing the pandects, institutes and edicts of Rome, the Partidas, *autos* and *fueros* of Spain, the ordinances of France and . . . everything that was ever written on the Civil law." These extraordinary powers he placed willingly in the service of the struggle to preserve Louisiana for the French, and yet, though he might frequently be found masterminding the strategic moves of his faction, he possessed none of the searing intensity of the younger Mazureau. A natural good humor made him always open to compromise, and he frequently proved capable of changing position without torturing his ego.

19. Henry S. Foote, *The Bench and Bar of South and Southwest* (St. Louis, 1876), 194; Sparks, *Memories of Fifty Years*, 430; Charles Gayarré, "The New Orleans Bench and Bar in 1823," in *The Louisiana Book*, ed. Thomas McCaleb (New Orleans, 1894), 55; Dufour, "Local Sketches," 233–34; Pearson, "Alexis de Tocqueville in New Orleans," 34; Edward Everett Diary, May 5, 1829, in Edward Everett Papers, MHS; Alexander Porter to Josiah S. Johnston, December 20, 1825, in Johnston Papers, HSP; *Louisiana Advertiser*, May 7, 17, 1826, November 13, 1827; *Louisiana Courier*, May 25, 1849.

Perhaps the personal tragedy of an insane daughter who divorced her husband, abandoned her children, and fell under the spell of a depraved paramour left the father with a clearer perception of what gave meaning to his life.[20]

Another of the impressive legal scholars of Louisiana, Justice François-Xavier Martin paired his exceptional judicial genius with an eccentricity notable even in a community which came almost to accept the bizarre as normal. He had left his native France for Martinique as a youth of eighteen, moving eventually to North Carolina, where he served in the legislature and produced a history of the state. In 1810 he arrived in New Orleans, and after a brief spell as attorney general, took the seat on the state supreme court which would be his place of greatest fame. Of all mankind, said John R. Grymes, Martin was the one best suited to be a judge, being "all head and no heart." He had no prejudices, no amusements, no wife, and no friends—nothing, seemingly, but an unquenchable thirst for knowledge and recurrent seizures of ambition to be sent to the United States Senate. No one doubted his mental qualifications for the post. He often demonstrated his prodigious memory with endless recitations from Horace, and his legendary analytical powers allowed him to knife through the most tangled legal questions to produce decisions remarkable for their clarity, precision, and conciseness. As he had done for North Carolina, so also did he produce for Louisiana a history of her growth and progress from colonial days through the great victory over the British in 1815.

Yet Martin generated hatred among many in New Orleans comparable to what a colleague called "Choctaw vengeance," for his tenure on the court threatened to be permanent. His peculiarities made him vulnerable to attack, it being easy to ridicule the old man whose short figure with its thick neck and massive head became one of the famous sights of New Orleans. An extreme miser, he could be seen each morning at the French Market, shabby and tattered, pinching and feeling everything in the stalls and always deciding on refuse meat and vegetables so that his expenditures would not exceed thirty cents a day. His sight failed him as he aged, leaving him almost blind by 1826. As his debility became more and more pronounced he tended to retire even more from social contacts, but he re-

20. Gayarré, "New Orleans Bench and Bar," in *The Louisiana Book,* ed. McCaleb, 68; *Louisiana Courier,* June 22, 1830.

mained, at least negatively, always a factor in the politics of the state. Many coveted his job.[21]

Peter Derbigny and Pierre Soulé also figured as mainstays of the foreign French faction. A former French nobleman, Derbigny had fled the Terror in 1793, and after a brief stay in St. Domingue roamed over the United States before settling in Louisiana in 1797. Governor Claiborne found him an "ultra-Frenchman" in 1804 and feared that he might be subversive to American control of the area, but by the 1820s Derbigny had established himself as one of the most moderate men in the community, so much so that he was to be the only foreign Frenchman ever to serve as governor of the state.[22]

Soulé understood nothing of moderation. After a turbulent early career, highlighted by rebellious flight from a Jesuit seminary and authorship of virulent newspaper attacks upon the restored Bourbons, he settled briefly in England after being expelled from France, then moved on to the West Indies, Baltimore, and New Orleans. Only twenty-five when he arrived in Louisiana in 1825, he soon rounded up letters of introduction to Andrew Jackson and departed to be a guest at the Hermitage, Jackson's estate near Nashville, supposedly to improve his English. By 1828 he was back in New Orleans as a student and eventual associate of Moreau Lislet, and in 1830 he began a tempestuous term on the city council. Some saw in him a striking resemblance to Napoleon, an impression which he took great pains to cultivate. He wore his raven hair long on his shoulders, framing penetrating black eyes set in a handsome face. With this striking countenance and vibrant voice he proceeded to act to the hilt the role of fiery spokesman for everything French, with a command of language thoroughly competent in English and brilliant in his native tongue. As much as any one influence could, his fiery partisanship inflamed old ethnic hatreds once again in the New Orleans of the 1830s.[23]

21. Sparks, *Memories of Fifty Years*, 410; Henry A. Bullard, "A Discourse on the Life, Character, and Writings of the Hon. François-Xavier Martin LLD.," *LHQ*, XIX (1936), 46; Alexander Porter to Josiah S. Johnston, January 5, 1831, in Johnston Papers, HSP; *Louisiana Gazette*, January 16, 1823.

22. Meynier, *Louisiana Biographies*, 13; Carter, ed., *The Territory of Orleans*, 12, 312.

23. *Biographical Directory of the American Congress*; Foote, *Bench and Bar of South and Southwest*, 201; Whitaker, *Life and Character in Louisiana*, 13; Dufour, "Local Sketches," 230; *Louisiana Courier*, August 26, 1828; Auguste Davezac to Andrew Jackson, April 11, 1825, in Jackson Papers, LC; Arthur Freeman, "The Early Career of Pierre Soulé," *LHQ*, XXV (1942), 972–80.

The richest man in New Orleans by repute and the greatest champion of the creole cause in the state by his own declaration, Bernard Marigny grew up in the midst of luxury, the pampered favorite of the affluent family of the de Marigny de Mandevilles, whose noble lineage once allowed them to play host to Louis Philippe when that prince's wanderings brought him to New Orleans in 1798. As a gesture to republicanism Marigny dropped the aristocratic trappings of his name after the Purchase, as he and his family had long since dropped most of the substance of their noble traditions. But he could never forgo parading his wealth, talking of his family heritage, reminding everyone of his grandfather and great-grandfather, and swearing "by the ashes of his ancestors." The sense of ownership so dominated him that it became almost an obsession—he converted his vast New Orleans holdings below the Esplanade into the Faubourg Marigny; stamped J'APPARTIENS À M. BERNARD MARIGNY on the great silver bell which guarded his country estate of Mandeville across Lake Pontchartrain; and burned his initials into the breasts of his slaves. Master of so much, he insisted upon being master of everything, and he fought passionately to become political ruler of his native state. He loathed both Americans and foreign French as intruders in the domain of the ancienne population, and he matched his hatred with a jealous animosity toward any other creole who might dispute his leadership.

From the very beginning of the American domination Marigny fought for creole control of Louisiana, seizing every means to cripple the Faubourg Ste. Marie and to crush the American power of Red River and the Floridas. His behavior during the British invasion had been so ambivalent as to raise real doubts as to his loyalty to the Union, and his critics frequently charged that he would have willingly surrendered New Orleans to the English had this been the only way to save his property from destruction. By 1822 his anger and pique at being continually kept from the power he coveted reached such a pitch that he decided to renounce Louisiana forever and sailed away for France after publishing a vicious "Good Evening" farewell piece in the New Orleans press reviling the whole population for their failure to accept his guidance. The next year he was back, having been unable, apparently, to find the position and prestige he sought in Europe, and determined once again to create it for himself at home.

With limited education and lacking the superior talents of the foreign French leaders, Marigny offered little to the people except a hatred of outsiders. Yet his vanity knew no bounds. He claimed to possess "in the highest degree every vice of a gentleman" and so admired his own oratorical powers that he saw nothing unusual in proposing himself to the city council as the principal speaker at the funeral services mourning the death of Jefferson. Inactivity or silence seemed impossible for him. He was ever on the move, impatient and reckless of ceremony, emitting constant sound, whether in word, song, or the peculiar chuckling laugh which accompanied the creation of the many puns which provided his major intellectual delight. "Creole of the Creoles" he has been called by some, a title which he would have accepted as his due. But wealth, name, and unremitting political struggle never managed to gain for Marigny the political ascendancy which he also felt to be his by right. It remained something he found impossible to understand or to forgive.[24]

Many of Marigny's most vicious attacks centered on Jacques Villeré, the first creole governor of Louisiana and successor to Claiborne, in no small part because of the admiration and affection felt for that gentle and courtly man in most quarters of the state. In Marigny's eyes, Villeré had committed the unforgivable sin of trying to work with the Americans, a fault made all the worse by his status as a highly successful contender for creole leadership. By the 1820s, however, Villeré began to show his years, having been born in 1761, and his always modest abilities proved hardly sufficient to meet the growing complexities of Louisiana politics.[25]

The creole community obviously expected much more from Denis Prieur, a young New Orleans favorite of the ancienne population who rose rapidly in the late 1820s to become almost a fixture as mayor of the metropolis. He was technically one of the foreign French, having been born in St. Domingue in 1791, but his residence in the state since infancy made him a creole in every sense but that of actual qualification. Handsome and gallant, he could be almost irresistible in his personal charm, and even the quarrel-

24. Dufour, "Local Sketches," LHQ, XIV (1931), 397; Whitaker, Life and Character in Louisiana, 83; Edward L. Tinker, The Palingenesis of Craps (New York, 1933), n.p.; "Andrew Jackson and Judge D. A. Hall (Report of the Committee of Inquiry of the Military Measures Executed against the Legislature of Louisiana, Dec. 28, 1814)," LHQ, IX (1926), 236; Marigny, "Campaign of General Andrew Jackson," 68; Ferdinand de Feriet to Janica de Feriet, November 21, 1823, in Feriet Family Papers, TU; L'Ami des Lois, February 24, 1824; New Orleans Argus, April 26, 1824; Louisiana Gazette, August 5, September 12, 1825, August 19, 1826; Louisiana Advertiser, November 1, 1827, July 4, 1834.

25. Alcée Fortier, History of Louisiana (New York, 1904), III, 184; St. Francisville Asylum, July 3, 1824; Louisiana Gazette, June 28, 1824; Alexander Porter to Josiah S. Johnston, February 15, 1826, in Johnston Papers, HSP.

some and termagant Anne Royall found herself completely captivated by his round, sunburned face, "silken voice and dove-like eye." Awareness of his many gifts made Prieur frequently careless in his actions. Impetuous and tactless, he many times committed himself to extreme positions on slight evidence, and he defied public censure by living in open concubinage with Harriet Rolls, a free woman of color who became the mother of his several children. Lacking in education and frequently yielding to what seems to have been an innate laziness, his actual accomplishments never fulfilled his great promise. But he remained the darling of the city, with a popularity impervious to fate or his many and varied indiscretions.[26]

With a popularity even greater than that of Prieur, Martin Duralde stood at the very apex of the creole hierarchy, his political influence enhanced by family ties reaching into practically every quarter of the state. The son-in-law of Henry Clay, Duralde had access to national leaders as well, while his highly remunerative position as recorder of mortgages in New Orleans provided a financial base independent of his notoriously naïve business sense. But his real power flowed as much from the attractiveness of his character as from any family connections or political offices. Simple and unassuming in manner, unaggressive and trusting in professional relationships, he enjoyed high favor all over the state, so much so that some said he might easily have won for himself any office in the gift of the people. Position beyond that of recorder of mortgages he never sought, however, seemingly immobilized by self-doubts as to his own abilities and by an awareness that in the eyes of many of his American associates he was "an amiable good man, little removed from idiocy & totally incapable of performing the duties properly of the most simple office." Yet his unquestioned stature among the creole population made him a constant factor in any formulation of Louisiana politics in his day.[27]

The political prominence which Duralde shied from found an eager

26. Anne Royall, *Mrs. Royall's Southern Tour, or Second Series of the Black Book* (3 vols.; Washington, D.C., 1830), III, 34; Benjamin Lundy, *The Life, Travels, and Opinions of Benjamin Lundy* (Philadelphia, 1847), 114; J. Merchant to James K. Polk, October 14, 1845, in James K. Polk Papers, LC; Denis Prieur Succession (#13,392), in Orleans Parish Second District Court Succession Records, 1846–1880, NOPL.

27. Etienne Mazureau to Henry Clay, September 19, 1825, Clay to James Brown, April 17, 1830, W. C. C. Claiborne to Clay, December 4, 1834, all in Clay Papers, LC; Henry Johnson to Josiah S. Johnston, December 10, 1825, in Johnston Papers, HSP; William Christy to John Tyler, April 13, 1841 (Christy file), Letters of Application and Recommendation During the Administrations of William Henry Harrison and John Tyler, in RG 59, GRDS, NA.

suitor in yet another native Louisianian, Dominique Bouligny, who would be successful at least to the extent of rising to the Senate of the United States. Despite an impressive appearance which caused Mrs. Royall to call him "one of the most noble and majestic looking men in Congress," Bouligny remained perhaps the most ineffectual and obscure of all the Louisiana political figures of the period. He sat mute during most of his term in Washington, and one gets the definite impression that this disturbed no one at home. Seemingly few people had much interest in anything he might have chosen to say.[28]

Between these foreign-French and creole leaders of New Orleans on one side and the American group on the other stood the imposing figure of Edward Livingston, unable to be identified completely with one or the other. In this, as in almost everything else, Livingston had but one major attachment: himself. There can be no doubt as to his high place in the history of jurisprudence. Roscoe Pound claimed that "Livingston will be held the great jurist of nineteenth-century America and one to rank with Bentham" among English-speaking peoples.[29] His legal genius generated the monumental Louisiana Civil Code, drafted with the aid of Moreau Lislet and Derbigny in 1825, and the visionary criminal code which won him the plaudits of scholars all over the world, though it was never adopted by the state.[30]

But many students of legal history have tended to confuse Livingston the codifier with Livingston the politician and man. One sees him as a great "democratic nationalist,"[31] and another claims that "Livingston assailed the leadership principle and energetically devoted himself to establishing a democratic unity of theory and practice through his conception of permanent legislation. Thus he leaps into the center of the world stage and becomes a principal and heroic personality in the decisive struggles which are taking place in our time."[32] Even his most recent biographer, a professional historian, has been unwilling or unable to look behind this figure of the printed word to find the Livingston that his contemporaries

28. Anne Royall, *Letters from Alabama* (Washington, D.C., 1839), 178; Carter, ed., *Territory of Orleans*, 526.

29. Roscoe Pound, *The Formative Era of American Law* (Boston, 1938), 167.

30. William B. Hatcher, *Edward Livingston* (Baton Rouge, 1940), 464–66.

31. Rufus Harris in foreword to Pound, *Formative Era of American Law*, 14.

32. Mitchell Franklin, "Concerning the Historic Importance of Edward Livingston," *Tulane Law Review*, XI (1937), 204.

knew.[33] These last recognized him for what he was—a legal scholar who had no rival, a lawyer who had no superior, and a man who had no apparent concern for personal integrity. He seemed incapable of thinking in terms of anything but his own advantage, his own enrichment, his own fame, or his own convenience, and even his great creative work was sullied by the stock-jobbing tactics with which he tried to sell his talents to the state and federal governments.

One perceptive acquaintance found him "unsocial and soulless, with every attribute of mind to be admired, without one quality of the heart to be loved."[34] His correspondence is unique, even for his day, for he seldom wrote except to ask for favors, publicize his latest accomplishment, or plot a profitable move against the unwary. Yet even while in public office he shamelessly ignored requests made upon his own time, and over and over again one reads in the letters of others such comments as, "from Livingston I have received no answer."[35] Old friends in need he could push aside with callous indifference, refusing on one occasion to offer even minor aid to a desperately destitute woman in whose home he had once been regularly received and honored.[36] Insistent upon his own rights to what was often a cruel degree, he ignored his public responsibilities at pleasure, frequently scorning to keep his own levees and roads in repair as required by law.[37] Such obstacles yielded to the effectiveness of his great legal skills, which enabled him to pursue a relentless grasping for wealth with a craftiness which, when added to an indifference to all considerations of equity, made his name one of the most hated and feared in the whole community.[38]

33. Regrettably, the adulatory approach of Hatcher's biography and of Charles H. Hunt's *The Life of Edward Livingston* (New York, 1864) makes them of little value.

34. Sparks, *Memories of Fifty Years,* 428.

35. See, for example, Edward Livingston to Martin Van Buren, March 17, 1829, Livingston to Nicholas P. Trist, October 16, November 7, 1830, all in Trist Papers, LC; Thomas F. Hunt to William S. Hamilton, July 26, 1829, in Hamilton Papers, LSU.

36. Mrs. R. Blodget to Harrison Gray Otis, October 30, 1824, in Harrison Gray Otis Papers, MHS.

37. *Louisiana Advertiser,* December 29, 1823; *Louisiana Gazette,* November 24, 1823, January 28, 1826.

38. See, for example, the record of his litigation in *Edward Livingston v. Benjamin Story,* United States Eastern District Court of Louisiana, Case #3380, 1834, in Federal Records Center, Fort Worth, Tex.; *Livingston v. Cornell,* 2 Martin (O. S.), 281–96; *Livingston v. Story,* 11 Peters, 351; *Story v. Livingston,* 13 Peters, 351; *Morgan v. Livingston,* Case #1373, all in

His rise to public prominence had its full measure of triumph and despair. A member of the powerful Livingston clan of New York, he graduated from the College of New Jersey (now Princeton) in 1781, won admission to the New York bar in 1785, and in 1794 became a member of the United States House of Representatives, where he soon distinguished himself as an ardent Democratic Republican.[39] Aaron Burr became his particular favorite, and only the adjurations of his older brother, Chancellor Robert R. Livingston, together with those of Alexander Hamilton, seem to have dissuaded him from honoring a pledge to give that problematic leader his House vote in the contested presidential election of 1800. As with so much else in his life, confusion and mystery still surround the exact role which he played in the final resolution of that question. The only thing certain is that his vote went finally to Jefferson, and that in 1801 the recipient of that support named him federal attorney for the southern district of New York.[40]

Early in his public career Livingston's sybaritic lifestyle earned him the sobriquet "Beau Ned," and his princely tastes soon had him deep in trouble as he joined to his new federal assignment the concurrent office of mayor of the city of New York, bestowed on him by the favor of Governor George Clinton. To his obvious discomfort, Secretary of State Albert Gallatin in 1802 began to hear rumors of delinquencies in Livingston's accounts, which by the summer of 1803 so convinced him of the new federal attorney's peculation that he urged Jefferson to prosecute him criminally, but the reluctant president settled for replacement in office. Given that option, Livingston re-

---

Conspicuous Cases in the United States District Court of Louisiana, Compiled by the Survey of Federal Archives in Louisiana (New Orleans, 1940); New Orleans Argus, July 1, 1828.

39. For Livingston's family connections and early congressional career, see Alfred E. Young, The Democratic Republicans of New York: The Origins, 1763–1797 (Chapel Hill, N.C., 1963), passim.

40. Details of Livingston's role in the election of 1800 may be found in William O. Lynch, Fifty Years of Party Warfare (Indianapolis, 1931), 119, 135; Noble E. Cunningham, The Jeffersonian Republicans: The Formation of Party Organization, 1789–1801 (Chapel Hill, N.C., 1957), 243–44; and Milton Lomask, Aaron Burr: The Years from Princeton to Vice-President, 1756–1805 (New York, 1979), 278, 281, 287–88. Robert R. Livingston's part in committing his brother's vote to Jefferson in 1801 may well have been determined by the crafty Virginian's hint of advancement for Edward in a letter offering the chancellor the post of secretary of the navy should he indeed win the presidency. His associates in the new administration, Jefferson promised, would be highly aceptable to him, "one of them, whom you cannot mistake, peculiarly so." Thomas Jefferson to Robert R. Livingston, December 12, 1800, in Robert R. Livingston Papers, Museum of the City of New York.

signed his post with a federal judgment of some $100,000 against his name, and for the rest of his life he and his followers tried repeatedly to brush away charges that he had diverted public moneys to his private use.[41] He eventually insisted that his only fault had been lack of oversight of his subordinates, placing the blame for the shortages in his accounts on an unnamed clerk, while his defenders proffered many, often conflicting, versions of what had happened. But an audit of his returns by the General Accounting Office in 1832, the absence of any contemporary suggestion of an agent's involvement, and the unqualified acknowledgment of his culpability in family correspondence of the period make Livingston's personal guilt essentially a certainty.[42]

Thus it was that in 1804 he brought himself to Louisiana, to a life new in locale and surroundings but hardly stripped of old habits and predilections. He was forty years old, tall and robust, with high shoulders which gave him an awkward, ungainly appearance. Large gray eyes, restless and constantly searching, looked out from beneath his highly arched brow, which curved far back to meet his deep black hair. He had one hundred dollars in cash and a letter of credit for one thousand more.[43] In a remarkably short time he was one of the richest men in the territory.

41. Dixon Wecter, *The Saga of American Society* (New York, 1937), 56, 89; Albert Gallatin to Thomas Jefferson, July 24, 1802, June 16, August 11, 1803, in Thomas Jefferson Papers, LC. The New Orleans *Argus,* June 30, 1828, prints four different defenses offered by Livingston's friends against the New York fraud charges. See also Auguste Davezac, "Fragments of Unpublished Reminiscences of Edward Livingston," *United States Magazine and Democratic Review,* VIII (1840), 376.

42. Edward Livingston, "Address to the People of the United States on the Measures Pursued by the Executive with Respect to the Batture at New Orleans," in *American State Papers, Public Lands,* II, 19. Strangely, this self-serving, unsubstantiated version of events has been uncritically accepted by a wide range of historians, including James Parton, George Dargo, John Niven, George Dangerfield, and the authors of the entries in the *Dictionary of American Biography* and A *Dictionary of Louisiana Biography.* The more circumspect Dumas Malone in his *Jefferson the President: First Term, 1801–1805* (Boston, 1970), 358, simply mentions Livingston's "troubles in New York, on which I pass no judgment here." The Livingston audit is Number 51,742, dated July 11, 1832, in Record Group 217, Miscellaneous Treasury Accounts of the General Accounting Office, 1790–1894, NA. The pertinent Livingston family letters include those to Robert R. Livingston from John R. Livingston, September 10, 1803, January 12, 1804, John Armstrong, February 7, 1804, and Edward himself, May 6, 1804, all in the Robert R. Livingston Papers, NYHS.

43. Sparks, *Memories of Fifty Years,* 428; Alexander Walker, *Jackson and New Orleans* (New York, 1856), 17; Carleton Hunt, "Life and Service of Edward Livingston," Louisiana Bar Association *Proceedings* (1903), 18.

Livingston plunged into the affairs of his new home with fierce dedication. In a matter of months he had launched speculations of ever widening
scope, at the same time engaging in political activities which made Jefferson, Gallatin, and Governor Claiborne suspect him of inciting trouble for
the government of the United States.[44] As early as September 1804 he represented the Baron de Bastrop in his attempts to gain federal recognition of
vast land grants in the Ouachita River area which were as suspect as they
were extensive, and in some mysterious manner which seems not to have
cost him a cent, he managed rapidly to acquire title in his own name to six-
tenths of the Bastrop lands.[45] Livingston's onetime hero, Aaron Burr, also
had extensive claims in the same area, and when General James Wilkinson
terrified New Orleans in 1807 with his electrifying charges of a conspiracy
against the city and nation headed by Burr, Livingston found himself sin-
gled out as one of the supposed agents of the conspirators. There is little
which can be said with certainty about Burr's true objectives, and Livingston's complicity in his plotting, whatever it involved, has certainly never
been proved. The questions posed by Wilkinson and others did, however,
raise myriad doubts.[46]

With an energy as restless as his eye, Livingston pursued his fortune in
haste. He collected handsome fees from the notorious Laffites to plead
their defense against piracy charges, or rather, he sent his partner, John R.
Grymes, to collect them, for timidity kept him away from the pirate kingdom at Barataria.[47] Together with Grymes he likewise sought to preserve
the monopoly granted by the territorial legislature to Robert Fulton and
Robert Livingston, allowing them exclusive rights "to navigate all vessels
propelled by fire and steam on the rivers in said Territory." Even Livingston
could not prevail against the determination of Henry M. Shreve to contest

44. Carter, ed., *Territory of Orleans*, 348, 512.
45. *United States v. The Mayor, Aldermen, and Inhabitants of the Cities of Philadelphia and
New Orleans*, 11 Howard, 609–61; James Wilkinson, *Wilkinson, Soldier and Pioneer* (New Or-
leans, 1935), 120–24; Carter, ed., *Territory of Orleans*, 294; Rowland, ed., *Letter Books of
Claiborne*, VI, 91, 156.
46. Wilkinson, *Wilkinson*, 122–24; Carter, ed., *Territory of Orleans*, 489; Ira Flory, Jr.,
"Edward Livingston's Place in Louisiana Law," *LHQ*, XIX (1936), 336; James Winston, ed.,
"A Faithful Picture of the Political Situation in New Orleans at the Close of the Last and the
Beginning of the Present Year, 1807," *LHQ*, XI (1928), 390.
47. Charles Gayarré, "Historical Sketch of Pierre and Jean Lafitte," *Magazine of Ameri-
can History*, X (1883), 295.

this grant, however, and when attempts to separate Shreve from any legal advice by buying up the services of all the lawyers in New Orleans failed, the grantees moved to offer the stubborn river captain one-half of the monopoly if he would advise his counsel to plead their case in such fashion as to guarantee a verdict favorable to the franchise. Shreve refused even this, and the monopoly claims finally collapsed shortly thereafter.[48]

Livingston's attempts to clear the federal court judgment against his name demonstrated dramatically the extraordinary sharpness and scope of his talents. He had little interest in paying out actual cash, but his ingenuity found in the growing needs of the American navy after 1815 a possible easy solution to his problem. In 1816 he contracted with the United States government to deliver a large quantity of live oak timber to proper naval ports, the price agreed upon, remarkably enough, being precisely sufficient to wipe out his government debt. His extensive plans included the cutting of a live oak stand on the eastern side of the Mississippi at Fort Darby near Bayou Terre aux Boeufs, but upon what right he proposed to claim this timber remained unclear to examining government inspectors. Unfortunately for his hopes, his agents failed him, and the government voided the contracts in 1818.[49]

All these disappointments meant little, however, in the light of his success in the monumental batture controversy. The intricacies of that complex legal struggle defy any simple explication. Suffice it to say that shortly after his arrival in New Orleans, Livingston successfully defended the claims of Jean Gravier to the tremendously valuable alluvial soil deposited by the Mississippi between the water's edge and the levee before the Faubourg Ste. Marie in a series of brilliant arguments which destroyed conflicting claims by the city corporation and the so-called front proprietors who held title along the old levee line. In usual clouded fashion, he emerged from this litigation with a large share of the lands whose title he had cleared for Gravier, only to find himself faced by the opposition of his avenging angel, Thomas Jefferson, whose agents seized the property as having always belonged to the federal government under international law. In the strenuous legal battle which ensued, Livingston carried his cause to

48. Hardin, "First Great Western River Captain," 32; Pfaff, "Henry Miller Shreve," 218–19.

49. "Contracts for the Year 1816" and "Increase of the Navy," in *American State Papers, Naval Affairs*, I, 431, 482, 553; Prichard *et al.*, eds., "Journal of Cathcart," 885.

success before the United States Supreme Court, but in the 1820s the United States had what seemed to be the final word when it appropriated his confirmed batture lots under a lien issuing from the old judgment against him in New York. He managed to salvage enough from the ensuing contest to clear his debt, but his relentless attempts to rewin what had been lost to the government continued for the remainder of his days, and much of his later activity in Jacksonian politics can be understood only in the light of this consuming determination.[50]

His political influence kept pace with his rising personal fortunes. Since his arrival in Louisiana he had sensed the value of alliance with the native population, leading him during the troubled days of territorial status to take a prominent role in attacking the policies of Jefferson and Claiborne which had seemed so restrictive and hateful to the creole group. He fought for a more liberal interpretation of the Treaty of 1803, drafted petitions for statehood, and organized relief for the impoverished Cuban and St. Domingan émigrés who had found refuge in Louisiana. With statehood finally won, he lent his great talents to defense of French traditions of jurisprudence, his authorship of the civil code winning for him the unqualified gratitude of the old population, as did his successful fight for federal court procedures likely to preserve Gallic predominance in the empaneling of Louisiana juries.[51] Not even his defense of Jackson before the court of Judge Dominick Hall in the dispute arising from the General's imposition of martial law during the 1814–1815 crisis weakened his position, for many Louisianians could understand the difficulties of that arduous time and willingly acknowledged Livingston's services before and during the great battle.

It was in his private life, however, that Livingston forged the strongest bonds tying him to the French faction in Louisiana. His first wife had succumbed to the constrictions of diphtheria in 1801, forcing him to find a home for his three children with a brother, John R. Livingston. They had

50. *Edward Livingston v. F. J. LeBreton Dorgenois* (Case 675), *Benjamin Morgan v. Edward Livingston* (Case 1373), *L. B. McCarty v. Edward Livingston* (Case 1374), all in *Conspicuous Cases in the United States District Court of Louisiana;* Edward Livingston, *An Answer to Mr. Jefferson's Justification of His Conduct in the Case of the New Orleans Batture* (Philadelphia, 1813), 15; *Louisiana Gazette,* January 17, February 6, December 12, 1821; Burns, "The Graviers and the Faubourg Ste. Marie," 414–15.

51. *L'Ami des Lois,* October 12, 1822; New Orleans *Argus,* June 21, 1826; *Louisiana Advertiser,* November 17, 1823.

not accompanied him on his trip into exile, and it was shortly after his arrival in New Orleans that he met and married Madame Louise Moreau de Lassy, whose life at nineteen had already been filled with violence and tragedy. A native of St. Domingue, she had married her first husband at thirteen; at sixteen she was a widow and mother of three children who died in infancy. The slave insurrection on the island took the lives of her father, grandmother, and two brothers, and scattered the remnants of the family. She finally made her way safely to New Orleans, joined eventually by her mother, an infant sister, and an older brother whom she worshiped, Auguste Davezac.

In the summer of 1805 she married Edward Livingston at a midnight ceremony in the chapel of the Ursuline Convent, and in 1806 gave birth to their only child, Coralie, or Cora, who grew to be her mother's great passion and her father's chief delight. The family closely identified with the French society of New Orleans, Madame Livingston presiding at regular soirees and dinners, where she loved to chatter in English and French over her newest literary interests or present her relative Jules Davezac, first president of the Collège d'Orléans, in readings from his poetry. Here Auguste would frequently display his oratorical talents in rehearsing appeals for the relief of Greece or in praise of some classical hero, and here Livingston himself seems to have been able to relax in an easy and affectionate relationship unknown in his public or professional life. Both his wife and daughter clearly adored him. His letters to Cora and the other children, models of sensitive and loving respect for their individuality and integrity as persons, reflect a side of the man totally at odds with his public record.[52]

But even within this warm and apparently exemplary family circle there existed something hidden, some sordid and unwholesome private climate which seems to have gathered around him. Few people knew the Livingstons better, for example, than Nicholas and Browse Trist. They had grown up under the Livingston roof, felt unquestionable attachment and gratitude to the couple, and generally identified with Edward's political positions. But when their stepfather considered on one occasion sending their half sister Mary to live with the Livingstons at her mother's death, the two brothers immediately joined in protest. Deeply troubled, Nicholas wrote

52. Louise Livingston Hunt, *Memoire of Mrs. Edward Livingston* (New York, 1886), 13–50; Elizabeth F. Ellet, *Court Circles of the Republic* (New York, 1869), 213–17. The extensive letters of Livingston to his children may be found in the Edward Livington Papers, PU.

his fiancée that his stepfather had become so fascinated by Cora that he would have his own daughter patterned after her, completely forgetting, he feared, "that Mrs. Livingston was notoriously a woman of intrigue; and the very *last* of all her acquaintances to whom Mary's mother would have entrusted her. . . . I had rather see my sister stung by a rattlesnake, than not be able to place the most implicit faith in her virtue and purity; which I could not do, were she brought up by Mrs. L."[53] His suspicions extended just as strongly to young Cora,[54] and it is unlikely that they stemmed from any simple puritanical misunderstanding of the Gallic temperament. The mother of the Trists had married a native Louisianian, as had Browse himself. This was no indictment of a group. Even Aglae, the young sister of Mrs. Livingston, seems to have shared her notoriety, and John Sibley once wrote to his daughter, the wife of Senator Johnston, that Aglae "will do to associate with Mrs. Eaton. I presume you have heard of her."[55] Sibley's allusion was to Peggy, spouse of John Eaton, Jackson's secretary of war. A great favorite of the General, she found herself nonetheless ostracized by a large portion of Washington society because of alleged sexual immorality.

If these suggestions of moral failing in the women of his household remained in some fashion hidden from Livingston, he could hardly have been blind to the reputation enjoyed by his brother-in-law, Auguste. Davezac had attached himself to the coattails of Livingston from the very beginning of their association, to become what Vincent Nolte called "factotum" to his more celebrated relative.[56] He worked with Livingston to embarrass Claiborne at every turn, leaving that harassed man to damn Davezac as the moving spirit behind the *Magic Lantern*, a paper boosting Burr and attempting, swore the governor, to "write down" every friend to the United States in Louisiana.[57] Trained in the law by Livingston himself, Davezac became his tutor's chief lieutenant, aiding him in his causes, living in his home, dashing off fulsome anonymous articles for the local press extolling the great virtues, services, and genius of his patron. Nolte, who loathed them both, maintains flatly that Davezac "made himself almost indispensable to [Livingston], in hunting up the evidence among the family

53. Nicholas P. Trist to Virginia Randolph, February 9, 1823 in Trist Papers, UNC.

54. Nicholas P. Trist to Virginia Randolph, May 20, 1823, *ibid.*

55. John Sibley to Ann Eliza Johnston, October 23, 1831, in Johnston Papers, HSP.

56. Vincent Nolte, *Fifty Years in Both Hemispheres* (New York, 1854), 89.

57. Rowland, ed., *Letter Books of Claiborne*, IV, 167.

papers of the French planters, and in procuring witnesses who were ready at all times to swear to anything that might be required of them."[58] In his own right, he made something of a reputation for himself as an effective criminal attorney, placing more reliance in his athletic oratory than in any profound knowledge of the law,[59] and winning renown of a sort on the municipal council for his pyrotechnics as defender of what he called the "bosom of the city," the old French Quarter, against the encroachments of the American faubourg.

Small and dapper, with a squinting eye and a face which sparkled with a "geniality bordering on sensualism," he reminded one observer of a "coarse and obscene" satyr,[60] an impression of moral depravity shared by a large part of the community. William Brent described him as "infamous, degraded and beastly"; Henry Johnson as "a man of talents, but of notorious bad character"[61]; and his vice, whatever it was, seems to have so appalled his contemporaries that no one ventured to spell it out on paper even to the closest of friends. Jackson's nephew, Andrew Jackson Donelson, received warning from one correspondent that Davezac "is in decidedly bad standing among his own neighbors. . . . I have no reference whatever to Mr. D.'s pecuniary concerns—my remarks apply to his moral character."[62] And Nicholas Trist once puzzled over a cryptic message from his brother-in-law in Boston to the effect that "Majr. Davezac of New Orleans is here; how I wish I knew whether he is a friend of yours; he is said to be an ———."[63] These attacks upon his character apparently worried Davezac not at all, his greater concern centering on perpetual monetary problems which frequently confined him to city limits as a public debtor.[64]

Marriage to Mrs. Livingston's younger sister tied yet another prominent New Orleanian, Henry Carleton, to the eminent jurist's family circle. An

58. Nolte, *Fifty Years in Both Hemispheres*, 89.

59. H. B. Trist to Nicholas P. Trist, May 18, 1825, in Trist Papers, UNC; Foote, *Bench and Bar of South and Southwest*, 194.

60. Foote, *Bench and Bar of South and Southwest*, 194.

61. William L. Brent to Henry Clay, September 17, 1829, in Clay Papers, LC; Henry Johnson to J. F. H. Claiborne, May 4, 1860, in J. F. H. Claiborne Collection, UNC.

62. J. J. McLanahan to Andrew J. Donelson, July 21, 1829, in Andrew Jackson Donelson Papers, LC.

63. Joseph Coolidge to Nicholas P. Trist, July 16, 1829, in Trist Papers, LC.

64. Auguste Davezac to Nicholas P. Trist, July 27, 1829, H. B. Trist to Nicholas P. Trist, August 3, 1829, *ibid.*

accomplished legal scholar in his own right, Carleton brought to his part-nership with Livingston and Davezac a reputation for honesty and probity unknown to the other two. Unlike his partners, moreover, Carleton pos-sessed a gentleness and sweetness of manner which made him one of the most beloved men in New Orleans society. He rarely enjoyed good health, a burden which might explain his eventual impatience with politics and the law. Forswearing the struggles of his earlier days, he would finally spend the last years of his life in Philadelphia, studying and writing on philosophy and religion.[65]

Also prominent in American circles of the capital, Alfred Hennen en-joyed a reputation as the best scholar in Louisiana, famed as a linguist, book collector, and barrister. A massive and sturdy man, with a great head of gray hair and florid complexion, he radiated serenity and good humor. Secretary of the State Bible Society, a model of old-fashioned piety and rigid polite-ness, he wore his hair in a short queue as late as 1866 and abstained abso-lutely from all forms of alcohol. He injected a rare moral tone into New Orleans politics, an influence unfortunately minimized, despite his schol-arship, by the limitations of a mind steeped in rigid formalism and such fa-natical religiosity that in early life his family feared it might cost him his sanity.[66]

Isaac T. Preston shared Hennen's reputation for good humor and dignity of manner, and like him ranked as one of the first members of the New Or-leans bar. A native of Virginia and a graduate of Yale, he captained a volun-teer company in the War of 1812, carrying over into his later life a military stride and manner which went well with his tall and heavy figure. Plain and deliberate, he often gave a first impression of being slow and indolent in thought and address, but as he warmed to his subject his mind snapped fast to its purpose, his speech flowing in easy exposition of clear and impressive logic. In many respects he championed a political program more liberal

65. Foote, *Bench and Bar of South and Southwest*, 194; W. K. Dart, "Justices of the Su-preme Court," 116.

66. Alfred Hennen to Mrs. James Hennen, July 22, 1803, in Hennen-Jennings Papers, LSU. See also Foote, *Bench and Bar of South and Southwest*, 195; Edward Everett Diary, May 6, 1829, in Edward Everett Papers, MHS; Gayarré, "New Orleans Bench and Bar," in *The Louisiana Book*, ed. McCaleb, 69; W. O. Hart, "The Bible in Louisiana a Century Ago," *PLHS*, IX (1916); Whitaker, *Life and Character in Louisiana*, 5; James S. Zacharie, "New Or-leans—Its Old Streets and Places," *PLHS*, II (1902), Pt. III, 65.

than anything acceptable to his Jacksonian colleagues, focusing particularly on democratization of civic rights.[67]

Whatever Hennen and Preston might have lacked in fire and color, John R. Grymes possessed in more abundance than could be comfortable in any man. Even with his close friends in a private circle, "he spoke, he looked, he was the great man. He was great in his frivolities, great in his burlesques, great in his humor, great in common conversation; the great lawyer, the great orator, the great blackguard, and the great companion, the great beau, and the great spendthrift; in nothing was he little." Kin to John Randolph and himself a Virginian, he was one of those men, said an associate, "who leap into manhood without the probation of youth," and at twenty-two he already enjoyed an extensive practice and fame as an eminent member of the bar.[68]

There was hardly a natural endowment which he did not enjoy in full measure. One finds the word *beautiful* in descriptions of him by practically everyone who has left them, and to these physical gifts he joined a superb intellect, a mastery of speech and logic, and a command of wit and sarcasm the envy of his associates. And yet, something in him was deformed and twisted, something which he alone could see, and which made himself and all the world revolting in his eyes. Perhaps he sensed that with all his powers he lacked some mysterious force which would have made it possible for him to exploit them to the fullest. With all his great talents, he never managed to do great things. And so he turned from himself and sought to find in the company of men some proof that greatness was a lie and that all mankind deserved to be despised. He could never be alone, yet remained the loneliest of men. Rarely in his office, he roamed the streets by day and the social centers by night, a great diner, a model of fashion, and a habitué of the ball. A self-confessed libertine, Grymes professed a disdain for all women, though he never complained against his wife, and continued to claim and support her after she fled from him—no one knew why—to live on Staten Island. Ridicule and contempt he wielded as favorite weapons against the world, but even in this he could not be what he claimed. For his scorn remained ever impersonal; he raged against mankind, yet was profligate in generosity to his fellow men. Money to him had no value. He made

67. Dart, "Justices of the Supreme Court," 118; Dufour, "Local Sketches," 537; Whitaker, *Life and Character in Louisiana*, 9.

68. Sparks, *Memories of Fifty Years*, 432.

fortunes, occasionally by very dubious means, and was always penniless, and it was said that he "owed everybody, loaned to everybody, gave to everybody, and paid nobody."[69]

The one regret to which he ever admitted was his inability to sit in the United States Senate, there to range himself against the great Webster, to test his skills in opposition to those he could not deny. But he lacked the funds, he said, to make the venture. He would go to the Senate in style or not at all, and so he slipped ever deeper into morose complaint against a society which he felt had paid him poorly, more poorly than even he deserved. Thus he went his way, brilliantly entertaining to those he pretended to despise; ridiculing knowledge and claiming to know everything; always at apparent ease, and always in a ferment of inner doubt. "He was at war with himself," said Sparks, "and consequently with all the world."[70]

In his later life Grymes looked back with nostalgic pleasure to the many times he had pitted his drinking prowess against that of John Slidell at the sumptuous Elkin's Club on Bayou St. John near Lake Pontchartrain. Slidell was a latecomer to Louisiana compared to Grymes, having arrived in New Orleans around 1821. They must have found much to talk about during their long, bibulous sessions, for gossip had it that Slidell had fled his native New York after wounding the manager of the Park Theatre in a duel which resulted from the impresario's discovery that the young man had forgotten the "distinctions usually maintained between the bed chambers of gay bachelors and dosy husbands."[71]

Whatever his past indiscretions, he put them behind him after his settlement in his new home, and though his bouts at Elkin's testify to the persistence of his love for the social life, they never seriously interfered with his ambition for political and economic advancement. He adjusted well to his new environment, with a fluent command of French gained during his legal studies on the Continent, and soon won attention at the bar and in the hustings for his shrewd and strong-minded intelligence. Possessed of none of the oratorical brilliance of Grymes and reserved even in conversa-

69. *Ibid.*

70. *Ibid.*; Foote, *Bench and Bar of South and Southwest,* 197; Gayarré, "New Orleans Bench and Bar," in *The Louisiana Book,* ed. McCaleb, 62; Whitaker, *Life and Character in Louisiana,* 8–9.

71. New Orleans *Daily True Delta,* April 4, 1858.

tion, his strength lay in his steadfast dedication to purpose and his willingness to bend his whole energy to its realization.[72]

John H. Holland and General Eleazar Ripley came from even farther reaches of the Union, figuring prominently in the New England Yankee community of the city. Holland had moved to New Orleans from Connecticut in 1801 as a boy of fifteen, but retained so strongly the impress of his native origins that all through life many persons mistook him for an Englishman. Portly and robust, with a round, fair face and blue eyes, he won renown as the unchallenged authority on his adopted city, about which admirers claimed he knew anything and everything. This fund of information and his position as leader of the Masonic movement in New Orleans added greatly to his political influence.[73]

Eleazar Ripley had no exclusive connection to any part of the state. He first settled in the Floridas at the little town of Jackson after a brilliant career in the army, which saw him decorated for gallantry at the Battles of Chippewa, Niagara, and Erie. His efficiency, regrettably, did not match his heroism, and his retirement from service in 1820 while commander of the troops at New Orleans came just in time to save Secretary of War John C. Calhoun the embarrassment of having to act on Andrew Jackson's demands that corrective actions be taken against him.[74] A man of considerable versatility, he could also look back upon an even earlier political career, which had taken him from his native New Hampshire and Dartmouth College to law practice in Maine, the Massachusetts senate, and the speakership of the Massachusetts house of representatives in 1811.

In the mid-1820s Ripley moved to join the New Orleans bar and to plunge himself into the political life of the metropolis. A commanding figure, he stood well over six feet in height, heavy without being fleshy, and with a ruddy complexion and blue eyes which won immediate attention. In

72. William Coleman, *Historical Sketch Book and Guide to New Orleans* (New Orleans, 1885), 93; Charles R. Craig, "John Slidell, Louisiana Politico, 1793–1847" (M.A. thesis, Tulane University, 1948), 5–6; Foote, *Bench and Bar of South and Southwest*, 202; Whitaker, *Life and Character in Louisiana*, 66.

73. Royall, *Southern Tour*, III, 35; New Orleans *Bee*, November 15, 1833.

74. Andrew Jackson to John C. Calhoun, January 17, 1820, in John S. Bassett, ed., *The Correspondence of Andrew Jackson* (6 vols.; Washington, D.C., 1927–35), III, 9; Calhoun to Jackson, January 22, 1820, in Jackson Papers, LC.

youth his hair had been deep auburn in color, but now in his middle age it clustered in thinning yellow ringlets above his high forehead. A wound suffered at the Battle of Fort Erie froze his neck in rigid and unbending posture, keeping him in almost constant pain and making him frequently irascible and contentious, though by nature he seemed genuinely friendly and convivial. Bombastic and florid in address, delighting in great figures of speech and hyperbole, he generally performed poorly in debate, though he was not lacking in fundamental intelligence. In all, he remained a rather pathetic man, ambitious and active, but pursued by the fear which few knew, that his endless suffering would one day unhinge his mind. From his wife he extracted the promise that she would never permit him to die in an asylum.[75]

Finally, there was Martin Gordon, originally of Virginia, a mysterious man who would make himself perhaps the most dominant figure in Jacksonian Louisiana and whose name has been practically ignored in the chronicles of the state. Unlike most of his political colleagues, he had no legal training and figured in none of the dramatic courtroom scenes of his day. Nor did he ever become governor, congressman, or senator, and perhaps this accounts to some degree for the obscurity which has been his lot. But it is a fate completely undeserved, for Gordon in his time ranked as one of the wealthiest and most successful of New Orleans business leaders, president of the immensely powerful Orleans Navigation Company, and a dominant force in the politics of his day. He surrounded himself with all the influence that great wealth could buy, deploying its seductions and his own innate craftiness in pursuit of the power he so desperately craved. Only the waspish Mrs. Royall has left us any description of him, and though her account is obviously one inspired by distaste, it so fits what his own actions suggest that perhaps it does him no injustice. To her he appeared to have "just been imported from the antipodes. . . . He was old, ugly, gangling, rawboned, stoop-shouldered, with a yellow, greenish, long stringy face, and cat eye; his iron countenance would appall the Pink himself, a great Russian bear . . . [and] monster of clownishness." Appealing he might not have been, but noteworthy he certainly was, and no other Louisianian ranked higher in the esteem and confidence of Andrew Jackson.[76]

75. *Louisiana Advertiser*, October 23, 1829, May 14, 1820; Foote, *Bench and Bar of South and Southwest*, 196; Royall, *Southern Tour*, III, 93; Charles R. Corning, "Eleazar Wheelock Ripley" (Typescript, n.d.), LSM, *passim*.

76. Whitaker, *Life and Character in Louisiana*, 80; Royall, *Southern Tour*, III, 32.

· VII ·

Birth of a Cause

Edward Livingston recognized Andrew Jackson as a prime presidential possibility as early as 1815. Anyone in the Tennessean's presence felt immediately the force of his personality and authority, but the sharp-eyed Louisianian sensed that the stunning victory over the British at New Orleans transcended all these qualities and transformed Old Hickory into a national hero with an open road to the White House. Livingston had grown up in an ambience which knew full well the blessings which could flow from close alliance with those in places of power, and in 1815 he saw on Jackson the stamp of future greatness.

Not everything seemed so clear only a short time earlier. The Livingstons had been somewhat perturbed in the days before the arrival of the backwoods warrior to take over the defense of their city, troubled by what might lie in store for them. Word of Jackson's temper and violence preceded him, creating among the ladies visions of all kinds of unpleasantness when common courtesy might force them to introduce this lion into their social circles. Some had even worried that he might gouge their floors with hobnailed boots. Jackson, it turned out, proved to be anything but the savage. His great personal dignity, his openness to close personal relationship, and the compelling charm which fell over anyone in his company worked upon those whom he met in New Orleans as they worked upon others in the years to come—to the perplexity and dismay of his enemies. Mrs. Livingston and her coterie were at first unbelieving, then captivated. Livingston watched and pondered.[1]

1. James, *Andrew Jackson,* 257; Charles Hunt, *Edward Livingston,* 197–98.

Seldom far removed from Jackson during the Louisiana campaign, at his own request Livingston became the General's aide-de-camp and military secretary, a spot he had sought even prior to the commander's arrival in New Orleans.[2] Jackson soon found himself surrounded by Livingston associates: Davezac as his judge-advocate; young Lewis Livingston, the jurist's son, as a commissioned captain in the engineers; and John R. Grymes as a member of his staff.[3] Through the whole crisis of the British attack, Livingston made himself invaluable to Jackson, and even after the enemy's withdrawal the General depended on the able legal advice of his aide in defending his martial law restraints on Judge Hall and the suspect Louisiana legislature. With his usual flamboyance, Davezac played an equally conspicuous role, prominent in almost every aspect of the celebrations attendant upon Jackson's remarkable victory.[4] When Rachel Jackson arrived to join her husband, Mrs. Livingston took pains to tutor the plain frontier wife in the rules of social behavior, making her own home a retreat in which the weary and beset Jackson could find what few moments of relaxation opened to him in New Orleans.[5] Before the General departed for the Hermitage, he heard carefully dropped hints from his aide that perhaps Jackson's services might one day be required in the presidency, to which the victorious soldier gave nothing but vocal disbelief.[6] But the suggestions could hardly have lowered Livingston in the eyes of an already grateful recipient.

"Je chante ce guerrier qui sauva notre ville," the citizens of New Orleans sang in Jackson's praise,[7] their enthusiasm for the champion who had deliv-

2. Edward Livingston to Andrew Jackson, September 21, 1814, in Donelson Papers, LC; John S. Bassett, *The Life of Andrew Jackson* (New York, 1916), I, 154.

3. Hatcher, *Livingston*, 215.

4. *Ibid.*, 215–25; *A Letter to Edward Livingston, Esquire, Delegate from Louisiana to General Congress at Washington City, on the subject of the Speech Delivered by Him, at Washington, at the Late Celebration of the Anniversary of the 8th. of January, 1815* (Natchez, Miss., 1828), 9–11. Livingston seems to have played a brave role in the 1814–15 campaign, though his arch foe, Vincent Nolte, insists that he left the battleground after December 23 and spent January 8 in a dressing gown anxiously pacing his gallery while the battle progressed. The same charge is made in the anonymous pamphlet cited above, which may well have been written by Nolte.

5. James, *Andrew Jackson*, 257.

6. James Parton, *Life of Andrew Jackson* (3 vols.; New York, 1860), II, 350. Parton offers no evidence for this statement, but there is little reason to doubt its accuracy.

7. Ruby Caulfield, *The French Literature of Louisiana* (New York, 1929), 71.

ered the "Booty and Beauty" of Louisiana from unspeakable danger magni-
fied by the fact that the enemy he had crushed was their traditional foe, the
British.[8] In him, moreover, the Louisiana French saw a duplicate of another
great hero, Napoleon, and the aura of military glory which surrounded
Jackson's name guaranteed the constancy of their affections.[9] No less ap-
preciative, the American segment of the community celebrated the New
Orleans campaign as a testimony to the vitality and endurance of their
young nation. The United States had offered no reassuring picture in the
winter of 1814, with the Louisiana capital feeling particularly abandoned
and distressed. "But oh! the Guardian Spirit of our country watched over
us," these Americans could recall in later days, "in the despair, and the
darkness of the hour when consternation and destruction sounded, a genius
appeared to reanimate our expiring hopes, and to brave the threatening
horrors of the storm: The heroic *Jackson* spoke, and all was calm!"[10] As Livingston himself once explained, others might read of Jackson's great gifts
and be told of the frightful terrors from which he had delivered them, but
Louisianians knew at first hand who he was and what he had done.[11]

The innumerable close personal friendships which tied Jackson to so
many leading figures in the state buttressed this already broad base of gratitude and affection to provide a strong foundation of future political support
in Louisiana. Like Davezac, who admitted that from his first meeting with
the General he fell under "the power of an irresistible spell,"[12] many others
retained warm memories of their wartime association with a valiant commander and were willing to pledge to him their support in his every under-
taking. General Jean B. Plauché, one of the most beloved and respected of
the creole citizens of New Orleans, was so overcome with gratitude to the
General during the victory celebration in the Place d'Armes in 1815 that
he threw down his sword and astonished the Americans, Jackson most of
all, by kissing his hero soundly on both cheeks.[13] He later urged his son to
pattern his life upon that of the General and stood ever ready to prove his

8. New Orleans *Argus*, June 21, 1828.

9. *Ibid.*; *Louisiana Advertiser*, September 20, 1828.

10. *Louisiana Gazette*, January 10, 1824.

11. *Ibid.*, June 2, 1826.

12. Davezac, "Reminiscences of Livingston," 369.

13. New Orleans *Argus*, November 15, 1827; J. B. Plauché to Andrew Jackson, June 8,
1822, in Jackson Papers, LC.

loyalty by acts of generosity in times of Jackson's need which reflected the obvious sincerity and selflessness which motivated them.[14]

Like Livingston, Grymes, and Davezac, Abner L. Duncan, another Jackson aide in 1814–1815, also understood the advantages to be won in keeping memories of Chalmette alive. He and his friends took pains over the years to apprise Jackson of their continuing fight against old enemies like Thomas B. Robertson and Fulwar Skipwith, whom Jackson continued to believe guilty of trying to surrender New Orleans to the British.[15] Jackson also knew that even more than Livingston, Duncan continued to be assailed politically as his principal adviser in the Louisiana legislature dispute of 1814–1815, and few things bound Jackson more closely to another than the suffering of attack in his cause. Thus Duncan became a valued friend and political sponsor of the General in Louisiana, host to his relatives or associates on their visits to New Orleans, and frequent supplicant for aid in acquiring whatever federal office might attract him.[16]

Isaac Baker's relationship with Jackson also reflected much more than simple political allegiance. A close friend of Andrew Jackson Donelson in his youth, Baker had himself been in some fashion or other a protégé or ward of the General. From his home in St. Martinville he made frequent pilgrimages to the Hermitage to visit with Jackson and report on the latest maneuvers of their common enemies.[17] "In my progress through life," he once wrote his benefactor, "I may safely say that after my father I owe you more obligations than to all other men living and, you cannot be ignorant, feel great solicitude for any and everything which regards you."[18]

14. Nolte, *Fifty Years in Both Hemispheres*, 210; J. B. Plauché to Andrew Jackson, June 8, 1822, in Jackson Papers, LC; Andrew Jackson to William B. Lewis, January 15, 1842, in William B. Lewis Papers, NYPL.

15. James Gadsden to Andrew Jackson, April 30, 1820, Jackson to John McLean, March 22, 1824, in Jackson Papers, LC; Thomas B. Robertson to Fulwar Skipwith, May 7, 1820, in Personal Miscellaneous Papers, LC; James Monroe to Fulwar Skipwith, September 15, 1823, in James Monroe Papers, NYPL.

16. James Gadsden to Andrew Jackson, April 30, 1820, James Scallan to Jackson, December 18, 1820, Andrew Jackson Donelson to Jackson, March 3, 1821, Abner Duncan to Jackson, December 12, 1821, A. P. Hayne to Jackson, October 7, 1823, in Jackson Papers, LC.

17. Andrew Jackson Donelson to Andrew Jackson, March 3, 1821, Jackson to J. C. Bronough, January 10, 1822, *ibid.*

18. Isaac L. Baker to Andrew Jackson, February 18, 1821, *ibid.*

Similar personal ties stretched from Jackson to many others in Louisiana. Lafayette Saunders had not only fought under him at New Orleans, but he had also married Mary Smith, daughter of Rachel Jackson's niece, in a ceremony at the Hermitage. And Clark Woodrooff had followed up his military service at Chalmette with an 1819 honeymoon of several weeks at the Jackson home in Nashville.[19]

General Walter H. Overton, for his part, had connections to Jackson not only through their shared military backgrounds, but also through membership in the family of John Overton of Tennessee, one of the old soldier's closest and most cherished friends. In like fashion, Thomas Butler's regard for the Hero of New Orleans stemmed from more than an impersonal attachment to his political principles. His brother, Adjutant General Robert Butler, had been the General's chief of staff at New Orleans, and both he and Jackson had enjoyed the hospitality of the Cottage on their way home from the great battle.[20] Another Floridian, the effusive John B. Dawson, prided himself on having been born in the Hero's own town of Nashville and found in the old warrior a personality which appealed to his own notions of emotional leadership. Jackson "sums up all my ideas of human perfectibility," he gushed to William S. Hamilton, "*Intelligent, Brave* and magnanimous. . . . Huzza for Jackson! In war, the spirit of the mountain storm, and in peace, the Widow's Friend, and the orphan's Father."[21]

Less demonstrative, perhaps, but certainly as sincerely devoted to their commander, Isaac T. Preston, Maunsel White, and W. L. Robeson had all served under the General at one time or another, Robeson winning considerable renown as the leader of the company in the forefront of Jackson's successful attack against Pensacola. They remained steadfast in loyalty to the General, White matching Plauché in the generosity of his personal assistance during many of Jackson's not infrequent financial crises.[22] Alfred Hennen, too, had renewed an old acquaintance with Jackson during his Louisiana campaign, and he and his wife kept this association alive in the years which followed.[23] All in all, the list of Jackson's close personal friends

19. Robinson, *Early Feliciana Politics*, 53–54, 103–108.

20. Butler, "West Feliciana," 103.

21. John B. Dawson to William S. Hamilton, June 29, 1824, in Hamilton Papers, LSU.

22. Maunsel White to Andrew Jackson, April 7, 1827, in Jackson Papers, LC; *Louisiana Gazette*, December 20, 1824.

23. Alfred Hennen to Andrew Jackson, November 8, 1825, in Jackson Papers, LC.

in Louisiana—Livingston, Davezac, Duncan, Grymes, Baker, Preston, Overton, White, Hennen, Robeson, Butler, Saunders—reads like a roll call of the eventual Democratic chieftains of the state. Jackson had, in effect, an already constituted cadre of leadership in Louisiana the moment he gave his consent to be entered in national politics and certainly before it could be well understood what political principles, if any, he might champion.

There could have been no better time for Jackson to look for political support in Louisiana than the early 1820s. The state lay almost helpless in the grip of despair and bewilderment, anxious for its future and searching for someone who might recognize its plight and crush the evils which had given it birth. Aggravating the effects of the national depression of the 1820s, which hit hard in Louisiana, a series of floods, broken levees, heavy rains, and rot struck the lower Mississippi valley, wiping away more than two-thirds of the area's crops for two or three years. Capital sources dried up, banks curtailed, and the state looked on incredulously as many of its oldest and heretofore soundest businesses began to close their doors. By the beginning of 1824, even the Mississippi itself seemed to waver, its water stage so low that the usual torrent of trade from the vast western interior diminished to scarcely a trickle.[24] Hard-pressed planters cursed the New Orleans factors and commission merchants and pushed through the legislature a state usury law clamping a 10- to 12-percent limit on interest rates. None of the leading men of the community rallied to continue the fight, however, when Governor Robertson vetoed the measure as an unwise and arbitrary extension of government power, and despite these real hardships, no strong demands emerged in the state for stay laws or replevin acts. Even the bitterest critics of Robertson, such as Isaac Baker, applauded his stern refusal to abandon what they considered the basic rules of sound economy.[25] A compromise of sorts finally calmed planter anger by creating the

24. *Louisiana Gazette*, November 6, 1822, July 8, 1823, January 8, 1824; St. Francisville *Asylum*, August 23, 1823; Josiah S. Johnston to Eliza Johnston, April 29, 1823, John Linton to Johnston, April 12, 1824, John H. Overton to Johnston, May 20, 1824, Walter H. Overton to Johnston, April 22, 1824, all in Johnston Papers, HSP; Nathaniel Cox to Stephen Austin, August 6, 1824, in Barker, ed., *Austin Papers*, Pt. 1, p. 872.

25. *Louisiana Advertiser*, June 3, 11, 12, 14, 19, 1823; Isaac L. Baker to William S. Hamilton, March 29, 1823, in Hamilton Papers, LSU; James Brown to Josiah S. Johnston, April 11, 1823, in Johnston Papers, HSP. For a discussion of different developments in a similar situation in Kentucky, see Arthur M. Schlesinger, Jr., *The Age of Jackson* (Boston, 1945), 31–32, 36.

Bank of Louisiana, designed specifically to provide funds to the agrarian group, but the stopgap measure brought only partial relief at best.[26] Moreover, what little help the bank did give could not offset the effects which even the limited talk about usury and stop laws had generated. Capital became more closely guarded than ever, and many northern and eastern investors began cautiously to pull their funds from the state.[27]

As trying as these economic tensions might be, experience led to a general acceptance that in the normal workings of the economic system things would eventually get better. No such optimism attached to those problems most Louisianians identified as having origins in the simple lack of knowledge about the state and indifference to its concerns which existed in Washington. With memories of the British attack in 1814 still fresh in Louisiana, its citizens found it inconceivable that even after the lessons of that terrible crisis the United States in the 1820s had still made not a single effort to provide the state the defenses necessary for its security. A state legislative committee issued a nervous warning in 1823 that Louisiana might well be considered "the Achillean Heel of these confederated States; for, from its geographical position, as well as from its scattered and spare white population, it is more accessible to the evil designs and actual inroads of a foreign foe, than any other state of the Union."[28] Governor Robertson filled his annual messages to the legislature with like sentiments, pointing out in 1822 that the state at that moment remained "as much exposed to invasion as it was seven years ago, when it experienced its horrors." Why does the United States build defenses at Mobile, he asked, while "New Orleans could be taken by a *coup de main?*" Because, he answered, "[ours] is unfortunately the only portion of the Republic, not only always unrepresented in what is termed the cabinet, but unknown by personal observation, as well to all its members, as, with few exceptions indeed, to all the legislators of the nation." The following year Robertson reported that his pleas had gone unanswered, and in words shaped more by the recognition of helplessness than by bitterness, he advised the assembly that Louisiana simply lay "too far from the center of power to be regarded at Washing-

26. *Louisiana Gazette*, April 7, 1824; Alexander Porter to Josiah S. Johnston, April 3, 1824, in Johnston Papers, HSP.

27. Dicks, Booker, and Company to William S. Hamilton, March 27, April 20, 1823, in Hamilton Papers, LSU.

28. *Louisiana House Journal*, 1823, p. 103. See also the *Louisiana Gazette*, January 3, June 28, December 20, 1821, June 3, 1822.

ton—distance seems to operate on them like time; and events which occur a thousand miles off, are like those which happened a thousand years ago."[29]

Public sentiment vented similar outrage over the marauding pirates in the Gulf, who terrorized the approaches to Louisiana and forced commercial insurance rates higher and higher because the federal government did nothing to provide adequate protection to American vessels in those waters. Repeated demands called for a naval squadron to patrol the seas off Cuba, and Robertson added to his complaints by questioning "the wisdom of the policy which has sent our naval force to Africa, whilst our own coasts, particularly those of the Gulf of Mexico, have been permitted for years to exhibit scenes of blood and rapine, unequalled in atrocity in the annals of the world."[30]

Mail service to Louisiana was primitive at best; the lack of a direct national road from New Orleans to Washington necessitated a twenty- to twenty-five-day journey to move correspondence from one of these cities to the other.[31] The whole state west of the Mississippi had serious need of federal improvements to the navigable streams which provided the region with its sole linkage to the outside world.[32] Not even in the vital function of the administration of federal justice did the central government show any concern for the interests of the state. The Judiciary Act of 1807 failed to create a federal circuit court for the western area of the United States, leaving Mississippi, Alabama, Indiana, Louisiana, Illinois, and Missouri with nothing but district judges, though the number of their federal cases exceeded those of the eastern states. These western district courts could try only those disputes involving sums in excess of five hundred dollars, an amount considerably higher than the fifty-dollar qualification in their eastern counterparts. Nor could the western states send on any appeals to the Supreme Court in criminal matters or in civil cases involving sums under two thousand dollars.[33]

29. *Louisiana Gazette*, January 10, 1822.

30. *Ibid.*; Alexander Porter to Josiah S. Johnston, January 12, 1821, Thomas B. Robertson to Johnston, December 24, 1822, in Johnston Papers, HSP.

31. *Louisiana Gazette*, July 28, September 19, December 15, 1824.

32. *Ibid.*, September 19, 1824; *Louisiana Journal*, June 15, 1826.

33. Curtis Nettels, "The Mississippi Valley and the Federal Judiciary, 1807–1837," MVHR, XII (1925), 203–206; *Louisiana Courier*, January 12, 1832.

Such restrictions convinced many in the West that an eastern conspiracy operated to strangle their growth, with some insisting that even the great Jackson had scarcely been able to survive a similar jealousy in his military career.[34] Caught up in much the same belief, Governor Robertson attacked the Adams-Onis Treaty of 1819 as one by which "our title to a province . . . has been most wantonly thrown away" to satisfy east coast interests.[35] The level of resentment occasioned by these affronts did not always match the seriousness of the offenses. New Orleans editors raged against a New York counterpart, for example, who had claimed that the mayor of their city jailed theatrical performers who muffed their lines. Was there no limit, they asked, to the absurdities which men would believe about their state?[36]

Nothing plagued Louisiana more than its inability to bring the vast acres of its public lands into private ownership. Therein, said Robertson in 1824, could be found "the principal cause of all the evils" besetting the state,[37] and the complexity of the situation made most men despair of any early solution. In part, the difficulty traced back to the confusion surrounding the status of private land claims in the state. The treaty of 1803 vested in the United States ownership of all soil in the Purchase territory not legitimately held by private title, and shortly after the transfer Congress passed legislation requiring all land titles in Louisiana to be registered in order to distinguish public from private holdings.[38] Lacking registration, no unrecorded title could be used as evidence in any court proceedings, but even this stringent measure did little to hasten entry of claims by the Louisianians. Many failed to register under the impression that the law did not apply to already established clear titles, an opinion held even by many attorneys,[39] while others lagged because most entries had to be made in New Orleans, requiring costly and time-consuming trips to the capital not only by the claimant but by his witnesses as well.[40] Some, especially the French-

34. *Louisiana Gazette*, May 2, 1822.

35. *Ibid.*, January 10, 1823.

36. St. Francisville *Asylum*, August 30, 1823.

37. *Louisiana Gazette*, January 8, 1824.

38. For these early land laws in the Territory of Orleans, see Carter, ed., *Territory of Orleans*, 408–14.

39. Henry Clay to ———, February 16, 1831, in Thomas Clay Papers, LC.

40. H. Lavergne to Josiah S. Johnston, December 11, 1830, in Johnston Papers, HSP.

speaking residents, simply paid no attention to these mysterious pronouncements by their new masters, confident in their belief that ownership
of property which they and perhaps their ancestors had held for decades
could never be questioned.[41] Faced with the obvious fact that to adhere rigidly to the time limit set for private entries would cause real and widespread
injustice, Congress repeatedly extended the period for registration, and the
Louisianians continued to make few attempts to meet the new deadlines.

Complicating this already confused picture immeasurably, a great number of claims presented to the United States clearly lacked credible authen-
ticity, many of such vast extent that they tied up literally whole sections of
the state in dispute. In the Ouachita area the federal government refused to
accept the claims of those holding under the Maison Rouge and Bastrop
grants of the late Spanish period, placing hundreds of thousands of acres in
question when claimants continued to press their suit against the ruling.
Some of the relatively few actual settlers in the area had purchased titles
from the large-grant claimants, others from the United States, while the remainder hoped eventually to be able to buy from the government under
preemption rights. Congress found itself caught squarely in the middle of
pressure from all these interests, with one group supporting the Spanish
grants and another assailing them as fraudulent schemes to deprive the
small settler of his proper rights.[42]

The Florida parishes faced equally baffling and disturbing problems, for
there the Spanish had denied that the Purchase included West Florida and
maintained possession until 1810, with many corrupt officials carelessly issuing or selling fraudulent land claims during the last seven years of their
control. Unfortunately, even many patents and grants legitimately conferred during the period of uncontested Spanish authority had never been
entered or registered because of incompetent or careless clerks, adding immensely to the confusion.[43] On a smaller scale, similar problems could be
found in practically every part of the state.

This persisting inability to guarantee land ownership had devastating

41. Alexander Porter to Josiah S. Johnston, January 19, 1831, *ibid.*

42. St. Francisville *Asylum*, August 22, September 19, 1822; *Washita Gazette* (Monroe),
October 24, 1825; *United States v. The Mayor, Aldermen, and Citizens of the Cities of Philadelphia and New Orleans*, 609 ff. See also the many letters of D. W. Coxe to Josiah S. Johnston
in defense of his Maison Rouge claims, in Johnston Papers, HSP.

43. Carter, ed., *Territory of Orleans*, 967–69; Henry Flower to Josiah S. Johnston, January
14, 1825, in Johnston Papers, HSP.

impact on Louisiana settlement. Few persons could be induced to purchase land for which a variety of claimants might show bogus Spanish titles, and the federal government could hardly open public lands to sale before determination of just what was and what was not public property. Confusion and inadequacy in the operation of the federal land office in Louisiana only deepened the problem, with agents making little effort to perfect surveys and plats for expansive areas incontestably owned by the government.[44]

As a consequence, the United States sold not a single plot of land in Louisiana until 1821, and as late as 1829 only 185,000 acres had been transferred to private ownership.[45] This count fell far below that of other states during the same period, understandably stimulating increasing demands for some change which would allow the region to share in the growing flood of western migration.[46] Adding to its disabilities, since Louisiana could collect no taxes from federal lands within her borders, construction of badly needed roads and bridges came to a virtual halt, the state refusing to improve property over which it had no control and from which it could expect no revenue. With settlers avoiding these federal acres, Louisiana watched helplessly as its sister states forged ahead in population and congressional representation. "The tide has passed [us] by," a state legislative committee reported sadly in 1824, lending support to Governor Robertson's repeated outbursts against the unchanging grievance.[47] "Louisiana is in the situation of a colony," he once protested. Is it nothing, he demanded, to permit the United States "to hold possession and exercise sovereignty over more than half the soil of our independent State? Ask the Virginians, who contend that the [United] States do not own soil over which a post road runs, or on which a post office stands in the ancient dominion."[48] From countless others in the state echoed the cry, "Send us people to settle!"[49]

44. L'Ami des Lois, May 14, 1822; Natchitoches Courier, February 21, 1825; K. McCrummen to Josiah S. Johnston, February 1, 1824, Thomas B. Brashear to Johnston, December 10, 1825, John Sibley to Johnston, January 3, 1826, in Johnston Papers, HSP.

45. Debates in Congress, 20th Cong., 2nd Sess., 46; 24th Cong., 1st Sess., appendix, 61–62.

46. See, for example, Henry Boyce to Josiah S. Johnston, February 1, 1824, Henry Bry to Johnston, November 5, 1824, in Johnston Papers, HSP.

47. Louisiana House Journal, 1826, p. 79.

48. Louisiana Gazette, January 10, 1823; Thomas B. Robertson to Josiah S. Johnston, November 7, 1821, in Johnston Papers, HSP.

49. Henry Boyce to Josiah S. Johnston, February 1, 1824, in Johnston Papers, HSP.

It was only natural in such a situation that men would turn to Andrew Jackson as a possible savior, for who more than he identified with the salvation of the state? A toast at a New Orleans dinner in 1823 spoke eloquently to the point: "The next President—may he be a man who knows that there is such a state as Louisiana, and that there has been such a day as the 8th of January!"[50] Even those outside the state looked upon Jackson as an obvious champion of its interests. John C. Calhoun reported to Governor Villeré in 1820, relative to a request upon the national government, that "the subject has been referred to Genl. Jackson whose local knowledge—and zeal to promote the interests of Louisiana will dispose him to give to it the attention it merits."[51] Reflecting much the same conviction, a plea sent to Jackson by New Orleans mayor Augustin Macarty in 1819 asked for aid in speeding the sale of United States lands in the city. "It would be deemed a fault, toward you, Sir," said Macarty, "to aim at any advancement without your participation."[52]

But not everyone in the state looked upon Jackson with the admiration and gratitude felt by Plauché, White, Baker, and those who sang his praises as the savior of New Orleans. The whole state might agree on the existence of problems which cried out for solution and complain against the neglect and injustice suffered at the hands of the federal government, but many saw the General as a false friend in whose custody the interests of the community would not be secure. The wounds which Jackson had inflicted upon French pride in Louisiana during his campaign against the British still stung in any number of important households. Louis Louaillier, for example, jailed by Jackson during his martial-law rule in 1815, was active in the 1820s recounting the insults and injuries he had suffered by command of the Hero of New Orleans. Others, such as Mazureau, found in Jackson the very distillation of everything they hated in Americans, and the Ajax of the Gallic forces never forgot that his own military advice had been unceremoniously disregarded by a backwoods soldier during the crisis of the invasion. He once entertained Edward Everett in New Orleans with "astonishing anecdotes of the ignorance of General Jackson relative to tactics,"[53] and later in his life he told Henry Clay, "I glory to have been engaged from

50. *Louisiana Courier*, January 10, 1823.

51. John C. Calhoun to Jacques Villeré, November 25, 1820, in Jackson Papers, LC.

52. Augustin Macarty to Andrew Jackson, December 30, 1819, *ibid.*

53. Edward Everett Diary, May 5, 1829, in Edward Everett Papers, MHS.

the beginning of the struggle against Dirtocracy," by which he meant, of course, Jacksonianism.[54]

To countless Louisianians, indeed, Clay rather than Jackson deserved to be the champion which everyone agreed the state so desperately needed. A westerner like the Tennessean, he could be relied upon to understand the needs and problems of the newer societies. Even more important, he had personal ties to Louisiana even stronger, perhaps, than those of Andrew Jackson. A brother, John Clay, had long been active in the business world of New Orleans, and two of his daughters made their homes there as well, one the wife of Martin Duralde, the great favorite of the creoles, the other the spouse of John Erwin, one of the best-known slave traders of his day. To these extensive family alliances Clay added a host of private friends such as Alexander Porter, James Brown, Josiah Stoddard Johnston, and Etienne Mazureau, and, like Jackson, he was himself no stranger to the streets of New Orleans.[55] Clay, moreover, had already by the 1820s made a clear record of his political ideas. His support of internal improvements and the protective tariff appealed strongly to the sugar-growing regions of interior Louisiana, while his championing of Clay's "American System" and the Second Bank of the United States made him a favorite with many of the commercial and business leaders of New Orleans.[56]

No one else in national life offered serious competition to the popularity and support enjoyed in Louisiana by the two westerners. Among the numerous "Down East" settlers in the Floridas and in the Ouachita area, John Quincy Adams did have a considerable following, but one based almost completely on his New England origins, which called down upon him the full force of the anti-Yankee sentiment so strong in Louisiana.[57] In addition, his dominant role as secretary of state in the crafting of the Adams-Onis Treaty of 1819 exposed him to the charge that he had ignored south-

54. Etienne Mazureau to Henry Clay, February 6, 1841 (Louis Hermann File), Letters of Application and Recommendation During the Administrations of Martin Van Buren, William Henry Harrison, and John Tyler, 1837–1845, in RG 59, GRDS, NA.

55. James Brown to Henry Clay, April 26, 1822, in Henry Clay Papers, LC; D. W. Coxe to Josiah S. Johnston, March 10, 1824, in Johnston Papers, HSP; H. B. Trist to Nicholas P. Trist, March 31, 1828, in Trist Papers, LC.

56. Joseph G. Tregle, Jr., "Louisiana and the Tariff, 1816–1846," *LHQ*, XXV (1942), 48.

57. St. Francisville *Asylum*, April 17, 1824; T. S. Slocum to Josiah S. Johnston, December 8, 1824, in Johnston Papers, HSP.

ern interests by surrendering American claims to Texas in that agreement with Spain,[58] and his supposed hostility to the Louisiana Purchase still rankled in the minds of many of the ancienne population.[59] Support for the political advancement of William H. Crawford of Georgia or John C. Calhoun of South Carolina attracted only a limited number of independent thinkers such as Thomas B. Robertson, who seemed to be drawn to Crawford primarily because he found so much to oppose in all the other major leaders of the day.[60]

Louisiana participated in only three presidential elections prior to 1824, all in the placid calm of the Era of Good Feeling which discouraged development in the state of any major factions grouped around contending national leaders. Its citizens had passively watched the legislature give their electoral votes to Madison and Monroe in 1812, 1816, and 1820, and then rushed once again into the consuming competitions of their local political scene, with all the unique ethnic and cultural tensions which made it practically a world apart from the rest of the Union. National politics seemed remote from Louisiana in the early 1820s, and whatever might have been said about Washington's neglect of the state could have been affirmed with equal justice of its own lack of concern over national political affairs except as they tended to impinge directly on its own interests. "In Louisiana," United States senator James Brown remarked in the spring of 1822, "our bales of cotton and hogsheads of sugar absorb all other considerations."[61] And Lafayette Saunders reported much the same thing to Jackson in 1823 when he wrote from his new home in the Florida parishes that "In this Country, Politics as well as all other considerations, yield in a great degree, to the cultivation of cotton and sugar."[62]

This political indifference generated spirited criticism in the local press,[63] perhaps unjustly, given the peculiar circumstances of the community. Except for those in the metropolis, few native Louisianians knew any-

58. *Louisiana Gazette*, January 3, 1821, January 10, 1823; St. Francisville *Asylum*, May 29, 1822.

59. *L'Ami des Lois*, January 17, 1823.

60. Andrew Jackson to J. C. Bronough, January 10, 1822, Isaac L. Baker to Jackson, February 14, 1823, in Jackson Papers, LC.

61. James Brown to Henry Clay, April 26, 1822, in Henry Clay Papers, LC.

62. Lafayette Saunders to Andrew Jackson, July 28, 1823, in Jackson Papers, LC.

63. *Louisiana Advertiser*, August 4, 1823.

thing at all about national affairs. They seldom read newspapers, content to allow their chieftains to manage the esoteric problems of political maneuvering.[64] Both amused and irked by the appalling ignorance of the outside world exhibited by his creole neighbors, Browse Trist regularly passed on to his brother Nicholas tidbits of their storehouse of misinformation.[65]

The state's continuing choice of presidential electors by legislative ballot added to a widespread feeling that national contests concerned only the political leaders of the state. Even those at that level seemed to give but little thought to federal elections. They clearly recognized the magnitude of the state's problems, particularly those involving unguarded frontiers and unsettled lands, but these had not become party questions. It appeared certain, at any rate, that in Louisiana Henry Clay would be the only major candidate to succeed James Monroe in the White House, and as much as any man in active politics he might be expected to defend its interests in the national councils. As late as 1822 most thought that Jackson had no intention of offering himself for the presidency, and with little serious competition to Clay in sight, the state tended to ignore the approaching campaign. In April of that year James Brown wrote to Clay from New Orleans that the Kentuckian remained "the only candidate for the P[residency] known here, and the only one having warm personal friends," so that his hope for Louisiana's five electoral votes seemed assured of realization.[66]

Nothing in the congressional campaigns in 1822 had any reference to the approaching presidential race except for a brief comment by William S. Hamilton in his opposition to Henry H. Gurley in the Second District. Fully aware of the hatred felt toward Yankees by many in his neighborhood, Hamilton attacked what he called a "new party . . . collecting the scattered forces" of Federalism to "overwhelm the South and the West," implying that Gurley, a New Englander, might be expected to assist Adams in the building of this northern despotism.[67] But Hamilton's thrust clearly aimed more at defeating Gurley than at affecting the presidential election, and it proved ineffective in any case, the Yankee experiencing little trouble in retaining his seat.[68] The battle in the western district between the incumbent

64. Alexander Porter to Josiah S. Johnston, January 19, 1831, in Johnston Papers, HSP.

65. H. B. Trist to Nicholas P. Trist, May 12, 1828, in Trist Papers, LC.

66. James Brown to Henry Clay, April 26, 1822, in Henry Clay Papers, LC.

67. St. Francisville Asylum, May 29, August 22, 1822.

68. Louisiana Gazette, July 9, 1822.

Josiah Johnston and William Brent developed into a vicious struggle re-volving almost completely around personal issues, with Brent finally win-ning a close victory by circulating anonymous pamphlets on the very eve of the canvass linking Johnston to attempts to guarantee the large grants at the expense of small settlers. Neither candidate had taken a stand on the presidential race.[69] At the same time, Mazureau had managed to line up such concentrated strength in New Orleans behind Livingston's try for the First District seat that no opposition offered, and the ex–New Yorker could now make ready to enjoy the rewards of his long fight in the French cause.[70] Whatever else had cemented the relationship between these two men, they certainly shared no agreement over the attractions of Andrew Jackson.

The General simply did not seem to be an issue in 1822. He had passed through New Orleans the previous year on his way to serve as governor of Florida and received a magnificent welcome, with celebrations at the the-aters, specially composed poetry proclaiming his fame, and brilliant trans-parencies commemorating his 1815 victory. But he must have left his friends with the firm belief that he would never seek the presidency, for even in late 1822, months after the Tennessee legislature had brought his name forward in July, his Louisiana admirers remained convinced he would not make the race. The dedicated Isaac Baker sadly accepted the fact and wrote to Hamilton that De Witt Clinton had now become his first choice for the White House: "I have so much gratitude and good feeling for Old Hickory," he assured the colonel, "that I would deem it a species of treason to abandon his standard beneath which I have always found promotion . . . and the kindest protection." But the General, Baker insisted, had no inten-tion of becoming a candidate.[71]

In early 1823, however, everything changed. Jackson's reply to the Dau-phin Committee in Tennessee confirmed his entry into the campaign, and as the publication of this correspondence began to appear throughout Lou-

69. Isaac L. Baker to Josiah S. Johnston, July 26, November 11, 1822, in Johnston Pa-pers, HSP; *Louisiana Herald*, June 9, 1824.

70. *Louisiana Gazette*, July 4, 1822; Samuel R. Overton to Andrew Jackson, June 9, 1822, in Jackson Papers, LC; Alexander Porter to Josiah S. Johnston, July 8, 1824, in Johnston Pa-pers, HSP.

71. Isaac L. Baker to William S. Hamilton, December 26, 1822, in Hamilton Papers, LSU.

isiana, the presidential race immediately assumed an entirely new configuration.[72] Not even the bitterness of the ethnic quarrel which had erupted in January with Moreau Lislet's Florida Bill and continued into the Fenno-Cuvillier militia dispute of the next several months, or the violent debate over usury and depression, could hide this fact from Mazureau, Duralde, and the other Clay champions who had for so long been sanguine in their expectations of delivering the state to Clay practically by default. Henceforth they had the General to contend with, and they entertained no doubts as to the magnitude of his threat. Now they faced the possibility that all their golden dreams of influence and patronage through Duralde's father-in-law in the White House could be totally blasted by this hated Tennessean with whom they had no alliances and whose friends in Louisiana had always been their most inflexible enemies. Fear made them rash, and early in February one of their spokesmen gave formal notice in the state legislature that he planned to call for a recess so that the assembly might caucus and nominate a successor to James Monroe. Obviously the Clay leaders wished to commit the state to their candidates as early as possible, hoping to convince Louisianians that Jackson should not be considered a serious aspirant to the presidency and that he had offered too late in any case. But they had moved too soon. Many of the members of the assembly felt it unwise to bind the state to any man so early in the campaign, preferring to hold out in hopes of profiting from a long courtship for their votes. At best, the Clay forces had failed to assess the assembly's probable reaction, and they retreated ingloriously from their call.[73]

Baker wrote immediately to inform Jackson of these developments. For their part, the General's adherents preferred to delay any Louisiana legislative pronouncement. The "opinions of the present members are so difficult to get at," Baker told Jackson, "that we think it rather unwise to risque a caucus until we see our way more clearly. . . . Clay's friends are in despair and talk with less confidence than two weeks ago."[74] Adhering to this original plan, Baker and his associates turned immediately to prepare the way for a move of their own, hoping to give "the voice of the people a chance

72. Lafayette Saunders to Andrew Jackson, July 28, 1823, in Jackson Papers, LC.

73. Isaac L. Baker to William S. Hamilton, February 14, 1823, *ibid.*; Alexander Porter to Josiah S. Johnston, February 16, 1823, in Johnston Papers, HSP; St. Francisville *Asylum*, February 13, 1823.

74. Isaac L. Baker to Andrew Jackson, February 14, 1823, in Jackson Papers, LC.

of being heard" and thus build up a strong force of public opinion which would avoid the charge of trying to dictate a popular choice. Especially did they hope for a pro-Jackson pronouncement from one of the large states, which would give their cause a sound prospect of success and ease the common fears that Jackson could make little headway against the more experienced candidates in the field.[75]

In mid-March the Clay faction moved once more to the attack, and again they blundered. What had been intended as an assembly caucus on the night of March 15 turned into a heated debate between Mazureau on one side, pleading for a vote endorsing Clay's candidacy, and Baker and Davezac on the other, demanding that no caucus be declared in session at all. Fearing another defeat, the Clay men hurriedly produced a list of resolutions in support of their favorite and allowed the meeting to disband without a formal vote of any kind. Within a few days they began to give wide circulation to their proposed caucus resolutions, now bearing the signatures of thirty-four of the slightly more than sixty members of the legislature, the preponderance of French names in the list testifying to the effective influence of Mazureau and Duralde.

The resolutions, themselves, however, did nothing to advance the Clay cause. The preamble's shaky defense of caucus nominations carried little conviction, and in the desire to win over those who still might not give credence to Jackson's candidacy, the resolutions themselves bestowed glowing praise upon the General, whose claims "upon his country," they conceded, "cannot be effaced." The assurance that Jackson himself would not "desire the suffrage of his fellow-citizens of Louisiana, when given at the hazard" of defeating the only westerner with a chance to win did little to erase the fact that the resolutions failed to enumerate the virtues of Clay or any other candidate and only provided a blanket endorsement of the Kentuckian. As Samuel Overton wrote in glee to Jackson, his enemies had played into his hands. "Louisiana cannot gainsay these declarations," he rejoiced, "and must ultimately give you an unanimous vote."[76]

The next year and a half buzzed with intrigue and ever mounting campaign propaganda. But most of the political agitation in Louisiana had

75. Isaac L. Baker to Andrew Jackson, February 26, 1823, *ibid.*

76. Isaac L. Baker to Andrew Jackson, May 3, 1823, Samuel R. Overton to Jackson, June 27, 1823, *ibid.; Louisiana Courier*, March 19, 1823; *Louisiana Advertiser*, March 18, 22, 1823.

nothing to do with the presidential campaign. In July of 1824 Louisiana had to elect a governor to succeed Robertson, and the passions aroused by this contest overwhelmed all other topics of public concern. Inevitably, the basic issues related to the now highly inflammatory ethnic antagonisms in the state, so local in their content that they pushed matters of national concern into the background.[77]

The insensitive and highly pro-American policies of the Robertson administration had inflamed the always smoldering ethnic controversy into the most dangerous domestic crisis known to the community since statehood. Economic depression, the Florida Bill, militia disputes, fear of the Holy Alliance, and Gallic conviction that the Americans had conspired to monopolize the public affairs of the state combined to make the 1824 gubernatorial election one of unprecedented virulence and ill temper. The French insisted that the established rotation tradition demanded choice this time of a Gallic governor, and long before the end of Robertson's term some proposed bringing old Jacques Villeré back to the chief executive's chair.[78] But still jealous of Villeré's popularity and furious at what he termed the ex-governor's capitulation to American control, Bernard Marigny returned from France in 1823 to seek the governorship for himself, throwing the Gallic forces into turbulent and raucous confusion. Adding fuel to the flames, Marigny condemned Villeré as a tool of Mazureau, a strange tactic indeed, joining together supposed pro-American principles and the reputed field marshal of the Gallic troops.[79]

77. Hatcher's statement in *Livingston*, 318, that "the national election was practically the sole issue in the 1824 state campaign" has no merit. Even a cursory reading of the newspaper comments of the period reveals that the presidential race went virtually unmentioned in the gubernatorial contest. Moreover, Hatcher says that the "Jackson forces made the mistake of dividing their support between the two [Marigny and Villeré]." Besides the error in assuming that there *was* a "Jackson force" in this election, Hatcher mistakes the position of Villeré, who was, if anything, a Clayite.

78. *Louisiana Courier*, February 5, 1824; St. Francisville *Asylum*, Feburary 27, August 16, September 6, 1823; Isaac L. Baker to William S. Hamilton, December 26, 1822, in Hamilton Papers, LSU.

79. *Louisiana Gazette*, November 28, December 5, 1823; *Louisiana Courier*, January 17, 21, February 9, March 23, May 1, 29, 1824; *L'Ami des Lois*, February 16, 1824; New Orleans *Argus*, April 26, 1824; Ferdinand de Feriet to Janica de Feriet, November 21, 1823, in Feriet Family Papers, TU.

Only a comparable disunity in the American camp held out any hope for eventual French success. There a three-man split had developed, with Henry Johnson, Philemon Thomas, and Thomas Butler all in the field, a fragmentation clearly to be laid at the door of Johnson. His Senate term expired in 1823, and although he had given repeated indications that he had every intention of offering for governor in 1824, he did not relish retirement into private life while waiting for Robertson's tenure to end. Several of his American colleagues grumbled at Johnson's voracious appetite for office, however, and put it to him bluntly that he should decide for one post or the other, his seat in the national Senate or the governorship, and leave the way open for someone else to win the remaining honor. Both Philemon Thomas and Thomas Butler eagerly awaited the chance to make the race for Robertson's place in 1824, and when Johnson indicated that he would prefer to keep his Senate seat, the Florida leaders interpreted this as a surrender by him of all gubernatorial ambitions. Thus they gladly gave him their support when he won reelection to the Senate over Judge Martin in January 1823, expecting in this way to rid themselves of a dangerous competitor for the governorship.[80]

By the fall of that year, however, Johnson's actions made it obvious that he had every intention of remaining in the gubernatorial race, something which had been rumored in the press for months, and in September he released his formal announcement, despite the fact that Butler and Thomas had already entered the field.[81] The outraged protests of the followers of the two Florida candidates gave Johnson little pause. The *Louisiana Advertiser*, backing his campaign, charged that Butler and Thomas had entered the race primarily to block Johnson's victory, their hatred of him so great that they would even suffer the governorship to fall to the French if in the process they might humiliate their rival.[82] The consummate professional, Johnson surveyed the state with an eye long accustomed to discerning the political lay of the land. Confident of a considerable vote in New Orleans, the Floridas, and along the coast, plus the backing of H. S. Thibodaux in Lafourche, he assured Josiah Johnston in October 1823 that "It is to me a

80. Isaac L. Baker to William S. Hamilton, December 26, 1822, January 14, 1823, in Hamilton Papers, LSU; *Louisiana Gazette*, March 13, 16, 17, 31, April 20, 29, 1824; *Louisiana Courier*, March 5, 1824; *Louisiana Herald*, February 18, 1824.

81. *Louisiana Advertiser*, September 5, 1823.

82. *Ibid.*, August 15, October 1, 1823.

matter of no consequence, whether Judge Butler and General Thomas withdraw from the contest or not."[83] He was already certain of success.

In December, Governor Robertson once again energized the Gallic community into bitter opposition by the deviousness of his policies. He announced that Mazureau could not be renamed attorney general at the expiration of his appointment unless he resigned his seat in the legislature, leading the Frenchman to accept this as a pledge of the governor's continued support. When he stepped down from his legislative position, Robertson promptly placed Isaac T. Preston in the attorney general's office, and French accusations of perfidy swirled through the state.[84] Mazureau immediately made a successful bid for his old assembly place and then moved to stimulate Gallic forces to even greater exertions in the governor's race.[85] Working closely with Davezac and Grymes, who had other objectives in mind, he also pushed Livingston's claim to the United States Senate seat vacated by the appointment of James Brown as American ambassador to France, but his involvement greatly angered the American wing of the assembly. Aided by rural French representatives who rebelled against sending a city man to Washington, they turned against Livingston and gave the Senate post to Josiah S. Johnston.[86]

This defeat further aggravated the decline in French unity and morale which continued in the raucous fight between the adherents of Villeré and Marigny in the gubernatorial campaign. With Mazureau properly perceived as the driving force behind the Villeré candidacy, Marigny summoned every means at his command to prevent the success of that partnership, for he had long been unable to decide which he hated most, the Americans or the foreign French. While Henry Johnson continued to win French support in rural areas aghast at the internecine Gallic fight in the city, the two creole candidates practically ignored the other contenders to

83. Henry Johnson to Josiah S. Johnston, October 24, 1823, in Johnston Papers, HSP; *Louisiana Herald*, September 17, 1823; *Louisiana Gazette*, November 7, 1823.

84. *L'Ami des Lois*, December 15, 16, 22, 1823; *Louisiana Gazette*, December 16, 17, 19, 23, 1823; *Louisiana Advertiser*, December, 5, 15, 19, 23, 1823.

85. *Louisiana Advertiser*, January 1, 1824.

86. Isaac L. Baker to William S. Hamilton, January 16, 1824, in Hamilton Papers, LSU; Joseph Walker to Josiah S. Johnston, January 5, 1824, Johnston to Eliza Johnston, January 15, 1824, in Johnston Papers, HSP; *Louisiana Advertiser*, January 8, 13, 14, 1824; *Louisiana Courier*, January 13, 1824.

wage their private war. Marigny announced publicly that he would use any means, even deception, to defeat his creole rival.[87]

The *Louisiana Advertiser* did everything in its power to keep the feud boiling, printing glowing accounts of Marigny to balance the campaign propaganda in the city's two French papers controlled by Villeré and Mazureau, the *Louisiana Courier* and the *Argus*.[88] Johnson's backers killed all Gallic attempts to convene a legislative caucus proposed to unite French strength around a single candidate,[89] and Marigny's suggestion to end the division by a pulling of lots came to naught.[90]

The intensity and vulgarity of this all-French battle made the performances of the American contestants seem insipid indeed and climaxed late in June 1824 with the appearance of a heated exchange in the columns of the *Louisiana Gazette*. "A Citizen" submitted a note reading:

> The editor of the Courier, C. de St. Romes, a man of universal talent, a writer, orator, soldier, horseman, distinguished swordsman, and marksman, Reared in the Grand Opera of Paris, inventor of the new and graceful step in dancing called "*Le Fendu*" which is performed by first loosening the suspenders and then with the activity of a harlequin bringing the posterior in contact with the floor and again vaulting into the air. This great man accuses Mr. Marigny of not speaking his language correctly. He ought to remember that it is not known that his candidate Mr. Villerie can speak at all; he once attempted to make a speech to both houses of the Legislature when he commenced by opening his mouth and ended with a gape. We have yet to look for a specimen of his writing.[91]

St. Romes replied the following day:

> We read this morning in the *Louisiana Gazette*, a very mean paragraph, from a very mean writer, *Bernard De Marigny, candidate for ever and ever* for

87. *Louisiana Courier*, June 24, 1824. For Johnson's successful campaigning against his rivals, see, for example, Reuben Kemper to Josiah S. Johnston, March 18, 1824, in Johnston Papers, HSP.

88. *Louisiana Advertiser*, December 4, 1823.

89. *Ibid.*, January 19, 20, 21, 1824.

90. *Louisiana Gazette*, March 19, 1824.

91. *Ibid.*, June 28, 1824.

the office of Governor, which he shall *never* get, notwithstanding all his journeys, and the handsome Spanish songs and *Boleros*, with which he treated
the voters of the upper Fourche; his promises to some, and his threats to others, in short, those delicate means which excited a feeling of pity in the mind
of every one. . . . we have often said and we do still say, that Mr. de Marigny
does not know two words of French.[92]

In such fashion did the Gallic host so divide itself that Johnson's sanguine predictions of success proved completely well founded in the July
elections. He carried every Florida parish but Thomas's own East Baton
Rouge and piled up a sufficient vote even in the interior French country to
outdistance Villeré and Marigny in the total count. Butler and Thomas
trailed very far behind. So Louisiana was to have two American governors
in succession, and the French could look with sorrow and growing wisdom
at the final tally. Their combined vote had exceeded that of the Americans
by 3,115 to 3,071.[93]

If nothing else, the gubernatorial election of 1824 highlighted the ideological emptiness of Louisiana politics of the period. No issues had been decided; indeed none had been discussed. The all-consuming concerns remained the old ones of ethnic dominance and personal ascendancy within
the contending factions. Nor had national interests been reflected in the
campaigns. The *Louisiana Courier* and the *Argus* both supported Villeré,
though the first backed Andrew Jackson and the second championed
Henry Clay. The Jacksonian *Louisiana Advertiser* endorsed Henry Johnson,
whose national loyalties probably lay with John Quincy Adams,[94] and the
pro-Adams St. Francisville *Asylum* served as the principal organ of the pro-
Jackson Thomas Butler. Mazureau, who loathed Jackson, had thrown all
his strength behind the senatorial bid of Edward Livingston, a pronounced
champion of the General, primarily because Livingston had long served
the French cause, which Mazureau headed in Louisiana. An intimate
friend of Clay, Josiah Johnston profited in the same race from the aid of

92. *Ibid.*, June 29, 1824; *Louisiana Courier*, June 28, 29, 30, 1824.
93. *Louisiana Senate Journal*, 1824, p. 3.
94. Isaac L. Baker to William S. Hamilton, June 15, 1824, in Hamilton Papers, LSU;
John Clay to Josiah S. Johnston, November 30, 1824, in Johnston Papers, HSP; *Louisiana
Gazette*, October 11, 1824.

such staunch Jacksonians as John B. Dawson, Martin Gordon, Isaac Baker, and Walter H. Overton,[95] none of whom liked Livingston and all of whom detested Mazureau. These same men during the same time span aligned in different combinations to contest the presidential election, but as yet no clear-cut national political affiliation had emerged in Louisiana comparable to that which developed over the course of the next decade. Even during the later period of greater devotion to national party identity, there would be not infrequent returns to the ethnic and personality loyalties so obvious in the governor's race of 1824, a tendency which kept Louisiana politics particularly unpredictable in the Jacksonian era.

Despite the intensity of the gubernatorial contest, the presidential campaign had not been completely forgotten. The uncertainty surrounding Jackson's candidacy until early 1823 inhibited somewhat any vigorous campaigning by adherents of the various nominees, and even such committed champions of Jackson as Livingston, Grymes, and Duncan held back from active participation in the General's cause until its prospects of success could be clarified.[96] But by midsummer Jackson's chances seemed far more favorable,[97] the campaign picked up speed, and the press began to devote greater attention to the claims of the various aspirants. Even then, however, interest remained largely concentrated in New Orleans and, to a lesser degree, in St. Francisville, the greater part of the rural section of the state remaining relatively placid during the whole contest.[98] James Beardslee, editor of the *Louisiana Advertiser*, acknowledged as the principal American paper in the state, took the lead in sponsoring Jackson's candidacy. P. K. Wagner of the *Orleans Gazette* and James M. Bradford of the *Louisiana Journal* (St. Francisville) joined him in vigorous support of the General, with intermittent and rather pedestrian assistance from J. C. de St. Romes, the foreign-French editor of the *Louisiana Courier*. Clay's chief advocacy came from R. D. Richardson of the *Louisiana Gazette* and Manuel

95. Walter H. Overton to Josiah S. Johnston, January 13, 1824, Martin Gordon to Johnston, March 10, 15, 1824, in Johnston Papers, HSP; Isaac L. Baker to William S. Hamilton, January 16, 1824, in Hamilton Papers, LSU.

96. See Baker's complaint against their inactivity in the legislative caucus fight of May, 1823, in Isaac L. Baker to Andrew Jackson, May 3, 1823, in Jackson Papers, LC.

97. Isaac L. Baker to William S. Hamilton, July 25, 1823, in Hamilton Papers, LSU.

98. Walter H. Overton to Josiah S. Johnston, November 22, 1824, John Linton to Johnston, November 14, 1824, in Johnston Papers, HSP.

Cruzat of the *Argus*, who had the distinction of being one of the rarities of the day, a creole newspaper editor, while John Quincy Adams won the backing of Joel K. Mead in the *Mercantile Advertiser* and George Bissett in the *Asylum*.

In Louisiana as elsewhere the campaign concentrated its greatest attention on the individual strengths and weaknesses of the candidates, although it did give substantial recognition to a variety of sectional and political problems which transcended this competition of personalities. Despite the large New England backing which gathered around him, for example, Adams's backers had to combat the fierce anti-Yankee sentiment so common in Louisiana and vigorously deny that his conversion to Jeffersonianism represented only a transient phase in a long political career, an interlude which would soon give way to the resurgence of the inborn Federalist tenets normal to a man bearing the Adams name. That charge severely damaged Adams, representing him as a threat to the western states, a deceiver whose opposition to the acquisition of Louisiana exposed his real intent to maintain a New England and eastern supremacy which amounted to nothing less than Federalism in new garb.[99] Not even the common admission that his illustrious career made him unquestionably the man best trained for the presidency could overcome these fears among the mass of the people,[100] allowing opposition spokesmen to claim that his candidacy found support only among a "few yankee pedlers and school masters stuck in every one of our villages, political priests, and federal lawyers."[101]

Crawford had so few personal contacts with Louisiana that his candidacy never attracted any sort of following in the state. At first there had been some rumors that Governor Robertson and William L. Brent might attempt to organize a faction in his support, but the folly of such a course became so quickly obvious that they both abandoned any such plans and rallied behind Clay.[102] The congressional caucus of February 1824, which

99. *Louisiana Gazette*, January 14, 17, February 7, 1823; *Louisiana Advertiser*, March 11, 1824; St. Francisville *Asylum*, May 8, 1824.

100. T. S. Slocum to Josiah S. Johnston, December 8, 1824, Charles T. Scott to Johnston, July 24, 1824, in Johnston Papers, HSP; *Louisiana Gazette*, July 26, 1823.

101. *Louisiana Gazette*, November 17, 1824.

102. William L. Brent to Henry Clay, September 3, 1824, in Henry Clay Papers, LC; James M. Bradford to Josiah S. Johnston, December 21, 1824, in Johnston Papers, HSP; *Louisiana Gazette*, May 5, 1824.

pronounced in Crawford's favor, produced little response in Louisiana except from those who seized it as an opportunity to denounce politicians who "have set themselves up as being better judges of the 'people's candidate,' than the people are themselves."[103] The Georgian's candidacy, nationwide as well as in Louisiana, did little more than kill the caucus as a nominating device for the presidency.[104]

In Louisiana, Clay and Jackson in effect had the field to themselves, backed by those bands of friends, relatives, and associates who expected so much from the political success of their favorite. Clay benefited particularly from the growing creole impatience with a national policy which had never seen fit to confer a federal political office of any significance on a native Louisiana, their expectation being that Duralde's influence would certainly change all that with Clay in the White House.[105] Jacksonians, in turn, never tired in their reiterations that the immense debt owed by Louisiana to Jackson for having saved its people from British slavery compelled it to support the Hero of New Orleans. The "very houses we occupy proclaim their choice of Jackson," they said,[106] adding the warning that only his attachments to Louisiana could be relied on to reverse the shameful neglect the state had suffered at the hands of an uncaring nation.[107]

The Clay forces early on adopted as a favorite tactic the ridiculing of Jackson as a political naïf totally devoid of governing skills, a "man on horseback" who might plunge the nation into tyranny or war,[108] at the same time praising the "statesmanship" of the great Kentuckian and the profound political wisdom he would bring to the presidency.[109] They also branded the General as a notoriously sadistic and despotic militarist,

103. St. Francisville *Asylum*, March 13, June 19, 1824; Alexander Porter to Josiah S. Johnston, April 3, 1824, in Johnston Papers, HSP.

104. See the comments on this point in Bassett, ed., *Correspondence of Andrew Jackson*, III, v.

105. *Louisiana Courier*, July 28, August 2, 1824.

106. *Louisiana Advertiser*, January 5, 1824; *Louisiana Gazette*, November 17, 1824.

107. *Louisiana Gazette*, December 1, 1824; *Louisiana Journal*, March 4, 1824.

108. Charles T. Scott to Josiah S. Johnston, July 24, 1824, in Johnston Papers, HSP; *Louisiana Gazette*, May 1, October 11, 1824; St. Francisville *Asylum*, August 16, 1823, April 3, 10, 17, June 26, July 10, 24, 1824; *L'Ami des Lois*, September 12, 1823, April 10, 1824; New Orleans *Mercantile Advertiser*, November 13, 1824.

109. *Louisiana Gazette*, May 1, 1824; St. Francisville *Asylum*, July 3, 1824.

known to have inflicted cruel punishment on men in his command for minor infractions of his arbitrary discipline. Jacksonians answered that these charges reflected the same perverse judgment which justified criticism of Jackson's martial law rule in Louisiana at the time of the British invasion. His actions, they claimed, always matched the seriousness of a particular crisis, just as his military rule in New Orleans had been absolutely necessary for the salvation of the city.[110] They added the additional jibe that men who opposed Jackson because of his military service did violence to the memory of Washington.[111]

The constant demeaning of Jackson's political skill and experience struck his admirers as especially wrong headed because they saw in that aspect of his record precisely the point which made him so attractive as a presidential candidate. The long political vacuum of the Era of Good Feeling seemed to them a contrivance of professional hacks designed to lull the public into a lassitude during which they might establish themselves in a perpetual circle of political control. They saw Jackson as a plain and straightforward nonprofessional who would protect the interests of the producing classes of the society and expel the conniving office gluttons from their long-held positions. Compared to Jackson, Dawson insisted, the "other candidates seem to be scientific, skillful politicians, untrammelled by principle,"[112] and Isaac T. Preston made this same point his most telling argument in the major Jacksonian rally of the campaign in New Orleans:

> Since the days of Washington, an usurpation has grown up, in our Government, which if not crushed by the power and virtue of the people will soon destroy the republic. . . .
>
> The people have presented *Jackson* as their candidate, and he must and will succeed. . . . Plain farmers! he is one of you! Industrious mechanics! Enterprising high minded merchants! he encourages industry and noble enterprize—Hardy seamen! you are his favorites. All these will unite for *Jackson*. And who fears his election? Not the brave; not the honest; he loves honesty, and makes no distinction among men but that of virtue; not the faithful public servant; he is the most faithful; not the Christian, he is one. No—it is the

110. *Louisiana Courier*, June 19, 1824.
111. *Louisiana Gazette*, June 10, 1824.
112. John B. Dawson to William S. Hamilton, June 29, 1824, in Hamilton Papers, LSU.

enemies of his country—the faithless public servant—those who prey on the vitals of the people. Let these, and these alone, shake and quake like Belshazzar of old for their time is come.[113]

Thus Jackson appeared in the eyes of his contemporaries as anything but a radical or an innovator. Soldier of the Revolution, Hero of New Orleans, he seemed to them a corrective force, the one man able to restore the nation to *old* ways, to the virtuous republican path made clear by Jefferson and Madison in 1798 and 1800. Class conflict, economic liberalism, or doctrinaire philosophies of any kind simply did not figure in this Louisiana campaign of 1824. Except as imported issues generated elsewhere, they would remain unknown in the state throughout the Jacksonian era.

Only with respect to the tariff did economics play much of a role in the campaign of 1824. Hatred of protective duties on imports flourished throughout Louisiana, not only in the cotton-growing sectors such as the Floridas and the Red River country, but also in New Orleans and the western interior as well. Brent denounced the Tariff of 1824 despite its continued support of duties on imported sugar, railing against the act's reaffirmation of protection and condemning it as "that unjust and unequal burthen upon the Southern States," and the St. Francisville *Asylum* labeled the same enactment an "odious and pernicious measure" ruinous to the whole nation but especially so to Louisiana.[114] His famous, or notorious, championing of the protective doctrine stimulated most of the attacks on Clay, raising charges that he would sacrifice the whole South to the "hemp growers in Kentucky, and the iron manufacturers of Pennsylvania."[115] Jackson's position on the tariff went practically unnoticed, though he also had voted for the 1824 act as a senator from Tennessee. His backers kept this vote hidden as much as possible, and to those such as William S. Hamilton who found this part of Jackson's past disturbing, defenders such as Dawson could write, "I want you to forgive the old fellow's vote upon the Tariff," with clear implication that it amounted to nothing but a minor oversight on the General's part, an indiscretion which sprang from his unfamiliarity with the devious ways of politicians.[116]

113. *Louisiana Gazette*, June 7, 1824.
114. *Ibid.*, September 29, 1824; St. Francisville *Asylum*, May 8, 1824.
115. St. Francisville *Asylum*, June 19, 1824.
116. John B. Dawson to William S. Hamilton, June 29, 1824, in Hamilton Papers, LSU.

Clay at least had the advantage that his protariff stand made him also a champion of the protective duties on sugar, and in a bizarre twist of logic which persisted in Louisiana for years, the sugar planters of Louisiana managed to defend high import rates on their own product while they condemned them on everything else. Clay represented to them a symbol of economic security, and this, plus his support of internal improvements and his many family connections, made him always a favorite in the sugar parishes of the state.[117] He exploited this situation to the fullest in the 1824 campaign, advising Duralde and other friends how to demonstrate that he had done more than anyone else to save the sugar duty in the last Congress while at the same time publicizing Jackson's protariff vote.[118]

As the campaign moved deeper into 1824, the strategies of the opposing camps tended to narrow around clearly defined themes. The Jacksonians reviled the attempted legislative caucus endorsement of Clay as an aristocratic technique clearly demonstrating the determination of professional politicians to keep power out of the hands of people, and to counter it they introduced in the state house of representatives a bill conferring the choice of presidential electors upon the voters. The Clay faction rejected such a measure as unthinkable. It would constitute nothing less than a repudiation of the legislative resolutions favoring their candidate, and even had they not feared the untested strength of the General's partisans in the state, they well knew that French legislators, among whom Clay had his greatest influence, would certainly oppose surrender of any of the paternalistic power so much a part of their tradition. They accordingly took an adamant stand against the proposed measure and sent it down to defeat. There could be no question of where the responsibility lay, for anyone could match the names on the pro-Clay resolutions with those recorded against the electoral bill. The Clay forces had lost another round in the battle for public approval.[119]

Having been balked in their proposals for a change in the electoral law,

117. Tregle, "Louisiana and the Tariff," 18 ff.

118. Henry Clay to Josiah S. Johnston, October 2, 1824, in Johnston Papers, HSP; William L. Brent to Clay, September 3, 1824, in Henry Clay Papers, LC.

119. *Louisiana House Journal*, 1824, p. 113; *Louisiana Herald*, April 28, 1824; *Louisiana Journal*, February 5, 1824; St. Francisville *Asylum*, April 17, May 8, 29, July 10, 1824; *Louisiana Advertiser*, April 3, May 24, 27, 28, June 11, 1824; *Louisiana Gazette*, May 21, June 26, 1824.

the Jackson leaders, sure of their strength in the city, hit upon a device by which they hoped to prove Jackson's standing as the true choice of the people. In mid-May a self-appointed committee made up of Jean B. Plauché, Bartholomew Grima, J. B. Labatut, W. C. Withers, and Isaac Preston wrote to all New Orleans candidates seeking election to the legislature in the approaching July canvass and asked for an expression of their feelings on the presidential contenders. They explained that the committee proposed drawing up an all-Jackson ticket, so that friends of the General might cast their ballots for men pledged in turn to cast *their* votes for him in November.[120] Assurances of loyalty flooded in from the Jackson candidates, and Davezac's reply set the tone in its praise for the "greatest services ever rendered to a whole nation by a *man*."[121] On June 5 Preston presided over an enthusiastic meeting in one of the most popular meetinghouses in New Orleans, Davis's Ball Room, where Davezac and General Ripley joined the chairman in rousing speeches honoring their favorite, following which the company resolved not to "support any candidate for the Legislature, who would, if elected, act in opposition to the will of a majority of the people."[122] A second meeting on June 22 adopted a Jackson legislative ticket made up of Labatut, Davezac, John R. Grymes, C. G. de Armas, P. A. Rousseau, and Alonzo Morphy, and appointed committees of ten to work in each of the city's wards to get out the vote for their nominees.[123]

The anti-Jackson forces immediately protested this "unauthorized" attempt by the General's "pretorian cohorts" to "dictate to the whole community," and protagonists of the opposing factions joined to repudiate the efforts to bind the legislative candidates to any pledge so early in the campaign. They insisted that they too had every intention of obeying the public will in the presidential question, but to make this the whole test of a man's fitness for an assembly seat, they maintained, would minimize the consideration due many other responsibilities perhaps even more important to the local interests of the community. Professing their great admiration and love for General Jackson, they then went on to assail his claims to the White House, with special emphasis on his violence and "insatiable ambition," and finally called a public meeting of their own, at which they

120. *Louisiana Gazette*, May 19, 1824.
121. *Louisiana Courier*, June 11, 1824; *Louisiana Advertiser*, June 3, 1824.
122. *Louisiana Gazette*, June 7, 1824.
123. *Ibid.*, June 24, 1824.

adopted an "Independent" legislative ticket, composed of two Adams men, Thomas Urquhart and George Eustis, and four who favored Clay, Etienne Mazureau, J. J. Mercier, Felix Grima, and Charles Maurian.[124]

While all of Louisiana sweltered through the most blistering June in memory,[125] these opposing forces swept the community with gales of continuous political controversy. Upset by the vigor of the Jackson leaders and disturbed by confidence in the enemy's camp that its candidate would poll a vote large enough to win without sending the election into the national House of Representatives,[126] the Clay men increased their emphasis on what they had come to consider one of the General's greatest weaknesses, his supposed lack of support outside Louisiana and Pennsylvania. Jackson's persistence in remaining in the race, they argued, could accomplish nothing except a division of the western states, which would weaken Clay sufficiently to keep him out of the House and deliver the presidency to Adams or Crawford.[127] The "prospect of Gen. Jackson's election," Richardson warned in his *Louisiana Gazette*, "however dazzling in the eyes of his admirers . . . [is] baseless, as illusive, and as evanescent as a soap bubble." The state, he argued, should not "allow the legitimate influence of Louisiana, on a decision of a most important national question, to be thrown away, on a chimerical and quixotic project of giving a public and irrefragable testimony of its gratitude."[128]

The July elections gave the Jacksonians four of the six legislative seats assigned to New Orleans, a result which the adherents of the General greeted as a sure harbinger of success in November. But the victory came at the price of stirring up new personal animosities which promised possible discord and dispute in the future. Marigny had thrown his considerable strength behind the Jackson ticket on the second day of the election, in exchange for a commitment that Davezac, a foreign Frenchman, would be put aside, and the latter bitterly resented his consequent exclusion from

124. *Ibid.*, May 19, 20, June 8, July 1, 5, 1824; *Louisiana Courier*, June 14, 17, 1824; St. Francisville *Asylum*, June 19, 26, 1824; *Louisiana Advertiser*, May 24, 1824.

125. John Sibley to Stephen Austin, July 8, 1824, in Barker, ed., *Austin Papers*, Pt. 1, p. 849.

126. Isaac Baker to William S. Hamilton, June 15, 1824, in Hamilton Papers, LSU.

127. *Louisiana Gazette*, February 24, August 24, 1824; St. Francisville *Asylum*, April 17, 1824.

128. *Louisiana Gazette*, June 29, July 3, 1824.

the assembly. Mazureau, too, had gone down to defeat, and he in turn denounced the ingratitude of Davezac and Livingston, complaining that after he had labored to give them political power, their first use of it had been
to promote the "Jacksonian pledge" in the legislative campaign which
helped bring about his own defeat.[129] Elsewhere in the state the elections
essentially ignored the presidential preferences of the candidates,[130] but results suggested that adherents of Clay had won a solid majority in the legislature.[131]

The congressional races, run concurrently with the state canvass, managed to proceed without a single question being raised as to the presidential
preferences of the men who would be called upon to cast the state's vote if,
as many thought, the election would devolve upon the House. No one offered against incumbents Henry H. Gurley in the Second District and Edward Livingston in the First,[132] though Livingston might well have had opposition had news of his recent activities in Washington not been delayed
in reaching New Orleans. They involved repeated efforts to place Davezac
in the recently vacated federal district judgeship in Louisiana, an appointment guaranteed to horrify a good portion of the community. "It was certainly a most shocking insult to the feelings of society," Judge Porter confided to his friend Josiah Johnston. "People said the candidate wanted only
two of the qualities necessary for the station—Integrity and Knowledge."[133] But the news came only after the election, and Livingston, like
Gurley, received practically the unanimous vote of his constituency.

The only real congressional contest of the year produced a stormy fight
between William L. Brent and Henry A. Bullard, who had come forward at
the solicitation of his friends to punish the incumbent for his slanderous
campaign against Johnston two years earlier. Even though Johnston had
now moved up to the Senate, Isaac Baker vented his psychopathic hatred
of Brent by convincing Bullard that the detractor of their friend must be
turned out, and in the optimism of his passion led the politically naïve Al-

---

129. Alexander Porter to Josiah S. Johnston, July 8, 1824, in Johnston Papers, HSP.

130. John H. Johnston to Josiah S. Johnston, June 8, 1824, Walter H. Overton to Johnston, June 24, July 10, 1824, Reuben Kemper to Johnston, March 18, 1824, *ibid.*; Isaac L.
Baker to William S. Hamilton, June 15, July 10, 1824, in Hamilton Papers, LSU.

131. *Louisiana Gazette*, July 10, 1824; *Louisiana Journal*, July 22, 1824; Henry Clay to Josiah S. Johnston, August 31, 1824, in Johnston Papers, HSP.

132. St. Francisville *Asylum*, July 10, 1824.

133. Alexander Porter to Josiah S. Johnston, July 8, 1824, in Johnston Papers, HSP.

exandria lawyer to believe that the whole western district shared his determination to oust the incumbent. Brent remained in Washington during the campaign, pleading illness in his family, while Bullard toured the parishes in exhaustive exertion. The turning point came when the irrepressible Baker overplayed his hand in publishing a pamphlet so violent in its attacks upon Brent that it aroused the public to his defense. Bewildered and hurt, Bullard finally wrote Johnston that all had miscarried, leaving Brent successful once again and the world indeed awry.[134]

As the summer months slipped away, the campaign grew wearisome in its repetitions. Despite the exertions of the press, public interest in the race began to lag, but behind the scenes political managers of the various factions filled their days with elaborate consultation and planning. The Clay camp expended the greatest energy, desperately looking for some way to boost its candidate's strength in the East. Crawford seemed certain to carry Virginia and Georgia, Adams dominated New England, and Jackson held the lead in the middle-Atlantic states. Clay had to pick up at least a few votes in these areas to get to the House. Once there he was safe, conventional wisdom being that congressmen would give their Speaker an overwhelming victory. Josiah Johnston spent the last months of the campaign scouring the eastern seaboard for Clay support, finally managing to strike an agreement with the Adams men of New York. Contingent upon Clay's carrying Louisiana, Thurlow Weed pledged to divert seven of his state's electoral votes from Adams to the Kentuckian, a move which would push Clay ahead of Crawford, keep the Georgian out of the House, and humiliate the New Yorker's pro-Crawford rivals such as Martin Van Buren.[135] It remained now for the Clay men to make sure of Louisiana.

Within the state, confusion and indecision mounted on all sides. Both the Jackson and Clay camps resounded with confident predictions of certain victory, but everyone recognized such talk as sheer bluster. Even old hands like Alexander Porter and John Linton, one of New Orleans' busiest

134. *Louisiana Herald*, June 9, 16, 23, 30, 1824; Isaac Baker to Josiah S. Johnston, March 5, 1824, John H. Johnston to Johnston, June 19, July 15, 1824, Henry A. Bullard to Johnston, August 5, 1824, all in Johnston Papers, HSP.

135. See, for example, D. Mallory to Josiah S. Johnston, November 4, 10, 1824, George M. McClure to Josephus B. Stuart, November 15, 1824, Stuart to Johnston, November 26, 1824, Henry Clay to Johnston, September 10, 1824, all in Johnston Papers, HSP; Harriet A. Weed, ed., *Autobiography of Thurlow Weed* (2 vols.; Boston, 1883), I, 128–29; Glyndon Van Deusen, *The Life of Henry Clay* (Boston, 1937), 177.

and best-informed factors, admitted their inability to fathom what the legislature's choice would be.[136] When the assembly convened in mid-November the state watched in fascination as the battle for votes raged among the members, who found themselves wined and dined and solicited by tenders of political honors.[137] When the issue finally came to rest, the Clay forces had been undone.

Much the smallest of the three contending camps, the Adams faction held the balance of power between the other two groups, and they had long recognized the possibility of using this advantage to win at least a part of Louisiana's five votes.[138] Their eleven legislative members, however, could not agree among themselves as to a preference between Jackson and Clay, and as late as November 18 they had not decided which of the two to support as a second choice. Clearly that determination would rest upon what offers came to them from the Clay and Jackson men.[139] Aware of Johnston's agreement with Weed and thus of their need for all five Louisiana votes, the Clay leaders were less willing than the Jacksonians to accede to the granting of the two votes which the Adams men demanded in exchange for their backing. They tried desperately to track down and round up five absentee legislators who would give them a clear majority in the assembly vote and thus an uncompromised victory. Those reinforcements could never be found, and on November 22 six Adams men joined the twenty-four Jacksonians to outvote the Clay ticket thirty to twenty-eight, giving three electoral votes to Jackson and two to Adams.[140]

Behind the result many saw a mass of intrigue. John Clay raged against what he called this "dirty Bargain" as the secret work of Governor Henry Johnson,[141] who had long been rumored sympathetic to Adams though he

136. Alexander Porter to Josiah S. Johnston, September 15, 1824, John Linton to Johnston, November 14, 1824, in Johnston Papers, HSP.

137. *Louisiana Gazette*, November 17, 19, 1824.

138. *Louisiana Advertiser*, June 3, 1824; St. Francisville *Asylum*, November 13, 1824.

139. John H. Johnston to Josiah S. Johnston, November 13, 1824, in Johnston Papers, HSP.

140. L. S. Hazelton to Josiah S. Johnston, [November 23], 1824, Reuben Kemper to Johnston, November 27, 1824, John Clay to Johnston, November 30, 1824, Walter H. Overton to Johnston, November 22, 1824, *ibid.*; David C. Ker to Andrew Jackson, November 23, 1824, in Jackson Papers, LC; *Louisiana House Journal*, 1824, p. 8; *Louisiana Gazette*, November 23, 1824.

141. John Clay to Josiah S. Johnston, November 30, 1824, in Johnston Papers, HSP.

had given a personal pledge of support to Clay.[142] No one ever satisfactorily explained why five members of the assembly simply failed to appear on the day appointed by law for the balloting, but in one case, at least, there is much to ponder. Placide Bossier, a strong Clay partisan, had remained home in Natchitoches to accept a challenge to a horse race tendered him by a known Adams sympathizer. As John Sibley wryly summed up the outcome to his expectant son-in-law, Josiah Johnston, "Bossier lost the Race & Clay the Election."[143]

The effect of the Louisiana vote on the New York balloting remains highly problematic. Weed insisted at a later date that the failure of Clay to carry the state released his group from its pledge to divert seven votes to the Kentuckian,[144] and Clay came out of the New York contest with but four of the total promised him. It seems impossible for Weed to have known of the Louisiana result at the time of the New York ballot, however, and the Clay camp most likely had simply been hoodwinked, for Weed must have realized the folly of allowing the Speaker to move ahead of Crawford and into a House vote, which he certainly would have won against the New Yorker's candidate, Adams.[145] As it was, the loss of Louisiana's five votes, even had Weed been true to his pledge, put Clay fourth highest on the electoral tally, trailing Jackson, Adams, and Crawford, and his name could not therefore be presented to the House when it met to resolve the deadlock in this election which had produced a majority for none of the contenders. Looked at in another way, the electoral count which gave Crawford forty-one votes and Clay thirty-seven would have read Clay forty-two and Crawford forty-one had the Kentuckian's majority held fast in the Louisiana legislature. Dr. Sibley's wry comment carried more truth than perhaps even he understood—Clay *had* lost the election in Louisiana, and now the nation could await the House choice from among his rivals. In Louisiana, as elsewhere, the result would be explosive.

"In the name of God and the Love of your Country prevent his Election!" John Clay pleaded with Josiah Stoddard Johnston as the House of Repre-

---

142. Henry Clay to Josiah S. Johnston, August 30, 1824, *ibid.*; Isaac L. Baker to William S. Hamilton, June 15, 1824, in Hamilton Papers, LSU; *Louisiana Gazette*, October 11, 1824.

143. John Sibley to Josiah S. Johnston, January 2, 1825, in Johnston Papers, HSP.

144. Weed, ed., *Autobiography of Thurlow Weed*, I, 128–29.

145. Van Deusen, *Clay*, 177.

sentatives made ready to choose the next president of the United States.[146] Like many others, he found the prospect of Andrew Jackson in the White House repellent and frightening.

But in Louisiana, Jacksonians delighted in the assurance that their candidate's plurality in the electoral vote of 1824 would finally bring him the rewards he so richly deserved. Even if the state had been forced to split its vote, they felt that the result saved them from the disgrace of ingratitude to its greatest benefactor. None exulted more extravagantly than James McKaraher, a Pennsylvania Irishman who had long been a loud and contentious part of the New Orleans scene. Sometime professor at the Collège d'Orléans,[147] McKaraher purchased the *Louisiana Gazette* from R. D. Richardson late in the presidential campaign and transformed that Clay sheet into the brashest and most fanatical of the pro-Jackson journals in the state. His wisdom now vindicated, on the morning following the choice of the Louisiana electors he proclaimed to his readers: "The market has been rummaged, and the wine cellars culled, presses have been bought, and writers hired to bring upon the State of Louisiana the contempt of her sister states, yet all have failed and *Jackson is Triumphant*. From New York to the Gulf of Mexico—Justice is done to the Hero of Orleans."[148]

In practically every subsequent issue, McKaraher kept up the flood of self-congratulation and thanksgiving, hailing this "triumph of the people" over evil politicians and giving wide circulation to a common Louisiana impression that the election was over. He labeled the procedures of the coming House choice mere formalities, bound to confirm Jackson as unquestionably the choice of the majority of the citizens of the republic.[149]

Much of the force of this argument in Louisiana could be traced to the peculiarities of her own constitution, for inevitably the function of the House in the coming presidential choice would be seen as comparable to that of the state's assembly when it regularly balloted in the official election of Louisiana governors. That the legislature picked from the two highest names on a list while the House would choose from three seemed no real difference at all. And everyone knew that no legislature had ever failed to name as governor the man with the highest number of votes—why should

146. John Clay to Josiah S. Johnston, November 30, 1824, in Johnston Papers, HSP.
147. *L'Ami des Lois*, April 30, 1823; *Louisiana Advertiser*, April 20, July 18, 21, 1823.
148. *Louisiana Gazette*, November 23, 1824.
149. *Ibid.*, December 14, 1824.

not the same respect be given to the public will in this presidential contest? The sanctity of this obligation had only recently been reaffirmed, when a brief attempt to bypass Henry Johnson for Jacques Villeré in the legislative gubernatorial election a few weeks earlier failed decisively, smothered under protests against any such shameful defiance of the people's will.[150] For McKaraher no doubt existed—the House was bound in honor to follow a similar course, and Jacksonians over the state agreed. Isaac Baker spoke for them all in his observation that "according to our Louisiana notions about pluralities the old general must be president."[151] In high spirits, they could hardly wait for the Hero to come into his own.

But wait they must, and once again attention turned to more localized political manipulations. Henry Johnson's resignation from the Senate to become governor required the selection of his successor in the opening days of the legislative session in November, and for the first time the full effect of Marigny's strategy during the July election could be measured. His efforts encouraged the creoles to demand a great share of national offices, and their full strength now gathered behind Dominique Bouligny for the Senate post. Livingston's disappointment at being passed over by his French friends found solace in their pledge that if he did not oppose Bouligny they would assure him of their complete backing against Josiah Johnston when he stood for reelection. Bouligny won the seat, and Johnston found himself on notice that he faced a major challenge to his own in January of 1825.[152]

With so much attention centered on the coming showdown for the presidency, it is surprising to find that in neither of these senatorial elections did questions of national factional loyalties play any part. Once again the ethnic issue pushed all other considerations aside: Livingston and the Clay enthusiast Bouligny had no difficulty in cementing their alliance, the eminent lawyer remaining thoroughly acceptable to the Gallic population because of past services and his ties to them by marriage. At the same time, avowals came to Johnston of support from Jacksonian and anti-Jacksonian

150. John H. Johnston to Josiah S. Johnston, November 18, 1824, Henry Johnson to Johnston, November 25, 1824, in Johnston Papers, HSP.

151. Isaac L. Baker to Josiah S. Johnston, December 21, 1824, *ibid.*

152. St. Francisville *Asylum*, July 24, 1824; Alexander Porter to Josiah S. Johnston, September 15, 1824, L. S. Hazelton to Johnston, November 21, 1824, David C. Ker to Johnston, December 3, 1824, in Johnston Papers, HSP.

Americans alike. He needed every bit of aid he could get, so skillfully did the Livingston forces manage their campaign. Marigny scampered to their side when told that a Johnston victory would make the senator a powerful favorite to succeed Henry Johnson as governor; old General Thomas willingly acceded to suggestions that he contest the seat, opening dangerous inroads into Johnston's American backing; and Florida legislators began to receive a flood of reports that the incumbent had been the major voice at Washington defending the hated Orleans Navigation Company, which monopolized commerce through the Canal Carondelet and forced the lake trade between New Orleans and the north-shore parishes to pay what many considered exorbitant fees and tolls.[153] Brent and Gurley, longtime personal enemies of Johnston, did what they could from Washington to oust Clay's great friend in favor of Livingston, Brent filling Ouachita and the Red River parishes with renewed tales of how the incumbent championed large land claims and defended the hated tariff, while Gurley added supposed confirmation of the senator's subservience to the Orleans Navigation Company.[154]

It required all the energies of Johnston's friends to save him from defeat. Livingston felt so certain of victory that Davezac was already in the field to succeed him in the national House.[155] But the phalanx behind Johnston proved too deep and strong. The French support which Livingston so much relied upon could not withstand the counterpressures exerted by Duralde and Henry Clay, and Philemon Thomas shifted his own votes to Johnston after the first ballot in the state senate. Meanwhile, Governor Johnson, W. H. Overton, and Isaac L. Baker, as well as others, vigorously denied all rumors unfavorable to Johnston, even when they had no knowledge of the facts, giving Martin Gordon, president of the Orleans Navi-

153. Reuben Kemper to Josiah S. Johnston, November 27, 1824, Alexander Porter to Johnston, December 10, 31, 1824, January 10, 20, 1825, Nathaniel Cox to Johnston, December 10, 1824, L. S. Hazelton to Johnston, January 10, 1825, Walter H. Overton to Johnston, January 4, 1825, in Johnston Papers, HSP.

154. Walter H. Overton to Josiah S. Johnston, October 29, 1824, January 4, 1825, Reuben Kemper to Johnston, November 27, 1824, Alexander Porter to Johnston, December 31, 1824, John H. Johnston to Johnston, December 21, 1824, John Moore to Johnston, January 10, 1825, ibid.

155. David C. Ker to Josiah S. Johnston, December 3, 1824, James Sterrett to Johnston, February 1, 1825, ibid.

gation Company and an ardent Jacksonian, time to amass in secret the backing of stockholders grateful to the Clay incumbent. The fact that Livingston's election would give New Orleans three of the state's five members of Congress also weighed heavily on Johnston's side. He won reelection by a thirty-two-to-twenty-seven vote,[156] causing that staunch Jacksonian, W. H. Overton, to exult, "Mr. Livingston will never be a Senator in Congress."[157] As in the gubernatorial campaign of the preceding July, tempers had run high in both senatorial elections, but certainly not because of rivalry between Clay and Jackson men. Once again ethnic loyalties and sheer personal antagonisms had determined the outcomes. It would be the last time they enjoyed such complete supremacy.

As the House election of a president in February drew closer, excitement in Louisiana mounted beyond anything felt in the days of the regular campaign. Crowds milled in post offices every mail day for news, and the uncertainty began to irritate even the most phlegmatic.[158] The Jacksonians strove to keep up their confidence with constant assurances of final success and celebrated the January 8 victory anniversary in New Orleans as a prelude to the promised festivities of the General's inauguration.[159] But through the press and in the circles of private conversation, clear hints and speculations began to suggest that all was not right in Washington. Rumor had it that Brent and Gurley would never cast their votes for Jackson, that Clay had been bought by the Adams party, and that corrupt alliances meant to divert the House from its duty.[160] McKaraher denounced such stories as sheer fantasy, promising that if any Louisiana congressman, "knowing as he does that nine-tenths of his constituents are in favor of

156. *Louisiana House Journal,* 1824, p. 67; Henry Clay to Josiah S. Johnston, October 2, 1824, John Moore to Johnston, January 10, 1825, Walter H. Overton to Johnston, January 11, 1825, Nathaniel Cox to Johnston, December 10, 1824, Isaac L. Baker to Johnston, January 10, 1825, Alexander Porter to Johnston, January 20, 1825, Martin Gordon to Johnston, November 28, 1824, February 1, 1825, in Johnston Papers, HSP.

157. Walter H. Overton to Josiah S. Johnston, January 11, 1825, in Johnston Papers, HSP.

158. Henry A. Bullard to Josiah S. Johnston, December 21, 1824, James M. Bradford to Johnston, December 21, 1824, *ibid.*

159. *Louisiana Gazette,* January 11, 1825.

160. James M. Bradford to Josiah S. Johnston, January 15, 1825, in Johnston Papers, HSP; *Louisiana Gazette,* January 5, 1825.

Gen. Jackson," should nonetheless "vote against the General, he will receive, as he will merit, the contempt and detestation of those whose interest he may betray."[161]

The long winter weeks stretched out, with extensive time for gossip and conjecture on all these moot points. Rain poured down in endless torrents from November to March, and roads almost merged with the swampland. There was little to do but sit and talk and wonder.[162] By mid-February the frosts had gone for good, and though the rains still pelted the countryside, men could look forward impatiently to spring. Those interested in public affairs, however, found little time to contemplate the vagaries of nature, for on February 28 the news from Washington finally arrived—Adams was to be president, and with the vote of Louisiana registered in his favor.

That morning McKaraher draped the *Louisiana Gazette* in black. Skulls and crossbones headed the dreary announcement and studded the paper's columns. "It may be as well for us," the story ran, "to record our own disgrace. To be the Heralds of our own infamy. Louisiana has, in the persons of her representatives, bound herself by a sacred compact to honor and obey his Excellency, J. Q. Adams. The deed is past and recorded, it must be, strictly, complied with." This submissive note recognizing the legality of the election behind him, McKaraher then burst with rage. He pronounced mighty curses on Clay and reviled Brent and Gurley, who had cast their votes for Adams while Edward Livingston proved loyal to Jackson. They were, said McKaraher, guilty of "shameful treachery, unparalleled in history. . . . they gave the whole vote of the state to one, who like a codfish, could not live one season in our waters. One whose secluded habits render him as ignorant of the feelings and habits of the western country, as though he had been all his life studying the Chinese alphabet in the centre of Pekin. . . . Treachery! Treachery! Treachery!" As for the two ingrates, the shameless subverters of the people's will, "Their funeral will take place as soon as a proper stage can be erected for their *elevation*."[163]

McKaraher's indignation mirrored a Jacksonian fury which swept across the nation. From Philadelphia the General received a passionate letter which very likely reflected his own brooding thoughts: "Louisianians! Degraded—Ungrateful Men!! To vote against you! Who under God, they are

161. *Louisiana Gazette*, February 8, 1825.
162. *Louisiana Journal*, March 24, 1825.
163. *Louisiana Gazette*, February 28, 1825.

indebted for the possession of their soil!—The Protector of the chastity of their wives and daughters!! You! Who saved them from the brutal lust of a mercenary soldiery! . . . The heart sickens at the thought." Isaac Baker hastened to assure Jackson that Brent and Gurley had damned themselves forever: "I scarcely think Brent will ever return to Louisiana," Baker wrote, and he went on to predict that the people would rise up to crush "Clay & Co." in 1828. Jackson unquestionably agreed. Andrew J. Donelson urged Louisiana followers of the General to launch immediate attacks upon Brent and Gurley, and Baker reported with great gusto the appearance in New Orleans of a doggerel poem entitled "A Defence of Col. William Lovetruth Bluster," obviously aimed at Brent.[164]

In some other quarters news of the Adams election brought joy and unanticipated elation. The *Argus*, the *Mercantile Advertiser*, and the *Asylum* congratulated the people on their escape from the clutches of the violent soldier into the custody of the statesman, and ridiculed the emotionalism of McKaraher.[165] Like the Natchitoches *Courier*, they insisted that Adams had been the second choice of Clay's backers in the state and that Brent and Gurley had thus truly reflected the popular will of Louisiana.[166] Such refusal to recognize the state's betrayal added to the Jacksonians' already towering anger, and they found in Clay's soon-announced appointment as secretary of state proof of Congressman George Kremer's charge that the Kentuckian had indeed sold himself to Adams.[167] McKaraher and St. Romes of the *Courier* threatened physical violence against C. W. Duhy, editor of the *Mercantile Advertiser*, for his defense of Clay and Adams, only adding to the troubles of Duhy, who had already been challenged to a duel by a furious Jackson sympathizer.[168]

Nothing incensed Louisiana followers of Jackson more than the torrent of blame and ridicule which now poured down upon the state from all quarters of the nation, and though it must have made McKaraher writhe, he printed it all for the enlightenment of his readers. In Philadelphia a

164. John Pemberton to Andrew Jackson, February 15, 1825, Isaac L. Baker to Jackson, March 21, 1825, in Jackson Papers, LC.

165. *Louisiana Gazette*, March 5, 17, 30, 1825; New Orleans *Mercantile Advertiser*, March 17, 1825; New Orleans *Argus*, March 8, 10, 1825.

166. Natchitoches *Courier*, April 4, 1825.

167. *Louisiana Gazette*, February 28, March 11, 18, 25, 26, 1825.

168. *Louisiana Courier*, April 5, 1825.

birthday banquet for the General toasted him with a typical sentiment: "Louisiana—Saved from British pollution by the valor of Jackson, to be a Harlot, in the hands of a Western Gambler. Her black ingratitude will call down the vengeance of Heaven!"[169] No wonder that friends reported Brent fearful that he might be killed should be ever return to the state.[170]

Despite their protestations of innocence, the votes of Brent and Gurley clearly ran counter to their previous commitments. Brent, especially, had pledged in May of 1824 to "vote the sentiments of those I represent" should the election go to the House,[171] and Gurley maintained immediately after the fateful ballot that he had wavered until the last moment and voted for Adams only when it appeared that it was impossible for Jackson to win.[172] It is clear, however, that as early as September 1824, both Brent and Gurley had already decided to abandon Jackson in the House, no matter what the electoral vote in Louisiana turned out to be.[173] Unable to prove this, Louisiana Jacksonians nonetheless remained convinced of Clay's perfidy and found it therefore easy to believe the worst of their representatives, especially since Brent figured prominently as a defender of the Kentuckian in all aspects of the controversy.[174]

In such fashion did the Jacksonians see all their dark forebodings of the previous months crystallize into reality. The professional politicians had been victorious over the people; dishonesty, bargain, and corruption had robbed the sovereign citizens of their republican birthright and plunged the nation back into the grip of the hated principles which had prevailed before Jefferson killed the evils of Federalism. Now again the aristocrats held sway—not the aristocrats of wealth, perhaps, but the aristocrats of irresponsible power. Jackson's close friend John Eaton vented his anger in the observation that "Corruption stalks thro our land—our politicians like

169. *Louisiana Gazette*, April 19, 1825.

170. *Ibid.*, March 30, 1825.

171. New Orleans *Mercantile Advertiser*, May 4, 1824. See also the claim of R. K. Call that Brent had replied to a query as to his choice in the House election with "Vox populi, vox Dei," thus giving Call the impression that Louisiana was safe for Jackson, in James, *Andrew Jackson*, 416.

172. *Louisiana Gazette*, March 11, 1825; Nathan Sargent, *Public Men and Events* (2 vols.; Philadelphia, 1875), I, 75.

173. William L. Brent to Henry Clay, September 3, 1824, in Henry Clay Papers, LC.

174. *Louisiana Journal*, May 5, 1825; *Louisiana Gazette*, April 7, 1825; New Orleans *Argus*, March 26, 1825.

the monks of old, claim to have everything of govt. science in their hands, & of right, apart from the people, an authority to rule." Those sentiments found echo in McKaraher's judgment:

> From this time forward; at least so long as the *"Era of correct principles"* shall prevail; let the shoemaker seal up his mouth with his own wax; the hatter not presume to intrude his smutty face into public concerns; the carpenter confine his sinewy arms to their proper sphere, the work bench; and let the blacksmith beware that his bellows does not blow opinions that are seditious, for the *"era of correct principles has commenced."* Let the people cease to think, and the printer to propagate their opinions—for who will respect them when their own representatives treat them with contempt.[175]

The Jacksonian cause had been born.

175. John Eaton to John Overton, April 3, 1825, in John Overton Papers, THS; *Louisiana Gazette*, March 8, 1825.

· VIII ·

THE SPIRIT OF '98

For a nation now held in the grip of evil and designing men—as the Jacksonians would have it—the United States in the early days of the Adams regime gave every evidence of remarkable well-being and optimism, certainly if Louisiana could be taken as any gauge. With the stringencies of the early part of the decade behind them, the spring and summer of 1825 appeared to some New Orleanians as the "heyday of their prosperity,"[1] and they looked with contented fulfillment at the proliferating speculations which pushed the selling price of their cotton and sugar to more and more rewarding heights.[2] Confident prophets predicted boom times in England which would keep the demand for southern staples firm, lending credence to other forecasts that American trade would soon be welcomed in the British West Indies, a certain stimulus to the commerce of Louisiana's great port.[3]

Even the violence of the Jacksonian protests against bargain and corruption gradually subsided. From the choleric James McKaraher there still came sputterings of the old fury—a nomination of Andrew Jackson for the presidency in 1828, in "opposition to the Usurper, *John Quincy Adams*,"[4] and claims of being threatened with reprisals if he did not cease his attacks

1. *Louisiana Gazette*, June 10, 1825.
2. New Orleans *Argus*, as quoted in the Natchitoches *Courier*, May 10, 1825.
3. New Orleans *Mercantile Advertiser*, May 18, 1825.
4. *Louisiana Gazette*, April 19, 1825.

upon the administration[5]—but these too evaporated in May, when McKaraher put the *Louisiana Gazette* up for sale. Its former owner, R. D. Richardson, who claimed McKaraher had never paid him a cent for the paper, rushed back to New Orleans, repurchased the paper, and promptly converted it into a vocal Adams-Clay mouthpiece.[6] The fusion of the St. Francisville *Asylum* and the *Louisiana Journal* in August under Fielding Bradford produced a new *Journal* independent in politics,[7] leaving Louisiana Jacksonianism practically without a voice. New Orleans' *Louisiana Advertiser* and *Courier* remained friendly to the General, but in a listless way which could only be called soporific compared to the erstwhile fulminations of McKaraher.

The Adams papers greeted the new administration with confidence and thanksgiving for the nation's deliverance from an unskilled and sadistic military chieftain.[8] William Brent wrote a glowing account of the "firm and undeviating republicans" making up the Adams cabinet, with assurances that the new regime would foster and maintain Jeffersonian principles.[9] The French community found particular satisfaction in the successful efforts of Martin Duralde and Brent to have the young creole Manuel Cruzat appointed as naval officer for New Orleans. At long last federal patronage had opened to a native Louisianian, proof of Henry Clay's commitment to his past promises.[10] Such signs of felicity and tranquility, such evident willingness throughout the state to accept the outcome of the House election when they had hoped to find rebelliousness and turmoil, unnerved the Jacksonians, at least for the moment. The behavior of Edward Livingston gave persuasive testimony to the fact. In late May when he and Senator Bouligny appeared at a dinner in their honor at the New Orleans city hall, his few words of regret at Jackson's defeat went almost unnoticed in the

5. *Ibid.*, April 20, 1825.

6. R. D. Richardson to Henry Clay, May 28, 1825 (Richardson file), Letters of Application and Recommendation During the Administration of John Quincy Adams, 1825–1829, in RG 59, GRDS, NA; *Louisiana Gazette*, May 19, 1825.

7. *Louisiana Journal*, August 27, 1825.

8. New Orleans *Mercantile Advertiser*, March 24, April 2, 1825; Natchitoches *Courier*, April 4, 1825; St. Francisville *Asylum*, May 28, 1825; *Washita Gazette*, May 21, 1825.

9. *Louisiana Courier*, March 25, 1825.

10. Martin Duralde to Josiah S. Johnston, May 24, 1825, Henry Johnson to Johnston, December 10, 1825, in Johnston Papers, HSP.

lengthy praise which he showered on the talents and integrity of President Adams. Following an observation that honest men might differ in opinions, he closed on a note which must have rankled many of his fellow Jacksonians—a hope that he had not offended the friends of Clay and Adams by his vote for the General in February.[11] Clearly, with Jackson's ship possibly going down for good, Livingston was making ready to jump safely to shore.

By midsummer the tensions of the 1824 campaign gave way to the excitement surrounding the rebellion of Bartholomew Grima and the Legion against General Robeson, flooding the state once again with charges centered on the foreign faction and monopolizing Americans. The year which had held such bright hopes in April and May waned fitfully to a close, beset by these internal convulsions and a demoralizing collapse of its prosperity. Dropping prices in the Liverpool market spread failure through the mercantile community in New Orleans, turning the promising season into the worst the state had experienced in fifty years. "I never witnessed such times in Louisiana," Alexander Porter sighed, while the planters throughout the countryside revived their old complaints against equally distraught financial houses in the capital.[12] The advent of a new year failed to bring its wonted surge of high spirits, the miseries of economic depression now compounded by the added grisly terror of smallpox in New Orleans.[13]

The politicians at least had the diversion of scrambling wildly for the new federal circuit judgeship which Congress seemed to be on the verge of creating for the area, gathering up all the tools of influence and persuasion available to them. Sick and irascible—"in the clutch of death," Porter said—ex-Governor Thomas B. Robertson, now a United States district judge, spent the days pouring out his wrath upon those who would expose him to the shame of losing the appointment, for he felt that he would be disgraced and discredited by being passed over.[14] Although favorably dis-

11. *Louisiana Courier*, May 24, 26, 1825.

12. *Louisiana Gazette*, December 3, 1825; New Orleans *Mercantile Advertiser*, January 7, 1826; Henry Johnson to Josiah S. Johnston, January 17, 1826, Nathaniel Cox to Johnston, December 1, 1825, Alexander Porter to Johnston, December 23, 1825, in Johnston Papers, HSP.

13. Walter H. Overton to Josiah S. Johnston, January 3, 1826, in Johnston Papers, HSP.

14. Thomas B. Robertson to Henry Clay, April 22, 1826, in Henry Clay Papers, LC; Alexander Porter to Josiah S. Johnston, February 27, 1826, in Johnston Papers, HSP.

posed to his pretensions, William Brent and Henry Gurley cautiously avoided any open sponsorship in this campaign year of 1826, but Edward Livingston pushed Davezac to frenzied activity on Robertson's behalf. Aware of the congressman's notorious disdain for the former governor, some saw this vigorous sponsorship as but another of Livingston's patronage grabs, a transparent effort to clear the way for Henry Carleton to fill the place vacated by a Robertson promotion.[15] Alexander Porter, himself a candidate for the job, warned Senator Johnston of these activities, with the admonition that it would not do to "put Mr. Liv.'s brother-in-law on the Bench here, and I could state ten good reasons for it, if you did not already know them all."[16] Congress finally ended months of increasingly bitter infighting for the appointment by deciding not to create the circuit court after all.

For those who looked to them as a means of visiting punishment on Brent and Gurley for their part in putting John Quincy Adams in the White House two years earlier, the congressional elections of 1826 brought only gloom and disappointment. They demonstrated almost nothing except the intricacies of the state's political life. Certainly the furor raised against the two berated traitors in 1825 implied a determined effort to turn them out of office at the first opportunity, but by the summer of 1826 the Jackson forces in the state seemed to have fallen completely apart. In the western district, despite the vocal eruptions of Isaac L. Baker, they could find no one to bring into the contest against Brent. W. H. Overton, their first choice, lay racked by a new siege of arthritis and crippled almost as effectively by financial worries.[17] Only another pro-Adams man, John Brownson, held out any promise of defeating Brent, leaving the Third District Jacksonians little other choice than to throw their uninspired forces behind his candidacy.[18] Because Brent's fate could not be a matter of indifference to the Adams and Clay leaders, Duralde threw his great personal

15. Alexander Porter to Josiah S. Johnston, February 18, 27, April 28, May 15, 1826, S. H. Harper to Johnston, April 8, 1826, Eleazar Ripley to Johnston, April 10, 1826, in Johnston Papers, HSP.

16. Alexander Porter to Josiah S. Johnston, February 18, 1826, *ibid.*

17. Walter H. Overton to Josiah S. Johnston, January 3, 1826, *ibid.*; *Louisiana Gazette*, September 6, 1826.

18. Isaac L. Baker to Josiah S. Johnston, May 6, October 5, 1826, December 15, 1827, in Johnston Papers, HSP.

influence into the balance, swung a heavy French vote behind the incumbent, and assured his reelection.[19] In short, voters of the western district had no real opportunity to register a clear pro-Jackson protest against the offending Brent.[20]

Gurley faced a more difficult task, for W. S. Hamilton had taken to the field with a full-scaled assault on Gurley's ballot for Adams in 1825, his supposed sympathy for abolitionism, and his record of support for such administration policies as internal improvements and American participation in the Panama Congress, seen by many as an antislavery meeting.[21] In the Floridas this kind of argument had a powerful appeal. No other part of the state gave greater allegiance to abstract concepts of states' rights and strict construction of the constitution, principles which Hamilton espoused with ease and conviction but which fellow southerners in his district thought Yankees like Gurley and Adams incapable of defending. An old foe, the powerful Orleans Navigation Company, tool of the New Orleans Jacksonian Martin Gordon, also opposed Gurley vigorously. All in all, he had good cause to be fearful of the final outcome of the campaign.[22]

But again the wily Duralde was at hand. Gurley's Second District included not only the Floridas but also the northern coast parishes of Iberville, West Baton Rouge, and Pointe Coupee. Here Hamilton depended on his fellow Jacksonian, Sebastian Hiriart, to prevent a massed French support of Gurley which might overcome his own expected lead in the Florida parishes. Duralde turned for help to Valerien Allain, a power among the French along the Upper Coast, and together, with the help of George Eustis, Allain's son-in-law, they convinced Hiriart that any aid to Hamilton would result in his own defeat in the race for the state senate. That prospect so frightened Hiriart, who had his heart set on eventually going to Congress himself, that he abandoned Hamilton to his fate. To make all this irresistible, Duralde and Allain promised as well that through Gurley the native Louisianians could expect to receive whatever offices they wished

19. *Louisiana Gazette*, November 7, 1826; Isaac L. Baker to Josiah S. Johnston, January 16, 1826, in Johnston Papers, HSP.

20. Alexander Porter to Josiah S. Johnston, August 31, 1826, in Johnston Papers, HSP.

21. *Louisiana Gazette*, May 30, June 24, 1826; *Louisiana Journal*, June 22, 1826; Baton Rouge *Gazette*, June 10, 24, 1826.

22. Henry H. Gurley to Henry Clay, August 20, 1826, in Henry Clay Papers, LC.

from the federal government. Clay, they said, would unquestionably succeed Adams in the White House, and who was not aware that the secretary
had recently followed up the appointment of Cruzat with the conferring of
the New Orleans postmastership upon yet another creole, Antoine Dupuy?[23] Against such intrigue from New Orleans the Jackson leaders offered
no resistance, and Davezac, Gordon, Marigny, Lacoste, and Grymes, who
might have offset this combination of Duralde and Allain, remained silent
and inert.[24] Hamilton carried all of Florida except Gurley's own East Baton
Rouge, but the incumbent swept the three coast parishes with such a majority that he squeezed into victory by a slim 135 votes.[25] In puzzled frustra-
tion, one despondent Jacksonian wailed, "Where are our leaders? What
plan, what organization have we?"[26] Certainly none had been apparent in
the campaign of 1826.

Only in New Orleans did the Jacksonians escape humiliating defeat, but
even there rejoicing languished, Livingston having apparently abandoned
the cause to assure his own reelection. Rumors circulated through New Orleans in May of 1826 that Duralde had received word from Clay that Livingston must be turned out,[27] and administration forces had drafted a
young creole, Peter E. Foucher, to contend against the incumbent. Once
again Duralde's political skills became apparent, this time through the
careful exploitation of the many obvious weaknesses in Livingston's position. The old stories of his New York defalcations cropped up again in the
press; reports represented him as a man so dishonored that he could carry
no influence in Congress; and repeated references to his many speculative
enterprises, such as the batture and Ouachita land schemes, detailed what
his critics called a pattern of public spoliation.[28] By this time, moreover,
complaints from judges and lawyers all over the state had begun to assail

23. Thomas F. Hunt to William S. Hamilton, July 30, 1826, September 24, 1826, Alexander White to Hamilton, July 22, September 24, 1826, John J. Burk to Hamilton, July 6,
1826, in Hamilton Papers, LSU.

24. P. K. Wagner to William S. Hamilton, July 30, 1826, *ibid.*

25. *Louisiana Gazette*, November 7, 1826.

26. P. K. Wagner to William S. Hamilton, July 30, 1826, in Hamilton Papers, LSU.

27. *Louisiana Journal*, September 21, 1826; New Orleans *Argus*, January 18, 1827.

28. *Louisiana Advertiser*, June 10, 1826; New Orleans *Argus*, June 20, 1826; *Louisiana Gazette*, June 30, July 3, 1826.

defects in the various Livingston legal codes,[29] a professional rebuke topped by the almost unanimous vote of the New Orleans bar condemning the introduction of Louisiana practice into the federal courts of the area, the means by which Livingston had assured selection of federal juries completely by lot.[30] That measure had resulted in a practical collapse of the enforcement of the revenue and slave trade laws in Louisiana and raised questions as to whether Livingston had not deliberately shaped the jury process to advantage himself in the many suits he brought before these very courts.[31]

Livingston knew full well the dangers he faced with Clay and Duralde in positions of such power under the Adams regime, a recognition which led him to the adoption of the cooperative policy towards the new administration revealed in his strange speech at the banquet in May of 1825. Upon his return to Washington later that year, he pointedly visited Adams to assure the president of his respect and to congratulate him upon his opening message to Congress, with which he agreed, he said, "in every part."[32] In the months which followed he gave warm encouragement to administration measures such as internal improvements and the Panama mission.[33] In claiming the character of a nonobstructionist Jacksonian he ran little danger of arousing any wide popular disfavor at home, for these policies seemed to elicit genuine support in most sections of Louisiana, if not in the Florida parishes.[34]

This conciliatory deportment greatly strengthened Livingston's position in his district, the Jackson organization in the state being nowhere firm enough to oppose it actively. Foucher had no real strength in his own right,

29. *Louisiana Advertiser*, January 3, 6, February 7, 10, 1826; Alexander Porter to Josiah S. Johnston, January 22, February 6, 1826, John H. Johnston to Johnston, February 13, 1826, Charles T. Scott to Johnston, January 27, 1826, in Johnston Papers, HSP.

30. Samuel Livermore to Josiah S. Johnston, January 5, 1825, in Johnston Papers, HSP.

31. *Louisiana Advertiser*, January 20, 1826; Samuel Livermore to Josiah S. Johnston, January 2, 1825, in Johnston Papers, HSP; George Eustis to Josiah S. Johnston, January 17, 1826 (Alexander Porter file), Letters of Application and Recommendation During the Administration of John Quincy Adams, 1825–1829, in RG 59, GRDS, NA.

32. Charles F. Adams, ed., *Memoirs of John Quincy Adams* (12 vols.; Philadelphia, 1874–77), VII, 77.

33. *Debates in Congress*, 19th Cong., 1st Sess., 151, 258, 1226–32, 2514.

34. John H. Johnston to Josiah S. Johnston, February 13, 1826, Isaac L. Baker to Johnston, April 9, 1826, Alexander Porter to Johnston, April 21, 1826, in Johnston Papers, HSP.

depending largely on family ties and the limited promise of some eventual political skills. Livingston held the singular advantage that a good portion of the community, especially among its lawyers and commercial leaders, wished above all else to keep him as far away from New Orleans as possible.[35] For this purpose, Washington sufficed. As another prop to his continuance in office, Livingston struck up an alliance with old Henry Schuyler Thibodaux, pledging to support the Lafourche patriarch in a run for the governorship in 1828.[36]

Even Duralde found it impossible to stimulate much interest in the 1826 campaign.[37] Reflective of this general lassitude, friends of the administration failed to see why they should exert themselves to turn Livingston out. He had caused them no trouble—why not let him alone, especially since few could find much enthusiasm for Foucher. The strongest newspaper endorsement of Livingston actually came from the staunchly pro-Adams *Argus*, which backed him as a capable man who stood neutral between Adams and Jackson, while the *Louisiana Gazette*, once again a Jackson sheet under James M. Bradford, gave steady if none too vigorous assistance. The *Louisiana Courier*, long a friend to Livingston and generally sympathetic to Jackson but unswervingly Gallic in its attachments, abandoned them both in its support of the creole, while the views of those Americans of the community who had always set themselves against Livingston found an outlet in the *Louisiana Advertiser*. With such support even among Adams partisans, and little unity among his enemies, Livingston piled up an overwhelming majority of some nine hundred votes.[38] Throughout Louisiana, and indeed in many other parts of the country, critics charged that he had succeeded only by deserting Jackson for the Adams camp.[39] Though obviously not true, such rumors told much of the sad estate of Louisiana Jacksonianism at this halfway mark in the Adams ascendancy.

Thus the long-awaited test of strength which the Jacksonians in 1825 had proclaimed would send Brent and Gurley to a deserved oblivion passed with little excitement and no avenging angels. Duralde had saved the two

---

35. Alexander Porter to Josiah S. Johnston, May 26, August 31, 1826, *ibid.*

36. Alexander Porter to Josiah S. Johnston, July 2, 1826, *ibid.*

37. *Louisiana Gazette*, June 17, July 1, 1826.

38. *Ibid.*, November 7, 1826.

39. *Ibid.*, September 15, 1826. For similar opinions closer to home, see the *La Fourche Gazette*, July 22, 1826.

Adams incumbents, if they had actually needed saving, and Livingston had scarcely been challenged. For weeks on end the newspaper editors could rake over the results to prove their indication of some profound attachment to the Adams or Jackson presidential cause, but the wiser heads in the state realized that the 1826 campaign had been hardly anything more than a compound of Duralde's skill and public indifference.[40] Local politics still provided no accurate index to sentiments on national issues. The real test of strength was yet to come.

Blame for the failures of the 1826 Jacksonian campaign in Louisiana only two years after the vigorous and impressive showing of 1824 did not really lie at the door of state leaders alone. Indeed, except for charging Adams with holding office by bargain and corruption, national leadership of the nascent Jackson party found little to complain about in the first months of Adams's administration. The General himself proved a model of responsibility after his loss, expressing no animosity toward his successful rival and urging his followers to acknowledge unreservedly Adams's constitutional right to the presidency. The business of the 1825–1826 session of Congress produced no major issues around which Jacksonians could rally any effective opposition, and the consequent political lull proved especially profound in Louisiana. Most parts of the state expended little time on theories of constitutional interpretation, a problem whose existence remained totally unsuspected by the great majority of French-speaking citizens along the coast and in the interior of the Lafourche and plains areas. Even in New Orleans, despite its great commercial and financial ambitions, the doctrine of limited powers in the federal government aroused little but academic interest. The dependence of the sugar planter upon the protective tariff left him suspicious of attacks on the legality of the system, and the tremendous need felt by the whole state for development of its communication and transportation facilities made opposition to internal improvements based on abstract questioning of the powers of the national government seem ludicrous to most Louisianians. Participation of the United States in the Panama Congress enlisted wide approval throughout the state, which felt such activity to be a natural expression of the nation's predominant posi-

40. *Louisiana Journal*, September 21, 1826; New Orleans *Argus*, September 6, 8, 19, 1826; *Louisiana Gazette*, July 17, 18, September 6, 15, 1826.

tion in western hemisphere affairs. Early attempts to find some basis for Jacksonian organization by challenging Adams and Clay in their support of such policies accordingly found no encouragement in Louisiana, where the friends of the General remained inert and acquiescent.[41]

Only the Florida parishes produced a clearly defined opposition to the administration based on political theory, for there among the large cotton plantations of the Felicianas the old traditions of southern Jeffersonianism had been deeply rooted by the many migrants from the states of the older South. William S. Hamilton took the lead in propagating these ideas, which he conceived to be the established principles of the great Revolution of 1800, a southern victory requiring constant protection from the insidious attacks of the Yankee Federalists, among whom, in his judgment, stood John Quincy Adams, no matter how much he might forswear the principles of his father. To Hamilton, the things which he understood Adams to favor—protective tariffs, internal improvements, strong executive power—unquestionably violated the Constitution, to which he gave a strictly literal reading.[42] Many others in the Floridas shared Hamilton's concept of the Union, a view defended vigorously as well in the pages of the *Louisiana Journal* (St. Francisville), professedly neutral in politics but openly distrustful of Adams and his principles. A constant stream of doctrinaire opposition poured out in the Floridas around the Panama mission, internal improvements, and the proposed national university and naval academy. "To our minds the constitution is clear," said the *Journal*, "and we are tired of seeing the assumption of powers which has been attempted by every branch of the government."[43] For Hamilton and most of those who concurred in his opinions, only Jackson, the firm exemplar of the principles of 1800, could save the nation from this threatening danger of centralization. To arrive at this decision required only an act of faith. But outside of the Floridas these issues went largely unnoticed. They had certainly stimulated no appreciable Jacksonian effort in the congressional campaign.

41. Alexander Porter to Josiah S. Johnston, December 23, 1825, April 21, November 27, 1826, Isaac L. Baker to Johnston, April 9, 1826, John H. Johnston to Johnston, February 13, 1826, L. S. Hazelton to Johnston, May 24, 1826, in Johnston Papers, HSP; New Orleans *Mercantile Advertiser*, March 9, 1825; *Louisiana Gazette*, November 5, 1825, June 7, 1826.

42. See Hamilton's address to the voters of West Feliciana during the 1826 campaign, in the *Louisiana Journal*, May 25, 1826.

43. *Ibid.*, May 19, 26, 1825, January 14, June 8, 1826.

What doctrinal dispute had been powerless to accomplish over the months an anonymous letter to the *Louisiana Courier* achieved in a single stroke, demonstrating pointedly that for the great majority of Jacksonians the only real issue in the coming campaign was Jackson himself. On August 30, 1826, the *Courier* ran a message from "D. A." reasserting the claims of the Tennessean to the presidency, reviling Adams as a usurper and northern bigot, exonerating the General from all blame in the controversial episodes of his past, and reviling all who opposed his political advancement in 1828.[44] Adams men rushed to the counterattack with violent pronouncements of their own, one of which said of Jackson: "I believe nature designed him for an oppressor. There is in his character, all the elements of tyrany; violence, audacity, inflexibility, impatience under contradiction, a superb and domineering port, an absolute tone. . . . He is organized for overthrowing and domineering."[45]

Nothing here smacked of rarified abstraction or speculative political theorizing. Instead, the reader could immerse himself in the excitement of personal insult, relish the flash of temper and individual vilification, all real and familiar experiences to the frontier temperament of Louisiana in the 1820s. Thus the 1828 campaign opened with a passion missing from the state since the same battle had been fought early in 1825. It would not close until the Jacksonian cause had come into its own.

The lethargy of the past few months now transformed into vigorous activity as both sides turned to the task of building up the propaganda outlets so vital to political success. Administration defenders began in much the better position, for they controlled the influential *Mercantile Advertiser* and *Argus* in New Orleans and the great majority of the country presses.[46] The Jacksonians had real cause for concern. Their sole dependable New Orleans paper, Bradford's *Louisiana Gazette*, carried such a burden of debt after its hectic career under McKaraher and Richardson that it finally collapsed

44. "D. A." sounds suspiciously like Auguste Davezac, though there is no proof of his authorship. Aside from the obvious hint of the anagram of his initials, this conclusion is supported by the strong similarity of style to be found in the letter and examples of Davezac's known writings. It was common knowledge, moreover, that he frequently composed political articles of this type, especially for the *Courier*.

45. New Orleans *Argus*, September 8, 1826.

46. *Louisiana Gazette*, July 17, 1826; P. K. Wagner to William S. Hamilton, July 30, 1826, in Hamilton Papers, LSU.

in December, while the *Louisiana Courier* under J. C. de St. Romes and the *Louisiana Advertiser* under James Beardslee held back from any formal enlistment in the cause of the General. St. Romes, a roly-poly foreign Frenchman who had fought under Jackson at Chalmette and remained devoted to his old commander, feared the loss of his job as public printer for the United States should he oppose the administration, so he extended no aid beyond giving unlimited space in his columns to his close friend Davezac.[47] Beardslee presented even more difficult problems. A northerner, he had established the *Advertiser* as a thoroughly American paper and had thrown its weight behind such candidates as Henry Johnson in the gubernatorial campaign of 1824. National politics found him seemingly torn between the two sides, for his background drew him to Adams but his close friendship with Eleazar Ripley kept the *Advertiser's* columns at least partly favorable to the General's cause.[48]

The sudden death of the *Louisiana Gazette* forced the Jacksonians to confront the crisis of their crumbling newspaper support. Ripley induced Beardslee to sell his publication to a committee of Jackson backers, and with John Penrice as it nominal owner the *Louisiana Advertiser* appeared in January of 1827 as the unchallenged mouthpiece of the party in Louisiana.[49] The editorial chair went to one of the most clamorous and uninhibited journalists of his day, Peter K. Wagner. A huge, barrel-like man, he had been in New Orleans since 1811, having come from Baltimore and a newspaper apprenticeship in the plant of his brother, publisher of the *Federal Republican*.[50] Notorious as the "Black Dutchman" because of his unkempt appearance and slovenly person, he cut a familiar figure in the coffee houses of the city, where he could frequently be found in the midst of friends, a small narrow-brimmed hat perched precariously atop his shaggy head, gulping his favorite "humble repast"—whiskey and oysters.[51] Mar-

47. New Orleans *Argus*, December 10, 1827; Auguste Davezac to Andrew Jackson, May 8, 1827, Jackson Papers, LC.

48. Alexander Porter to Josiah S. Johnston, May 26, 1826, in Johnston Papers, HSP.

49. Ripley denied being the prime actor in the venture, but it is clear that he was closely related to the move. See the *Louisiana Advertiser*, June 1, 1827, June 12, 1828, and Alexander Porter to Josiah S. Johnston, January 12, 1827, in Johnston Papers, HSP.

50. New Orleans *Daily Picayune*, November 18, 1883.

51. *Louisiana Advertiser*, February 7, 1827, May 23, 26, June 12, 1828; New Orleans *Argus*, June 25, 1828.

ried into the prominent family of Judge Joshua Lewis,[52] Wagner forever paraded his lowly origins, and when in the early 1820s he finally acquired his own paper, the *Orleans Gazette*, he poured out a steady stream of invective upon anyone he envied or suspected of feeling superior to his kind. He heaped his wrath particularly upon Governor Robertson for the veto of the usury bill in 1823,[53] and the violence of his language on that occasion must have been remembered by Ripley and his associates in 1827. With Wagner's talents for demagoguery clearly for hire, his *Gazette* having failed in 1823, and Jacksonian needs so great, the new enterprise got underway amidst exuberant optimism. It would prove a profitable bargain for all concerned.

At almost the same moment, Edouard Louvet arrived in New Orleans to begin the *Propagateur Louisianais* as a French-language counterpart of the *Advertiser*, and though his venture survived only through July 1827, in that short time he acquired a reputation for fanatical Jacksonianism second only to that of Wagner himself.[54] Meanwhile, the faithful began to exert themselves in the rural parishes as well. Isaac Baker besieged the editor of the *Attakapas Gazette* (St. Martinville) to win him to the good cause, and since their exchanges involved not ideas but subscriptions, Baker began to entreat his Jacksonian friends throughout the state to send him aid. By June he could report success. The *Gazette* had "come over."[55]

The Florida segment of the party kept pace. Some time between late 1826 and July of 1827, Jacksonians purchased Fielding Bradford's *Louisiana Journal* and turned it over to the management of Archibald Haralson, whose general editorial approach so mirrored that of Wagner's as to suggest a close working alliance between their two publications.[56] Shortly thereafter the town boasted a second Jackson sheet, the *Crisis*.[57] Along the coast, Godwin B. Cotten launched the Donaldsonville *Creole* to offset the *La Fourche Gazette* of Adams,[58] while back in New Orleans, St. Romes finally

52. New Orleans *Daily Picayune*, November 18, 1883.
53. *L'Ami des Lois*, June 12, 1823.
54. New Orleans *Argus*, January 13, August 1, 1827.
55. Isaac L. Baker to William S. Hamilton, December 18, 1826, June 3, 1827, in Hamilton Papers, LSU.
56. *Louisiana Journal*, July 28, 1827.
57. St. Francisville *Crisis*, May 10, 1828.
58. *Louisiana Courier*, November 14, 1827.

came out openly for Jackson in November 1827, despite his patronage fears.[59]

Alarmed by this burst of Jacksonian energy, administration forces shored up their own news outlets. The Natchitoches *Courier* followed a clearly pro-Adams line despite shallow pretensions to neutrality,[60] and Stephen Henderson of the Baton Rouge *Gazette* adhered to a similar course of non-violent attachment to the president.[61] Not satisfied with such dignified and restrained support, Josiah Johnston installed Thomas J. Pew at the *Louisiana Messenger* (Alexandria) for more vigorous attack, later moving Pew down to New Orleans in the fall of 1827 to assume control of the more important *Mercantile Advertiser*.[62] The Adams press, however, found its true Titan in John Gibson of the *Argus*, who could match the insults and invectives of Wagner blow for blow. They made a ludicrous pair, Gibson a wisp of a man only slightly over five feet in height and weighing but 118 pounds, a dwarf beside the leviathan bulk of his antagonist. His minute size had no room for timidity, and his long journalistic career in New Orleans found him embroiled in physical conflict at one time or another with practically every one of his fellow editors, though his courage on one occasion could not quite bring him to accept Wagner's challenge to a duel with broadswords. Gibson's personal integrity had no greater standing in the community than that of his giant competitor, giving his enemies full play to charge him with a remarkable assortment of libidinous and venal misdeeds.[63] With all his failings, however, he remained the most gifted of his craft in the state, regularly adopting novel and pioneering methods which eventually became standard in the presses of his contemporaries. Under his guidance the *Argus* quickly began to rival the *Advertiser* in circulation among the American readers in New Orleans.[64]

From 1826 through 1828 the state almost sank under the weight of endless campaign propaganda from this battery of presses and countless speak-

59. New Orleans *Argus*, December 10, 1827.
60. Natchitoches *Courier*, September 25, 1827.
61. Baton Rouge *Gazette*, November 10, 1827.
62. Henry A. Bullard to Josiah S. Johnston, November 24, 1827, Alexander Porter to Johnston, April 16, 1828, George Eustis to Johnston, October 31, 1827, in Johnston Papers, HSP.
63. *Louisiana Advertiser*, June 17, 1828; New Orleans *Argus*, August 20, 1829.
64. New Orleans *Argus*, August 6, 1829.

ers' platforms. Charges and countercharges followed one upon the other in much the same pattern to be found over the nation, but with an emphasis on certain issues which had particular urgency in the minds of Louisianians. For Jacksonians the driving compulsion to action resided in the deep resentment aroused by the method which had brought Adams to the presidency, a bitterness intensified by the conviction that the base intrigue responsible for that outrage had resulted in the people of Louisiana being charged with shameful ingratitude toward the man who had saved them from destruction. Now they felt that Louisiana must redeem its honor by reversing the reprehensible vote for Adams given by Brent and Gurley in 1825. Behind all that had happened they saw more than the need to repudiate the malfeasance of Brent and Gurley. These miscreants they now reduced to relative insignificance as pawns in an overarching plot by professional politicians to set themselves above the will of the people and create an aristocracy of perpetual officeholders. Thus Andrew Jackson became in their eyes an instrument through which the people must reassert their sovereignty, his candidacy and election not only a necessary personal reward for unparalleled services but a confirmation that the American people had not lost their liberties.[65]

This sentiment quickly expanded to embrace the conviction that Adams, now in possession of his ill-gotten office, meant to establish overwhelming power in the national government through a protective tariff, internal improvements, and creation of national educational and armed services institutions. What most Louisianians had earlier viewed as nothing more than foolish abstract political theory suddenly appeared to be rebirth of a Federalist grasp for tyrannical power once thought killed forever by Thomas Jefferson. Jackson champions rushed to proclaim that only he could lead the nation back to the principles of the Revolution of 1800, making this appeal to an old tradition perhaps the major theme in their drive to put Andrew Jackson in the White House. "The cause of General Jackson," the New Orleans merchant W. L. Robeson proclaimed in 1827, "is emphatically that of the People of the United States opposed to their

65. Isaac L. Baker to Josiah S. Johnston, January 16, 1826, Walter H. Overton to Johnston, August 18, 1827, in Johnston Papers, HSP; Natchitoches *Courier*, October 22, 1827; *Louisiana Journal*, August 31, September 14, October 21, 1827; *Louisiana Advertiser*, May 31, October 10, December 14, 17, 21, 1827; *Louisiana Gazette*, June 9, 12, August 7, 26, September 9, 1826.

unprincipled misrulers; a controversy between patriotism, virtue, and political integrity on one side, and usurpation, vice, and hypocrisy on the other; a contest involving the rights of every citizen in our country and one in which each individual should take an active part."[66] The clash of the Adams administration with Governor Troup of Georgia confirmed these fears of executive tyranny, leading the *Louisiana Gazette* to reprint a Frankford *Argus* editorial which it found expressive of its own ideas:

> Ever since the administration of Jefferson . . . government has been deviating gradually from its republican task, until at length it would be difficult to recognize his principles in the conduct of any of its departments. A national Bank was then thought to be unconstitutional and anti-Republican; now it is a favorite of government. Then, it was thought the states possessed, in relation to their reserved powers, some degree of independent sovereignty, and that no state could be made accountable for the acts of its government, to any national tribunal; now there is no act of sovereignty which a state can exercize in defence of itself against the encroachments of the general government.[67]

As Jackson had once saved Louisiana from the British, now he was ready, said his advocates, to save it from this internal menace. A "republican of the old school of 1798," he had contributed more than any . . . west of the Allegheny mountains, to bring about the reformation of 1800." Indeed, "without his exertions," the argument ran, "we should now be laboring under federal misrule," and for this is he "relentlessly pursued by the minions of aristocracy; by apostate republicans; by the coalition of 1824."[68]

Skilled Jacksonian campaigners painted this revival of Federalism as part of a great sectional clash between East and West, highlighting dark plots by the hated centralists to despoil the younger and rising sections of the nation. They recalled that just as in 1824 when Louisianians had rallied to Jackson because he had not been a cabinet member, "They prefer him now to John Q. Adams, because the administration of the latter is founded on principles repugnant to the spirit of Republican institutions— manufacturers have been fostered at the expense of southern agriculture;

66. W. L. Robeson to Alfred Balch, November 11, 1827, in Jackson Papers, LC.
67. *Louisiana Gazette*, November 2, 1826.
68. *Louisiana Journal*, August 31, 1826.

and commerce, the offspring of labour and industry, has been depressed and shackled in its operations; and while one part of the Union has been the exclusive object of executive solicitude, the South has been contemned, calumniated, denounced, sacrificed."[69]

Jacksonians accused Adams of deliberately throwing the weight of federal favor to New England with an internal improvements program destructive to the interests of Louisiana. The great mass of eastern canals being planned by the government, to be built, said these critics, with money partly collected from the New Orleans custom house, were "intended to divert the produce of the West from this city." Not "a spadeful of dirt has been removed in order to improve the navigation of our rivers" or to link them by canals; and where, they asked, "is the boasted National Road over which the mail it was said, would glide in ten days from Washington to New Orleans?—Where is the military road, intended to run from the city to the Fort of Plaquemines—where are the Canals which were to connect the Mississippi with the Lakes?"[70] Clearly, they would never be forthcoming from a man whose whole record breathed antagonism to Louisiana, and who, with his fellow New Englanders, had tried to keep its people out of the Union with charges that they were as "ignorant of republicanism as the alligators of their swamps."[71]

Denouncing the American System as the boldest attack on the West and South ever made, despite its support by Clay, Louisiana Jacksonians represented it as a desperate attempt to choke off the migration of settlers to the new West. The tariff had no purpose in their eyes except to keep eastern men at their looms—to enrich New England towns at the expense of trade with Europe, upon which the South and West depended for the marketing of their produce.[72] Nothing outraged them more then the report that Adams had described the existing land policy of the United States as "eminently successful," a sentiment made more hateful by his refusal to support Senator Thomas Hart Benton's proposal to sell western lands for twenty-five cents an acre. Such disdainful disregard for the state's peculiar concerns in a problem which had plagued it since 1803 struck them as un-

69. *Louisiana Courier*, October 27, 1828.
70. *Ibid.*
71. *Louisiana Advertiser*, October 16, 1828.
72. *Louisiana Courier*, November 9, 1827.

forgivable.[73] With such a background to exploit, Jacksonians could glory in the identity of their hero with the West as a whole, and with Louisiana in particular.

Nonetheless, they recognized the dangers facing them in the complications of the tariff controversy. In the first place, their criticism of protection was unequivocal. "The object of the tariff," Wagner reported in the *Advertiser*, "is to enlarge and multiply the manufacturing establishments of the Northern and Middle States, to open new sources of employment for their people, to increase their wealth and population, and consequently add to their political strength and importance. . . . It is not the American System, but the system of corrupt political traffickers at Washington, who are buying the Northern votes for the Presidency with the sweat of the southern planters."[74] But how would the Louisiana sugar grower react to such a diatribe, caught up as he was in the protective system as much as any New England woollens manufacturer? The Adams men did everything in their power to stress the havoc which would visit the sugar industry under a Jacksonian antitariff policy, and Brent warned the sugar planters that the enemies of the administration meant to include them in their plans to destroy the protected interests of the country.[75] Gibson's *Argus* gave unqualified support to the Adams-Clay tariff policy as the only means by which America might be made economically self-sufficient, with capital to build roads and canals and expand the marketing of all American products. The Jacksonians, Gibson warned, would destroy all this and keep the United States a colonial dependency of Britain in matters of trade and industry.[76]

Fear of alienating the sugar-planter vote forced the Jacksonians, therefore, to the unconvincing argument that the sugar duties did not really belong to the Adams-Clay protective system at all, having been laid entirely for revenue purposes before Louisiana became part of the Union. John Slidell stressed the close relationship of the sugar industry to slavery and urged the sugar planters to realize that their greatest danger came from antislavery fanatics, not antitariff men,[77] while the *Advertiser* proclaimed that

73. *Louisiana Advertiser*, October 2, 1828.
74. *Ibid.*, October 4, 1828.
75. Tregle, "Louisiana and the Tariff," 30.
76. New Orleans *Argus*, June 14, 1828.
77. Tregle, "Louisiana and the Tariff," 30.

Jacksonians opposed only *new* tariffs designed to create monopolies for Rhode Island and Massachusetts manufacturers.[78] The so-called Tariff of Abominations of 1828 came therefore as a great deliverance to Louisiana Jacksonians, for while its schedules certainly ran counter to their objections to protectionism, the measure as a whole had aroused protests from the manufacturing areas not happy with high imposts on raw materials processed by their mills and plants. "The secret is out," Wagner proclaimed to his readers upon receipt of the details of the congressional action. "It appears," he maintained, "that the pretended friends of domestic manufacturers are determined to adopt such a tariff as will promote their own interests exclusively," and he praised the attempt to grant privileges to Louisiana's sugar, Kentucky's hemp, and Pennsylvania's iron equal to that dispensed to New England's cottons and woollens. "This wise and just distribution of national favor," Wagner observed, "has given mortal offence to those who were clamorous for an increase of imports, so long as they thought the system would bear hard upon the southern planters and benefit themselves exclusively. . . . Thus we see unmasked, the false professions of the tariff-men in favor of Louisiana."[79]

As controversy grew more and more heated around issues like the tariff and the American System as a whole, Jacksonian language tended frequently to spill over into wild exaggeration subject to interpretation not really reflective of its actual intent. The consequence has been a variety of judgments as to just what these economic and public policy battles tell us about the essential nature of the politics of the 1820s and 1830s and of the America in which it was played out. Some years after delivering his seminal essay "The Significance of the Frontier in American History," Frederick Jackson Turner closed his *Rise of the New West* with a sentence which looked more to the future than to the past: "And on the frontier of the northwest, the young Lincoln sank his axe deep in the opposing forest."[80] The Turnerian thesis to which these works gave birth stressed the formative impact of the western movement on American life and provided the foundations of a long-persisting interpretation of the American character as having been shaped by this meeting of man with the retreating wilder-

78. *Louisiana Advertiser*, June 4, 1827.
79. *Ibid.*, March 17, 1828.
80. Frederick J. Turner, *Rise of the New West* (rpr. New York, 1962), 226.

ness, frequently extending into applications far beyond anything envisioned by the famous historian. It saw in the constant repetition of that frontier contact the molding force of a virgin land which nurtured sturdy independence, freedom from ancient restraints, leveling of imposed inequalities, and the ascendancy of what would come to be called "the common man"—in substance, Jacksonian democracy. In 1945 a young Harvard historian, Arthur M. Schlesinger, Jr., challenged this pervasive view in *The Age of Jackson*, arguing that in truth the driving force behind Jacksonian democracy came "in the main from the seaboard, not from the forest."[81] His work, quickly identified as the "wage-earner thesis," opened a whole new era of Jacksonian scholarship as historians reacted to his contention that an eastern workingmen's movement rather than one of western frontiersmen determined the character of the era. Schlesinger maintained that the period reflected vividly a main theme in the nation's history, "that enduring struggle between the business community and the rest of society,"[82] a theme dramatically highlighted in Jackson's destruction of the Second Bank of the United States. This avowal that class conflict provided the key to understanding a critical phase of American history did not go unchallenged, other scholars arguing that the era might more accurately be described as one in which men sought to break open a closed circle of business leadership rather than to challenge the business ethic per se. Later studies have looked to religious and social identities, party loyalties, and simple unclassifiable responses as truer guides to the political character of the period—in at least one instance going so far as to question its claim to having been an egalitarian age at all.[83] The better picture of Louisiana in the Age of Jackson is to be found outside the wage-earner construct.

In none of their attacks upon protectionism, internal improvements, or eventually the Bank of the United States did Louisiana Jacksonians display any indication of hostility to the business complex as a class or endorse the concept that the relatively dispossessed members of the community found themselves in that status because of economic exploitation by bankers or commercial barons. Their arguments reflected instead a sharp response to

81. Schlesinger, *Age of Jackson*, 283.

82. *Ibid.*, 307.

83. For a comprehensive survey of Jacksonian historiography, see Edward Pessen, *Jacksonian America: Society, Personality, and Politics* (Homewood, Ill., 1978).

conflicting sectional interests dividing East and West or aligning wealthy, slaveholding planters against manufacturers in distant northern centers. They opposed the tariff not because it made some people rich but because it favored one section over another, and internal improvements because they had relatively less importance for an agrarian region than for an industrial one. They did, unquestionably, frequently laud the virtues of the "honest mechanic" and rage against aristocrats and wealth, but almost always in the context that the pejorative terms applied to behavior or attitude rather than to status.

Much in this approach could be traced back to old associations of the Adams family and Federalism with a social aristocracy which felt itself superior to the average American. The obvious dissimilarity between John Quincy Adams and Andrew Jackson led the followers of the General to a belief that in the difference there must be a fault, and because Jackson so epitomized the western ideal, the flaw inevitably fell to the New Englander. This provided as well a satisfying response to those who praised the president's superiority over his rival in education and training, for those very qualities might now be labeled as the trappings of prideful snobbery rather than as sound reasons for political preferment. Adams also had to carry the burden of the sins of his father, the Jacksonians repeatedly warning that he would unhesitatingly reinstate the alien and sedition laws of 1798 at the first opportunity. In effect, they pictured the cub as determined to realize the old bear's hope of making the presidency "into a kingly throne, with all its appendages of hereditary nobles, and all the trappings of kingly splendour," a dream which must now be crushed by Jackson as it had been by Jefferson in 1800.[84]

It was easy to pose the virtues of the Savior of New Orleans against the fripperies of his opponent:

> General Jackson has read a great deal, and probably with as much judgment and effect as any man living. He has not skimmed the surface of every art or science or revelled away life in the pleasures of literature. This is the essence of mental indolence. To loll in an armchair and look over the pages of every book that is written, is the resort of a weak mind to wear the polish of the diamond without possessing the richness of the mineral. The educa-

84. *Louisiana Advertiser*, August 30, 1828; Baton Rouge *Gazette*, October 25, 1828.

tion of General Jackson resembles rather the hickory tree of the forest; a tree rough without but more substantial in use than the smooth sicamore. . . . Although not a bookworm he made his bread by the practice of the law, of which Mr. Adams was incapable, although he is rolling in wealth drawn from the Treasury of the United States.[85]

For Wagner there could have been no more pleasant task than this of castigating a supposed social aristocracy, for he had long nursed these hatreds against men whose success and prestige seemed to be indictments of his own plebeian background and financial failures. He delighted now in extending the "aristocrat" label to all those who refused to back Jackson, anxious to pillory them as snobs who held themselves aloof from the workingman. Ridiculing the "arrogance which overgrown wealth, assumed talents, and inflated pride give to some of their would-be leaders,"[86] he provided much of the campaign fodder to be found in the official pronouncements of the Jackson organization. At a January, 1828, convention of the General's partisans, General Ripley pointed out that when Jackson first went to Congress, the

old principles of democracy which had carried us triumphantly through the revolution; and which had also been victorious in the formation of our national constitution, stood in danger of being supplanted by aristocratic tendencies . . . our immense and profitable commerce, during the Revolutionary wars of France, poured in upon us the opulence of the East and of Europe. And this sudden acquisition of wealth created a corps of monied patricians in the commercial states who seemed to commence a crusade against those doctrines of democracy which had established the independence of the nations. . . . Distinctions in society between "well born" and the "base born" began to be introduced. . . . At length by the election of Thomas Jefferson, the great moral revolution was completed. The democracy of the nation once more triumphed, and the citizens regained their former peace and tranquility. . . . [But] the most pernicious circumstance associated with this administration, is the revival of the party in the eastern metropolis, which had first introduced the germs of aristocratic distinction; and whose conduct dur-

85. Baton Rouge *Gazette*, September 23, 1828.
86. *Ibid.*, October 6, 1827.

ing the late war, was a tissue of frenzy and folly. . . . Mr. Adams has brought back that party into power which had been beaten and broken down by the Giant force of our democracy.[87]

The constant theme in all of this proclaims that aristocrats assumed airs of social superiority which made them scorn and avoid the mechanic and yeoman. Wealth gave them arrogance, the charge went, but at no time did Wagner or his associates challenge or even inquire into the system by which that wealth had been accumulated, leaving the clear impression that all would have been satisfactory had the aristocrats only condescended to shake the hand of the honest workingman and agree to commingle with him as an equal.

"I wish not to be understood as condemning the honest acquisition of wealth," one of the *Advertiser*'s correspondents wrote,[88] and Wagner himself in May of 1828 printed a long defense of the Bank of the United States against charges that it "caused a scarcity of specie and embarrassment of trade." All banks, Wagner advised, possessed great power for good and evil, but deserved no criticism on general principles.[89]

This reluctance to oppose anything more than the social snobbery of the wealthy could undoubtedly be traced in part to the fact that Wagner, the *Advertiser*, and indeed the Louisiana Jackson movement altogether, had become closely allied to Martin Gordon, one of the most affluent men of the state and president of unquestionably its most feared and criticized business enterprise, the Orleans Navigation Company. Holding a complete monopoly over the traffic in the Canal Carondelet–Bayou St. John link with Lake Pontchartrain, its high tolls and irresponsible management aroused popular resentment to such a pitch that for years petitions called upon Congress to abrogate the charter which the company had received from the territorial government.[90] But with the help of Senator Josiah Johnston, Gordon managed to thwart these moves and eventually began to

87. *Ibid.*, February 7, 1828.
88. *Ibid.*, November 16, 1827.
89. *Ibid.*, May 10, 1828.
90. *Louisiana v. New Orleans Navigation Company*, 2 Martin (O.S.), 309; David B. Morgan to Josiah S. Johnston, January 5, 1827, in Johnston Papers, HSP; *Louisiana Gazette*, January 29, 31, February 2, 11, 1825; *Louisiana Journal*, February 9, 1826; New Orleans *Argus*, March 19, 1827.

urge the state to purchase the company at his own valuation of its stock.[91] Behind the scenes, Wagner acted as his chief publicist in this cause, presenting himself as nothing more than a disinterested citizen working for the elimination of the canal tolls. His messages, however, returned always to the same conclusion: "the only just, the only equitable, and the only practical mode of getting rid of the tolls imposed by that Company [is] the *Purchase of their stock at par.*"[92]

At least one other consideration blunted any likely development of a class-based mechanic or workingman movement in Louisiana—the unusually high wages workers could command in the state and especially in the city of New Orleans. Their exceptional status made them unlikely subjects of any complaint against economic exploitation by aristocrats, Wagner contenting himself with paternalistic advice that they should deposit their surplus funds in the new savings bank to be opened shortly in the city.[93]

Inevitably, the flood of invective against Adams and his eastern power base widened to include attacks upon the president's antislavery views, which obviously invited the observation that the social ideas and loyalties of Louisianians had long been hateful to the man now seeking their suffrage for four additional years in office. They accepted as a matter of course that such sentiments formed a natural part of the Yankee mentality, as Gurley had every reason to know from his political career in the state. Upon Adams accordingly there now descended the full weight of this conviction, the Jacksonians railing against his kind as a perpetual threat to this basic interest of the South and praising the General for standing always ready at the slightest notice to expend his strength and fortune in the preservation of southern values.[94] Adams confirmed his critics in their view by purchasing a slave prince, Abduhl Rahhaman, whom he then manumitted and restored to his tribe in Africa. When Bostonians hosted the prince at a public dinner, Wagner blasted northern aristocrats who shied away from white

91. Martin Gordon to Josiah S. Johnston, March 10, 15, November 28, 1824, February 1, 1825, in Johnston Papers, HSP.

92. *Louisiana Advertiser*, November 20, 1828.

93. *Ibid.*, April 24, 1827; New Orleans *Argus*, February 17, 1820; Edward Everett Diary, May 5, 1829, in Edward Everett Papers, MHS.

94. *Louisiana Gazette*, June 6, 12, July 10, November 22, 1826; *Louisiana Journal*, September 14, 1826; *Louisiana Courier*, November 7, 9, 1827, October 21, 22, 1828.

Irish and Germans and yet would gather to honor an old Negro, making the issue a cause célèbre in his pages for weeks.[95] Two other cases before Congress, however, raised issues of much greater import to slaveholders, challenging as they did the very constitutional guarantees of the slave system. Both related directly to Louisiana. During the British invasion of 1814–1815, the United States military forces had commandeered much civilian property for the use of their troops, among the requisitions being slaves belonging to Francis Larche and Marigny d'Auterive of New Orleans. Their Negroes having been subsequently killed, the owners petitioned for compensation, and in 1826 a congressional committee disallowed the claim, refusing to recognize slaves as property. When the d'Auterive request met the same fate in 1828, Livingston and Gurley launched a full-scale constitutional debate in Congress, but to no avail. The Jacksonian press seized on these two cases as irrefutable evidence of the malice of their foes, and though Adams had played no part in the controversy, they placed full responsibility for its outcome at his door.[96]

With this plenitude of hatred and emotionalism coursing through the campaign, Louisiana could be thankful for escaping the tensions of at least one problem generating fear and conflict in other quarters of the Union. The issue of anti-Masonry simply did not emerge in the state except as it provided yet another opportunity to belabor Adams for encouraging a movement without any attraction for Louisianians. Masonry had deep roots in the state, possibly even enlisting in its membership Père Antoine, guardian of St. Louis Cathedral. No Louisiana political figure was so stupid as to identify with an anti-Masonic policy which would have put him at odds with essentially the entire community, Roman Catholic and Protestant, French and American.[97]

95. *Louisiana Advertiser*, October 21, 23, 25, 30, 1828.

96. *Louisiana Journal*, June 15, 1826; New Orleans *Argus*, January 31, 1828; *Debates in Congress*, 20th Cong., 1st Sess., 899, 903, 904, 989–91, 1048, 1475, 1486.

97. See, for example, these accounts of Masonic activity in New Orleans and elsewhere, which indicate the inclusive nature of its membership: *L'Ami des Lois*, May 5, 1823; *Louisiana Journal*, May 26, June 30, 1825, March 9, June 15, 1826; *Washita Gazette*, August 9, October 11, 1825; *Louisiana Courier*, August 15, 1825, January 7, 1826, January 5, September 14, October 22, 1828, March 14, April 11, 1829; *Louisiana Gazette*, March 21, April 18, 1825; Clarence W. Bispham, "Fray Antonio de Sedella," *LHQ*, II (1919), 36.

In resisting the Jacksonian attacks, defenders of Adams had little choice but to concentrate their own fire on the personality and past deeds of the General, for his partisans presented little in the way of a consistent ideology or program which could be opposed. No one could reasonably argue for snobbery or repudiate the republican virtues of the Revolution of 1800, more or less confining the president's adherents to vigorous denials that the charges against their candidate possessed any validity. They did stress Jackson's equivocal personal position on the tariff, at the same time maintaining steady predictions of disaster to the sugar industry should his antiprotection friends ever control the nation. Defiantly, they asked for one specific example of despotism or antidemocratic behavior on the part of Adams himself.[98]

Against Jackson personally, the possibilities of attack were limitless. It required little ingenuity or effort to rekindle the always smoldering resentment felt toward him in much of the Gallic community, and Louisiana once more reverberated with the outraged protests of those who could never forgive his supposed suspicions of their loyalty in 1814–1815. Old Louis Louaillier, a state legislator whom Jackson had jailed in 1815, again took to the hustings, describing in angry denunciation his arrest for inciting rebellion after the Battle of New Orleans, reviling Jackson as a man whose easy recourse to arbitrary acts and violence made him unfit to be president.[99] Lurid accounts of how New Orleans would have been put to the torch by Jackson's command had the British pierced his lines at Chalmette sent renewed thrills of horror through the property holders of the city. Moreover, the Adams press charged, the General had shown no change of heart since those terrible days. It "would be carrying our gratitude beyond all bounds and forgetting what we owe to ourselves," an Adams meeting proclaimed in 1827, "were we to declare in favor of him, who, after thirteen years' reflection, without any, even semblance of, proof, still persists" in his shameless libel against the loyal people of Louisi-

98. New Orleans *Argus*, March 28, April 12, May 17, June 1, 1827, April 15, 18, June 14, 21, 1828. The Jacksonian strategy was obviously to keep the General personally clear of any antitariff statement which might alienate Pennsylvania. See, for example, John Eaton to Andrew Jackson, March 4, 1828, J. Floyd to Sam Houston, March 15, 1828, in Jackson Papers, LC.

99. New Orleans *Argus*, September 17, 24, 1827.

ana.[100] Nowhere else in the nation, perhaps, did the campaign against the intemperance and violence of Jackson find an audience with more reason to accept its validity.[101]

Warming to the attack, defenders of the president pronounced Jackson's candidacy as the height of folly. To them the election of 1824 had resulted from no bargain and corruption but from the wise judgment of the people that their interests would be better served by the expert and experienced leadership of Adams and Clay than by the reckless adventurism of a military political amateur.[102] Jacksonians they derided as foolish hero worshipers, or worse, as men who wished to use the General to climb to positions in which they themselves could exploit the people. They cited Carleton and Davezac as revealing examples of the ambitious and grasping office seekers crowding Jacksonian ranks,[103] coupling them as well to military cronies who desired to place the nation under a "man on horseback." "The more I have an opportunity of observing the zeal and intemperance of the officers of the Army relative to the Presidential Election," John Sibley wrote Senator Johnston, "the more I am convinced of the Expediency of our Government to keep an Eye to the Army. If we had such an army as they say we ought to have and they could procure the Election of their military Chief to be President we should all be rode down."[104]

No wonder then that the campaign of 1828 aroused the fears of the community—for if their leaders could be believed, then clearly they must choose between a would-be king and a potential military despot.

100. Baton Rouge *Gazette*, October 20, 1827, quoting the New Orleans *Argus*. That there was considerable truth in these charges is revealed by Jackson's 1827 statement that in 1814, "I went on my way to duty, they [the French Louisianians] went off to dance." See James A. Hamilton, *Reminiscences* (New York, 1869), 69.

101. Alexander Porter to Josiah S. Johnston, November 17, 1826, in Johnston Papers, HSP; New Orleans *Argus*, March 24, September 10, 1827, October 23, 1828; *Louisiana Courier*, July 8, 1828; *Louisiana Advertiser*, August 21, October 21, 1828.

102. New Orleans *Argus*, November 20, 1827, May 13, 14, 1828.

103. *Ibid.*, March 17, 24, September 5, 14, 1827; Baton Rouge *Gazette*, October 20, 1827; Natchitoches *Courier*, July 10, August 21, 1827.

104. John Sibley to Josiah S. Johnston, October 30, 1827, in Johnston Papers, HSP. The resentment of the Jacksonians at such charges is revealed clearly in Isaac L. Baker to William S. Hamilton, March 22, 1825, in Hamilton Papers, LSU; *Louisiana Advertiser*, September 28, 1826, September 13, 1827, February 16, 1828.

Andrew Jackson on the eve of his 1824 presidential bid.
Portrait by Samuel Lovett Waldo (1819), courtesy Historic New Orleans Collection.

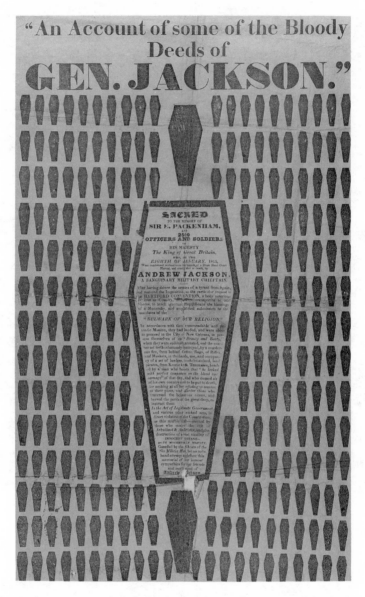

Pro-Jackson campaign broadside of 1828, designed to counter the infamous "coffin hand bill" which attacked Jackson for "bloody deeds" as a military commander. It represents Jackson as guilty of executing General Pakenham and hundreds of British soldiers intent on enjoying the "beauty and booty" of New Orleans in 1815. *Courtesy Louisiana State Museum.*

Henry Clay, "Harry of the West," idol of Louisiana Whigs.
*Engraving by T. Johnson from a photograph by Rockwood,
courtesy Historic New Orleans Collection.*

Edward Livingston, who foresaw Jackson's future while serving
as his aide at the Battle of New Orleans. *Print from Alceé Fortier,*
History of Louisiana, *courtesy Historic New Orleans Collection.*

Alexander Porter, ardent champion of Henry Clay and the keenest and most articulate observer of Jacksonian Louisiana. *Portrait attributed to Matthew Jouett, courtesy Louisiana State Museum.*

Caricature silhouette of Etienne Mazureau, field marshal of the foreign French in Jacksonian Louisiana. *Courtesy Historic New Orleans Collection.*

John Slidell, years after his fateful battle with Martin Gordon
for control of the Louisiana Jackson party. *Carte de visite photograph
by E. Anthony, courtesy Louisiana State Museum.*

John Randolph Grymes, the decidedly "uncommon man"
of Louisiana Jacksonianism. *Portrait by Theodore F. Moise (1842),
courtesy Historic New Orleans Collection.*

Jacques Villeré, first creole governor of Louisiana and gentle advocate of ethnic harmony in the state. *Print by Pointel du Portail, courtesy Historic New Orleans Collection.*

Bernard Marigny, fiery Jacksonian protagonist of creole ascendancy. *Portrait by Thomas Sully (1808), from John S. Kendall,* History of New Orleans, *courtesy Historic New Orleans Collection.*

General Jean B. Plauché, exemplar of creoles who saw in Jackson
the hero who had saved them from British spoliation. *Print from Alceé Fortier,
History of Louisiana, courtesy Historic New Orleans Collection.*

Edward Douglass White, Whig victor in the bitterly contested gubernatorial
election of 1834. *Crayon drawing, courtesy Louisiana State Museum.*

· IX ·

Democracy Triumphant

The torrent of argument and debate flowing from the campaign of 1828 engulfed Louisiana and brought it for the first time in its history to a consuming involvement in a national election. Much of this excitement unquestionably derived from the disputed outcome of the preceding contest and from the personal relationships, good or bad, which tied so many Louisianians to Andrew Jackson. But to an even greater extent, perhaps, the state assembly in 1825 added immensely to this heightened popular participation in the political process by abolishing legislative choice of presidential electors and transferring the selection to the qualified voters of the state.[1] Edward Douglass White reported his assessment of how this affected the populace in a jocular note to Nicholas Trist which reflects a rather caustic view of the political sophistication of his neighbors:

> The influence of this fall has pressed hard on our biliary ducts, and another cause has helped to derange them in their function—politics—so called; for every man who has been told, and has faculties enough to remember the fact, that there are two men candidates for the presidency, considers himself a politician engrossed by politics. As for us we are for Fitz Jack, and the reasons are obvious—1. He lives nearer us; 2. He is a good fighter, which suits us, who are bellicose. 3. He knows nothing about the Science of Government; neither do we and therefore despise the knowledge and deem it

1. Moreau Lislet, ed., *Digest of the Acts of the Louisiana Legislature*, I, 451.

hurtful. 4. We are hostile to all former usages in the United States, saving the one which tends to preservation, and Fitz Jack has some character in that way.—5. We are tired of the monotonous system, and want to change it: we are glad to find our brethren in London agree with us, and advise us to vote for Fitz Jack. 6. Davezac says the work of separation is begun, and that we shall make Fitz Jack emperor of the West. We can't all be Heroes, but it is still something to be Heroites. We are told all the folks in Virginia have feelings like our own. I hope it's true.[2]

The memories of popular reaction against the attempted caucus nomination in the 1824 campaign made political leaders wary of any such devices during the 1828 canvass, legislators in January of 1827 rejecting caucus calls out of hand.[3] Emphasis shifted instead to public assemblies in every parish and town of the state, at which resolutions and recommendations tolled off the repetitive claims of virtue and vice to be found in the contending candidates. The scale and frequency of these meetings far exceeded anything comparable in 1824, giving them an especially impressive new organizational unity which for the first time indicated the beginning emergence of a modern political party system. Vigilance committees and committees of correspondence sprang up all over the state, dedicated to keeping their adherents both informed and loyal.[4] In no sense honorary or transient, they met regularly to rally their forces and to maintain disciplined support of their favorites, functioning down to ward units in the city of New Orleans.[5]

Centralized guidance of these new party activities also appeared at the state level for the first time in the 1828 campaign. In November of 1827 Adams delegates elected from each parish gathered in convention at Baton Rouge and elected Thomas Urquhart of New Orleans president, appointed a slate of five presidential elector candidates, and listened to Mazureau's

2. Edward D. White to Nicholas P. Trist, November 29, 1827, in Trist Papers, LC.

3. Alexander Porter to Josiah S. Johnston, January 27, 1827, in Johnston Papers, HSP; *Louisiana Advertiser*, January 25, 1827.

4. *Louisiana Advertiser*, August 6, December 25, 28, 1827, January 5, 7, 8, 11, 15, 1828; *Louisiana Courier*, December 1, 1827; March 5, June 21, 24, 1828; Baton Rouge *Gazette*, July 14, 1827; New Orleans *Argus*, September 28, 1827, October 3, 17, 22, 24, 30, 31, November 15, 1827; Natchitoches *Courier*, July 17, September 1, 25, 1827.

5. New Orleans *Argus*, March 29, October 20, 27, November 1, 1828.

scathing denunciation of the Jacksonians.[6] The General's backers held their own meeting in New Orleans late in January 1828, with 120 delegates from 27 of the state's 30 parishes in attendance, providing the audience for General Ripley's blast against the aristocracy of the Adams administration.[7]

The frenzy of the campaign allowed hardly a moment's peace throughout 1827 and 1828. January 8 and July 4 celebrations turned into rousing political rallies, with Jacksonians contributing especially aggressive and vocal excitement to the gatherings. Slidell, Davezac, General Robeson, Nathan Morse, and Ripley proved the most energetic of these oratorical minutemen, but friends and enemies duplicated their efforts all over the state.[8] In rough and tumble competition each side delighted particularly in seizing upon an opportunity to embarrass the opposition, with the Jacksonians again demonstrating greater adeptness at the game. When Commodore David Porter visited New Orleans in July of 1827, for example, to be honored at a public dinner in gratitude for his past naval services, both the Jackson and Adams camps agreed that no reference would be made to the quarrel with Adams which had caused Porter's resignation from the navy, or, for that matter, to any political issue whatsoever. Ignoring their pledge, the Jacksonians took control of the meeting, allowing their friends to launch noisy demonstrations at every mention of their hero's name, and forcing poor Porter to sit neglected through an evening of Jacksonian adulation.[9]

Activity begat optimism. Each month saw the champions of both sides

6. The five electors chosen were Jacques Villeré, Charles Bushnell, Andrew Le Blanc, Neuville Declouet, and Benjamin Morris, according to the Baton Rouge *Gazette*, November 10, 1827; New Orleans *Argus*, November 20, 1827.

7. Chosen as Jacksonian electors were J. B. Plauché, Trasimond Landry, T. W. Scott, Alexander Mouton, and Placide Bossier, who had undergone a substantial change of outlook since his 1824 horserace. *Louisiana Advertiser*, January 16, 1828. The Louisiana experience in the campaign was quite similar to that prevailing in most parts of the Union. See, for example, Culver H. Smith, "Propaganda Technique in the Jackson Campaign of 1828," in *East Tennessee Historical Society's Publications*, VI (1934), 44–66; Erik M. Eriksson, "Official Newspaper Organs and the Campaign of 1828," in *Tennessee Magazine of History*, VIII (1924), 231–47.

8. *Louisiana Advertiser*, July 6, 1827.

9. *Ibid.*, July 25, 1827; Maunsel White to Andrew Jackson, August 4, 1827, in Jackson Papers, LC.

more and more certain of eventual victory, though in their expressions of confidence, an occasional muted note of fear might indeed be heard. Alexander Porter watched somewhat uneasily as the campaign progressed, concerned because he perceived the Jacksonian ranks to be "composed of men who have reason *to wish for much,* and the stimulus of self interest gives great energy to their movements."[10] By late 1827, though still confident, he confessed a growing distress as campaign hysteria pushed the state to a level of excitement it had never before known. "A spirit of proscription is abroad, such as I never expected to see for a difference of opinion," he informed Johnston in yet another message. "I have been trying to rouse a *friend* of ours," he continued, with obvious reference to Governor Johnson, "who has great influence if he would exert it. If he thinks to escape by neutrality he is mistaken. He is marked already, and he will share the fate of every man who does not bow down before the idol and worship it."[11] Only Henry Clay seemed to be confident and without fears. "Louisiana, at this time" he told Edward Everett late in 1827, "is one of the safest and best organized states in the Union."[12]

Preoccupation with the presidential campaign became so intense that it dominated both the gubernatorial and congressional elections as well, a situation which would have hardly seemed possible only four years before. The gubernatorial campaign had actually begun immediately after Henry Johnson's inauguration in November of 1824, and the first two years of his administration gave every indication that the old issues would still prevail, with Americans and French lining up in opposing camps. Most Americans looked to Josiah Johnston as their only hope of uniting the several sectional factions in their ranks, planning to bring his name forward so early and with such backing that it might forestall the expected quadrennial emergence of General Thomas into the field.[13] Even such ardent Jacksoni-

10. Alexander Porter to Josiah S. Johnston, January 27, 1827, in Johnston Papers, HSP. See also John Slidell to Joel K. Poinsett, March 27, 1827, in Joel Poinsett Papers, HSP; Eleazar Ripley to John McNeil, April 30, 1827, in Miscellaneous Manuscripts, NYHS.

11. Alexander Porter to Josiah S. Johnston, December 8, 1827, in Johnston Papers, HSP.

12. Henry Clay to Edward Everett, November 7, 1827, in Edward Everett Papers MHS.

13. L. S. Hazelton to Josiah S. Johnston, March 30, 1825, Henry A. Bullard to Johnston, October 23, 1825, John Linton to Johnston, November 24, 1825, Nathaniel Cox to Johnston, November 26, 1825, Alexander Porter to Johnston, April 11, 1826, in Johnston Papers, HSP.

ans as Isaac L. Baker, W. H. Overton, and Martin Gordon pledged to support that strategy, despite Johnston's known devotion to Clay,[14] and again it appeared as if Louisiana's ethnic fixation would isolate the state election process from national party concerns. As the presidential campaign grew more heated, however, a clear change of sentiment began to emerge, plainly confessed by Baker in a frank communication to Johnston in October of 1826. The administration party, Baker complained, had become so violent and proscriptive toward anyone not of their persuasion that Jacksonians felt they must "look to ourselves," and without a tremor Baker continued with open hints that many American voters in Attakapas now looked to the Jacksonian Marigny as their next gubernatorial candidate.[15]

Fully aware of these changing attitudes, Johnston held back from any open announcement of his candidacy for other reasons as well, chiefly because he knew the uncertainties of popular elections in Louisiana and much preferred the security of his Senate seat. "I am too old to be thrown out of public life," he advised his friends as early as 1825, thus preparing them for his final refusal to enter the race,[16] and though Porter and others continued to push his pretensions,[17] Johnston did not relent from his decision. By June of 1826 he had definitely taken himself out of the campaign.[18]

Even without him the field soon overflowed. As expected, Gurley and the Baton Rouge partisans of Philemon Thomas announced the old general's candidacy in April of 1826;[19] determined to erase the ignominy of his 1824 defeat, Marigny again roamed the countryside convinced that Jacksonians all over the state would rally to his support;[20] Henry S. Thibodaux offered from the Lafourche area, much to the delight of the Adams forces, who expected him to cut into the French vote of Marigny;[21] Bouligny took

14. Isaac L. Baker to Josiah S. Johnston, November 1, 1825, Martin Gordon to Johnston, February 1, 1825, Walter H. Overton to Johnston, October 2, 1826, *ibid.*

15. Isaac L. Baker to Josiah S. Johnston, October 5, 1826, *ibid.*

16. Josiah S. Johnston to John Linton, October 9, 1825, *ibid.*

17. Alexander Porter to Josiah S. Johnston, April 11, 14, 1826, *ibid.*

18. Alexander Porter to Josiah S. Johnston, June 21, 1826, *ibid.*

19. Alexander Porter to Josiah S. Johnston, April 14, 1826, *ibid.*; Natchitoches *Courier*, November 5, 1827; *Louisiana Advertiser*, June 29, 1827.

20. *Louisiana Gazette*, April 6, 7, 10, 1826; Baton Rouge *Gazette*, February 2, 1827; Isaac L. Baker to Josiah S. Johnston, October 5, 1826, in Johnston Papers, HSP.

21. Alexander Porter to Josiah S. Johnston, January 27, August 30, 1827, in Johnston Papers, HSP.

to the stump vigorously, apparently oblivious to the fact that he had practically no following;[22] Derbigny announced in August of 1827, hoping to attract a strong French-American Adams vote because of his reputation for moderation in the ethnic question;[23] and finally, with a French New Orleanian like Marigny utterly impossible to support, Florida Jacksonians united behind Thomas Butler.[24]

Meanwhile, a host of contenders girded for battle over the state's three congressional seats in a campaign completely unlike that of 1826 in its clear linkage to the presidential preferences of the candidates. All three incumbents offered for reelection, Brent being opposed by General W. H. Overton and Charles T. Scott, Gurley by Lafayette Saunders, and Livingston by Edward Douglass White. Gurley felt reasonably safe, Saunders having only recently come to Louisiana, and Brent and Livingston seemed to share an optimistic sense of security. In the case of these last two, confidence blithely ignored the facts. The closeness of his relationship to Jackson and the intensity of his dedication to the General's cause aroused Overton's previously dormant adherents, concentrating opposition to Brent in a way which neither Brownson nor Bullard had been capable of in 1826. As for Livingston, he now had to contend with one of the most popular men in the state.[25]

The climactic campaign year of 1828 opened on a note of nervous excitation which would be sustained with hardly a break until the great presidential question reached resolution in November. Clay's printed defense against the revived bargain and corruption charges of the Jacksonians reached the state shortly after the New Year, sent on by Johnston and others, to meet with immediate and acerbic response.[26] It included sharp attacks upon Clay's critics, that by Brent couched in especially offensive language. The libels of Clay, he said, came from a frustrated group of fanatics, "headed by a military chief, without talents, and whose life is a history of

22. Henry A. Bullard to Josiah S. Johnston, October 23, 1825, ibid.; Louisiana Courier, June 15, 1827.

23. Alexander Porter to Josiah S. Johnston, August 30, 1827, in Johnston Papers, HSP; New Orleans Argus, August 22, 1827.

24. Baton Rouge Gazette, November 3, 17, 1827.

25. Louisiana Advertiser, February 5, April 8, 1828; Alexander Porter to Josiah S. Johnston, May 21, 1828, in Johnston Papers, HSP.

26. Henry A. Bullard to Josiah S. Johnston, January 10, 1828, in Johnston Papers, HSP.

immorality, bloodshed, and violation of the laws of God and of his country. . . . If Genl. Jackson does not establish his assertion (which he cannot), he ought to stand forth to the world, as a proven base calumniator, as unworthy of public or private confidence, and avoided by every man who has a respect for virtue and for Honor."[27]

So Brent had once again done violence to the Hero of New Orleans, and while Louisiana Jacksonians shook with rage, news from the east sent the Adams party, especially its French segment, into a temper of its own. This time the culprit was Livingston, who in addressing a Washington banquet on January 8 so praised Jackson's behavior in New Orleans in 1814–1815 as to seem insulting to the Louisiana French. On the same occasion, General Robert Desha of Tennessee toasted Livingston as the "first and only *Honor* in the Louisiana pack," who "though beaten in the Presidential game, by the *Knave* from that state . . . shall shine conspicuously, while the *Knave* 'will stand before the world as a proven base calumniator, unworthy of public or private confidence, and avoided by every man who has a respect for virtue and for honor.' "[28] Desha had thus thrown Brent's words "in his own teeth,"[29] with results that reverberated as far away as Louisiana itself.

Over and above all these flamboyant campaign dramatics, the Adams party recognized that their best hope of defeating Jackson lay in giving increasing and ever wider emphasis to the charge that his ungovernable temper, violent behavior, disdain for constitutional forms, and primitive ignorance of statecraft made him unsuitable for the office of president of the United States. It required little political insight to conclude that nothing better supported that representation than the supposed record of his behavior at New Orleans in 1814–1815. The Adams English-language press in the city had early on leaped to attack this vulnerability, led by John Gibson in the *Argus*, whose columns in July 1827 suggested that the next January 8 celebration should feature a great parade with banners portraying the constitution of the United States pierced by Jackson's sword, Judge Hall in prison, Louis Louaillier about to be shot, the Louisiana legislature driven

27. William L. Brent to [Tobias Watkins], June 4, 1827, Dominique Bouligny to Henry Clay, December 3, 1827, in Henry Clay Papers, LC.

28. New Orleans *Argus*, February 12, 20, May 3, 6, 1828; *Louisiana Advertiser*, February 13, 1828; *Louisiana Courier*, February 11, 1828.

29. Robert Desha to Andrew Jackson, January 21, 1828, in Jackson Papers, LC.

from its hall, flames consuming the city of New Orleans, and the six Tennessee militiamen once executed by Jackson's order being led to the firing
squad.[30]

The effectiveness of this kind of attack so alarmed Jackson's national
committee leadership that they cast about desperately for some design to
counteract its damaging impact. How better to strike back, the General's
chief strategist, William B. Lewis, finally decided, than to have Jackson return to the very scene of his supposed greatest crimes, there to give the lie
to the base charges against him, in the midst of a grateful populace who
knew the truth of his services and heroism. Out of that decision came a
well-crafted scenario which provided the climactic event of the 1828 campaign in the state.

In February 1827 the Louisiana legislature invited Jackson to be its guest
in New Orleans on January 8, 1828, to join in celebration of his great victory on the plains of Chalmette. It is not clear if this move had in some
fashion been engineered by Lewis or had simply been seized by him as a
most welcome vehicle for the carrying out of his plan to counter the repre-
sentations of Jackson as a violent misfit. In either case, it caught the Adams
forces in the state completely off guard.[31] When General Pierre Lacoste
proposed this gesture of respect in the state senate, Jackson's opponents
feared to resist the move, not wishing to appear spiteful or to drive voters
to the General out of a sense of sympathy. Nor did they wish to give the impression of being so unsure of their strength that they would tremble at his
presence in their capital. Relying on their control of the legislature, they
decided to join in the invitation, boast of their magnanimity, and then take
over the celebration themselves as proof that Jackson's visit could not be
understood as any mark of political favor or sign of overwhelming support
by the people of the state.[32] At this point the Jackson leaders committed a
tactical blunder which almost spoiled their victory. Overjoyed at the ease
of their success, they neglected to ask for any appropriation of state funds to
receive the General or meet his expenses. On record as having joined in
the invitation, the Adams men felt safe in rejecting all pleas for state
money, forcing the Jacksonians to rely upon popular subscription to raise

30. New Orleans *Argus*, July 18, 20, 1827.

31. *Louisiana Advertiser*, February 27, 1827; New Orleans *Argus*, March 10, 1827.

32. Alexander Porter to Josiah S. Johnston, January 9, 1828, in Johnston Papers, HSP;
New Orleans *Argus*, June 6, July 18, 1827.

the funds to support Jackson's visit. Martin Gordon took the lead in that effort, but the Jacksonians suffered additional humiliation when many amused Adams men offered to help and added their names to the subscription list.[33]

But at least the visit had been assured, for Jackson quickly sent word that only the "interposition of Divine Providence" would keep him away from the celebration,[34] and now plans could be laid to wring the utmost political propaganda out of the event. Everything centered on using the January 8 celebration to convince the United States that Jackson's enemies had maliciously misrepresented his character and falsified the record of his behavior, as would be proved by the outpouring of admiration and respect bestowed upon him by the grateful people of Louisiana. "It is the first time our Legislature have given you any testimony of good feeling," Isaac Baker wrote his old chief, "and it will at once prostrate the Demagogues who have hitherto stifled the feeling of Louisiana in your behalf. The effect through the Union would be such as would dispose all to feel grateful for your manifold Services." Apparently with total seriousness, Baker then assured the General that if the Adams partisans dared label his visit "politics" the indignation of the Union would overwhelm them.[35]

On December 13, 1827, the steamship *Pocahontas* left New Orleans and headed toward Nashville to take on board the honored guest of Louisiana. Fog and murky nights delayed her passage while William B. Lewis fretted in Tennessee, fearful of some slip-up which might make useless the long weeks of planning. The "importance of the occasion requires absolute certainty with regard to our movements," he advised Jackson, and proceeded to instruct the General in alternate plans to be followed should the *Pocahontas* fail her deadline.[36] But the official escort finally arrived. Sick and uncomfortable, Jackson nonetheless set forth on the journey, issuing determined orders that no stops be made en route except at Natchez, where the New Orleans committee would meet him, for he thought thus to escape enemy charges of electioneering.[37]

33. *Louisiana Courier*, June 23, 25, September 11, 1827, March 22, 31, 1828; New Orleans *Argus*, November 24, 28, 29, 1827.

34. Andrew Jackson to Henry Johnson, April 18, 1827, in Jackson Papers, LC.

35. Isaac L. Baker to Andrew Jackson, April 21, 1827, *ibid.*

36. William B. Lewis to Andrew Jackson, December 24, 1827, *ibid.*

37. Andrew Jackson to William B. Lewis, December 19, 25, 1827, in Lewis Papers, NYPL.

Meanwhile in New Orleans celebrants paraded Nashville-grown "Jackson Beef" through the city streets and offered elk meat as a special delicacy of the occasion. At daybreak on January 8 a three-gun salute from the official steamboat cortege announced Jackson's arrival three miles above the city, answered by twenty-four blasts from the guns at the Place d'Armes—the festivities had begun. They would last for four days, beginning with the long procession of the eighteen boats through the mist and fog down to the hallowed plains of Chalmette, where the General answered the long and flowery welcomes with a justification of his martial-law rule during the days then being celebrated and rejoiced in the reunion as a "deep testimony" refuting the calumnies aimed at destroying his good name.[38]

His words carried particular significance, for they spelled out what would remain his unchanging and defiant justification of his actions during the critical days of the 1815 campaign:

> When I review the measures then adopted, and the circumstances with which we were surrounded, I think now as I did then, that they were necessary for the preservation of the country: without them that country would have been sacrificed. The substance of law which ordinarily governs the actions of society, was then suspended by necessity, by the controlling principle of self-preservation, so far as the course of military operations extended. The whole scope of those operations, according to the genius of our invaluable institutions, had for its object the substantial support of this great principle; to have forborne in a case of unquestionable necessity would have resulted in a sacrifice of substance for form; constitution, laws, and all, would have been forever lost.[39]

Through the din of continuous salvos from Chalmette and the Place d'Armes, the party made its way back to New Orleans, landing at the levee fronting Marigny's estate, where Jackson marched ashore bareheaded to the acclaim of the throngs who massed along his way or hung dangling from windows, ship riggings, and roof tops. Père Antoine greeted him at the cathedral, where a choir intoned a "Te Deum" and the altar displayed a banner proclaiming VICTORIA A DEO ET JACKSON DATA. Cantatas, receptions, theatrical performances, balls, and banquets filled the four-day stay,

---

38. *Louisiana Advertiser*, December 29, 1827, January 8, 1828; *Louisiana Courier,* January 5, 7, 1828; Speech of Lucius C. Duncan at January 8, 1828, celebration in Jackson Papers, LC.

39. Jackson's Address to Citizens of New Orleans, January 8, 1828, Jackson Papers, LC.

until finally an exhausted General and his lady set out once again for the Hermitage.[40]

Behind them they left a city which for months would argue and debate the significance of his visit. From the conflicting reports it is impossible to reach any certain conclusion, for Adams observers all reported a coldness exhibited toward Jackson by all but those imported by the committee to swell the crowds and shout the huzzas, while just as unanimously Jacksonians rejoiced at the magnificent success of their venture. "On the very spot where you are charged with violating the Constitution," R. K. Call exulted to Jackson, "you have been hailed as its redeemer, and its champion."[41] To A. P. Hayne, everything "connected with the late wonderful celebration at New Orleans, now that it is over," appeared like a dream. "The World had never witnessed so glorious, so wonderful a celebration—never were *Gratitude & Patriotism* so happily united," he exclaimed in a congratulatory message to Jackson.[42]

Of all the commentaries on the celebration, none caused anything like the sensation produced by a series of articles sent to the New York *American* by that bitter critic of everything Jacksonian, Vincent Nolte. In a typically contemptuous vein, Nolte referred slurringly in these letters to various Jacksonian committeemen, calling one a "cabinet maker by trade," labeling another "*a successful bricklayer* alias architect," and heaping general ridicule on what he called sycophants trying to strut in the role of president-makers. His reports played right into the hands of Wagner, who jumped at this opportunity to resume his role as the great spokesman for social equality and respect for the workingman. Nolte's characterization of the Jacksonians as "low cartmen, dirty woodsawyers and contemptible bricklayers" provided the meat for endless columns in the *Advertiser*, which warned the "mechanics" and "all those who support themselves by the sweat of their brow to keep aloof from a faction, who, if they had the power, would convert them into hewers of wood and drawers of water for those spurious nobles of the land."[43] John Slidell demanded a public apology from Nolte, and when the latter refused, the friendship of the two men shattered. More fe-

40. *Louisiana Advertiser*, January 9, 14, 16, 21, 23, 1828; *Louisiana Courier*, January 10, 16, 18, 1828; New Orleans *Argus*, March 26, 1828.

41. R. K. Call to Andrew Jackson, March 11, 1828, in Jackson Papers, LC.

42. A. P. Hayne to Andrew Jackson, March 12, 1828, *ibid.*

43. Nolte, *Fifty Years in Both Hemispheres*, 345; *Louisiana Advertiser*, March 10, 1826. See also the *Advertiser*'s later discussions on March 12, May 26, June 5, 12, 28, 30, 1828.

rocious than Slidell, F. B. Ogden tried to kill Nolte in his home, but failed. As late as 1829, when the outspoken merchant made his last farewell to New Orleans, his friends guarded the way to his ship to prevent other attempts upon his life.[44]

The weeks between January and July of 1828 continued the rounds of ceaseless political activity. Shortly after Jackson's departure, his adherents assembled their state convention in New Orleans, where Ripley and others addressed themselves to the glorification of their cause while Marigny and Overton took on the more pragmatic task of committing the party to individual candidates in the congressional and gubernatorial races to avoid a scattering of their votes. But Scott's friends argued that this would be offensive to men who had remained loyal to the General for years, and the Florida delegates balked at giving up Butler for Marigny. The fiery creole believed his gubernatorial chances had been greatly enhanced by his prominence during Jackson's visit, when he had presided at the major banquet in the General's honor, but now he began to grumble that the Florida men would make Derbigny governor and give Adams the vote of the state.[45]

Jacksonian spirits lifted considerably in April, when Denis Prieur swept to an easy victory over Anathole Peychaud in the New Orleans mayoral race and seven of the ten council seats also fell to supporters of the General's cause.[46] The municipal election had been largely waged along Adams-Jackson lines, but the administration forces pretended to see no indication here of the real presidential preferences of the people. Many extraneous factors had indeed influenced the mayoral campaign, chief among them the great personal popularity of Prieur and the equally profound antagonism against Peychaud because of his foreign French birth.[47] For Wagner, aristocracy provided the key again. "It was diverting to see the arch smile on the face of the laboring mechanic," he wrote, "when rejecting with a dry sneer a ticket proffered to him by a hand never before extended to him in token of friendship or with the frankness of equality."[48]

As the July elections approached, political leaders over the nation

---

44. Nolte, *Fifty Years in Both Hemispheres*, 346–47.

45. John Erwin to Josiah S. Johnston, January 16, 1828, Alexander Porter to Johnston, January 24, 1828, in Johnston Papers, HSP; *Louisiana Advertiser*, February 5, 1828.

46. *Louisiana Courier*, April 8, 1828.

47. T. J. Pew to Josiah S. Johnston, May 31, 1828, in Johnston Papers, HSP; New Orleans *Argus*, April 9, 11, May 13, 1828.

48. *Louisiana Advertiser*, April 15, 1828.

turned their eyes to Louisiana for some glimmer of light which might indicate the trend of public favor, for these contests introduced what would be a steady progression of important electoral decisions throughout the country, climaxing with the great presidential choice itself. Edward Everett advised his brother as early as March to watch carefully for the outcome of this "most important event" in Louisiana,[49] Brent felt that the November decision in the state would be fixed by the results of the July canvass,[50] and Alexander Porter predicted that success of the Adams forces in the summer campaigns would greatly influence later elections in Kentucky.[51]

With so much at stake, New Orleans became tremendously agitated and tense as the political battles raged toward their climax, radiating much excitement to the rural parishes as well. In February, fire destroyed the state house and the Pontalba mansion in the heart of the city, leading to disturbing reports of a phantom incendiary plotting to put the whole town to the torch.[52] The following month a rumor of Henry Clay's death spread dismay everywhere, adding a pall of darkness to an already cloudy scene.[53] Then in June John Gibson flooded the community with the inflammatory "coffin hand bills" depicting Jackson as a murderer for his execution of several militiamen under his command during the late war. Tempers now reached the breaking point. Sheltered young ladies came close to exchanging blows while furiously debating the question of Jackson's character, and one writer in the Advertiser moaned that the "ordinary courtesies of society are trampled upon, and in every circle dividing lines are drawn— harmony and good understanding are banished; and in their place are introduced topics calculated only to exasperate and offend."[54]

The politicos, meanwhile, steeled themselves for exhausting last efforts. Thibodaux had died of an abscessed liver in October, leading to a scramble

49. Edward Everett to [Alexander Everett], March 15, 1828, in Edward Everett Papers, MHS.

50. William L. Brent to James G. Taliaferro, May 9, 1828, in James G. Taliaferro Papers, LSU.

51. Alexander Porter to Johnston, May 21, 1828, in Johnston Papers, HSP.

52. New Orleans Argus, February 4, 7, 9, 12, 1828.

53. Ibid., March 26, 1828.

54. Ibid., June 13, 1828; Louisiana Advertiser, June 11, August 23, 1828. Gibson publicly admitted the printing of the "coffin handbills." See New Orleans Argus, August 11, 1829. John Binns, Recollections of the Life of John Binns (Philadelphia, 1854), 246, describes the origins of these famous campaign items.

for his votes in which Derbigny came off much the best.[55] The foreign Frenchman's strength seemed to grow in proportion to the malignity of the campaign, for his determination to stand as a moderate between the extremists of both the Adams-Jackson and the French-American quarrels appealed to many Louisianians frightened by the intensity of the political storms disturbing the community. Despite his moderation, moreover, he clearly benefitted by being the only Adams man in the governor's race, while Jacksonian power still fragmented on the split between Butler and Marigny.[56] Not even the fever of fanatical Jacksonianism could prevail over old ethnic hatreds.

The congressional campaign presented contrasting studies in boundless exertion and comfortable indolence. Overton threw himself into his task with an energy even his friends found difficult to believe, while Brent remained listless at his post in Washington.[57] Much the same pattern prevailed in the Livingston-White contest, with the incumbent almost unbelievably careless of his own congressional future. Skillfully coached by Henry Johnson and Alexander Porter, White neglected his duties as city judge in New Orleans to conduct a lengthy tour of the Lafourche area, capitalizing on his old and steady friendships among the French population.[58] Livingston did nothing but urge Davezac and St. Romes to greater and greater efforts in the *Courier,* while he lolled in Washington and at Montgomery Place in New York, attentive only to his criminal code. He apparently felt that public recognition of his superiority over White made defeat by such a young upstart out of the question. A letter to his constituents in June announced his inability to return home for the elections because of the great press of his duties in Congress, and elaborated on his willingness to suffer such dangerous personal inconvenience for the good of those he represented. His references to White insultingly patronized and belittled his opponent, clearly implying that no person with sense could fail to understand the difference between his own genius and the shallow talents of

55. New Orleans *Argus,* October 29, 1827; George Eustis to Josiah S. Johnston, October 31, 1827, Alexander Porter to Johnston, December 8, 1827, in Johnston Papers, HSP.

56. George Eustis to Josiah S. Johnston, October 31, 1827, January 11, May 11, 1828, Alexander Porter to Johnston, December 8, 1827, James Hull to Johnston, June 3, 1828, Henry A. Bullard to Johnston, November 25, 1827, July 4, 1828, in Johnston Papers, HSP.

57. John H. Johnston to Josiah S. Johnston, August 6, 1828, *ibid.*

58. Alexander Porter to Josiah S. Johnston, April 16, May 21, 1828, *ibid.*

a city judge.[59] At almost the same moment, he sent a note to Jackson describing his leisurely life at his sister's home in Red Hook, New York, making not a single reference to the Louisiana campaigns. In the ease of his own optimistic security, he obviously cared little about the fate of his fellow Jacksonians at home.[60] But for the exertions of his relatives and the worried assistance of Wagner and Martin Gordon, Livingston would have had no campaign at all. As it was, the Jacksonian committees raised quite a clamor for the absent congressman, and it may well have been that Livingston relied on Wagner and Gordon not being able to abandon him in a campaign so vital to their own interests.[61] The Gurley-Saunders race presented problems of a wholly different character. Jacksonian strength clearly dominated in the Second District, but Saunders had so little personal appeal that even his friends made ready to concede his defeat.[62]

The July elections surpassed in excitement even the most exaggerated forecasts of the campaign. Confusion reigned from the opening of the polls, primarily because each side, with seemingly good cause, had come to believe absolutely that the other planned monstrous frauds to steal the election. As early as June the *Argus* charged the Jacksonians with buying large plots of ground which they then parceled out to their followers to qualify them as tax payers entitled to vote. The evasiveness of Wagner's denials convinced the Adams men that they had hit upon the truth,[63] and they made preparations of their own to prevent being swamped by what they called illegal voters. Two of the official election supervisors of Orleans Parish, Judges Preval and Pitot, nominally politically neutral, agreed to step down from their positions as commissioners, forcing the other eligible judges in the parish to serve in their place. But one of these was White, who clearly could not function in such a capacity, being himself a candidate. Governor Johnson hurriedly dispatched Derbigny to Donaldsonville to receive White's resignation, meanwhile signing an appointment for Felix

59. *Louisiana Advertiser*, June 19, 1828; *Louisiana Courier*, June 3, 1828.

60. Edward Livingston to Andrew Jackson, June 20, 1828, in Jackson Papers, LC.

61. Alexander Porter to Josiah S. Johnston, June 27, 1828, in Johnston Papers, HSP; *Louisiana Advertiser*, January 28, February 1, May 10, 19, 21, June 21, 23, 30, July 4, 1828; *Louisiana Courier*, June 3, 21, 23, 24, 26, 28, 1828; New Orleans *Argus*, February 12, 28, May 3, 6, 7, June 30, 1828.

62. Alexander Porter to Josiah S. Johnston, June 27, 1828, in Johnston Papers, HSP.

63. New Orleans *Argus*, June 7, 1828; *Louisiana Advertiser*, June 10, 1828.

Grima to fill White's place on the bench and round out the three-man election board. In the process he had guaranteed a pro-Adams majority on the
panel of election judges, for Grima was not only a supporter of the president but a brother-in-law of Mazureau.

The plan soon took on clearer shape. No longer attorney general, Mazureau nonetheless commanded great respect as a legal authority, and his
insistence persuaded the judges to disregard the tax rolls for 1828, declaring
them invalid for having been made up by assessors appointed after the date
stipulated by law. This meant, he argued, that the 1827 rolls must be used,
which would result in the exclusion from the polls of the newly propertied
Jacksonians, who naturally did not appear on the 1827 list. With the Mazureau opinion as their guide, the two pro-Adams election judges prepared
to face the opposition.[64]

For the full three days of the election the Jacksonians performed near
miracles to get their supporters to the polls. Twenty hacks and carriages
coursed through the city streets, carrying the faithful to the voting site and
trailing banners of blue silk blazoned with the motto, JACKSON AND THE
PEOPLE. But at the polls the Adams judges held fast, refusing to accept some
two hundred persons as legitimate voters. Slidell and Grymes protested
each unfavorable decision with all the vigor they could command, though
each felt near death from the Spanish dengue fever ravaging the city, a disease not fatal but so painful as to incapacitate its victims for weeks.

The Jacksonians had not come to all this with entirely clean hands.
They relied essentially upon the unfinished state of the 1828 tax lists, hoping to push as many of their partisans through to the polls as possible,
whether legitimate taxpayers or not. Many of the rejected clearly belonged
to this class, and it would have been almost impossible for the election
judges to have successfully denied the ballot to two hundred legitimate voters.[65] Outside the city, as always, a greater decorum prevailed, though passions could run high, as they did in Donaldsonville, where S. J. Tournillon,
stepfather of the Trists, almost came to blows with E. D. White after reading a fiery pro-Livingston appeal in his presence.[66]

64. *Louisiana Advertiser*, July 7, 12, 15, August 21, 1828; New Orleans *Argus*, July 14,
August 23, 1828.

65. *Louisiana Advertiser*, July 15, 1828; New Orleans *Argus*, July 9, August 29, 1828;
Richard Davidson to William S. Hamilton, August 15, 1827, in Hamilton Papers, LSU.

66. H. B. Trist to Nicholas P. Trist, August 20, 1828, in Trist Papers, LC.

The results gave the Adams forces an overwhelming victory. Derbigny piled up such a vote over Butler and Marigny that his total exceeded their combined tally, leaving the disappointed creole humiliated and angered by his poor third-place showing.[67] Marigny's old hatred of the Florida section flared anew, for he thought himself betrayed by their support of Butler. "Je me vengerai en Novembre," he muttered to his friends in dark threats to abandon the Jacksonian cause itself, if that might allow him the pleasure of striking back at those who had once again thwarted his greatest ambition.[68] Old General Thomas, supposedly neutral to the end, finished last in the race.

The Jacksonians suffered staggering losses in the New Orleans legislative delegation as well, every seat going to the opposition, and only the solid support received in the Floridas prevented their being completely eclipsed in the assembly. Statewide, they managed to win six of the seventeen senate seats and twenty-one of the fifty in the house, with three of the members of that body being of uncertain party affiliation.[69]

Of the three Jacksonian congressional candidates, only W. H. Overton had been successful, in a victory largely attributable to William Brent's continued absence from the state. With the sale of his Louisiana lands shortly before the campaign, Brent became virtually a nonresident, loathed by the Jacksonians because of his violent attacks upon the General and detested personally by most of the men of his own party because of his slanders against Josiah Johnston.[70] As had been expected, Henry Gurley edged out Lafayette Saunders, though by a mere thirty votes, for despite his newness in Louisiana the young challenger profited from a large party following.[71] Edward D. White won the campaign's most decisive victory by capturing every parish but one in the district, polling 1,780 votes to Livingston's 1,173. The incumbent lost even his base in New Orleans, compelling proof of the collapse of his once strong creole support.[72] Sectional and eth-

67. *Louisiana House Journal*, 1828, p. 5.

68. John H. Johnston to Josiah S. Johnston, August 6, 1828, in Johnston Papers, HSP.

69. New Orleans *Argus*, July 29, 1828.

70. John H. Johnston to Josiah S. Johnston, August 6, 1828, in Johnston Papers, HSP; Josiah Baker to Nicholas P. Trist, July 26, 1828, in Trist Papers, LC.

71. Lafayette Saunders to Andrew Jackson, July 18, 1828, in Jackson Papers, LC.

72. Alexander Porter to Josiah Johnston, March 7, July 19, 1828, in Johnston Papers, HSP.

nic hatreds, together with the indolence of Livingston, had pretty well done the Jacksonians in.

With resounding cheers and editorial bombast, the preponderance of Adams supporters celebrated their splendid victory as a sure harbinger of repeated success in the November presidential elections. Some, however, cautioned against misplaced confidence. Happy at the success of his friends, Porter nonetheless warned Johnston that the July vote "must not be understood *by you* as indicative of the sentiments of the state on the Presidential election. Not a single one of our elections turned exclusively on it."[73] But it was clearly good politics to impress the opposite opinion upon observers in other parts of the nation, and the Adams press did its best, with some effect. Henry Lee, one of the General's trusted publicists, wrote to Jackson from New York that the "defeat of Mr. Livingston and the failure of our ticket in La. produced an unpleasant thrill in this quarter."[74] Even more upset, James A. Hamilton, son of the great treasury secretary, shared his anger with Van Buren in a note which revealed at least some insight into the Louisiana campaigns: "That creole Mongrel Louisiana has again stuck the fang of her ingratitude in the sides of her Benefactor by the late administration Triumph in that State. As it respects Livingston he almost deserves his fate, for his neglect of his Constituents & apathy to his own interests. There is always a Lion in the path to the Sluggard. It is what I expected & the result does not surprise me."[75]

Eventually, however, indignant complaints that the election had been stolen by the corrupt practices of the Adams men restored some confidence to Jackson's followers.[76] They still had November in which to redeem their cause. By August the recent defeat seemed important only as an object lesson highlighting their own errors. Baker repeatedly pushed W. S. Hamilton to greater efforts in the Floridas, the urgency of his language reflecting the new determination of the party: "Something must be done to counteract the plans of H. Johnson, Duralde & Co. for giving the vote of the State to Adams. . . . we are not organized. . . . You, Dawson, Butler, Hickey & Law-

73. Alexander Porter to Josiah S. Johnston, July 27, 1828, *ibid.*

74. Henry Lee to Andrew Jackson, August 13, 1828, in Jackson Papers, LC.

75. James Hamilton to Martin Van Buren, July 31, 1828, in Martin Van Buren Papers, LC.

76. Lafayette Saunders to Andrew Jackson, July 18, 1828, Edward Livingston to Jackson, August 12, 1828, Henry Lee to Jackson, August 15, 1828, in Jackson Papers, LC.

rence in the West [of the Floridas] must communicate often with Moore, Morgan, Goff, Penn, etc. in the East."[77] Moved by the same spirit, Ripley and Hennen spent most of their summer in active campaigning, while some of their imaginative colleagues busied themselves in mailing pamphlets to their neighbors bearing what purported to be the personal greetings of Jackson himself.[78]

Despite the warnings of Porter and others, overconfidence generated by their July successes almost drained the Adams party of energy during the last critical weeks of the campaign. Still primarily concerned with local elections, the French in the interior parishes simply relaxed after the great summer victory, to the dismay of the administration men who recognized them as the principal strength of the Adams party in the state.[79] "The struggle here will be fierce," an obviously distraught Porter advised Johnston. "The Jackson party," he lamented, "are more active than ever, and certainly if ever zeal and devotion merited success, theirs deserve it. Were it not for *one* or *two* persons in this state I know not what would become of the administration here."[80] Even the carefully chosen T. J. Pew, Johnston's protégé as editor of the *Mercantile Advertiser* from whom so much had been expected, abandoned his post for a private trip which took him away from his paper for several months through the whole climax of the November canvass.[81]

Long before the day of decision arrived, the Jacksonian press mounted an intensive campaign urging its followers to verify their enrollment on the finally completed 1828 tax list to prevent a repetition of the July exclusions.[82] With Denis Prieur and the county sheriff on their side, they hoped this time to dominate the polls themselves. Their efforts redoubled with receipt early in November of the news of Jackson's great victory in Pennsylvania, which voted before Louisiana, and in a moment they covered the city with handbills announcing the tidings. Isaac Preston delivered one of his rousing speeches at a great party rally the following night, urging his fel-

77. Isaac L. Baker to William S. Hamilton, August 10, 1828, in Hamilton Papers, LSU.

78. New Orleans *Argus*, October 22, 1828; *Louisiana Journal*, October 4, 1828.

79. For an analysis of this support, see Alexander Porter to Josiah S. Johnston, April 16, June 27, July 27, in Johnston Papers, HSP.

80. Alexander Porter to Josiah S. Johnston, September 20, 1828, *ibid.*

81. T. J. Pew to Josiah S. Johnston, November 29, 1828, *ibid.*

82. *Louisiana Courier*, October 13, 1828.

low Louisianians to climb aboard the General's bandwagon, and for the next few days Wagner ran in review the whole argument which he and his colleagues had developed over the months in favor of the Hero of New Orleans. With a final effort he pleaded, "Louisianians! remember that Andrew Jackson is a man of the South, a slave holder, a cotton planter."[83] Belatedly, the Adams forces began to bestir themselves anew, with George Eustis presiding over a great administration meeting on the eve of the election and Gibson's *Argus* reciting once again the old and familiar sins attributed to the General.[84]

This time, victory belonged to the Hero of New Orleans. Sloughing off the indolence which had threatened them, the Adams camp brought its full force into the field, polling even more votes than they had won in the July canvass, and this despite the pressures of the rolling season which made so many demands on the time of sugar planters. But the Jacksonians had done their work even better since that summer defeat. Hundreds of additional voters now made their way to the polls, many newly enfranchised by the purchase of simple vehicle licenses made possible by party support, while the northern cotton parishes spilled forth other hundreds who had remained inert in the gubernatorial campaign. With Prieur and his cooperative sheriff controlling the polls in the capital, it was the Adams men who this time found difficulty in reaching the voting booth.[85]

Jackson carried all of Florida and every parish north of Red River save Avoyelles, plus Orleans, Iberville, West Baton Rouge, Lafayette, and Pointe Coupee. Adams won every major sugar parish except Iberville, but his popular vote of 4,076 fell short of Jackson's 4,603. Within the sugar parishes, predominantly Gallic in population, it would be difficult to single out the factor which most attracted them to Adams. No doubt a combination of factors swayed their vote—Duralde and the tariff had meant Clay and Adams. New Orleans had broken almost down the middle, 747 to 665 in favor of Jackson, while the heavily American cotton sector to the north had given an overwhelming preponderance to the victor.[86]

"I am almost mad with joy," an old friend of the General proclaimed in

83. *Ibid.*, November 1, 3, 1828; New Orleans *Argus*, November 1, 1828; *Louisiana Advertiser*, November 4, 1828.

84. New Orleans *Argus*, November 4, 1828.

85. *Ibid.*, November 4, 5, 6, 1828; *Louisiana Advertiser*, November 7, 1828.

86. *Louisiana Courier*, November 25, 1828; Tregle, "Louisiana and the Tariff," 30–31.

a hastily scrawled note informing Jackson that Louisiana had at last paid its debt of gratitude. "I thank God," he rejoiced, "that I have lived to see the downfall of the Yanky Dynasty!"[87] In the Floridas, cotton planters and "resin heels" joined in singing:

> To establish a monarchy was Johnny Q's intentions
> Whilst Clay as premier, was to serve the lads with pensions,
> Who could best defame our Hero by some unfounded tale
> Or, in supporting aristocracy; pen or tongue did never fail.
> Huzza, huzza, huzza, huzza, huzza!
> By unity like free-born men, we have won the day![88]

The Age of Jackson had begun.

---

87. David C. Ker to Andrew Jackson, November 6, 11, 1828, in Jackson Papers, LC.
88. St. Francisville *Crisis*, November 22, 1828.

· X ·

DEMOCRACY REGNANT

Now let our side come in—or let us never *labor* as I have labored!" an exuberant Louisiana Jacksonian exclaimed as he greeted the beginning of Old Hickory's tenure in the White House.[1] That frank expression of expectation mirrored a sentiment common to many in the Jacksonian fold anxious to enjoy the fruits of their momentous triumph. They gave little time now to talk of principle or usurpers and even less to an old pledge by Wagner that "Jackson has too much greatness of soul to imitate the poor, vindictive policy of Mr. Clay, in removing people from office because they differ from him in opinion."[2]

Instead, they joined the Jackson press in support of what they called the "doctrine of reform," urging the new president to effect the "complete political purgation" demanded by the people in the great victory of 1828. The Adams-Clay regime had polluted government service with corrupt and irresponsible men, ran the new theme, and Jackson must now be given the freedom to wipe away this ugliness from the American scene. Moreover, said Archibald Haralson of St. Francisville's *Florida Gazette*, the "President is the only person to judge of the means (provided always that they be constitutional) by which such an end is to be accomplished." Nor should the people ever complain, "for it is for their benefit that the act is done."[3] True to his preachments, Haralson did his best to aid reform by finding some fed-

1. William Haile to William S. Hamilton, May 20, 1829, in Hamilton Papers, LSU.
2. *Louisiana Advertiser*, March 26, 1827.
3. *Florida Gazette* (St. Francisville), June 27, 1829.

eral job in which he might himself replace an enemy to republicanism, for after many years service to the Jacksonian cause, as he wrote his friend Thomas Butler, "My mouth is yet open."[4]

Many mouths opened in Louisiana when Jackson finally defeated Adams in the 1828 campaign, insistently seeking to be filled. Edward Livingston figured prominently among them, for it must have been galling to find himself turned out of office almost at the very moment of the General's triumph. He denied any great disappointment at his loss to White, but a note to Jackson shortly after that melancholy affair in July clearly meant to work on the sympathies of his old chief. Should the General be elected in November, it plainly implied, Livingston would be grateful to be remembered in the obscurity of his Louisiana surroundings, from which, he sighed, it might have been better never to have emerged.[5]

His conduct during the presidential campaign actually gave him small claim on Jackson's gratitude. He had, in truth, essentially ignored the contest altogether, enjoying leisurely days at his sister's home during the fall of 1827, "quietly employed in preparing systems that will most probably never pass whoever may be president," while "you politicians," he wrote Johnston, "are exercising your electioneering talents."[6] In August of 1828, he did give a speech at Harrisburg, Pennsylvania, supporting the General, but only because his private professional duties required his presence in that city to check into an involved inheritance case.[7] Otherwise he confined his activities to speculations concerning New York affairs and to general advice sent on for Jackson's consideration. He contributed no more to the national victory than he had to the one in Louisiana, and that was very little indeed.[8]

Jackson's success in November, however, stimulated Livingston to a new burst of energy. Upon confirmation of Jackson's election he immediately set out for Louisiana to exploit the newfound power of his party, anxious to

4. Archibald Haralson to Thomas Butler, December 29, 1828, in Thomas Butler Papers, LSU.

5. Edward Livingston to Andrew Jackson, August 12, 1828, in Jackson Papers, LC.

6. Edward Livingston to Josiah S. Johnston, October 22, 1827, in Johnston Papers, HSP.

7. *Louisiana Advertiser*, November 6, 1828.

8. The claim of his biographer that Livingston was a major force in both these campaigns is insupportable in fact. Unfortunately, this glorification of Livingston permeates Hatcher's work. See his *Livingston*, 316, 218, 219.

win the United States Senate seat held by Dominique Bouligny, whose term was soon due to expire. Intent upon reaching New Orleans before the legislature balloted in January of 1829, he stopped nowhere en route except at the Hermitage, where his short visit aroused conjectures that Jackson had chosen him to be the next secretary of state.[9] Ripley and others of his friends at home snapped up these rumors as a compelling reason for Louisiana Jacksonians to unite behind him for the Senate. Only then would the repudiation of July be cleared from his record, thus justifying Jackson in granting whatever place he might deign to bestow.[10]

The thing would require some doing, however, for the Louisiana legislature unquestionably remained under the control of the Clay faction. Both the *Advertiser* and the *Courier* jumped to build up a great noise for the returning Livingston, charting his journey homeward every day, until finally a sumptuous dinner at Davis's Ball Room welcomed him back to New Orleans. Excusing his absence from Washington as a service to many constituents who required his presence in the city to advise them on a vital legal problem, Livingston launched into one of the strangest political speeches of the new era, in effect declaring himself the only man capable of representing the state properly in the Senate. With a grateful nod to Gordon, he pledged his best efforts to get the United States to purchase the Orleans Navigation Company, "at a modest price."[11] Trying to help, Jacksonian members of the legislature attempted to cut the Clay faction's strength in the assembly by challenging the legitimacy of the New Orleans house delegation because of alleged fraud in the July elections, but the move got nowhere.[12]

Only a miracle could make Livingston a United States senator, Alexander Porter had once said, confident of the anti-Jacksonian strength in the assembly.[13] He had not reckoned with Henry Johnson. That glutton for office stepped down from the governorship in November 1828, and apparently feeling that Bouligny had simply been warming his Senate seat until

9. Gulian C. Verplanck to Martin Van Buren, December 6, 1828, in Van Buren Papers, LC; Edward Everett to Alexander Everett, December 15, 1828, in Edward Everett Papers, MHS.

10. Archibald Haralson to Thomas Butler, December 29, 1828, in Butler Papers, LSU.

11. *Louisiana Courier*, December 9, 11, 22, 1828; *Louisiana Advertiser*, December 6, 8, 9, 16, 22, 1828, January 12, 19, 1829.

12. New Orleans *Argus*, December 2, 8, 1828.

13. Alexander Porter to Josiah S. Johnston, July 27, 1828, in Johnston Papers, HSP.

his return, promptly announced for the latter's place. As the January election approached, the two rivals agreed to unite behind whichever of them won the higher vote on the legislature's first ballot, but when that proved to be Bouligny, Johnson brazenly refused to honor his pledge and remained in the race. Bouligny's outraged supporters threw their votes to Livingston out of sheer hatred for the ex-governor, giving him the senatorial seat and leaving a bewildered Henry A. Bullard to exclaim, "I have this day seen the most singular election ever known in the state."[14]

Livingston was not the only one who scrambled for place in the new regime. Hardly a week after the election, David C. Ker wrote the General demanding the dismissal of Beverly Chew as collector of customs at New Orleans. Chew, it seems, had committed the unpardonable crime of opposing the president-elect, with a commitment "so virulent," Ker swore, "as even to refuse permission to us to hoist a flag on the church [of which he was a vestryman] or to have the bells rung on the 8th of January in honor of the day—because they could not celebrate that glorious victory without honoring also the Chief who atchieved it. . . . An early example ought to be made of this man." Ker and Gordon had a ready suggestion for Chew's successor—Gordon himself. By late 1828 the Virginian clearly stood out as one of the major figures in the Louisiana Jackson party, in large measure because of wealth accumulated through the hated Orleans Navigation Company. Wagner and the *Advertiser* jumped to his command; Livingston respected and feared his strength and money; Grymes, Preston, Ripley, and Slidell courted his favor. Now he sought truly commanding dominance by winning the collector's office, for as Ker pointed out to Jackson, the man who held that position could "wield at will the whole mercantile body" of New Orleans and go far toward establishing himself as the political boss of the community.[15] He had read Gordon's designs perfectly.

Unlike most leading Jacksonians in the state, Gordon could not claim a long or intimate relationship to the General, nor had he fought under him at Chalmette, for at the time of the Battle of New Orleans he had prudently retired to safer precincts of the Union.[16] It was not until late 1827,

14. Henry A. Bullard to Josiah S. Johnston, January 12, 1829, John Erwin to Johnston, January 12, 1829, Alexander Porter to Johnston, January 13, 1829, *ibid.*

15. David C. Ker to Andrew Jackson, November 15, 1828, in Jackson Papers, LC.

16. *Louisiana Courier*, October 22, 1831.

when he headed the committee planning Jackson's campaign trip to New Orleans, that Gordon actually traveled to Nashville to meet the old warrior, carrying with him a letter of introduction from Grymes.[17] Now again in December 1828 he set out for Washington with a double purpose in mind—to sell his Orleans Navigation Company to the government and to get the promise of Chew's job.[18]

His trip proved profitable indeed. By the time of his return to New Orleans in March 1829, Jackson had been inaugurated and the first federal appointments in Louisiana announced. They included two which Gordon had promoted, placing John Slidell in the United States attorney's post for the eastern district of Louisiana and John Nicholson in the office of United States marshal. Gordon strutted among his friends, proudly describing the intimacy of his contacts with the president while in Washington despite the crush of office seekers penning in the old man, and carefully cultivating the impression that national governmental patronage must now be sought only through him.[19]

In May his own appointment as collector verified those claims, reinforced shortly thereafter by the naming of Wagner as naval officer, Ker as postmaster, Preston as register of the land office, W. L. Robeson as receiver of public moneys, James McFarlane as surgeon of the United States marine hospital, and S. H. Harper as judge of the eastern district court, all of them members of Gordon's circle, if not altogether beholden to him.[20]

Such examples of so-called reform brought quick and angry response. The Louisiana French seethed at the dismissal of Cruzat and Dupuy from the jobs now given to Wagner and Ker, especially since the list of new appointments included not a single creole,[21] while the unblushing political

17. John R. Grymes to Andrew Jackson, November 3, 1827, in Jackson Papers, LC.

18. Alexander Porter to Josiah S. Johnston, December 4, 1828, D. B. Morgan to Johnston, February 6, 1829, in Johnston Papers, HSP.

19. Martin Gordon and Edward Livingston to Andrew Jackson, [January ?], 1829 (John Slidell file), Alfred Hennen to Lafayette Saunders, February 2, 1829 (Saunders file), Letters of Application and Recommendation During the Administration of Andrew Jackson, 1829–1837, in RG 59, GRDS, NA; Joseph Saul to Andrew Jackson, March 31, 1829, in Jackson Papers, LC.

20. *Louisiana Courier*, May 13, 1829; *Louisiana Advertiser*, March 30, 1829.

21. New Orleans *Argus*, May 20, 1829; W. C. C. Claiborne to Henry Clay, June 5, 1829, in Henry Clay Papers, LC.

proscription applied against Chew and other Adams sympathizers gave even some Jacksonians uneasy pause.[22] Outraged friends convened a great public meeting to protest the removal of Chew, who had served as collector for eleven years and won praise as a "popular man and a good officer" even from such an avid Jacksonian as Lafayette Saunders.[23] Irritated by the fuss, the Jacksonians staged a gathering of their own a few nights later, where they reaffirmed the party doctrine of reform in resolutions which defended the recent dismissals as necessary because the enemies of Jackson had used patronage to prevent his coming into office, "without any regard to the decorum of official station, and in defiance of public opinion." They hailed Gordon as a "man of the people," once a "mechanic," who "had lent his body as a rampart to Jackson [while] the bullets whistled about his ears" at the Battle of New Orleans, though most people knew full well that he had been in Cincinnati on that great occasion.[24]

Responding to the loud clamor over removals, the Jacksonians dismissed much of the noise as proceeding from the camp of Clay partisans always ready to "lay hold of everything to excite opposition to the present administration."[25] But however much this might have convinced the general public, it did little to assuage mounting resentment against Gordon among powerful forces within the party itself. For the new list of appointments was barren not only of creoles but of Florida Jacksonians as well. Haralson's mouth, together with those of many of his colleagues, remained still open, a disturbing fact which John B. Dawson brought quickly to the president's attention. "There is a voice from Florida," he wrote the General, "that whispers to you, that thus far you have overlooked her, and believe me sir, 'twas Florida that [gave] you this State. The noisy clamours of

22. New Orleans *Argus*, May 5, 1829, February 6, 1829, D. B. Morgan to Josiah S. Johnston, November 15, 28, 1829, in Johnston Papers; Dorothy C. Barck, ed., *Letters from John Pintard to His Daughter* (4 vols.; New York, 1940), III, 81.

23. New Orleans *Argus*, May 16, 19, 1829; *Louisiana Courier*, May 16, 1829; Lafayette Saunders to Martin Van Buren, May 8, 1829 (Beverly Chew file), Letters of Application and Recommendation During the Administration of Andrew Jackson, 1829–1837, in RG 59, GRDS, NA.

24. *Louisiana Advertiser*, May 16, 18, 20, 1829; New Orleans *Argus*, May 20, 21, 1829; *Louisiana Courier*, May 20, 1829.

25. Archibald Haralson to Andrew J. Donelson, August 18, 1829 (Haralson file), Letters of Application and Recommendation During the Administration of Andrew Jackson, 1829–1837, in RG 59, GRDS, NA.

New Orleans may have told better abroad, but it was the silent work of modest and noiseless Patriotism in Florida that gave us victory."[26]

Complaints of neglect in the Floridas became so pervasive that the *Political Gridiron* of East Feliciana, fearful of party disunity, felt compelled to warn against reading anything significant into what it called the carping criticism of men who had little claim upon the president, but such an obvious gloss hardly sufficed to hide the truth.[27] Gordon's treatment of Col. William S. Hamilton, one of the General's most loyal and effective supports from the very beginning of his political career, gave disturbing evidence of his determination to control everything Jacksonian within the state. Already grooming Ripley for Congress, the collector now moved to shift him back to the Floridas as the agent of the New Orleans clique in that strongly Jacksonian area. The success of this venture required removal of Hamilton from the scene, and Ripley urged the colonel to accept Gordon's offer of aid in acquiring the post of federal surveyor general for the territory south of Tennessee. Knowing Hamilton's reluctance to assume an office located outside the state, Ripley pledged to have the surveyor's headquarters moved to Baton Rouge. But he advised Hamilton not to delay acceptance of the appointment, even if it meant settling in Mississippi while awaiting transfer of the post to Louisiana. The cautious Hamilton, however, declined to be trapped. He refused to accept the appointment without proof of its being shifted to Baton Rouge and finally determined that Ripley and Gordon had in fact made no attempt to relocate the office. Recognizing finally that the plan had simply been a device to get him out of the state and open a clear avenue to Congress for Ripley, the enraged Hamilton declined the post and sent off a biting report of the devious scheme to Jackson and his old schoolmate, John Eaton, loaded with venom against the "cold, selfish, and cunning" Yankee who had set to work "like a Burr or a Clay to manage and to master."[28] Clearly, Gordon meant to rule or ruin. With such a break in the Jacksonian ranks as early as 1829, the latter possibility seemed real indeed.

26. John B. Dawson to Andrew Jackson, May 26, 1829, *ibid.*
27. Quoted in New Orleans *Argus*, July 28, 1829.
28. Eleazar Ripley to William S. Hamilton, May 21, September 7, 1829, Alexander Barrow to Hamilton, October 28, 1829, Hamilton to J. P. Turner, November 25, 1829, Hamilton to Andrew Jackson, November 5, 1829 [rough draft]; Hamilton to George M. Graham, December 11, 1829, in Hamilton Papers, LSU.

Meanwhile, the New Orleans Jacksonians luxuriated in their newfound ascendancy. With Prieur in the mayor's office and a majority of their adherents on the municipal council, they began to build an effective distribution of city patronage through contracts and control of the police force.[29] For his part, Gordon swept the collector's office clean of old appointees, replaced them with minions of his own,[30] and then turned to plague the secretary of the treasury with incessant demands that he be allowed to expand his staff. He insisted on an additional deputy collector; argued the necessity of appointing full-time inspectors year-round rather than only in the busy season; and urged the hiring of a corps of special watchers for the ships in port. An exasperated Secretary Ingham finally gave way to anger, bluntly informing Gordon that "I regret to be obliged to resist in this as in many other cases the incessant importunity for patronage; but it is indispensable that it should be understood from this place that offices are not made for the incumbents, but for the public." Unabashed, Gordon continued his badgering until Ingham ended the exchange by going directly to Jackson, whose threats to "apply the Correction" finally brought the collector to heel.[31]

Frustrations of this kind may well explain the collector's response to the visit of Anne Royall in his offices at just about the time of Ingham's rebuke. That roaming virago answered his blunt query as to her business with an equally blunt rejoinder that she had called to see how he was conducting his affairs. "No wild beast caught in a trap, looked more astonished," she later remarked, "and wrinkling his skinny face without speaking a word he stalked back again" to his desk.[32]

Far away in Washington, ensconced now in new senatorial dignity, Livingston had greater opportunities than ever before to realize the perquisites of office. Davezac he provided for with an appointment to assist William Pitt Preble in the discussions of the Maine border at the Hague,[33] and then

29. New Orleans *Argus*, May 25, 26, 27, 28, 29, 30, July 3, 18, October 1, 1829.

30. *Louisiana Courier*, June 6, 1829.

31. S. D. Ingham to Martin Gordon, October 28, November 12, December 21, 1829, February 12, March 19, 1830, Letter Books of Secretary's Correspondence with Collectors of Small Ports, in RG 56, GRDT, NA.

32. Royall, *Southern Tour*, III, 32.

33. Edward Livingston to Andrew J. Donelson, April 19, 1829, in Donelson Papers, LC; William P. Preble to Martin Van Buren, July 6, 1829, Preble to Andrew Jackson, January 17, 1831 in Van Buren Papers, LC.

for a time seriously considered accepting Jackson's offer to become minister to France. In a "long and gloomy" interview with Martin Van Buren in Philadelphia early in the new president's term, however, he gave the secretary of state to understand that he and his wife could not accept such a post while there remained any possibility that the Jackson administration would be so primitive in its "social phases" as to "lead to degradation and contempt in the eyes of foreigners and of good society in general." Van Buren took this to mean that the Livingstons foresaw the "probability that they would be the persons most exposed to annoyances at a foreign court, from any scandal that might obtain circulation upon that point." In May, Livingston declined the position, pleading the press of financial problems, but only a few days later he gave every indication of having changed his mind. By then it was too late. The post had gone to W. C. Rives of Virginia, much to Van Buren's satisfaction, for he had expressed definite opposition to Livingston from the beginning.[34] For the Louisianian it meant resigning himself to life as a United States senator.

At least this elevated position gave him his best chance to end at last the twenty-five-year-old judgment still pending against him in the New York federal courts. That tangled problem had not been simplified by his activities in New Orleans, becoming even more complicated as a consequence of its eventual connection to the intricate complexities of the batture controversy. By 1820 Livingston had won clear title to a major part of that extremely valuable property along the Faubourg Ste. Marie levee by compromise with the city of New Orleans and the "front proprietors" behind the embankment, but the United States in 1822 recorded its claim of $100,014.89 against him in the Louisiana federal courts and seized his batture lots to satisfy his government debt. Finally sold at auction, they left an unpaid balance against him of $9,511.47, a sum that the resourceful senator now sought to escape paying.

His reputation as a lawyer had not been won for nothing. He knew that certain of the seized lots had been released from the government lien by the federal attorney in order that they might be sold prior to the general auction to pay the cost of filling in the property as required by city ordinance. When this lifting of the lien on these few units had been announced, however, his private creditors won seizure of them in the state courts, resulting

34. John C. Fitzpatrick, ed., *The Autobiography of Martin Van Buren. Annual Report of the American Historical Association for the Year 1918*, Vol. II (Washington, D.C., 1920), 229, 251–52, 259; Hamilton, *Reminiscences*, 138.

in a judgment ordering their sale to meet his local debts. Almost immediately the state supreme court reversed that judgment, but because no steps had been taken to stay the order of the sale, the lots passed into the hands of private buyers purchasing under affirmed clear title guaranteed by the state recorder of mortgages.[35]

There the matter stood until March 1829, when Livingston became a United States senator, John Slidell assumed office as federal attorney in New Orleans, and Samuel H. Harper donned his robes as judge of the eastern district court. Jacksonians all, they had little cause to complain of any inequities in distribution of the patronage. Slidell had a particularly close connection to Livingston, for the latter had carried his recommendations for the federal attorney's job to Washington in January and had been the first to inform him of his appointment. Now Livingston asked for help. Responding to his requests, Slidell brought suit against the purchaser of one of the lots sold by state court order, demanding payment of the $9,511.47 still outstanding against the senator. He argued that because the lifting of the lien was irregular, the property purchased by Daniel T. Walden remained subject to the United States claim upon Livingston, and although Walden had bought it with clear title from the state, Harper decided he must pay the amount demanded or surrender his lot to the government. Overruled even in his attempts to make Livingston at least a party to the suit, Walden finally capitulated and paid the $9,511.47. Proud of such success in one of his first ventures, Slidell hurried to inform the treasury department that this "finally disposes of the judgment against Mr. Livingston."[36] He also had paid his debt.

On October 6, 1829, Governor Derbigny died of injuries sustained a few days earlier when bolting horses had flung him from his carriage, plunging

35. *United States v. Daniel T. Walden*, Records of the Eastern District Court of Louisiana, Case #2670, 1829, FRC; John Slidell to Stephen Pleasanton, May 6, 1830, in John Slidell Letter Book, TU; Sale to Daniel T. Walden, in Record Book 1, Conveyance Office, Parish of Orleans, 480.

36. *United States v. Daniel T. Walden*, Records of the Eastern District Court of Louisiana; John Slidell to Stephen Pleasanton, July 18, 1829, in Slidell Letter Book, TU. For the difficulties encountered by Livingston in clearing the claim in the New York district attorney's office, see Hamilton, *Reminiscences*, 140. Even here Livingston's procedure was so irregular that Hamilton wrote: "It was a piece of jugglery with which I did not choose to be supposed to be connected."

the state into a bizarre confusion over the gubernatorial succession which would have been the delight of later Savoyards. The Constitution of 1812 made no provision for a lieutenant governor but designated the president of the senate as the successor to the governor's office should any vacancy occur. In conformity to this principle, Arnaud Beauvais became governor upon Derbigny's death, but when the legislature met in January 1830 and the senate necessarily elected a new presiding officer, Jacques Dupré, many insisted that since Beauvais was no longer president of the upper chamber he must surrender his executive chair to Dupré, who was. When the cha-grined Beauvais complied with these demands, the absurdity of counte-nancing an endless succession of presidents of the senate moving up to the governorship impelled the legislature to call for a special election in July to select a chief executive for a full four-year term.[37] So after a respite of only a few months, Louisiana faced anew the rigors of a major political cam-paign, and for the first time since the great victory of 1828 the Jacksonian forces could test the effectiveness of their organization in a contest on the state level.

Tempers already frayed by the nonsense of the gubernatorial succession grew increasingly testy as old ethnic disputes once again tended to confuse the political scene. Despite his inability to capture the governorship, Ber-nard Marigny, still muttering threats of vengeance against the Americans, had managed to generate a force more and more at odds with those hoping to build Louisiana political parties along lines which conformed to prevail-ing national norms. The *"creole feeling,"* Porter reported to Johnston with his usual insight, kept "getting stronger every year and every day in the state."[38] By 1830, indeed, its strength fired the French-speaking citizens to a fixed commitment to approach the gubernatorial canvass as if Jackson and Clay had no relevance to the election. That determination, after all, simply reflected their long-standing conviction that the choice of state of-ficers should be unrelated to national issues or personalities. Equally re-sponsive to the ethnic imperative, some of the American leadership tried to commit members of their community to an agreement that the election would be waged on a no-party basis, allowing them to unite behind the strongest American candidate whatever his national party ties. But that

37. New Orleans *Argus*, October 13, 1829; Bullard and Curry, eds., *New Digest of the Laws of Louisiana*, 399.

38. Alexander Porter to Josiah S. Johnston, January 23, 1830, in Johnston Papers, HSP.

kind of campaign inevitably spelled disaster for Jacksonian hopes of seizing control of the governorship, for the party's major strength unquestionably lay in the Florida parishes, whose leaders had long ago demonstrated that even their dedication to Andrew Jackson could not bring them to support a French candidate for office, however strong his credentials. The Jacksonians consequently had no French-speaking champion to push forward to exploit the creole feeling, for the memories of Marigny's humiliation in 1828 still burned among the natives in their ranks, none of whom wished to be a second victim on the altar of Florida prejudices. Even the consuming ambition of Marigny could not prod him into a battle which he knew he could not win.[39]

By contrast, this hardening of Gallic unity immeasurably strengthened the Clay forces in the state. Their support had always been grounded primarily in the French parishes, despite the absence of anything approaching complete Gallic loyalty to their cause. Thus they had no difficulty in finding strong native candidates who also shared their national political attachments, and to their relief the American segment of their party now revealed a significant if not complete willingness to support these French-speaking colleagues.[40] The major activating force behind this congealing unity unquestionably came from Clay himself, giving an ironic twist to a campaign supposedly free of national party overtones. He arrived in New Orleans early in 1830, at the very beginning of the contest, and quickly threw himself into meticulous direction of his camp's strategy, with an eye to 1832 as well as to the immediate problem. The greatest threat to his success lay in the possible fragmentation of the Gallic vote among Duralde, Beauvais, and A. B. Roman, all of whom had announced for the governorship. Such division could easily throw the victory to an American, and since Clay had effectively kept his own American supporters from entering the field, this would have been unquestionably an American Jacksonian.[41]

39. Alexander Porter to Josiah S. Johnston, February 25, 1830, *ibid.*; W. L. Robeson to W. S. Hamilton, February 6, 1830, in Hamilton Papers, LSU.

40. T. J. Pew to Josiah S. Johnston, January 31, 1830, Alexander Porter to Johnston, March 10, 1830, in Johnston Papers, HSP; Benjamin F. Linton to William S. Hamilton, September 1, 1830, in Hamilton Papers, LSU.

41. Henry Clay to Josiah S. Johnston, March 11, 1830, John H. Johnston to Johnston, February 28, 1830, in Johnston Papers, HSP; Benjamin F. Linton to William S. Hamilton, September 1, 1830, in Hamilton Papers, LSU.

With his usual willingness to sacrifice his own personal ambitions, Duralde virtually eliminated this danger by withdrawing his candidacy to throw his weight behind Roman, eventually joined by such ardent Gallic Jacksonians as Alexander Mouton, Placide Bossier, and Benjamin Metoyer. Some rumors even placed Denis Prieur in this alliance, while the traditionally pro-creole *Louisiana Courier* made little attempt to keep up its pretense of neutrality in the conflict.[42]

These defections by no means exhausted the difficulties besetting the Jacksonians. Gordon could agree with the French on at least one thing— he wanted no Florida governor. His hold on the Louisiana Jackson party would have been seriously threatened by the victory of a man from the region which so bitterly resented its neglect in the patronage distribution he claimed to have managed. He also knew that Hamilton would almost certainly be the choice of the Florida Jacksonians for the governorship, and he had little doubt where he stood in that old campaigner's esteem after the manner in which he and Ripley had tried to maneuver him out of the state.

Without even bothering to check with him, Gordon, Ripley, Wagner, and Carleton announced Overton's candidacy in the *Louisiana Advertiser* immediately following the legislative call for the July election.[43] Compared to Hamilton, Overton represented in every respect a safer risk for the New Orleans faction, which knew full well that the more than normally inflamed rural resentment against the city made a choice of one of their own group an impossibility. At least he would owe his advancement to the Gordon wing of the party, and they in a sense could claim him as one of their protégés, something which would have been ridiculous in the case of Hamilton, with the massed Florida voters at his back.

For his part, Hamilton had no great confidence in his own electability, never underestimating the reality of Gordon's power, for all the resentment it might have engendered. The announcement of the coming election

42. Henry Clay to James Brown, April 17, 1830; W. C. C. Claiborne to Clay, May 23, 1830, in Henry Clay Papers, LC; Richard Davidson to William S. Hamilton, February 4, 1830, John R. Dunn to Hamilton, April 12, 1830, John Nicholson to Hamilton, April 22, 1830, Charles A. Bullard to Hamilton, May 1, 1830, Alexander Mouton to Hamilton, June 1, 1830, in Hamilton Papers, LSU.

43. Walter H. Overton to William S. Hamilton, March 5, 1830, P. K. Wagner to Hamilton, January 21, 1830, in Hamilton Papers, LSU; Alexander Porter to Josiah S. Johnston, February 10, 1830, in Johnston Papers, HSP.

moved him to seek out the advice of Wagner, an old friend whose support he had won on earlier occasions. What, he asked Wagner, could Florida expect of the Gordon group in the ensuing campaign? Now even closer to Gordon than ever before, Wagner cooly lied to Hamilton that the collector had been in constant communication with Overton before the two men decided to bring the general's name forward only three days before receipt of the colonel's letter in New Orleans. Confident that Overton's chances of success made him the strongest possible candidate, Gordon felt compelled to support him, Wagner reported. Hamilton must have writhed at the patronizing tone of Wagner's final comment on the collector's position. "He long since expressed a wish to me and he now repeats it," the ex-editor turned naval officer wrote, "that you should be the successor of J. S. Johnston in the senate."[44]

Convinced now that he could expect no aid from Gordon, Hamilton might well have declined the poll had not other voices made themselves immediately heard. Hatred of Gordon and his White House clique, as that faction was now called by its enemies, so permeated the country parishes that it suddenly seemed possible that it might give Hamilton a united rural support from his party which could hardly have been foreseen. Isaac L. Baker volunteered his active aid in the prairies, assuring Hamilton that "Your being opposed by old Martin Gordon would only make me stick more close to you . . . he is playing the devil with our party and should be kept in check."[45] From his Florida compatriots, too, came renewed pledges of support, most of whom seemed to share Robert Haile's wish "to see a country candidate succeed above all measure, even if for no other reason than that it would sorely dissapoint [sic] a certain New Orleans Set, who arrogate so much to themselves, that not content with seizing and taking under their especial protection the affairs of General Jackson as connected with this state, [they] wish likewise to extend their hated influence over the whole government."[46] Equally anxious to put an American in the governor's chair, the old Adams partisans in the Floridas offered their aid to Hamilton too, though the colonel prudently placed no great reliance in their protests of friendship.[47]

44. P. K. Wagner to William S. Hamilton, January 21, 1830, in Hamilton Papers, LSU.

45. Isaac L. Baker to William S. Hamilton, April 18, 1830, ibid.

46. Robert Haile to William S. Hamilton, January 27, 1830, ibid.

47. Alexander Barrow to William S. Hamilton, January 25, 1830, John T. McNeill to Hamilton, January 25, 1830, ibid.

Even in New Orleans Gordon's leadership stimulated some opposition, for not all city Jacksonians found it pleasing to trot at the collector's heels like faithful hounds. W. L. Robeson, Isaac Preston, and Samuel Spotts, the surveyor of the port, grew more and more critical of the White House phalanx at the very moment that some of the Clay Americans in the capital began to question their party's obvious determination to throw its weight behind Roman. Robeson and Richard Davidson, one of these disgruntled Clayites, did their best to keep Hamilton in the race, promising him at least some support in the metropolis.[48]

The greatest factor in upsetting Gordon's plans proved to be General Overton himself. Drafted by the White House set without his consent, Overton agreed to remain in the race only if he could be assured that the Florida wing of the party would back his candidacy. He had no desire to contend against his old friend Hamilton, and he seemed quite sincere in his pledge to step aside in the latter's favor should he ascertain that this was the wish of the Florida region.[49]

Dismayed at the possible crash of all his schemes, Gordon hit upon a stratagem designed at least to extricate himself from an embarrassing position should that indeed become necessary. He arranged a gathering for March 20 at Davis's Ball Room to choose delegates to a Donaldsonville meeting with Jacksonians from other parishes called to decide upon a single candidate for governor. But just prior to the session at Davis's, Gordon and his close followers met together at his home and there determined to push Overton no matter what the cost. If successful at Donaldsonville, well and good. If it proved impossible to put Overton across, then Gordon might still claim credit for advancing the plan by which a candidate had finally been agreed upon. Watching these tactics, Robeson refused to have anything to do with Gordon's proposals. Instead, he reported everything to Hamilton with a caustic observation concerning the White House clique. "I think it impolitic for them or for officers of the Federal Government to be interfering publicly in state politics," he complained. "Let them go to H—— their own way. Mr. G[ordon] is certainly laboring under severe mental derangements, or he must be politically speaking an unprincipled man."[50]

48. W. L. Robeson to William S. Hamilton, February 6, 1830, Richard Davidson to Hamilton, April 9, 1830, *ibid.*
49. Walter H. Overton to William S. Hamilton, March 5, 1830, *ibid.*
50. W. L. Robeson to William S. Hamilton, March 21, April 20, 1830, *ibid.*

The Donaldsonville convention collapsed in complete failure. Only eight delegates appeared for the meeting, so insignificant a number that no sessions ever convened.[51] Overton had already become convinced that he could expect no support in the Floridas, and true to his pledge he retired from the race in favor of Hamilton, leaving Gordon completely abandoned.[52] The collector had, in effect, been essentially cut out of the campaign. The *Louisiana Advertiser* came forward in May with a halfhearted endorsement of *two* candidates, Hamilton and David Randall, who offered primarily in the hope of taking votes from Roman in the Lafourche area and along the coast, where he had something of a personal following. Except for this feeble gesture, however, and a few scattered attacks upon Roman as a defender and proponent of the protective tariff, the *Advertiser* remained singularly quiet throughout the ensuing campaign.[53]

The effectiveness of Clay and Duralde gave Roman an overwhelming victory. He carried most of the French parishes easily, losing but three to Beauvais and two to Randall, while Hamilton had difficulty even in some parts of Florida, actually dropping St. Tammany to his creole rival. The New Orleans vote demonstrated clearly the disastrous consequences of the disarray in the city's Jacksonian ranks, giving Roman a total of 587, Beauvais 460, Hamilton 191, and Randall 3. The determining factor in all this, one of his disappointed backers, Benjamin F. Linton, told Hamilton, had been the guiding genius of Clay, working diligently from his base in the city. Despite the repeated declarations that ethnic loyalties would take precedence over national party affiliations in the race, Linton maintained, Clay kept his American followers solidly behind Roman, while the Jacksonians failed to give a comparable unified support to Hamilton. All told, the Clay candidates outpolled the Jacksonians 5,116 to 3,164.[54] But those who knew Louisiana politics best reminded the rest that no message as to presi-

51. M. G. Penn to William S. Hamilton, April 23, 1830, John J. Burk to Hamilton, April 25, 1830, W. Winfree to Hamilton, May 2, 1830, Montgomery Sloan to Hamilton, May 6, 1830, John T. McNeill to Hamilton, May 6, 1830, *ibid.*

52. John R. Dunn to William S. Hamilton, April 12, 1830, *ibid.*; *Louisiana State Gazette and Creole* (Donaldsonville), May 15, 1830.

53. *Louisiana Advertiser*, May 14, 1830; Montgomery Sloan to William S. Hamilton, May 6, 1830, in Hamilton Papers, LSU.

54. *Louisiana House Journal*, 1831, p. 7; Benjamin F. Linton to W. S. Hamilton, September 1, 1830, in Hamilton Papers, LSU.

dential probabilities in 1832 should be read into the contest. The state had obviously not given up its attachment to a political system operating on two distinct levels—one local, one national—and each had its own dynamics.

For Jacksonians, the 1830 campaigns could only be seen as disastrous. In the congressional races, old Philemon Thomas had little trouble winning the seat recently vacated by Gurley, for again the Jacksonians split their ranks. Ripley had made his bid for the place with the blessing of Gordon and the *Louisiana Advertiser*, while the Floridians rallied behind Lafayette Saunders again to thwart this invasion of their region by an agent of the White House coterie. The angry blasts of the *Advertiser* that it "had expected better things" of Saunders only widened the breach and in effect insured Thomas's election.[55] Edward Douglass White continued so popular in the First District that no one offered against him, and in the western district Henry Adams Bullard finally succeeded in his political ambitions. Overton had decided not to seek reelection to Congress even before the gubernatorial issue arose, wishing to keep a closer watch on his still unsettled business affairs. He pledged his support to young P. A. Rost of Natchitoches, but his protégé's vigorous attempt to win favor as an avowed Jacksonian candidate could not offset his own personal liabilities. A foreign Frenchman to begin with, he committed the incredible blunder of voting in a legislative session against an apportionment bill which would have added strength to his own district. Against such competition even Bullard could win, giving the Adams men a clean sweep of the congressional seats.[56] At the same time, however, the legislative canvass assured a majority for the Jacksonians in the assembly. And in the New Orleans mayoral elections they also triumphed, but there their standard bearer had been Prieur, whose popularity notoriously transcended party loyalties.[57]

55. *Louisiana Advertiser*, May 14, 1830; Lafayette Saunders to William S. Hamilton, November 4, 1829, Hamilton to Saunders, December 14, 1829, in Hamilton Papers, LSU.

56. Alexander Porter to Josiah S. Johnston, February 10, 1830, Henry A. Bullard to Johnston, February 12, 1830, Thomas Curry to Johnston, March 30, 1830, in Johnston Papers, HSP; Walter H. Overton to William S. Hamilton, March 5, 1830, in Hamilton Papers, LSU; *Attakapas Gazette*, May 15, 1830.

57. New Orleans *Argus*, April 6, 1830. As usual, both parties claimed control of the legislature at first, but by 1831 it was generally conceded that the Jacksonians had the edge. See Alexander Porter to Josiah S. Johnston, January 12, 1831, in Johnston Papers, HSP.

On the surface the Jacksonians seemed to accept their defeats placidly enough. Gordon maintained that he had not really been involved, a claim faithfully seconded by Maunsel White, a close confederate of the collector and Andrew Jackson's New Orleans factor. Shrugging off the recent elections as indicating no weakness of the *real* Jacksonian strength in the state, White reported to the president that his important Louisiana friends were "as true as steel but some who wished to get office by your popularity have been disappointed, and they deserved it." Then came the revealing final comment: "They were not our choice."[58]

But the impact of the 1830 failings could not really be dismissed so easily. Gordon's electoral humiliation intensified an earlier public embarrassment when various blunders on his part in interpreting certain trade regulations provoked a furious howl from the mercantile community and brought him another stinging rebuke from Secretary Ingham.[59] A week following Roman's victory, he was telling friends he had decided to give up the collector's post,[60] though he fixed no date for this action and his comments may well have been designed to provide a face-saving escape should his interim appointment to the office fail to receive Senate approval in the newly convened session.

Elsewhere, violence attending the campaign still agitated Ouachita Parish, climaxed by the killing of General Ferdinand Morgan in a brawl resulting from charges by the Morehouse faction that Morgan had defrauded Jacksonian candidates by stuffing the ballot box during the canvass. The parish remained in an uproar for months, and when the accused came to trial, party hatreds seemed fully personalized in Bullard as chief prosecutor and Ripley as principal defense attorney. Acquittal of the defendant by what Bullard claimed to be a politically biased jury only exacerbated the tensions. "We are here now so effectually divided," one observer wrote Johnston, "that society does not exist for any one except with those of his side. The line of demarcation is traced with blood."[61]

58. Maunsel White to Andrew Jackson, January 29, 1831, in Jackson Papers, LC.

59. S. D. Ingham to Martin Gordon, March 18, 1830, Letter Books of Secretary's Correspondence with Collectors of Small Ports, in RG 56, GRDT, NA.

60. Joseph Saul to Andrew Jackson, July 13, 1830, in Jackson Papers, LC.

61. Henry Bry to Josiah S. Johnston, December 24, 1830, Henry A. Bullard to Johnston, December 9, 1830, in Johnston Papers, HSP; F. A. McWilliams to William S. Hamilton, September 11, 1830, in Hamilton Papers, LSU; *Louisiana Advertiser*, January 5, 1831.

The Floridas experienced no such bloody affray, but tempers flared and emotions ran high. "Florida failed to do her duty, & is forever disgraced," Alexander Barrow, one of the region's leading planters and politicos, raged. "The Jackson party in Florida and I may say throughout the state," he ranted in a letter of sympathy to Hamilton, "deserve to be ruled forever hereafter by a rod of iron, and I wish from my soul that all *Americans* who voted for Roman were placed on his sugar farm under the lash of his drivers." If Louisiana was ever to have an American governor again, Archibald Haralson groused to Hamilton, "it will be by French sufferance. . . . I think the American population at the mercy of the French." He ended on a despairing note: "We may all say as much as we please about the practicability of uniting Florida in the support of any American candidate. It can't be done."[62] Most troubling and laden with prospects of continued Jacksonian failings, reports had it that even heretofore loyal Florida adherents to the American cause had defected to Roman, some going so far as to claim that Thomas Butler had begun to look more favorably upon Clay than Jackson and that he had indeed voted for the creole against Hamilton. His defeat so embittered the colonel that he retreated into practical retirement after the election, though he kept up a busy conspiracy by letter with some of his cohorts, who engaged in stealthily checking old church records in the hope of proving Roman too young to meet the age requirement established for the governor's office by the constitution. All in all, 1830 had certainly been no time of glory for Louisiana Jacksonianism.[63]

The new year brought little promise of better things to come. January saw prodigious efforts to reunite the party for the defeat of Senator Johnston's bid for reelection, but again the doctrinaire Florida faction made success almost an impossibility. By insisting that Johnston's protariff record must constitute the main public issue in the contest they naturally drove sugar-area legislators to energetic moves of their own in Johnston's defense. The incumbent, moreover, had many personal friends among Jacksonians irritated by Florida efforts to whip their party into line behind J. B. Dawson. Again the Jacksonians failed, managing to gather but twenty-two votes for

62. Alexander Barrow to William S. Hamilton, July 12, 1830, Archibald Haralson to Hamilton, July 31, 1830, in Hamilton Papers, LSU.

63. R. Davidson to W. S. Hamilton, April 9, 1830, Archibald Haralson to Hamilton, July 31, October 30, 1380, E. W. Taylor to Hamilton, October 13, 1830, John Nicholson to Hamilton, November 16, 1830, *ibid.*

the iridescent Dawson against Johnston's twenty-nine. Dejected by yet another defeat, Robert Haile admitted to what must have been a general feeling among his colleagues. "I am," he confessed to Hamilton, "a good deal staggered with the virtual [collapse] of our party in this state."[64]

Upon an already weakened cause there now fell the confusion of the Peggy Eaton affair and the first real awareness of the inner tensions threatening the unity of the central Jacksonian forces. The trouble stemmed from the unwillingness of some Washingtonians to admit the secretary of war's wife to capital society because of alleged sexual immorality, despite her obvious place in the affections of the president. Jackson fumed at what he took to be an attack upon Peggy's reputation akin to that which his enemies had waged against his own Rachel in the stormy days of the election of 1828, when they had charged her with adultery because of her union with him before her first marriage had been legally dissolved. Floride Calhoun, wife of Vice-president John C. Calhoun, figured as a leader of the anti-Eaton protagonists, and the furor over the dispute soon drove a wedge between Jackson and the South Carolinian. Secretary of State Martin Van Buren, anxious to supplant Calhoun as heir apparent to the General, seized the opportunity to champion the Eatons and thus establish himself in the good graces of the president. Early rumors of a Calhoun–Van Buren split in the administration began to be heard in New Orleans in late January, but they aroused little interest. St. Romes in the Louisiana Courier tried to smooth over the reported quarrel as an insignificant difference between two ambitious men, making it quite obvious, however, that Calhoun as a southerner certainly warranted greater trust than the crafty New Yorker. More cautious, the Louisiana Advertiser ignored the story until the position of the president could be more clearly understood, a wise move which saved it from the embarrassing gyrations forced upon St. Romes by the eventual revelations of the break between Jackson and his vice-president.[65]

64. John H. Johnston to Josiah S. Johnston, January 8, 10, 11, 1831, Alexander Porter to Johnston, January 12, 1831, James Porter to Johnston, January 10, 1831, in Johnston Papers, HSP; Robert Haile to William S. Hamilton, January 19, 1831, in Hamilton Papers, LSU; Louisiana Advertiser, January 1, 6, 7, 8, 11, 1831; Louisiana Courier, December 2, 3, 1830; January 4, 11, 1831; New Orleans Bee, January 10, 1831.

65. Louisiana Courier, January 27, March 7, 15, 29, April 28, May 4, 6, June 2, July 12, 20, 23, September 17, October 1, 1831; Louisiana Advertiser, May 11, June 20, July 3, November 15, 1831.

By July the *Courier* had come so far around as to label Calhoun "a malignant spirit," encouraging men to the same reckless attack upon helpless women as that turned upon Rachel Jackson herself in 1828.[66]

The strident quarrel over Peggy Eaton inflamed additional differences between Jackson and Calhoun which eventually resulted in dissolution of the cabinet, a development which threw a pall of depression over the once buoyant Jackson forces in the state.[67] Their enemies ridiculed the spectacle of St. Romes shifting ground with almost every issue of the *Courier*,[68] charged that the president had turned Washington into a brothel,[69] and noted with pleasure that even some of the oldest friends of the administration seemed shaken by the recent developments in the national capital.[70] Upset by the turn of events, Gordon and Henry Carleton launched a vigorous campaign to counteract the opposition propaganda by giving the Washington *Globe* a wider circulation in New Orleans, going so far as to visit all subscribers to the pro-Calhoun *United States Telegraph* to urge transfer of their subscriptions to the official Jacksonian organ.[71] Their efforts underscored an awareness of how seriously the party's local press had failed it in this critical period, with St. Romes increasingly incompetent and the *Advertiser* bereft of passion and fire since Wagner had left its editorship to take on public office.

Increasing bitterness surrounding the tariff and nullification controversies soon threatened to raise issues of even greater import than the embarrassments of the cabinet crisis and Eaton imbroglio. It must have been particularly disheartening for the Louisiana Jacksonians to realize that again they faced a situation laden with possibilities of disaster for their own cause far beyond those threatening their rivals. The difficulties sprang from the peculiar economy of the state, resting as it did upon the two great staples of cotton and sugar. Cultivators of the first shared the general southern antipathy to the protective tariff system, while producers of the second felt their

66. *Louisiana Courier*, July 12, 20, 23, 1831.

67. Alexander Porter to Henry Clay, June 10, 1831, in Henry Clay Papers, LC; Porter to Josiah S. Johnston, September 2, 1831, in Johnston Papers, HSP.

68. New Orleans *Mercantile Advertiser*, October 1, 1831.

69. *Ibid.*, August 13, 1831.

70. Alexander Porter to Josiah S. Johnston, September 2, 1831, in Johnston Papers, HSP.

71. *Louisiana Courier*, June 20, 1831.

very existence to depend upon duties shielding them from the destructive competition of the West Indies. Associated with a national party generally considered hostile to the protective policy, Louisiana Jacksonians frequently felt the distrust of the sugar parishes, which regularly gave majorities to candidates friendly to Clay and his American System. Moreover, what support might have been won in the cotton parishes by an antitariff stand could hardly compensate for the enmity it engendered in the sugar regions, for the speculative fears of free trade proponents seldom matched in intensity the dread with which a sugar planter faced the prospect of a slash in the import duties on his commodity.[72]

The rising importance of the sugar industry to the Louisiana economy added substantially to the complexities of the problem. The total value of the state's annual production of sugar and molasses had forged ahead of that of the cotton crop of 1828,[73] and the turn of the new decade saw vast new acres opened to the cultivation of the cane.[74] At almost that very moment, rumors that the Jackson administration planned drastic reductions in the sugar duty spread fear and uncertainty through the industry.

Secretary of the Treasury Ingham in January 1830 circularized the planters for information on their operations and profits, stirring up memories in Louisiana of earlier warnings by Governor Beauvais and Henry Gurley that the 1830 sessions of Congress would inevitably witness an assault upon the sugar tariff.[75] Fearful of such attacks from the antitariff forces, the Louisiana sugar interests began to feel that they could no longer support the state's old policy of denouncing all protection except that on their own product. "We must join somebody," Alexander Porter remarked at the time, "neutral we cannot be."[76] Sensing the futility of trying to maintain an alliance with the southern free traders, the Louisiana legislature finally took the full step toward partnership with the avowed protariff forces, and in March of 1830 the assembly passed an almost unanimous resolution in support of protectionism, declaring it harmless to the property of the South

72. Tregle, "Louisiana and the Tariff," 48–53.

73. Ibid., 57.

74. See, for example, the *Southern Agriculturist*, I (1828), 236, 337; Edmund J. Forstall, *The Agricultural Productions of Louisiana* (New Orleans, 1845), 7.

75. Tregle, "Louisiana and the Tariff," 58–59.

76. Alexander Porter to Josiah S. Johnston, December 13, 1830, in Johnston Papers, HSP.

and pledging its support to "such measures as those that are contemplated by the law of 1828, on the tariff."[77]

Jacksonian attack upon the measure came immediately and forcefully, for it could hardly be considered anything other than a victory for Clay and a rebuke to their own tariff program. But later attempts in Congress to reduce the sugar duties vindicated the wisdom of the assembly's policy when southern antitariff forces lined up solidly against the Louisiana staple.[78] Left with no other argument, the Jacksonians in the state could only maintain that all had been well until the legislature shifted position to join forces with eastern manufacturers. Whatever fate now befell the sugar industry, they claimed, would be completely the responsibility of the Clay forces. Licking their wounds, they fell back to the old position that only the antiprotection policy of the southern states truly secured the sugar tariff, because its duties had never formed part of the hated American System but derived from a constitutional application of the tariff-for-revenue doctrine.[79] Even they realized, however, that few sugar planters would accept such rationalization,[80] and Ripley told Bullard bluntly that it had become "the settled and determined policy of the Jackson party to break down the aristocracy of Louisiana, consisting of the sugar interest and the Banks—and that to punish Louisiana for committing itself on the subject of the tariff, the duty on sugar must and will be taken off." This had been a private warning, but it so shocked Bullard that he could find no other reply than "God have mercy on us."[81]

With the excitement of the cabinet dissolution almost certain to push

77. *Louisiana Senate Journal*, 1830, p. 55; *Louisiana House Journal*, 1830, p. 70; Henry Clay to James Brown, April 17, 1830, in Henry Clay Papers, LC; Clay to Josiah S. Johnston, March 11, 1830, in Calvin Colton, ed., *The Private Correspondence of Henry Clay* (New York, 1856), 255.

78. Tregle, "Louisiana and the Tariff," 69.

79. *Louisiana Courier*, November 6, 13, 15, December 22, 1830, February 17, March 10, May 19, August 27, September 17, 1831.

80. D. B. Morgan to Josiah S. Johnston, December 4, 1830, in Johnston Papers, HSP; Wade Hampton to Goodhue and Co., February 6, 1831, in Wade Hampton Papers, UNC; *Rémarques Sur la Culture de la Canne à Sucre, à la Louisiane, et Sur la Diminution des Droits Sur les Sucres Etrangers* (New Orleans, 1831), 8; *Letter of Mr. J. S. Johnston, of Louisiana, to a Gentleman in New York; In Reply to an Article on the Expediency of Reducing the Duty on Sugar* (n.p., n.d.), 5–8.

81. Henry A. Bullard to Josiah S. Johnston, December 9, 1830, in Johnston Papers, HSP.

the nullificationists to a more radical stance, the Louisiana Jacksonians had to tread very carefully between two extreme positions, trying to woo the sugar planters without appearing to embrace the American System and at the same time attempting to maintain the backing of the free-trade wing of the party without seeming to encourage the heresy of nullification. How they must have envied the Clay men their easy course of embracing the tariff and cursing the South Carolina aberration without reservation.

The reorganization of the cabinet produced yet another problem, for Livingston's ascendancy to the Department of State required Louisiana to select a senator to fill his place. Failure to put one of their own in the seat would leave Louisiana Jacksonians unrepresented in Congress, additional evidence of the decline of their fortunes at the very moment that the approaching 1832 campaign required at least some sign of their party's vitality in the state. Fearful that Governor Roman might fill the vacancy with a Clay partisan, they quickly demanded a special legislative session to make the choice, reminding Roman that any other procedure would be a marked insult to all those Jacksonians who had helped him win office.[82] With the governor's acceptance of their challenge, the campaign moved into full swing.[83] Taking advantage of the November timing of the session, which made it difficult for sugar planters to attend because of the rolling season, the Jacksonians decided to make the tariff a principal issue in their campaign strategy,[84] at the same time stressing a particular attraction of their candidate, Henry Carleton. The *Louisiana Advertiser* made much of this point, emphasizing Carleton's brother-in-law relationship to Livingston, now high in the official family of the president. "It would be madness," the *Advertiser* lectured the legislators, "to shut your eyes to advantages like these."[85]

But even with this clever strategy, things did not go well. A meeting called by the *Courier* and *Advertiser* to choose delegates to the Free Trade Convention in Philadelphia ended in a ludicrous rout of the antitariff forces. Clay men packed the hall, put Dr. A. E. McConnell in the chair, and howled with delight as he denounced Jackson for seeking a second term, reviled free traders as nullifiers, and adjourned the gathering until

82. *Louisiana Courier*, May 14, 1831.
83. *Ibid.*, October 1, 1831.
84. Alexander Porter to Josiah S. Johnston, October 29, 1831, in Johnston Papers, HSP.
85. *Louisiana Advertiser*, November 11, 1831.

September 1, 1939.[86] Even the attempts to picture Gordon as the savior of the state's industry because he had recently exposed and halted the introduction of liquified sugar into the nation under the duty-free label of "syrups" failed miserably when it turned out that White and Porter had for weeks warned the collector of the fraud without stirring him to the slightest action. He had moved only after finding an opening which allowed him to claim credit for ending the deception himself.[87]

The fatal blow to Jacksonian hopes of winning the Senate seat came, ironically enough, from Livingston himself. On the eve of the legislature's choice, with Jacksonians as far away as Natchitoches being dragged from sick beds to make the poll, word arrived in New Orleans of Davezac's appointment as *chargé d'affaires* to the Hague, and once again the old odor of nepotism which seemed to cling to the Livingston name ruined whatever chances Carleton might have had. A Jackson member of the legislature told Porter that "he supposed the next thing would be that Carleton if elected would go out minister to England or France, and Harry Lockett [another Livingston relative] be made one of the judges of the Sup. court of the U. States, and this he could not stomach."[88] Evidently other Jacksonians shared his disgust, for though their party had a majority in the assembly, Roman's secretary of state, George A. Waggaman, won the election by a substantial margin.[89] For the Jacksonians, 1832 looked bleak indeed.

Elsewhere in the Union, however, Jacksonian party prospects brightened day by day. Each month seemed to expose more clearly the basic weaknesses of Clay's position. Unacceptable to the South because of his tariff views, unable to shake Jackson's grip upon the West, and frankly uncertain as to the potential of the anti-Masonic movement growing in the East, Clay appeared to be continuously losing ground in his campaign for the White House. The victory of the Jacksonians in the Kentucky elections of 1831, followed closely by the anti-Masonic nomination of William Wirt, spelled disaster in the eyes of most of Clay's Louisiana friends, and Josiah

86. *Louisiana Courier*, September 3, 1831.

87. *Ibid.*, October 17, 22, 1831; Alexander Porter to Josiah S. Johnston, September 2, 1831, Martin Gordon to J. A. Barker, September 20, 1831, in Johnston Papers, HSP.

88. Alexander Porter to Josiah S. Johnston, December 1, 1831, Charles A. Bullard to Johnston, November 12, 1831, in Johnston Papers, HSP.

89. Alexander Porter to Josiah S. Johnston, December 1, 1831, *ibid.*

Johnston's mail pouch grew heavier with predictions that if the Kentuckian remained in the race he would destroy his own party.[90]

Completely aware of his slipping fortunes, Clay had no desire to bind his friends to a fruitless campaign. At a gloomy conclave in Washington on December 7, 1831, he confessed that he thought his chances hopeless and urged withdrawal of his name from the contest. But when his followers could see no alternate candidate who might take his place, he agreed to continue the fight, primarily, as he told Edward Everett, because he had become convinced that his withdrawal would have toppled his faithful adherents from their control of state governments in places like Louisiana and Maryland.[91]

Reports of Clay's own pessimism must certainly have reached Louisiana through his family connections if in no other way, and after the long series of victories over their enemies in 1830 and 1831 the Clay party now faltered and proceeded to fall slowly apart. Duralde and his associates, normally the vitalizing spark of the Kentuckian's forces in the state, suddenly seemed to be paralyzed in the grip of a sense of futility, despondent and inactive.[92] To the ever watchful Porter they appeared "to have taken leave of their senses,"[93] while apprehensive opportunists such as T. J. Pew, editor of the *Mercantile Advertiser*, found their inertia clear warning of impending disaster. For Pew the remedy was simple enough—he deserted to the Jackson camp.[94]

The apathy and despair of their opponents gave new life to the once battered forces of the president. Soon after Pew's shift in loyalties, the editors of the New Orleans *Bee*, a rapidly growing publication once bitterly opposed to the administration,[95] also joined the growing coalition. Even the strident voice of Gibson now fell practically mute. As the Clay forces sank deeper into lethargy, Jacksonians all over the state met in enthusiastic

90. Alexander Porter to Josiah S. Johnston, September 1, 1831, Charles A. Bullard to Johnston, November 12, 1831, Thomas Curry to Johnston, November 15, 1831, *ibid.*; New Orleans *Mercantile Advertiser*, November 15, 1831.

91. Edward Everett to Alexander Everett, December 8, 1831, in Edward Everett Papers, MHS.

92. Thomas Curry to Josiah S. Johnston, January 26, 1832, in Johnston Papers, HSP.

93. Alexander Porter to Josiah S. Johnston, March 18, 1832, *ibid.*

94. Thomas Curry to Josiah S. Johnston, January 26, 1832, *ibid.*

95. New Orleans *Bee*, January 11, 1833.

gatherings to reaffirm their faith and to organize their strength for the coming electoral battles.[96] A boisterous party conclave in New Orleans early in January 1832 culminated in nominations of presidential electors and the choice of delegates to the Baltimore convention for the naming of Jackson's running mate. Van Buren and Martin Gordon won particular plaudits from the participants, with the collector receiving acclaim as the Hero of the Second Battle of New Orleans, as overgenerous reference to his role in blocking the importation of syrups to evade the sugar duty.[97]

Already thoroughly aroused from their earlier lassitude and ineffectiveness, Jacksonians joined together in even greater solidarity when the United States Senate, by the casting vote of John C. Calhoun, rejected Van Buren's appointment as ambassador to Great Britain. Storms of protest reminiscent of the 1825 charges of bargain and corruption once again reverberated throughout the nation, with the *Advertiser* cursing this victory of a "new coalition" as one designed to "degrade [our] chief magistrate in the eyes of his own country and of foreign nations."[98] Gordon broadcast his devotion to the president and his martyred defender with brilliant transparencies draped from the balcony of his home on Royal Street,[99] while the party faithful thronged to a public meeting in New Orleans called as a testimony of admiration for Van Buren.[100] Such acclaim completely drowned out the feeble praise for the Senate's action at a pitifully small anti–Van Buren demonstration staged by Clay sympathizers, evoking from a disgusted Porter the despondent admission that for men of his persuasion the political prospects seemed "more gloomy in this State, than I ever knew them."[101]

This impressive resurgence of strength and optimism in the state's Jacksonian ranks covered over what might have developed into a major break in the party. The Florida leaders of the administration forces had lost much of their enthusiasm for Jackson because of his refusal to bend to South Car-

96. *Louisiana Courier*, January 10, 13, 27, 1832.

97. *Ibid.*, January 10, 11, 1832; *Louisiana Advertiser*, January 13, 1832.

98. *Louisiana Advertiser*, February 10, March 9, 1832; *Louisiana Courier*, February 10, March 5, 1832.

99. *Louisiana Courier*, February 23, 1832.

100. *Ibid.*, March 5, 10, 1832; *Louisiana Advertiser*, March 9, 10, 1832.

101. Alexander Porter to Josiah S. Johnston, March 18, 1832, Dr. Duncan to Johnston, April 17, 1831, Johnston Strawbridge to Johnston, May 12, 1832, in Johnston Papers, HSP.

olina's view of the Union as subordinate to a state's right to interpose its sovereignty between federal power and the citizenry. More and more this turned them to an open acceptance of John C. Calhoun as their true champion. W. H. Overton, meanwhile, had played a major part in the attack upon John Eaton, husband of the notorious Peggy, convinced in his own mind that the president had fallen under the spell of evil men dominated by the crafty Van Buren.[102] With all his sympathy for Calhoun, however, Overton had no leanings toward nullification, which clearly distinguished him from the Florida doctrinaires. Alexander Barrow, appalled at Jackson's admission that he considered protection perfectly constitutional, openly advocated nullification to the president's face during a conversation late in 1831. His comments in letters to Hamilton leave little doubt that the colonel as well as John B. Dawson shared these views, which Barrow defended as the original faith of 1798. Barrow actually considered embracing the doctrine openly and publicly in December 1831, but he recognized the dangers latent in such a course. "Dawson you know," he wrote to Hamilton, "is the declared candidate for the office of Governor and if . . . [he] was to come out in favor of the nullifiers, there is no telling what loss he would sustain by it."[103]

Outside the Florida parishes the nullification doctrine attracted little support, a reality fully appreciated by those tempted to endorse it. By 1832 the Louisiana Jackson party's overwhelming commitment to the president's stand on national sovereignty made opposition futile and would almost certainly have ended Dawson's hopes for the governorship in 1834, a prospect particularly distasteful now that the future of the Jacksonians seemed so bright. Barrow and Dawson held their tongues.

Their silence attracted no great attention, for the passions once aroused by divisions on nullification and the tariff dissipated appreciably as 1832 wore on. The fiery attacks upon protectionism by the South Carolina nullifiers did much to swing Louisiana Jacksonians toward a defense of the system hardly distinguishable from that of the Clay party itself, and the tariff debates in Congress during the spring and summer stimulated the *Courier* and *Advertiser* to comments which they would have damned only a few

102. *Louisiana Advertiser,* September 6, 1832, December 6, 1834; Walter H. Overton to Josiah S. Johnston, April 29, 1832, in Johnston Papers, HSP.

103. Alexander Barrow to William S. Hamilton, September 3, December 9, 1831, in Hamilton Papers, LSU.

months earlier.[104] No major difference emerged in the approaches of the two parties to the proposed Tariff of 1832, except for the greater Jacksonian push for acceptable compromise features in the measure. Gone now were the wonted attacks upon the tariff as a conspiracy to enrich eastern manufacturers, replaced by regular pronouncements in the *Advertiser* that the true Jacksonian creed had always recognized "free trade absurdities" as the tool of British economic colonialism. Those still clinging to antitariff principles common to Jacksonians only a few months previously found themselves damned as "those who pant for a 'solemn league and covenant' between Carolina nullifiers and English manufacturers."[105]

This remarkable blurring of party distinctions led to a demonstration of bipartisan accord which must have appeared like a dream to those who could remember 1825 and 1828. At a great antinullification meeting in New Orleans on June 17, 1832, leaders of both parties gathered to condemn the South Carolina doctrines convulsing the nation. The Jacksonians clearly meant to use the occasion to urge adoption of the proposed tariff compromises then pending in Congress, but when the Clay leaders threatened to withdraw rather than support any kind of reduction in the duties, the two sides agreed to a simple blanket resolution condemning nullification as anarchy. Significantly, even some of the Jacksonians insisted that no concessions could be made in tariff adjustment until South Carolina renounced its heresy, a position most strongly held by the Gallic members of both parties who, Porter reported, "were all for marching off to S. Carolina and fighting."[106]

Passage of the Tariff of 1832 shortly thereafter eased the sectional antagonisms to a degree by providing for a modest reduction in most duties, although it clearly retained the principle of protection. Louisiana Jacksonians generally praised its more moderate schedules, and even the Clay faction eventually gave it their somewhat reluctant support, for loss of a half-cent total in the sugar rates seemed small enough price to pay for what everyone hoped might be a permanent tariff settlement. At least the Jacksonians had been brought to a point at which they no longer threatened de-

104. *Louisiana Advertiser*, May 28, June 29, August 21, 1832; *Louisiana Courier*, October 8, 1832.

105. *Louisiana Advertiser*, August 21, 23, September 26, 1832.

106. *Ibid.*, June 29, 1832; *Louisiana Courier*, June 28, 1832; Alexander Porter to Josiah S. Johnston, June 17, 1832, in Johnston Papers, HSP.

struction to the whole system of protective imposts. The Calhounites had been effectively silenced,[107] and the radical states' rights cause which had loomed so large in the first years of the Jacksonian movement found itself now without any major champion in Louisiana. From the Florida parishes came no word of protest against the president. Clearly, no one determined to rule the state at the head of his party could afford to cast off Andrew Jackson as an ally. So Barrow and Dawson continued to hold their tongues.

This defusing of nullification and the tariff as issues in the coming campaign of 1832 left the Bank of the United States as the center of controversy around which the election would revolve. Essentially an imported disagreement in Louisiana, the quarrel over the rechartering of the financial giant would probably never have developed in the state without outside stimulus. Not that this made the consequences of the struggle any less real or important in the community. The New Orleans branch of the Second Bank of the United States served the whole Mississippi valley, especially facilitating the solution of the complex exchange problems growing out of the position of New Orleans as the place to which the flood of western produce came to be sold but not the place at which the West bought most of the things required to satisfy its own needs. By acting as the major channel through which bills of exchange finally found their way to the points of greatest need in the vast national marketing system, the New Orleans branch performed one of its most valuable services, at the same time filling the additional and equally important role of providing ready credit and discount services to the multifarious commercial interests of the metropolis.

The branch and its officers established such a record of efficiency and liberality in New Orleans that few found any reason to complain against it prior to the beginning of the titanic struggle between Jackson and the Bank's imperious president, Nicholas Biddle. Even in the long history of bitterness directed toward financial houses in the city by the planter class of the parishes, the national bank generally escaped any major criticism. Nor had there been any serious public sentiment against banks in principle in Louisiana during the pre-Jackson period, for one can discount the many attacks found in the press as the normal complaints of a society which generally felt that banks were not evil but too few and that favored citizens received special privileges in the parceling out of available funds. The anti-Jackson composition of the state's congressional delegation makes its vote in favor of re-

107. Tregle, "Louisiana and the Tariff," 90–92.

chartering the Bank in 1832 and 1834 in no way unusual, but that this position enjoyed wide sympathy back home seems confirmed by the extensive expressions of support Samuel Jaudon, the branch cashier, managed to drum up for the Bank from a broad spectrum of the community's mercantile and financial institutions. After Jackson's bank veto, Samuel H. Harper advised Secretary Taney that the banking houses of New Orleans represented a "mixed character" so far as their political attachments could be determined, and that the directors of only one of them had refused to sign a memorial recommending renewed charter of the Bank of the United States.[108]

There is no history of any antibanking or antibusiness bias even among the men who formed the nucleus of the Jackson party in the state. Martin Gordon, Isaac T. Preston, W. L. Robeson, James W. Breedlove, J. B. Plauché, William G. Hewes, William C. Withers, J. B. Labatut, S. W. Oakey, Harvey Elkin, Nathan Morse, Joseph Saul, Peter Laidlaw, Henry Lockett, Samuel Spotts, John Hagan, and many others, Jacksonians all, had a long record of being among the most active bank directors and businessmen of the community. Maunsel White as late as 1832 continued to serve as one of the branch bank's board of directors, a position earlier held by other prominent Jacksonians including Hewes, Hagan, and Gordon himself. Up in Rapides Parish, W. H. Overton, for all his dedication to Jackson, had considerable uneasiness about his old comrade's anti-Bank policy, which he ascribed to his having fallen under the spell of the evil Martin Van Buren. "I had hoped," he confided to Josiah S. Johnston, "that with slight modifications the charter of the bank would have been renewed & the interests & currency of the country remain in its present satisfactory state." In Washington, Edward Livingston apparently felt much the same. Before Jackson made opposition to the Bank a matter of party and personal loyalty, Livingston did everything he could to facilitate its salvation, on one occasion telling Charles J. Ingersoll, a Pennsylvania Jackso-

108. Abernethy, "Early Development of Commerce and Banking in Tennessee," 317; Samuel Jaudon to Nicholas Biddle, February 11, 1832, in Nicholas Biddle Papers, LC; "Memorial of the President and Directors of the Louisiana State Bank for the Rechartering of the Bank of the United States," *House Executive Documents*, 22nd Cong., 1st Sess., No. 153; "Memorial of the Bank of Orleans, for a Renewal of the Charter of the Bank of the United States," *House Executive Documents*, 22nd Cong., 1st Sess., No. 184; "Memorial of the New Orleans Canal and Banking Company for Renewal of the Charter of the Bank of the United States," *Senate Documents*, 22nd Cong., 1st Sess., No. 108; Samuel H. Harper to Roger B. Taney, October 23, 1833, Letters from Banks, in RG 56, GRDT, NA.

nian, that he "denounced all substitutes for the present Bank of the United States and every kind of other fiscal contrivance as absurd and impracticable," adding that he thought it "impossible to administer the Treasury of the United States without just such a Bank."[109]

Prior to Jackson's veto the Louisiana press more or less tended to ignore financial questions altogether. There had been some threats against banks and monied aristocracies, to be sure, but these had generally been of much the same type as Wagner's 1828 campaign against those supposedly antimechanic in sentiment, which meant that they stressed social snobbery as the great offending sin or else made completely unsupported assertions that aristocrats used the Bank of the United States to buy political control of the country.[110]

It was not until late May of 1832 that the Jacksonian press began to give any appreciable space to the great Bank fight, and that primarily in the form of reprints from Francis P. Blair's Washington *Globe*. Local editors copied these with little additional comment for the most part, or contented themselves with observations typical of one in the *Advertiser:* "Thank God, that the American people are too intelligent to be led astray by the hirelings, and paid mercenaries of an ambitious aristocracy, who would be the *noblemen* of the land."[111] But one would look in vain for any analysis of flaws in the Bank's financial structure or for any explication of how its business practices did harm to the nation's economy or threatened the political

109. W. H. Overton to Josiah S. Johnston, April 29, 1832, in Johnston Papers, HSP; Charles J. Ingersoll to Nicholas Biddle, February 10, 1832, in Biddle Papers, LC. George D. Green in *Finance and Economic Development in the Old South: Louisiana Banking, 1804–1861* (Stanford, 1972), 219, disputes the assertion that the Bank quarrel constituted an "imported issue" in Louisiana and denies that any significance should attach to Jacksonian membership on the branch bank's board of directors, maintaining that such an interpretation "wrongly assumes that Jacksonians on the board of the New Orleans branch were therefore disloyal to the party." Actually, he continues, "Biddle appointed them at the suggestion of William Lewis, one of Jackson's 'kitchen cabinet,' in order to give political balance to the board." Green obviously misses the point here, which is that Maunsel White, Martin Gordon, and others friendly to the Bank before Jackson's veto saw nothing in their relationship to it at odds with loyalty to their party. The wrong assumption is Green's, that they presumably agreed to serve on the branch board only to please the president and William B. Lewis.

110. See, for example, the typical comment of St. Romes in the *Louisiana Courier*, February 1, 1831.

111. *Louisiana Advertiser*, August 11, 1832.

freedoms of its people. It sufficed to know that Jackson found it necessary to do battle with the institution. That alone made it evil.

The president's insistence that the Bank was unconstitutional, financially despotic, and politically corrupt created an inevitable furor, and Louisiana learned that one of the principal complaints against Biddle and his associates charged them with deliberately using the New Orleans branch to drain capital from the West to the coffers of the East. Despite the unlikelihood that such claims had any basis in fact beyond the admitted and regular transfer from New Orleans of funds which had accumulated there through the Mexican trade,[112] the Louisiana Jacksonians seized upon the president's message outlining his reasons for the Bank veto as the greatest state paper since Washington's farewell address, happy that they now had something around which to wage their campaign.[113] Again they could go forth to crush the evil of Federalism, to do battle with aristocrats.

Despite an increase in the number of original articles in the Jacksonian press blasting Biddle's "Octopus," local papers came nowhere close to matching the veritable avalanche of print spewed out against the Bank in the columns of the administration's chief mouthpiece, the Washington *Globe*. Jacksonians outdid themselves in flooding the state with Blair's publication. One dismayed Clay supporter reported to Johnston that the mail to his small town in the Floridas had become so heavy because of the mass of *Globes* being delivered that the bag had to be carried slung on a pole between two men, whereas in earlier times a single clerk had been able to manage it easily under one arm. The "Extra Globes are sent gratis all over the country," he moaned. "You see them everywhere."[114]

In such fashion did Jackson's veto and Blair's pen succeed in inflaming Louisiana Jacksonianism against the Bank. Maunsel White, only recently a director of the New Orleans branch, not only bestowed lavish praise upon the president for striking at such a vicious economic tyrant but actually bestowed upon his blameless newborn son the name of Andrew Veto Jackson White.[115] Forced to act by the approaching end to the Bank's charter and

---

112. *Debates in Congress*, 22nd Cong., 1st Sess., appendix, 39; Erik M. Eriksson, "Official Newspaper Organs and Jackson's Re-election, 1832," in *Tennessee Magazine of History*, IX (1925), 55.

113. Thomas G. Davidson to F. P. Blair, September 6, 1832, in Blair-Rives Papers, LC.

114. D. B. Morgan to Josiah S. Johnston, October 13, 1832, in Johnston Papers, HSP.

115. Maunsel White to Andrew Jackson, December 14, 1832, in Jackson Papers, LC.

the instability of the eastern financial market, already upset by the cholera epidemic raging in the nation, Biddle reluctantly ordered the New Orleans branch to curtail its discount and exchange services. The branch's compliance produced such financial hardship in the metropolis that by late August credit had almost completely dried up in the city, leading even friends of the Bank to protest the severity of its curtailment. Biddle may well have hoped to demonstrate the value of his institution's services by making them unavailable, but if that had been his strategy it played instead right into the president's hands. In the eyes of many, the Bank's actions seemed to prove exactly what Jackson had always maintained—perhaps, they said, no private institution should be allowed in a republic to possess power to cause such distress at will. Further questions as to the Bank's propriety mounted with the *Advertiser*'s report that Josiah Johnston, one of its major Senate defenders, was indebted to the institution for as much as $36,000, clear evidence in the minds of some that such a loan must have constituted a subsidy for attack upon the president.[116]

The war upon the Bank in Louisiana came at a most opportune time for the Jacksonians, for it did not require them to defend a policy which would almost completely deprive the state of access to banking capital and services, as would have been true only a few years earlier. The new decade had seen a veritable rash of additional banks in the community, pushed by planters who hoped to play one house against the other and enthusiastically supported by businessmen in New Orleans anxious to link banking with internal improvement projects while they also tested the new device of using mortgages on urban property as pledges for stock. Between 1830 and 1833 chartered banks in the state other than the Bank of the United States increased from four to eleven, with a jump in capitalization from $9 million to $39 million. Curtailment of the Bank's functions in New Orleans produced serious distress, but these new financial establishments allowed the state to ride out the storm.[117]

116. John Linton to Josiah S. Johnston, October 5, 1832, in Johnston Papers, HSP; *Louisiana Advertiser*, September 25, October 16, 1832.

117. Trufant, "Review of Banking in New Orleans, 1830–1840," 32; Stephen Caldwell, *A Banking History of Louisiana* (Baton Rouge, 1935), 56–58; G. D. Green, *Finance and Economic Development in the Old South*, 22–23; Alexander Porter to Josiah S. Johnston, February 14, 1832, Thomas Butler to Johnston, February 23, 1832, L. Hodge to Johnston, March 8, 1832, John Linton to Johnston, October 5, 1832, in Johnston Papers, HSP; *Louisiana Courier*, January 20, 1832.

In the face of such an explosion of Jacksonian vigor, the Clay forces had little chance to escape their own slough of despondency and inactivity. Not even the successful return of their three incumbent congressmen in the July elections revived their spirits, for as was so often true in Louisiana these contests once again swung primarily on personal factors and augured no success for Clay in November. Bullard defeated Alexander Mouton, a young creole handicapped by opposition from the powerful Dupré clan based more on family than political differences.[118] In the First District White had again gone unchallenged, and in the Floridas General Thomas repeated his victory over a Jacksonian opposition still divided by the pretensions of the Yankee from New Orleans, Eleazar Ripley.[119]

The last months of the campaign changed nothing. Clay was already defeated.

On the morning of October 25, 1832, Dr. James S. McFarlane pushed his way through a New Orleans crowd of early risers gathered around the still bodies of two men at Poydras Street and the levee. Uneasy but curious, they watched his quick inspection of the dead. Then they broke in panic, scattering through the streets of the city, down to the Exchange, out to the faubourgs, carrying the terrifying news. The cholera had finally come to New Orleans.

By the next day death was rampant in the city, and as the disease began to radiate out into the parishes, mounting consternation spread with it. In ten days New Orleans lost one-tenth of its people, while the rest struggled through scenes of horror unparalleled even in this place of recurrent plague. The whole state plunged into a surrealist nightmare. Sheets of rain poured down from skies perpetually reddened by the blaze of great fires of burning "goudron" belching suffocating smoke designed to keep away infection. Cannon boomed constantly, day and night, in the hope that they might stir the air and waft away the sickness. The grim signs of death loomed everywhere—silent homes occupied only by the dead; stacks of corpses piled high one upon another, abandoned in cemeteries, burned in open lots, or dumped into great common graves in the enveloping swamps. There was nothing to do but wait. Some encased themselves in binding plasters of burgundy pitch, while others downed a so-called cholera pre-

118. Thomas Curry to Josiah S. Johnston, May 6, 1832, in Johnston Papers, HSP.
119. *Louisiana Courier*, July 6, 1832.

ventative composed of "pure French brandy mixed with plenty of red pepper." But the disease had its way.[120]

In the very midst of this terror came the election of 1832; it is remarkable that anyone at all felt any interest in going to the polls. Many who went were dead before the counting of their ballots. It may well have made little difference in the outcome, considering the collapse of Clay's forces, but the cholera struck most viciously in those parishes of the Kentuckian's greatest strength. "No human exertion could get the French to the polls," Porter wrote to Johnston in explanation of the overwhelming Jackson victory,[121] and the returns bolster his findings. The total ballots cast in the rural sugar parishes fell far below normal, while the strong pro-Jackson region of Florida, relatively untouched by the disease, brought its full force to bear. The final tabulation gave Jackson 4,873 votes to Clay's 2,207, and once again the Hero of New Orleans had carried Louisiana.[122]

Under the circumstances of this peculiar campaign, abandoned almost from its start by Clay men, who felt their champion had been deserted elsewhere in the Union, and climaxing in the worst epidemic the state was ever to know, who could find in the election of 1832 any proof of the political or economic faith of Louisiana? Only one thing remained beyond dispute—the Jackson party had surpassed its rival in energy, spirit, and organization. Even without the cholera, victory almost certainly would have been theirs. It had turned not on issues clearly setting them apart from their opponents, but on the magnetism and will of Andrew Jackson.

120. For the plague of 1832, see Jo Ann Carrigan, *The Saffron Scourge: A History of Yellow Fever in Louisiana, 1796–1905* (Lafayette, La., 1994); Halphen, *Mémoire sur le Cholera-morbus*, 57; Spear, *Ancient and Modern New Orleans*, 34; H. B. Trist to Nicholas P. Trist, November 7, 1832, in Trist Papers, UNC; New Orleans *Bee*, November 4, 1834.

121. Alexander Porter to Josiah S. Johnston, December 6, 1832, in Johnston Papers, HSP; see also Martin Gordon to William B. Lewis, November 12, 1832, in Miscellaneous Papers, MHS.

122. *Louisiana Advertiser*, November 28, 1832.

· XI ·

DEMOCRACY DISCORDANT

In all of his public life only one action by Edward Livingston ever met with the almost universal acclaim of the people of Louisiana. And yet as perversely ironic as it must have seemed, he could not claim it as his own. For what he had done was to fashion a state paper aimed at destroying the theory of nullification, and it bore the name of Andrew Jackson.

The proclamation embodying the president's reply to the South Carolina ordinance of nullification reached New Orleans on Christmas Day of 1832, amidst a wild mixture of terrible rains and bursts of thunder which seemed to underscore the temper of the great dispute. It produced excited and unreserved praise for the chief executive, with even his traditional enemies blessing his name. That archdefender of the Union, Alexander Porter, seemed almost converted to the ranks of the General as he gave thanks for Jackson's energy and "indomitable will,"[1] and others of like mind rushed plans for a great public meeting in New Orleans on January 2 to allow the people an opportunity to voice their support of the president's stand.[2]

As had been true in 1832, public sentiment against nullification united both Louisiana parties in opposition to the South Carolina doctrine. Dominique Bouligny presided over the January meeting; John R. Grymes helped draft the resolution declaring the Union an "indissoluble compact";

1. Alexander Porter to Josiah S. Johnston, December 26, 1832, in Johnston Papers, HSP; *Louisiana Courier,* December 26, 1832.

2. *Louisiana Courier,* December 28, 1832.

and Governor Roman reinforced these popular expressions with an official declaration to the state legislature which called upon Louisiana to honor her motto of "Justice, Union, and Confidence" with a pledge to "surround the President with all the force possible by expression of general approbation" of his actions.[3]

By now even the Florida nullifiers had somewhat modified their position, at least vocally if not in substance. When the legislature proceeded to consider Roman's recommendations, the committee to whom the question was referred voted unanimously in opposition to the South Carolina vision of the Union but divided as to the proper course to be pursued by the national government. One segment of the committee offered resolutions which would have fully justified the complaints of the southern states against the tariff and called for immediate reduction of duties to a revenue-only level. But this would have meant a repudiation of the 1830 resolutions in favor of the tariff of 1828, as well as a practical abandonment of the state's claims to protection of her sugar industry. Alert to the danger, the legislature turned back these attempts to damn the tariff along with nullification, and once again the state officially ratified its support of protection.[4]

Leadership in this antitariff campaign had been taken by the Florida Jacksonians and John R. Grymes, with the latter responsible for the major presentation of their arguments. It is difficult to deduce from the evidence exactly what doctrinal position Grymes held in this whole affair, for he could pronounce violent strictures against nullifiers, affirm the sanctity of the Union, and then, as on this occasion, attempt to prevent the inclusion of a condemnation of secession in the resolutions attacking nullification. But at least he voted in favor of reprobating both when the measure came to the test, which was more than Alexander Barrow and several of his fellow Florida delegates could bring themselves to do.[5] Clearly the nullification flame still flickered in the Florida area, but prudence again prevented any public acknowledgment of it by the leaders of the region. Too much was at stake in the coming attempt to win American control of the state to allow all to be lost in defense of an idea which had become so obviously

3. *Ibid.*, January 3, 1833; New Orleans *Bee*, January 3, 1833; *Louisiana House Journal*, 1833, p. 4.

4. *Louisiana House Journal*, 1833, pp. 42–44, 72–74.

5. *Ibid.*, 73–74.

hated by the majority of the citizens and which had been condemned by the man whose personality seemed destined to maintain its spell over the political affairs of the community.

Writing to Hamilton from New Orleans shortly after the defeat of the antitariff resolutions in the legislature, Alexander Barrow reported that he had tried to follow the colonel's advice to keep mum on his ideas concerning states' rights, but the debate on nullification forced him to drop a few observations on the issues in dispute. "I am now put under the ban," he complained, "and am denounced as a nullifier, as all are considered here nullifiers who do not laud the proclamation, and pronounce General Jackson to be immaculate." Clearly, his conflicting loyalties troubled him deeply. "I am no nullifier, as you know," Barrow protested, in a strange departure from many of his earlier comments to Hamilton, "but all my sympathies are with them, and as the nullifiers are contending against laws which are unconstitutional, unjust, oppressive and ruinous to the South, I never will consent to see them put down by military force." His final observation gives the key to the reluctance of his group to do more than sulk and complain against the wickedness of the tariff. "The popularity of Jackson is so overwhelming—the belief in his purity is so deeprooted—and the spirit of man worship is so prevalent," he wrote, that it appeared futile to resist.[6] Nullification had indeed aroused little sympathy in Louisiana. Public opinion remained so hostile to the doctrine that even men with the views of Barrow shied away from any open support of it, largely out of fear that they might be taken for secessionists.

Louisiana gave additional demonstration of its devotion to the Union with vigorous support of the Compromise Tariff of 1833, which provided for a gradual reduction of duties to a flat rate of 20 percent ad valorem over a ten-year period. As early as December 1832 Johnston had warned Porter that some such arrangement would be the only way to save the nation from schism, and Porter had replied in a fashion which would sum up the later reaction of the state in the face of the accomplished fact: "Be it so," was his comment. "It will nearly ruin me, and it will totally ruin others, but I trust we all have patriotism enough to bear this and much more for the sake of the Union."[7]

6. Alexander Barrow to William S. Hamilton, February 19, 1833, in Hamilton Papers, LSU.

7. Alexander Porter to Josiah S. Johnston, December 20, 1832, in Johnston Papers, HSP.

Porter's judgment of the feelings of his neighbors proved sound. The slash in the sugar duties at first induced what Governor Roman called "a kind of panic," but this soon subsided in the hope that the years would bring some measure of salvation to the industry. A sugar planter himself, Roman assured Johnston that the people recognized that no alternative to the compromise had been open to their congressional representatives— "we all agree," he remarked, "that you have done your best for the interest of the state."[8] But as early as 1834 the nullification threat had so dissipated that politics could produce the strange spectacle of a Florida antitariff candidate for governor belaboring his opponent for having voted to reduce duties on sugar in 1833 in order to save the Union.

The appearance of unity demonstrated by Louisiana Jacksonianism in the face of the nullification crisis quickly shattered on old ambitions. Democratic success in the election of 1832 once again emboldened Gordon to bid for complete mastery of his party under the General's banner, for now success might well mean political control of the state during at least the next four years. To attain that end he was willing to jeopardize the solidarity of the Jacksonian organization in the state.

No real cause of dissension threatened the party except Gordon's determination to have his colleagues accept his status as Andrew Jackson's alter ego in Louisiana. He ruled the custom house with a grip of iron, terrorizing merchants in his disfavor, demanding unquestioning obedience from his subordinates, and dispensing his patronage with a zeal which had already called down admonitions from the treasury department under Secretary Samuel D. Ingham.[9] Wagner, now naval officer of the port, served as his principal lieutenant, pandering to his notorious hypochondria and acting frequently as confidential secretary in the political maneuverings of the White House clique.

From the beginning of his tenure as collector, Gordon alienated many of his fellow Jacksonians, particularly W. L. Robeson, Isaac Preston, and Samuel Spotts, who resented his tyranny and blamed him for their party's rout in

8. A. B. Roman to Josiah S. Johnston, April 20, 1833, *ibid.*

9. Edward Didier to S. D. Ingham, May 15, 1830 [copy], Collector's Letter Books of Correspondence Received, 1830, New Orleans; P. A. Rousseau to Samuel Spotts, April 3, 1833 [copy], Charges Against Custom House Officers, 1833–1841, both in RG 56, GRDT, NA.

the disastrous gubernatorial campaign of 1830. Spotts seems especially to have incurred Gordon's wrath, their antagonisms frequently bubbling up in disputes over their respective duties in the custom house.[10] As surveyor of the port, Spotts exercised wide authority over inspectors, watchers, and other minor customs officials who generally owed their appointments to joint recommendation from his own office and that of the collector. Unlike Wagner, Spotts did not owe his job to Gordon's influence and always remained an outsider in the latter's eyes, to be spied upon, harassed at every turn, and pressed to accommodate Gordon's political and patronage demands.[11] Clearly, if the collector meant to retain his self-proclaimed role as the president's chief friend and adviser in Louisiana, he could brook no independence of action on the part of Spotts or any other federal officeholder in the state, countenance no resistance to his plans or to his will.

In some fashion not entirely clear, John Slidell transgressed against this majesty of the collector, suddenly to find himself a man marked for destruction. There is no proof, but a strong probability, that the misunderstanding had its roots in a situation which developed in September 1832, when three boatmen in the custom house service—Alexander Smith, James McFarlane, and William Whitney—seized the brig *Primero de Mahon* as she tried to smuggle cigars and rum into Louisiana. Gordon retained the informers' fee of $5,179.59 and later divided it with Spotts, Wagner, McFarlane, and Whitney, but refused to render any share to Smith. The latter protested in vain, for Wagner and the collector had forced Whitney to sign a false statement that Smith had not participated in the seizure of the brig. Unable to obtain redress in any other fashion, Smith finally sued Gordon for his share of the fee and won judgment against him in February 1834.[12]

No evidence links Slidell to this dispute, but Smith may well have enlisted his aid, for Thomas Slidell and Robert M. Carter served as his lawyers in the case, the first a brother to the federal attorney and the second his

10. Disputes between Gordon and Spotts are recorded in their correspondence with various secretaries of the treasury. See, for example, S. D. Ingham to Martin Gordon, March 19, 1830, Letter Books of Secretary's Correspondence with Collectors of Small Ports, Louis McLane to Gordon, April 21, 1833, McLane to Samuel Spotts, April 21, 1833, Letters Sent by the Secretary of the Treasury to Collectors of Customs, all *ibid*.

11. Samuel Spotts to Louis McLane, April 4, 1833, Charges Against Custom House Officers, 1833–1841, *ibid*.

12. *Alexander Smith v. Martin Gordon* (copy of parish court proceedings), *ibid*.

close friend and associate.[13] Whatever the cause, by December 1832 Gordon had determined that Slidell must be crushed. He made no overt break with his associate, however, leaving Slidell to grow increasingly puzzled by the collector's mounting coolness and refusal to cooperate in government cases requiring their joint action.[14] The breach soon became so wide that Slidell could ignore it no longer, especially since his appointment was to expire in March. On January 7, 1833, he wrote to the president requesting renewal of his commission and asking that any attacks upon him by Gordon be judged in the light of the known vindictiveness of the collector.[15] To Gordon himself Slidell the next day proposed an end at least to their official bickerings. "You have thought proper for reasons best known to yourself," he wrote the collector, "to change the friendly relations which have hitherto existed between us, but I wish you to understand that I am at all times prepared to give you every information in my power in any official matter upon which you may think fit to consult me." All he asked was an end to "captious correspondence."[16]

There was to be no placating the adamant Gordon. Already he had won Henry Carleton to his side in an alliance which assured support from Livingston, the only Louisiana Jacksonian in the national capital. Having thus cut Slidell off from any defense in Washington, he then demanded of President Jackson that he choose between his federal attorney and collector at New Orleans, since it was obvious that they could no longer work together in harmony, suggesting at the same time that Carleton would be the perfect choice to succeed his errant colleague.[17]

On March 15 Slidell received the news. He was not to be reappointed, Livingston's brother-in-law having been named in his place.[18] Taken completely by surprise, he soon managed to get an abashed Carleton to admit that the whole thing had been planned by Gordon, thus confirming his fears of early January. He had received not a single complaint from the president nor the slightest sign of his impending dismissal.[19]

13. *Ibid.*

14. John Slidell to Martin Gordon, December 13, 1832, in Slidell Letter Book, TU.

15. John Slidell to Andrew Jackson, January 7, 1833, *ibid.*

16. John Slidell to Martin Gordon, January 8, 1833, *ibid.*

17. Andrew Jackson to Martin Gordon, April 9, 1833, in Jackson Papers, LC; John Slidell to Henry Carleton, March 16, 17, 1833, in Slidell Letter Book, TU.

18. John Slidell to Henry Carleton, March 16, 1833, in Slidell Letter Book, TU.

19. John Slidell to Henry Carleton, March 17, 1833, *ibid.*

In a matter of days Jackson discovered himself in the middle of a noisy battle among his followers in Louisiana. Furious at the intrigue against him, Slidell enlisted the aid of practically every prominent Jacksonian in the state, and most of them affixed their signatures to a protest against his removal which charged bluntly that Gordon's attempts to dominate his Jacksonian colleagues spelled possible disaster for the party.[20] They forwarded a copy of the remonstrance to Martin Van Buren as well, in the hope, as Slidell wrote the vice-president, that he at least would be able to prevent the memorial from falling into the hands of the very people around Jackson who had furthered Gordon's plans. Slidell clearly meant to warn against Livingston. Determined to impress upon Van Buren the significance of what might appear on the surface a simple petty quarrel, he also took pains to make the ambitious vice-president recognize the personal stake he himself had in maintaining the unity of a party anxious to see him as Jackson's successor in the White House:

> To preserve its organization and moral force it is necessary to destroy an impression which has been gradually gaining ground and which my removal has served to confirm; that an individual of all others the most unpopular in this community, possesses in everything relating to Louisiana, a controlling influence with the president. This influence has been acquired by a course of persevering intrigue and by the systematic denunciation of everyone who may have the misfortune to excite the ire of Mr. Gordon and is boasted of by him in a tone calculated to degrade the president and disgust his warmest friends. The crisis has now arrived and the question must be decided, whether the single voice of Mr. Gordon is to be more potential at Washington than the expressed and unanimous wish of the whole party. . . . The occasion calls for frankness and I assure you with the utmost sincerity, that if this man be not put down, the party that has uniformly supported General Jackson must inevitably be broken up. . . . The harmony of the party cannot be affected by his dismissal, it must be destroyed if he be not put down.[21]

But the wily Van Buren, in a position to observe Jackson's reaction to the remonstrance, sensed immediately the indiscretion of interfering in a matter which had so disturbed the president, and he brushed Slidell off

20. John Slidell to Martin Van Buren, March 27, 1833, in Van Buren Papers, LC; Andrew Jackson to Martin Gordon, April 9, 1833, in Jackson Papers, LC.

21. John Slidell to Martin Van Buren, March 27, 1833, in Van Buren Papers, LC.

with regrets that his letter had come too late for any corrective action.[22] The president had reason indeed to be agitated, for the petition in Slidell's favor carried the endorsement of several of his closest friends in Louisiana, like Maunsel White and J. B. Plauché, as well as those of Trasimond Landry, Sebastian Hiriart, and J. B. Labatut, all of whom had given long service to the General's cause and whose loyalty to his interest could hardly be challenged.[23]

Suddenly confronted with the realization that he had acted solely upon the charges of Gordon alone, Jackson reacted in typical Jacksonian fashion. Having done this, he never doubted for a moment that it was the right thing to have done. So now he had to write hastily to Gordon for some evidence of Slidell's misconduct which he might use to convince his Louisiana friends that the removal had been proper. "Send me a copy of your letter upon which I acted," he advised the collector, "with such a justification for your application for Mr. Slidell's being superceded as you have in your power, shewing the want of harmony between you and in what of his acts it consisted."[24] Slidell was clearly to be given no hearing at all.

The implacable Gordon needed no encouragement. Aware of the efforts in Slidell's behalf, he moved quickly to guarantee Jackson's continued support by a heavy-handed but nonetheless effective device. At what must have been the same moment that the Slidell memorial made its way to the president, the collector mailed a one-thousand-dollar donation to Francis P. Blair from himself and nine associates, to attest to their "support of the true Democratic and American principles proclaimed and acted upon by our illustrious chief magistrate."[25]

On the very day that the president sat drafting his own letter to Gordon announcing the arrival of the Slidell remonstrance, Blair hastened to the White House to report on Gordon's gift and to read to Jackson the letter which had accompanied it. As Blair repeated the message's encouragement to "go on—the friends of Jackson will support you," the General's eyes filled with gratitude. "Why . . . Mr. Blair," he said, "these friends of mine mean to pay back through you the thousand-dollar fine imposed on me at New Orleans," and he related the whole story with great gusto to Van

22. Martin Van Buren to John Slidell, April 20, 1833, *ibid.*

23. Andrew Jackson to Martin Gordon, April 9, 1833, in Jackson Papers, LC; John Slidell to Martin Van Buren, March 27, 1833, in Van Buren Papers, LC.

24. Andrew Jackson to Martin Gordon, April 9, 1833, in Jackson Papers, LC.

25. F. P. Blair to Martin Gordon, April 11, 1833, in Miscellaneous Papers, NYHS.

Buren that evening at dinner. As for Blair, he was similarly affected. "I need not say to you," he wrote Gordon, "how deeply I feel the obligation I owe to you personally for the early and active part you took in my behalf. . . . it is easy to say you have given a support to the Globe, which has almost taken its burden off my shoulders."[26]

Such powerful friends at court soon stood Gordon in good stead. Late in March a committee of New Orleans merchants headed by W. L. Robeson drafted a petition to Secretary of the Treasury Louis McLane requesting the immediate removal of the collector because of his tyrannical and oppressive conduct in office.[27] Informing William B. Lewis of this attack, Gordon placed the blame for it squarely upon Slidell, and then widened the campaign to destroy his enemies by adding his old foe Spotts and John Nicholson, the United States marshal at New Orleans, to his list of those officeholders opposed to the best interests of the president. His move shows clearly the scatter-gun nature of his campaign and how well he understood Jackson's easily aroused paranoia:

> In a former communication to the President of the United States, I recommended the Same course with respect to the Surveyor [Spotts], namely that he ought not again to be nominated for that appointment, and earnestly recommended our very worthy and true friend, Col. H. D. Peire, to succeed him.
>
> Respecting Mr. Nicholson, I will remark that he had never given the President that support which he ought to have done; I have always considered him as *a disguised ennemy* [sic], and I may say with great truth, that he has opposed the present Administration, *as far as he dared to go.* He has never, nor has Captain Spotts, ever contributed one cent towards the support of our Cause; they have always been found associating with our most vindictive, and malicious political ennemies.[28]

Transmitting the letter to the president, Lewis advised Jackson that "Gordon, no doubt, is a good deal excited at the course of these gentlemen, but he is a true and sincere friend, and worth a regiment of *lukewarm* or *pre-*

26. *Ibid.*

27. Committee of Signers of Memorial to Roger B. Taney, June 16, 1833, Charges Against Custom House Officers, 1833–1841, in RG 56, GRDT, NA.

28. Martin Gordon to William B. Lewis, March 27, 1833, in Jackson Papers, LC; for Nicholson's reactions to these charges, see John Nicholson to Andrew Jackson, April 8, 1833, Miscellaneous Letters Received, Secretary of State, in RG 59, GRDS, NA.

tending friends."[29] Jackson needed little encouragement to give Gordon the benefit of the doubt, having already instructed Secretary McLane to forward a copy of the charges against him to the collector, with the promise that "no opinion will be formed upon the subject until you shall have had full opportunity for defense."[30] The signers of the memorial were meanwhile advised that their complaints must be made in more specific form for any action upon them to be considered.[31]

While Robeson worked vigorously with his fellow merchants to draft the bill of indictment, Slidell and Spotts accumulated additional evidence of malpractice by Gordon, and in July and August 1833 a veritable barrage of accusations against the collector poured down upon the treasury department. They charged him with making false oaths against sea captains for personal reasons, demanding exorbitant storage and drayage fees not required by the treasury, and forcing merchants to have papers notarized by his brother-in-law despite their already proper form.[32] The most serious indictment alleged fraud involving the collector's paying excessive rent to himself for the use of one of his buildings as a storehouse even though he knew of the availability of United States property suitable to the purpose.[33]

The meager and obviously controversial evidence now available makes it impossible at this late date to decide the question of Gordon's guilt in these matters. But the weakness of his rejoinders to the accusations against him adds credibility to their accuracy. Only one deposition in the records actually denies the charges, the other letters and comments submitted in his behalf being simple avowals of friendship and confidence in his integrity.[34] Slidell and his associates continually urged Secretary Roger B. Taney to appoint a committee of inquiry to assess the complaints against Gordon and committed themselves to abide by its findings, but no such action was

29. William B. Lewis to Andrew Jackson, April 26, 1833, in Jackson Papers, LC.

30. Louis McLane to Martin Gordon, April 16, 1833, McLane to Samuel Spotts, April 16, 1833, Secretary's Letter Books of Correspondence with Collectors of Small Ports, in RG 56, GRDT, NA.

31. Committee of Signers of Memorial to Roger B. Taney, June 16, 1833, Charges Against Custom House Officers, 1833–1841, *ibid.*

32. Memorial against Martin Gordon, *ibid.*

33. R. F. Canfield to William J. Duane, August [?], 1833, *ibid.*

34. Deposition of Charles J. Gow, November 1, 1833, *ibid.*

ever taken.[35] Increasingly irritated by the turmoil among his Louisiana partisans, Jackson moved to end the imbroglio by giving Gordon an indisputable sign of his support. When the collector advised the president in July that he would resign from office rather than continue to serve with Spotts, Jackson summarily dismissed the surveyor as well as Robeson as receiver of public moneys.[36] Unlike Gordon, they had been given no opportunity to defend themselves.

Slidell, meanwhile, had journeyed to Saratoga Springs to lay his own case personally before Van Buren, only to be told by the vice-president that an "acknowledgment of injustice on Jackson's part was out of the question." True to his promise, however, Van Buren did finally write the president to explain that Slidell would be satisfied with the offer of any public office "of sufficient respectability to wipe away the effect of what had been done, such as a chargé's," it being understood that he would decline accepting so as to devote full time to his private practice.[37] Not even this was to be granted him, for in November Gordon journeyed to Washington on official leave, determined to block any action against himself and to settle his account with Slidell as well. This time he was at least more specific in his claims, if no more generous with his proof. Jackson obviously welcomed this new confirmation of his own fairness in the matter, and hastened to advise Van Buren of these new developments:

> Mr. Gordon (Collector of New Orleans) is now here. From testimonials submitted Mr. Slidel[l] has imposed upon the Secretary of the Treasury and myself in his recommendation of an appraiser for the port of New Orleans— the man had been suspended as an inspector for intemperance twice and then permitted to resign. This is charged to be in the knowledge of Mr. Slidel[l]—it is stated further by Mr. Gordon that Slidel[l], Nicholson and Grimes are all Calhoun men and nullifiers . . . and he asserts that they all three are your and my bitter opponents at all their elections. . . .
> Knowing that you had a favourable opinion of Mr. Slidel[l] as well as my-

35. John Slidell to Roger B. Taney, October 18, 1833, R. F. Canfield to Taney, December 28, 1833, *ibid*.

36. Martin Gordon to Andrew Jackson, July 2, 1833, Letters from Collectors of Customs, in RG 56, GRDT, NA; *Louisiana Courier*, August 1, 1833; New Orleans *Bee*, February 1, 1834.

37. Martin Van Buren to Andrew Jackson, August 6, 1833, in Van Buren Papers, LC.

self this letter is written to put you on your guard against this man, that you may not break your shins over stools not in your way—and that you may be guarded in any communication you may happen to make with him.[38]

For Slidell this was the end. Nothing more came of the charges against Gordon, but Slidell, Spotts, and Robeson found themselves cast out without mercy, for what appears to have been the single sin of incurring the wrath of the collector. Gordon could with good reason now feel that his claims to special place in the confidence of the president had been vindicated. But he had yet to reckon with the United States Senate, and humiliation of members of his own party, however satisfying, could not give him that mastery of the state government which he so ardently craved. In the spring and summer of 1834, his victory over Slidell would seem evanescent indeed.

Although pure malice alone might have sufficed for Gordon's attacks upon Slidell and the many others in his disfavor, he unquestionably had much more at stake in the months following the campaign of 1832 than simple spiteful gratification. To the political dominance which he sought, he now added the additional goal of snatching up the scepter of financial power which he knew would fall from the hands of the Bank of the United States when Jackson removed the federal deposits from that institution. In short, his program for 1833–1834 looked forward to placing a successor of his own choosing in the governorship to succeed Roman, creation of his own bank in New Orleans, and winning for it the federal funds when these were removed from Biddle's "Monster." With such political patronage and financial power, he would indeed be master of the state.

That strategy had required as a first step the purging from his party of those who might challenge his claim to its leadership, and so Slidell, Spotts, Nicholson, and Robeson had been doomed. Meanwhile, as early as December 1832, he made it quite clear to Secretary McLane that great caution must be exercised should the federal deposits be transferred to some local institution. "We have already experienced the baneful influence of the Bank of the United States *using the funds of the General Government to affect political objects,*" he explained, "and great care and circumspection will be

38. Roger B. Taney to Martin Gordon, November 11, 1833, Letters to Collectors of Customs, in RG 56, GRDT, NA; Andrew Jackson to Martin Van Buren, November 19, 1833, in Van Buren Papers, LC.

necessary to guard against like evils being exercised by *Local Banks*, making *use of the same means for like purposes.*"[39] Already active in the affairs of the Louisiana State Bank, Gordon in January 1833 succeeded in establishing the Mechanics and Traders Bank of New Orleans, whose claims to the deposits he pushed in correspondence with members of Jackson's cabinet, his letters filled with condemnation of all competitors as enemies of the administration. Confident of his support in Washington, he boasted openly that he was certain to be allowed to handle the public funds when Jackson finally removed them from Biddle's clutches.[40]

While waiting for that happy occasion he could turn his attention to the coming state campaign of 1834. Gordon had learned much since the debacle of 1830, chiefly that the only hope of a Jacksonian victory in the gubernatorial race depended on a fusion of his White House set with the Florida leadership. Fortunately for his plans, a link between the two factions was not only available but practically panting for an opportunity to be of service. John B. Dawson had finally reached the minimum age required of Louisiana governors, and he now moved to take over command of a Florida Jacksonian party left without guidance by the crushing defeat of Hamilton in 1830. Unlike his old tutor, Dawson had firm ties to General Ripley despite the latter's Yankee origins. An association with Wagner growing out of Dawson's ownership of various newspapers in the Floridas paved the way to an understanding with Gordon, and as early as November 1831 Dawson announced his candidacy to succeed Roman.[41] Aware of the strength of a Gordon-Dawson coalition, the Clay forces turned to Edward Douglass White as their candidate, convinced that no other man in the state possessed a popularity so strong among both the French and American populations.[42]

Before the battle between Dawson and White could get up any momentum, however, the Jacksonian ranks shattered in the Gordon-Slidell feud early in 1833. Encouraged by the loud denunciation of his dismissal by so many of their colleagues, Slidell and his friends moved boldly to seize con-

39. Martin Gordon to Louis McLane, December 21, 1832, in Jackson Papers, LC.

40. *Louisiana Courier*, February 12, 1833; William L. Hodge to Josiah S. Johnston, January 1, 22, 1833, in Johnston Papers, LC; Martin Gordon to Amos Kendall, October 15, 1833, Gordon to Roger B. Taney, November 22, 1833, Letters from Banks, in RG 56, GRDT, NA.

41. Baton Rouge *Gazette*, November 26, 1831; New Orleans *Bee*, May 10, 1834.

42. Baton Rouge *Gazette*, September 1, 1832.

trol of the Jacksonian leadership from the White House clique, fully convinced that they would be able to drive Gordon from office once they had made their case before Jackson and the treasury department. Their numbers were by no means insignificant, including as they did Slidell, Spotts, Robeson, Nicholson, and General Overton. But the full measure of their strength became evident in August 1833, when their recent acquisition of the *Louisiana Advertiser*, the state's leading Jacksonian newspaper, allowed them to bring forward Denis Prieur as their own candidate for governor.[43] Prieur had long been out of favor with Gordon, who had tried in 1832 to replace him in the New Orleans mayoralty with one of his own favorites, H. D. Peire.[44] Surviving that attack with ease, Prieur had announced for governor a few months later, but his candidacy had not been taken in any way seriously.[45] Now with Slidell and the enemies of Gordon united behind him, he became a threat of major importance, for aside from his famed personal drawing power, he might well exploit his newfound support to convince the creole population that his chances of success were by no means illusory. Against two American candidates such as Dawson and White, a combination of disaffected Jacksonians and loyal creoles could well prove irresistible. In addition, the likelihood that White would be a major contender suffered a serious blow from a tragic accident which almost removed him from the contest. The explosion of the Red River steamboat *Lioness* on May 18, 1833, snuffed out the life of Senator Josiah Johnston and so seriously injured White that it would be months before his recovery was assured.[46] In this state of uncertainty, Prieur's possibilities of victory could hardly be taken lightly.

The extent of Gordon's concern at this unexpected retaliation of his victims reveals itself starkly in the deluge of vilification which now poured down on Prieur from the organs of the White House clique. Chief among these, the *Louisiana Courier* and *Bee* of New Orleans abandoned earlier claims to independence from the internal quarrels of the party to launch strident onslaughts against Slidell and his associates. Their attack matched in brutality anything known in the many violent political wars which preceded it. They assailed Prieur as an ignorant city man who knew nothing

43. *Louisiana Courier*, August 10, 1833; New Orleans *Bee*, August 7, 1833.

44. *Louisiana Advertiser*, March 31, April 5, July 21, 1832.

45. New Orleans *Emporium*, November 26, 1832.

46. *Louisiana Courier*, May 25, 1833.

of the problems of the rural countryside, as an immoral and corrupt figure in his private life, a venal dictator and bungling incompetent in his management of the affairs of the metropolis, and the pawn of "a petty-half-way-pretended-Jackson party, which is now in direct opposition to the President."[47]

This vicious onslaught simply replicated in large measure the tactics which Gordon had used so effectively against Slidell. Not once did it advance a single concrete example of how anyone on Gordon's enemies list had betrayed Jackson or his party. Nowhere did it proffer any explanation of why they should suddenly find themselves labeled with the favorite stamp of "aristocrat." Nothing was forthcoming, in short, but a continuous flood of denunciation and condemnation by unsupported assertion, all reflecting the primary article of Jacksonian faith as purveyed by the followers of the White House coterie: to refuse acknowledgment of Martin Gordon as the unchallenged leader of Louisiana Jacksonianism was to stand convicted as an enemy of the president and as a nabob who would spit upon the workingman.[48]

A second challenge to Gordon's leadership suddenly came unexpectedly from General Overton, once considered a pliable instrument of the collector's will but now in open rebellion. Overton had his eye on the Senate seat of the late Josiah Johnston, and since he had been one of the main signers of the anti-Gordon memorial sent to Jackson in Slidell's defense, he naturally held high place on the collector's roll of traitors. Upon him too there now fell the full weight of the custom house press. "What folly!" cried the Bee. "Can it be that Mr. Overton has been so deceived by some half-a-dozen doubtful friends of the Administration, as to take such a step, one that will bring upon him in the end, should he not resign, disgrace and humiliation?"[49] What Jacksonian could support Overton, the Bee demanded, when it was known that he "is in heart a Calhoun man, and a nullifier . . . as we have strong reasons to believe." Determined to cut Overton off from any support in Washington, Wagner, in typical subservience to Gordon, wrote Francis P. Blair to warn that "Col. O. is strongly attached to Mr. Calhoun and if elected to the senate would be inclined to support him and all his

47. Ibid., August 29, 1833; New Orleans Bee, August 9, 14, 23, 26, 28, 30, 1833.

48. See, for example, Louisiana Courier, August 10, 29, 1833; New Orleans Bee, July 8, 1833.

49. New Orleans Bee, July 8, 1833.

projects." Overton stood high in his estimation, Wagner assured Blair, proceeding then to suggest that "three or four lines in the Globe, written in a
decided and positive tone, would fix his fate."[50]

Thus the summer and fall of 1833 reverberated with assaults upon Gordon's enemies from editors who remained singularly quiet about the
charges against their own favorites. The *Bee's* assertions that it possessed
complete data refuting the charges made against the collector were never
followed by publication of any of these supposed facts,[51] nor did any hint
ever appear in its columns that Dawson's flirtation with nullification had
been by all odds more serious than Overton's admitted attachment to Calhoun during the Eaton affair, a sympathy totally unrelated to the South
Carolinian's constitutional theories.[52]

Gordon's spokesmen continued their slashing denunciation of Overton
but could find no satisfactory candidate loyal to them to back in his place,
which resulted in the bizarre exhibition of the supposedly official Jackson
papers reviling the senatorial nominees of both parties with judicial impar-
tiality. For however great their hatred of Overton, it paled into nothingness
when compared to that which they felt for Alexander Porter, the Clay aspirant to the office. Not content to challenge his political ideas, the *Bee* labeled Porter as an ignorant alien unable to write good English and lacking
eligibility for the office because he had never become a citizen of the
United States. These were remarkable charges indeed in light of Porter's
gifts as one of the most polished and witty correspondents of the state and
his long tenure on the Louisiana Supreme Court, especially coming from
men who had always proclaimed themselves the understanding friends of
immigrants in their fight against "alien and sedition law aristocrats."[53]

Prieur, meanwhile, continued to add additional worries to the Gordon
camp by remaining a candidate to succeed himself as head of the city gov-

50. *Ibid.*, August 7, 1833.

51. *Ibid.*, September 6, 1833.

52. See Overton's comments on his feelings toward Calhoun in Walter H. Overton to
Josiah S. Johnston, April 29, May 23, 1832, in Johnston Papers, HSP, and his observations
on the Eaton affair in Walter H. Overton to John Overton, December 21, 1830, in John
Overton Papers, THS; *Louisiana Advertiser*, September 5, 1832; New Orleans *Bee*, August
5, 1833.

53. New Orleans *Bee*, December 7, 1833.

ernment. Reelection had always been rather easy for an incumbent mayor, and the *Bee* charged Prieur with deliberately contriving to retain his city post long enough to use the New Orleans police to coerce votes in his favor in the gubernatorial contest.[54] As a countermeasure, the Gordon forces brought forth John H. Holland as their mayoral candidate, and then unleashed a vigorous assault disputing Prieur's eligibility for the office. In the midst of continuous reference to the incumbent's immorality, the *Bee* ran at its mast the legislative act of March 14, 1820, which required the mayor and recorder of New Orleans "to be chosen from among the citizens who are heads of families."[55] There could be no misunderstanding the meaning of this device, a clear allusion to the notorious fact that Prieur's only family consisted of his colored paramour and their children.

It is easy to imagine Gordon's fury—engaged as he was to the limit of his strength against Prieur, Overton, Slidell, and Porter—when in November 1833 Secretary Taney announced selection of the Union and Commercial Banks of New Orleans as the institutions chosen to receive the public deposits in Louisiana, bypassing the collector's Mechanics and Traders Bank completely.[56] Having clashed for one reason or another with all of Taney's predecessors, Gordon had never been a particular favorite at the treasury department, his political strength depending primarily upon the president and his personal advisors like Francis P. Blair and William B. Lewis. The reasons underlying Taney's choices remain obscure and may indeed have been based on judicious financial, rather than personal or political, considerations. With a cash capital of $7 million, the Union Bank had been the major single force easing the financial tension in New Orleans in the fall of 1832, and its regulations restricting stockholders to citizens of the state presumably guarded against the kind of foreign influences charged against the Bank of the United States.[57] William G. Hewes, president of the Commercial Bank, had long identified with the Jackson party and labored diligently to persuade Taney that his institution deserved the deposits because

54. *Ibid.*, September 2, 1833.

55. *Ibid.*, October 4, 1833.

56. Roger B. Taney to Martin Gordon, November 4, 1833, Letters to Collectors, in RG 56, GRDT, NA; *Louisiana Courier*, November 21, 1833.

57. *Louisiana Courier*, January 9, 1833; Matthew Morgan to Louis McLane, December 21, 1832, Letters from Banks, in RG 56, GRDT, NA.

of its semipublic character as provider of the city's water supply.[58] Hewes was also closely allied to William D. Lewis, cashier of the Girard Bank of Philadelphia, and Reuben M. Whitney, a onetime director of the Bank of the United States anxious to become coordinator of the pet-bank system, their scheme envisioning a partnership between the New Orleans and Philadelphia pets which might ensure financial stability when they became custodians of the public moneys. Taney always denied any connection to Whitney, but the irrepressible meddler clearly enjoyed close contact with those involved in decisions determining pet-bank selections, and his influence may well have proved profitable to Hewes and the Union Bank directors.[59]

To Gordon, Taney's action came as a humiliating and costly defeat. His oft-repeated boasts that Jackson would surely adopt his recommendations in the selection of the pet banks collapsed around him, and he now saw himself as the laughingstock of New Orleans. For he had long reviled the Union Bank as a tool of the friends of Henry Clay,[60] and now Hewes might be seen as yet another challenge to his Jackson party leadership. All the more embarrassing, when Taney's decision reached Louisiana it was widely known that Gordon was at that very moment in Washington attempting to make sure that his own bank became one of the pets while he clinched the destruction of his intraparty enemies. Particularly galling, the Union and Commercial Banks turned out to have been sponsored by his old foes, Slidell and Nicholson.[61]

The defeat at least gave him a ready-made explanation for Porter's vic-

58. William G. Hewes to Roger B. Taney, October 27, 1833, Letters from Banks, in RG 56, GRDT, NA; Hewes to George Poindexter, March 21, 1834, in John F. H. Claiborne Collection, MSA.

59. Reuben Whitney to William D. Lewis, November 2, 4, 5, 1833, in Lewis-Neilsen Letters, HSP; John M. McFaul, *The Politics of Jacksonian Finance* (Ithaca, 1972), 64–69; Carl Brent Swisher, *Roger B. Taney* (New York, 1935), 223, 244, 283. The extent of Whitney's involvement in the Treasury Department's review of possible pet bank choices in New Orleans is suggested in John A. Brown to Reuben M. Whitney, October 1, 1833, Letters from Banks, in RG 56, GRDT, NA.

60. Roger B. Taney to Martin Gordon, November 4, 1833, Letters to Collectors, John Slidell to Taney, October 21, 1833, John Nicholson to Taney, October 29, 1833, Miscellaneous Letters Received, all in RG 56, GRDT, NA. Martin Gordon to F. P. Blair, December 13, 1833, in Jackson Papers, LC.

61. New Orleans *Bee*, December 6, 14, 1833; Washington *Globe*, December 30, 1833.

tory in the Senate election in December. Overton had withdrawn from the race at the last moment, to paeans of praise from the *Bee*, which suddenly discovered in him a man whose talents and loyalty deserved the universal admiration of the people of Louisiana. The move bespoke no particular rapprochement with the Gordon faction; Overton, as in 1830, once again simply deferred to a man who seemed better able to guarantee Jacksonian victory, this time to Joseph Walker of Rapides, his own parish. But the sacrifice came too late to give much propulsion to Walker or to unify his badly divided party, and Porter carried the day.[62]

Not one to overlook an opportunity to point out how disaster followed upon rejection of his advice, Gordon immediately took up his pen not only to rage against those who had bested him in the pet-banks competition but to open the eyes of Jackson, Blair, and Lewis to another of their "hidden enemies," Roger B. Taney. The sole factor leading to the victory of Porter—"a foreigner by birth, an *alien* by the laws of our country," Gordon proclaimed in an angry note to Blair—was Taney's incredible appointments. Directors of the Union Bank he condemned as minions of Henry Clay, then blasted William G. Hewes as "the brother in Law of that immaculate George Poindexter [a United States senator from Mississippi and one of Andrew Jackson's most hated enemies], under whose control, and at whose wink, he is the willing menial." "We are cursed with *Traitors* in our *Ranks*," he raged, but these might have been overcome, he maintained, had it not been for their "being supported—nay, cultivated by the effects produced on our party in the public Deposits. . . . We have been defeated but not conquered. . . . Believe me to be without hypocrisy or dissimulation."[63]

In a companion letter to William B. Lewis, these veiled accusations against Taney became more specific. As early as 1832, Gordon wrote, he had warned Secretary McLane of the "identical evils which have been fastened upon us by Mr. Taney." They had already lost the party a Senate seat, he observed, and would likely bring a Jacksonian defeat in the coming gubernatorial campaign, and yet Taney, he charged, continued to aggravate the problem by giving "countenance and support . . . to officers in the Customs at this port, who are politically opposed to us." In a closing move, he cast his net even wider. "When at Washington," he told Lewis, "I was a

62. Martin Gordon to F. P. Blair, December 13, 1833, in Jackson Papers, LC.
63. Martin Gordon to William B. Lewis, December 16, 1833, *ibid.*

close observer of passing events, and I must now confess to you, that I observed much to be displeased and mortified with.—Individuals for whom you and the President entertain the highest regard, are in fact and in truth *not* your political friends."[64]

Thus it became Taney's turn to be read out of the party by Martin Gordon, obviously a dangerous man to cross. But some hope remained, in spite of Taney's "treachery." By late December the Slidell-Prieur faction had seen enough in the correspondence from Washington to convince them that their opposition to Gordon would prove fruitless, and that his position in the confidence of Jackson remained unshakable. Spotts was now dead,[65] Robeson removed from office, and Overton once again at peace with the White House clique. All at once the Prieur campaign simply collapsed. On December 18, 1833, John Gibson bought up its principal news organ, the *Louisiana Advertiser,* and promptly announced for White,[66] leaving Prieur to abandon his candidacy in January. The latter made no open truce with the Gordon faction, but in some fashion an agreement clearly had been reached between the opposing camps. Without the slightest embarrassment, the *Bee* welcomed the mayor back into the Jacksonian fold of which it was guardian, explaining unblushingly that Prieur had never been attacked in its columns for any personal defects but only because of the "false friends by whom he was surrounded."[67] In March, Holland withdrew from the mayoral campaign for "causes beyond my control,"[68] assuring the unopposed reelection of Prieur.[69]

Now the opposing camps could concentrate their forces for the climactic struggle between White and Dawson. In many ways it would be the most bitterly contested election of the Jacksonian period in Louisiana, at least equaling in intensity the presidential battle of 1828. For just as in that national contest, high stakes and passionate commitments pushed the rival partisans to extraordinary efforts. And just as in that earlier clash, the Jacksonians set out to fight what they claimed to be the all-important war of the people versus the aristocracy.

64. Martin Gordon to Andrew Jackson, December 14, 1833, *ibid.*
65. *Louisiana Courier,* July 12, 1833.
66. *Ibid.,* December 23, 1833.
67. New Orleans *Bee,* January 6, 1834.
68. *Ibid.,* March 17, 1834.
69. *Ibid.,* April 8, 1834.

The opportunities to develop such a theme were many in 1834, and the Jacksonians missed none of them. By January the Bank of the United States had resumed its curtailment policy and once again money and credit became practically unavailable in Louisiana. At first the Jackson press simply refused to admit the existence of any hardship, ridiculing the reports of financial depression as the propaganda of those who would falsely maintain that removal of the deposits had brought ruin and economic suffering to the state.[70] But as the Bank continued to tighten its credit and discount activities in the early months of 1834, the painful consequences of that policy could no longer be denied. Many, some ardent Jacksonians among them, now concluded that the economic woes attendant upon the Bank's contraction had indeed been made inevitable by the president's rash removal of the deposits, and a great pro-Bank meeting gathered in New Orleans on February 19 to protest that policy, presided over by S. W. Oakey, a longtime supporter of the administration.[71]

As the economy grew more and more stringent, the administration press began to flood the country with reams of oratory from Thomas Hart Benton and the *Globe* insisting that the Bank's worst crimes could be found in New Orleans, where thousands of dollars had reportedly been kept out of circulation or shipped to the East to create panic in the Mississippi valley and spread disaffection against Jackson's Bank policies. This led Democratic editors in Louisiana to belated recognition that the economic distress of 1834, instead of being denied, might be turned into the most dramatic argument against Biddle's hated institution.[72] Swearing vengeance against the "Monster" for needlessly producing this misery in the society, the *Courier* repeatedly claimed that those who supported such a cruel and irresponsible enemy of the people revealed themselves as the aristocrats against whom Jacksonians had always warned. "Who can show an instance

70. *Louisiana Courier*, February 10, 1834; New Orleans *Bee*, February 18, 1834.

71. "Memorial of New Orleans Citizens," *Senate Documents*, 23rd Cong., 1st Sess., No. 187; "Memorial and Resolution of Tradesmen and Others of New Orleans," *ibid.*, No. 188; *Louisiana Courier*, February 20, 1834.

72. Thomas Hart Benton, *Thirty Years' View* (2 vols., New York, 1854), I, 465, 485, 541, 544; *Debates in Congress*, 23rd Cong., 1st Sess., 257–59, 702–15, 1007; Washington *Globe*, January 23, March 6, 10, April 1, 12, 1834; *United States Telegraph*, February 20, 1834; *Louisiana Courier*, February 20, 24, March 7, 8, 13, May 1, 7, 1834; New Orleans *Bee*, March 14, April 5, 1834.

of friendship extended on the part of the Bank to a poor man?" St. Romes demanded. "Banks are established for the benefit of the rich," he argued, with the final question: "Will the poor lend their aid to sustain and perpetuate an institution from which they can derive no advantage, and which threatens their liberties, by its extensive powers and the corrupting influence which it is enabled to exercise over the country, in the shape of bribery to one and influence to another? . . . Is it not better that the people should sustain the President, of whose honesty there can be no question, rather than side with an institution unknown to the constitution?"[73]

C. W. Duhy, editor of the *Merchants' Daily News* (New Orleans) and a onetime bitter enemy of Jackson who had been won over to the General's cause by the outright monetary bribes of H. B. Trist,[74] soon launched a campaign on the same tack, managing to bring the old anti-Federalist arguments of the Jacksonians completely up to date. Remnants of the old Federalist party, he warned, reenergized in the anti-Jackson camp, would restore the alien and sedition laws and "bind our interests, nay, our very thoughts, to the wheels of the political waggons driven by Webster and Biddle."[75]

Relishing their revived role as champions of the people, Jacksonian editors showed not the least embarrassment at the reminders of the opposition that Marigny, a prominent Jacksonian, was at that very moment doing all in his power to push through the legislature a charter for his Citizens Bank which would bind the state's credit to a bond issue of $12 million to facilitate the raising of capital for his purely private enterprise.[76] To this, as well as to pointed reminders of Gordon's long presidency of the notorious Orleans Navigation Company[77] and the extensive financial and commercial activity of Jacksonians like Maunsel White, J. B. Plauché, William G. Hewes, S. W. Oakey, and others, the *Courier* answered for its followers with the standard refrain: "The *Argus* seems to think that Aristocracy necessarily implies *wealth*. This is a great error. Aristocracy is a thing of the *head* and

73. *Louisiana Courier*, February 20, 24, 1834.
74. H. B. Trist to Nicholas P. Trist, April 30, 1832, in Trist Papers, UNC.
75. *Merchants' Daily News* (New Orleans), February 13, 1834.
76. *Louisiana Advertiser*, February 12, 21, 18, March 7, 8, 11, 31, 1834; *Louisiana Courier*, February 18, 1834; New Orleans *Argus*, July 2, 1834.
77. *Louisiana Advertiser*, June 2, 1834.

the *heart*, not of the *pocket* or the *purse*. . . . Now, everybody knows that Bernard Marigny is a democrat in theory and practice—that he has intermixed with, and has in fact been one of the people, from his earliest years—that he is plain and unostentatious in his manners, and that he pays as much deference to the poor as to the rich."[78] And when the puzzled defenders of White asked then if it were not well known that their candidate was loved for the friendliness of his manner and the simplicity of his life as contrasted to the gaudy effulgence of Dawson, the *Bee* seized upon this as the best proof of White's duplicity, that he should act like a democrat while harboring a hatred of the common man.[79]

So nebulous and empty of specifics were the arguments of the Jacksonians against the "aristocracy" of the Bank and its supporters that they scarcely deserve the name *arguments* at all. Skillfully contrived, they appealed to the jealousies and hatreds of the many who felt that their economic plight must indeed be the result of some conspiracy against them. Consistent or meaningful economic facts or demonstrations of how the Bank specifically injured the interests of the common Louisianian appear nowhere in this tangle of campaign oratory, whose recurrent theme could be summed up in one sentence: those for Jackson and Dawson were men of the people; those in the opposite camp were "aristocrats." This was not something to be explained, analyzed, or demonstrated. It sufficed simply to declaim it.[80]

Much more consequential than anything to be found in these pseudo-economic rantings, the Jacksonian assault upon the Constitution of 1812 as a document preserving the dominance of the "aristocracy" in the political life of the state addressed a clearly substantive issue. As early as January 1833 calls sounded in the legislature for a poll of the citizenry to ascertain their feelings on the matter of constitutional revision.[81] They failed of passage, but the argument remained alive in the months of the 1834 gubernatorial campaign. The Jacksonians generally favored abolition of the tax qualification for voting, reduction of the appointive powers of the gover-

---

78. *Louisiana Courier*, July 2, 1834.

79. New Orleans *Bee*, June 21, 1834.

80. See, for example, the speeches of Pierre Soulé and Alfred Hennen at the Dawson rally of June 7, 1834, in New Orleans *Bee*, June 9, 11, 1834.

81. *Louisiana Senate Journal*, 1833, p. 11.

nor, and a more equitable apportionment of representation in the state legislature.[82] All such demands had unquestionable legitimacy as integral
components of a liberal democratic credo, a rise-of-the-common-man type
rebellion against conservative public policy. But in this instance, given the
political history of Gordon and Dawson, the purposes behind their advancement of these principles must be highly suspect. For them, more than
being a matter of abstract political commitment, the question of constitutional change tied directly to the particular opportunity that each saw in
the election of 1834. In Dawson's case, he clearly meant to use it to attract
support of his candidacy from those sections of the state like north-central
Louisiana and his own Florida parishes, more and more restive under the
political dominance secured to the Gallic southwestern region by the Constitution of 1812. Alliance with the formidable Gordon camp of New Orleans might well bring him to the governorship, in position to humble
French pretensions and reorder the political dynamics of the state.

Like most New Orleanians, Gordon knew that both Gallic and American rural sections feared and indeed hated the city. The cosmopolitan population of the great metropolitan center made it essentially neutral in the
ethnic rivalry between the Gallic southwest and the American parishes, its
habitual course of action being to ally with those sections that might best
advance the city's own interest in a particular matter. Indeed, the ethnic
contest had little importance to Gordon, whose main objective always
centered on engineering whatever arrangement might secure for him the
political supremacy he had so long sought. Being the principal factor in
putting the Jacksonian Dawson in the governor's chair, in his judgment,
would do precisely that. Indeed, no other course seemed open to him, for
the pervasive attachment to Henry Clay in the southwestern sugar parishes
made the likelihood of any combination between them and the New Orleans Jacksonian White House clique remote indeed. Aside from any ethnic considerations, moreover, proposals to revise the fundamental law
might also strengthen his position in New Orleans by the promise of at
least partially redressing the notorious inequities in legislative representation imposed on the great metropolitan center by the existent constitution.
With such potential for advancing the ambitions of both Dawson and Gor-

82. New Orleans *Bee*, May 13, 30, July 2, 4, 1834; *Louisiana Advertiser*, June 26, 1834;
Merchants' Daily News, April 24, June 27, 1834.

don, constitutional reform became, therefore, a major rallying cry of the Jacksonian campaign in 1834.[83]

It lent itself particularly well to the strategy of attacking the E. D. White forces as elitists resistant to any change which might give greater political power to a larger number of Louisianians, the Jackson press constantly harping on how the Constitution of 1812 restricted the suffrage to those who paid taxes and limited officeholding to men of property. The *Louisiana Democrat* (Clinton) charged that "there is more aristocracy entwined in our State Constitution and Government, then in all the other states of the Union, but it is also true that it is early doomed to be eradicated. The democracy are coming to the rescue." Not even the supposed iniquities of the Bank of the United States provided a better whipping boy for those who would claim to speak for the rights of the people.[84]

In his constant harangues in the *Merchants' Daily News*, Duhy made it inescapably clear where the Jacksonians perceived this aristocratic system to be most firmly entrenched. Avoiding any overt reference to creole parishes of the state, he nonetheless claimed that aristocrats ruled "in districts where ignorance is the principal trait in the character of the population," imposing their will through parish judges, curates, sheriffs, and the influence of family ties. The power of these aristocrats, Duhy charged, rested in the archaic strictures which they had cemented into the Constitution of 1812, allowing them to maintain a "contempt for the masses of the people." He even managed to link together the two favorite Jacksonian targets: "Connected by a similarity of views, with the monied aristocracy throughout the Union, this faction has been emboldened of late by the successful efforts of the United States Bank in oppressing the middling classes and alarming the poor." And who, a writer to the *Bee* asked, had been most responsible for the aristocratic features of the Constitution of 1812? His answer: Alexander Porter. "*Will you,*" he demanded, "*have Alexander Porter to reign over you? If so, elect his pupil, his adopted child, his willing and obedient servant, Edward D. White!*"[85]

The White camp responded to these attacks with arguments compounded of rather transparent rationalization and hardheaded analytical

83. *Merchants' Daily News*, April 24, June 27, 1834; New Orleans *Bee*, July 3, 4, 1834; New Orleans *Courier*, June 28, 1834.

84. Reprinted in New Orleans *Bee*, May 13, 1834.

85. *Merchants' Daily News*, February 13, 1834; New Orleans *Bee*, June 24, July 1, 1834.

realism. The restrictions of the Constitution of 1812, they maintained, imposed such modest restraints on suffrage and officeholding that no man willing to work should feel burdened by them. Calls for universal suffrage and readjustment of legislative representation, according to this view, reflected no championing of expanded popular rights but aimed instead at enfranchising the indolent masses of the Florida parishes, thus providing Dawson the electoral power needed to destroy the delicately structured ethnic balance built into the Constitution of 1812, which for more than twenty years had allowed the state's Gallic and American factions to live together in reasonable equity and harmony.[86] In direct appeal to creole voters, the New Orleans *Argus* warned that a Dawson victory would mean shifting control of the state to their old American antagonists, with a consequent elimination of all French influences in the legislature and courts and a move of the state capital to the Florida parishes. The end result would be to make French-speaking Louisianians "strangers in their own land."[87]

From the very beginning of the campaign the Jacksonians recognized that White's greatest strength lay in the creole sections of the state and had begun to challenge his reputation as a particular favorite of the native population.[88] Aware of the ever present sensitivity of the creole sugar parishes to any threat against their basic industry, from April 21, 1834, until the end of the election the *Bee* highlighted its masthead with the running line, "THINGS TO BE REMEMBERED AT THE POLLS. REMEMBER, that Edward D. White voted in favor of a law, calculated to bring distress and ruin upon the great flourishing interest of our state." And on the very eve of the balloting they exploited another opening which the always unpredictable White provided them. Jacksonian papers raised a great fuss over a report by Isaac Johnson that during a campaign visit to Bayou Sara, White had asked a friend if he was a creole, pronouncing the word as "creowl." "No," the friend was said to have replied, "but I have a negro in my kitchen who is."[89] John Gibson in the *Louisiana Advertiser* and other White supporters at first denounced the story as totally false, stressing that its source, Johnson, was Dawson's brother-in-law, but their later attempts to characterize the incident as simply a "trifling pleasantry" tend to confirm that it actually hap-

86. New Orleans *Argus*, July 8, 1834.

87. *Ibid.*, July 9, 1834.

88. *Merchants' Daily News*, February 3, 1834.

89. *Louisiana Courier*, July 4, 1834.

pened.[90] But even that likelihood apparently did little harm to White's strength among the creole population, most of them seemingly accepting the whole exchange as just more evidence of White's notorious strangeness. His behavior, in any case, may well have been adjudged harmless compared to that of Dawson, who at almost the same time had thrown himself into a campaign brawl at Donaldsonville with drawn dagger, but only, his defenders said, to restore order.[91]

In the more pedestrian routines of campaigning, the White camp dutifully extolled their candidates's record in Congress, stressing his efforts in the always troubling question of disputed land titles in the state and defending his vote for the Compromise Tariff of 1833 as actually protective of the Louisiana sugar industry rather than damaging to it as charged by the Democrats. They denounced his Jacksonian opponent as an enemy of internal improvements and a nullifier at heart, condemned the Jackson administration's war against the Bank of the United States as the destructive folly of an ignorant old man, and made much of the fact that even Dawson admitted opposing the removal of the deposits despite his conviction that the Bank of the United States should be dismantled.[92] For Dawson the man they had nothing but contempt, dismissing him as a "painted butterfly," limited in ability, and notoriously the pawn of Martin Gordon, the would-be "Pacha" and "viceroy" of the Jackson party in Louisiana.[93]

In all this storm of controversy, Dawson did indeed play a highly unusual part for a Louisiana politician: he said practically nothing for himself. His specific views on nullification, internal improvements, the tariff, and removal of the deposits remained largely unspoken, leaving it to Duhy, Robert J. Ker of the *Bee*, and St. Romes of the *Courier* to fill their pages with explanations of what they were "assured" Dawson really believed.[94] In obvious counterthrust to Jacksonian charges of Dawson's subservience to Gordon, they paraded White in the meantime as devoid of any ideas of his own, dependent in all things upon Alexander Porter, the aristocratic and

90. *Louisiana Advertiser*, July 1, 3, 1834.

91. New Orleans *Argus*, July 1, 1834; *Louisiana Advertiser*, June 21, 1834.

92. New Orleans *Argus*, May 7, 1834.

93. *Louisiana Advertiser*, February 12, 14, April 23, 25, June 30, 1834; Baton Rouge *Gazette*, May 3, 1834.

94. New Orleans *Argus*, April 19, May 27, 1834; *Louisiana Advertiser*, January 15, May 2, 1834.

foreign master who controlled all aspects of his candidacy.[95] For their part, White's supporters tried to blunt this attack by urging Irish voters to rally to his side as one of them, claiming his Hibernian ancestry as a guarantee of his attachment to their interests, but the effort never managed to gain much momentum.[96]

Rejection by the United States Senate of Gordon's reappointment as collector of the port provided additional tension in the last weeks of the campaign.[97] His great offense, the *Courier* proclaimed, "consists in his being a staunch democrat, and therefore an eye-sore to the ruffle-shirt gentry. . . . What generous heart will not envy Mr. Gordon martyrdom?"[98] It was slightly more difficult to weep for Martin Gordon Jr., who at his father's rejection had been pushed forward unsuccessfully by the Jacksonians as a substitute, though not yet twenty-one.[99] The expostulations of the New Orleans Jackson press fed upon the effusions of the *Globe*, which trumpeted the praises of both Gordons as the firmest of the president's allies and mourned their fate as victims of Nicholas Biddle and New Orleans "smugglers," Blair's description of the merchants who had opposed his friend and financial patron.[100] Forced to keep pace with Blair, the *Bee* and the *Courier* lashed themselves to ever more violent denunciations of those who opposed their champions.[101]

Nothing better captured the frequently mindless extremism of this campaign than the uproar that erupted upon the report that Mazureau had replied to the vigorous pro-Dawson speeches of Pierre Soulé with the charge that most Jacksonian votes could be purchased for a glass of whiskey. What more striking proof of the aristocratic tendencies of the White party could be found, cried the *Courier*, than this shameful attack upon the humble

95. See New Orleans *Bee*, May 30, 31, 1834; *Merchants' Daily News*, March 17, 24, May 13, 1834.

96. *Louisiana Advertiser*, July 4, 1834; New Orleans *Bee*, May 2, 16, June 19, 1834; New Orleans *Argus*, June 5, 1834; Alexander Porter to J. Burton Harrison, June 9, 1834, in Harrison Papers, LC; Wendell H. Stephenson, *Alexander Porter, Whig Planter of Old Louisiana* (Baton Rouge, 1934), 81–87.

97. New Orleans *Bee*, June 16, 1834.

98. New Orleans *Courier*, June 13, 1834.

99. John Riddle to Roger B. Taney, June 24, 1834, in Levi Woodbury Papers, LC; *United States Telegraph*, May 31, June 5, 1834.

100. Washington *Globe*, May 30, June 4, 11, July 10, 11, 1834.

101. New Orleans *Bee*, June 16, 18, 1834; New Orleans *Courier*, June 16, 18, 1834.

drink of the working man.[102] Even Marigny, ludicrously enough, felt impelled to appear before a Dawson gathering to declaim: "Those aristocrats who are moved by the love of personal interest, will be defeated, and triumphant democracy will be seen rising as they fall. . . . They believe that because they have a few bankers on their side, that they will have a majority. . . . In the great contest between Great Britain and the United States, who was it that triumphed? The drinkers of Bordeaux and Chateau Margaux, or the drinkers of whiskey? When the Bostonians repulsed John Bull, was Claret or Whiskey drank?"[103]

In New Orleans the election proved as hectic as the campaign itself. Burly Irish draymen blocked suspected White voters from the polls, with little interference from John Holland, the county's deputy sheriff, otherwise occupied as a Dawson poll commissioner. Both sides crowded their partisans into the narrow stairway leading to one of the polling booths where election judges had placed a barrier across the head of the stairs, narrowing the approach to the officials' desk, and as the crowd pushed and pulled to get their own men through the opening the whole mass frequently went crashing down to the bottom landing.[104]

The returns gave White an impressive victory, not only in New Orleans but throughout the state as well, showing him defeating his opponent by a vote of 6,065 to 4,149. He carried the city by a margin of 958 to 542 and every parish south of Red River except Plaquemines, while Dawson captured the Floridas and the Red River region except for Avoyelles and Concordia.[105] Jacksonians fared almost as badly in the congressional campaigns. Among them only Ripley won his race, profiting from predicted support in the traditional Jacksonian stronghold of the Floridas and the scattering of votes among three opposing candidates. In the First District, Henry Johnson took the seat vacated by White, defeating young Charles E. Gayarré in a campaign which saw the ex-governor courting his old creole support by suddenly appearing regularly at mass, though not a Catholic. And in the western district Rice Garland won over the Jacksonian Joseph Walker.[106]

---

102. New Orleans *Courier*, June 28, 1834.
103. *Ibid.*, June 30, 1834.
104. *Ibid.*, July 9, 1834; *Louisiana Advertiser*, July 8, 9, 10, 1834.
105. *Louisiana House Journal*, 1835, p. 10.
106. New Orleans *Bee*, June 28, July 17, 1834.

Sadly, the *Courier* surveyed the wreckage of Jacksonian hopes and blamed everything on "that humbug, the Deposites."[107] Little in the record would seem to support that judgment, a lame rationalization hardly convincing even to those who propounded it. The economic distress of 1834 had indeed affected rural parishes as well as the financial centers of New Orleans, leading Browse Trist to the conviction that White's victory "was owing in a great measure to it." But most observers seemed to agree that few followers of the General broke with his party on that issue.[108]

Distribution of the returns underlines the principal verity of this clangorous contest: no ascendancy of an aristocracy over the people, no victory of Chateau Margaux over whiskey, had much to do with the outcome. Behind all the various maneuverings and tactics, behind all the frenzied campaign rhetoric, the old and still vibrant question of Gallic or American rule continued to dominate the Louisiana political scene. The election of 1834 added to that abiding issue the even more inflaming consideration that in this campaign American victory would clearly have meant dominion over the state by Martin Gordon and his White House coterie. Secure in the protections of the Constitution of 1812, Gallic south Louisiana was simply not yet ready to submit to the invader.

Its successful resistance had in large measure been assured by what remained a besetting weakness of the Jacksonian cause, the constant unwillingness of its principal leaders to surrender individual ambition to party solidarity. The Dawson-Gordon alliance never managed to repair the breach of the Slidell-Prieur challenge in New Orleans, and even many of the candidate's closest Florida advisers remained clearly uncomfortable in their association with the collector and his White House clique. Old frictions between adherents of Dawson and General Ripley never completely dissipated, and the always smoldering antagonisms between southerners and Yankees, nullifiers and unionists, prevented a united support of Dawson's candidacy even in those American precincts most important to

107. New Orleans *Courier*, July 11, 1834.

108. H. B. Trist to Nicholas P. Trist, August 27, 1834, in Trist Papers, UNC; E. G. W. Butler to Thomas Butler, April 27, 1835, in Butler Papers, LSU; Henry A. Bullard to Gulian C. Verplanck, January 18, 1834, in Gulian C. Verplanck Papers, NYHS; Maunsel White to Andrew Jackson, April 18, 1834, in Jackson Papers, LC; William G. Hewes to George Poindexter, March 21, 1834, in John F. H. Claiborne Collection, MSA; R. J. Walker to William C. Rives, July 17, 1837, in William C. Rives Papers, LC; Baton Rouge *Gazette*, June 21, 1834.

him. The pine woods area of the eastern Florida parishes, for example, harbored growing suspicion of the more affluent St. Francisville political leadership which he personalized. The wounds of internecine party conflict, especially those provoked by Gordon and his hacks, had cut deep—too deep to be easily forgotten.[109]

Buoyed by the joy of victory, White's supporters spent little time analyzing their success. In New Orleans a boisterous throng paraded through the city streets at the news of their triumph, bands blaring "The Rogue's March" before the home of St. Romes and intoning "The Dead March" before that of Jerome Bayon, publisher of the *Bee*. The following evening raucous crowds assembled outside Martin Gordon's residence on Royal Street to shout cries of "Whiskey! Whiskey!" and to rail at the dejected leader of the scattered Jacksonian forces.[110] Within, Gordon may well have listened and pondered his unhappy fate. The puzzle remained ever the same—Louisiana insisted on voting for Jackson but would have little to do with Jacksonians.

109. New Orleans *Argus*, July 1, 1834; Lafayette Saunders to Thomas Butler, January 31, 1830, in Butler Papers, LSU; Eleazar W. Ripley to Levi Woodbury, January 25, 1835, in Woodbury Papers, LC, in which Ripley blames "personal antipathies" within the party for Dawson's defeat, supports John Nicholson's retention as federal marshal, and subtly warns against letting Gordon sow seeds of further division in Jacksonian ranks.

110. New Orleans *Courier*, July 11, 12, 1834; New Orleans *Bee*, July 14, 1834.

· XII ·

Valedictory

Midway in his governorship, Edward Douglass White found himself mired in controversy of such variety and intensity that he despaired of the success of his administration. All his troubles, he concluded, had their origin in the circumstances of the election which had brought him to power. As he confided to his friend, the eminent legal scholar Peter S. Duponceau:

> I came in under the disadvantage of what was called a splendid triumph—an overwhelming majority. I say disadvantage, in this sense, that it presented numbers who had been, as they conceived, the chief instrument in the result of my election, and who had consequent wishes to gratify. I was very soon brought into collision with some of my warmest *friends*, that is, of persons who had contended stoutly in the canvass. In proportion to the height of expectation was the bitterness of disappointment, especially when a needy editor happened to be in the case, who had my name in his paper, and who believed, or affected to believe, that it was he who had elected me. It seemed as if fate had conspired to produce a conjuncture. The unwonted sounds of war were in the land. I had to raise a force of militia for Florida. All the elements of petty policy & ambition were at once called into action. Add to which that a number of offices, objects of general cupidity, and which had never before been vacant, now lost their incumbents & had to be filled anew.[1]

Regrettably, the keen analytical powers demonstrated in this remarkably accurate summation of his problems appear to have failed him as he la-

1. Edward Douglass White to Peter S. Duponceau, March 27, 1837, in Simon Gratz Collection, HSP.

bored almost desperately to contain them. Nor does he seem to have appreciated how at least some of the turmoil of his time in office flowed from his
own indiscretions.

The days immediately following his impressive victory carried no hint of
impending difficulties. In Washington, Blair's *Globe* ascribed the Jacksonian defeat to the state's tax requirement for the suffrage, in gloomy observations which seemed resigned to continued Whig electoral success, while
Duff Green's *United States Telegraph*, mouthpiece for the Calhoun party, rejoiced that "the defeat in Louisiana must be gall and wormwood to the cor-
ruptionists . . . a sign that their war cry of the 'victory at New Orleans,' is
beginning to lose its savour among the people."[2]

A great festival in New Orleans on August 3 celebrated White's triumph
as a resounding repudiation of the "crimes" and "corrupt appointments" of
the Jackson administration and gave the governor-elect a platform from
which to demonstrate his confidence and independence, the *Argus* having
already pointed out that Alexander Porter's intention to spend the summer
touring the middle and eastern states gave the lie to charges that the senator planned to serve as "viceroy" through his protégé. As testimony to its
assurance that a new epoch had indeed been born, the *Argus* rechristened
itself the *Whig* on August 7, a move which, taken in tandem with the Jacksonian adoption of the Democratic label at its Baltimore convention in
1832, signaled popular acceptance of the party nomenclature of the next
two decades. Even some of White's erstwhile enemies seemed ready to wish
him well, the St. Francisville *Phoenix* in the fortress of Florida Jacksonianism venturing the view that though he had been backed by aristocrats in
the campaign, he himself did not belong to that elitist clique and might be
expected to demonstrate his distance from them. The economic strictures
attendant upon the Bank's severe curtailment of credit in 1832 and 1833
appeared now to have completely ameliorated, with specie plentiful and
the commercial market brisk and confident. Bank capital continued to rise,
plans for a New Orleans to Nashville railroad engaged the energies of a
good portion of the state's financial community, and all parties joined in
celebrating the extinguishing of the national debt early in 1835.[3]

2. Washington *Globe*, July 29, 1834; *United States Telegraph*, August 4, 1834.

3. New Orleans *Argus*, July 24, August 2, 1834; New Orleans *Courier*, August 2, 1834;
New Orleans *Bee*, November 21, 1834, January 24, 26, 1835; Maunsel White to Andrew
Jackson, November 29, 1834, in Jackson Papers, LC; William G. Hewes to Roger B. Taney,
June 10, 1834, Miscellaneous Letters Received, in RG 56, GRDT, NA.

But hidden dangers lurked beneath these apparently tranquil waters, none more potentially destructive than the old preoccupation with ethnic division. Some ominous rumblings of factional disarray had been heard back in 1833 when the rapid creation of new banks raised questions in creole circles about American predominance among presidents, cashiers, and directors of the city's financial houses. As one of their number commented in a letter to the *Bee* urging his fellow creoles to a more vigorous competition, "Shall we not throw off that lethargy, which is said to characterize us? . . . I respect [the Americans] and admire their enterprise—but I think they ought to be satisfied with their share of power."[4] That sentiment continued to grow. In January 1835 the approaching end of the United States Senate term of George A. Waggaman turned the Louisiana legislature to the task of retaining him in office or selecting a successor, and this time creole pride worked against the Whig faction. They first inclined to continue their support of the incumbent, a favorite of Roman, whom he had served as secretary of state from 1830 to 1833, until the Democrats surprised them by uniting behind the young creole historian, Charles Gayarré. Their wonted reliance on Duralde to win creole support no longer sustained them, that one time champion now in financial ruin as a consequence of a lack of business sense which had him deep in law suits, raising questions about his honesty even in his own community. The Whigs scampered for some alternative to the American Waggaman, finally managing to win Roman's consent to stand for the position himself. But time had run out. Gayarré swung three creole Whigs to his side and won the seat.[5]

Trying to explain how a Whig-dominated legislature found itself electing a Democrat to the United States Senate, Henry Adams Bullard advised his Massachusetts friend Amos Lawrence that "the truth is we have raised up in our Louisiana politicks an element unknown in the other states, an element difficult to manage or to estimate its effects—I mean *creolism*—a kind of *national native* feeling—principally operating on moderate minded natives of French origin."[6] This kind of fixation on old ethnic pas-

4. New Orleans *Bee*, May 22, 1833.

5. *Louisiana Advertiser*, January 14, 1835; H. P. Dart, "Autobiography of Charles Gayarré," 9–27; W. C. C. Claiborne to Henry Clay, December 4, 1834, in Henry Clay Papers, LC.

6. Henry A. Bullard to Amos Lawrence, February 28, 1835, in Amos Lawrence Papers, MHS.

sions began to mount in the weeks and months after White's election, with consequences which eventually added much to the troubles besetting him.

That inextinguishable firebrand John Gibson, the excitements of the 1834 campaign behind him, had quickly returned to one of his favorite pastimes, blasting the Catholic clergy for alleged discrimination against those not of their faith and circulating stories about nuns sure to offend creole sensibilities.[7] Repeated American calls in the legislature for revision of the state constitution early in 1835 revived Gallic fears that their foes meant to strip them of the protections built into the Constitution of 1812, leading to angry exchanges over even mild proposals to expand the suffrage by modest general tax levies.[8] Equally divisive quarrels erupted in the New Orleans city council, defenders of the "bosom of the city" returning to familiar insistence that the original section of town be given a greater share of the steamboat landings so profitable to the upper faubourg. "It is time," one of their protagonists proclaimed, "that the first inhabitants of the country should be reinstated in their rights and advantages, with regard to the port." Responding to the attack, spokesmen for the commercial sector renewed complaints that the predominantly Gallic council discriminated against the upper faubourgs in allocating funds for street paving, charging as well that Mayor Denis Prieur deliberately blocked James Caldwell's efforts to provide the city with gas lighting because of his connection to the American community. And this despite the fact, Gibson grumbled, that these newcomers had raised New Orleans from a village to a "great and populous city," and were the "bone and sinew, the mainsprings" of its business and commerce.[9]

Although White played no part in this recrudescence of ethnic hostilities, he stood on its fringes, vulnerable to its possible expansion. Despite the support given him by the native population in the 1834 election, there was no escaping that he really was not one of them, and the heightened creolism that so alarmed Bullard kept alive in some quarters memories of the "creowl" story and earlier complaints that he had indeed displaced legitimate creole candidates like Prieur, Beauvais, and Duralde in the governor's race.[10] But for the moment he remained untouched.

7. *Lousiana Advertiser*, July 23, 28, 1834, March 23, 1835.
8. New Orleans *Bee*, January 21, 23, 24, 27, 1835.
9. *Louisiana Advertiser*, February 28, March 19, 1835.
10. *Ibid.*, January 23, 1834.

E. D. White, as he invariably signed himself, took the oath of office on February 2, 1835, and then delivered a pedestrian inaugural address promising to maintain the supremacy of the law, ensure faithful performance by public officials, and secure everyone in his rights, including along the way a defensive explanation of why he had voted for the Compromise Tariff of 1833 with its reduction of sugar duties. It had been necessary, he said, to save the Union. Perhaps so, but his return to the topic only reminded the influential sugar interest of what remained for them an unpleasant and hurtful reality.[11] And so he began his term with no great reservoir of faith and trust to sustain him in times of trouble.

They came soon enough, in an explosion of anger and resentment at his various appointments to office. He should have been forewarned of the pitfalls in that area by recent fulminations of Gibson, whose columns in the *Advertiser* flailed right and left at the malign influence of foreigners in the nation's political life and called for an outright ban upon their holding public office. He opposed them, he said, not on any basis of narrow prejudice about place of birth but because they did not understand English, American institutions, or the meaning of freedom, and could not be relied upon in any situation which might pit the United States against their former homeland. He stressed that he did not number creoles in that group, but made it equally plain that he did mean to include even naturalized foreign-born citizens, particularly those who he implied remained loyal to their "darling France."[12]

For whatever reason, he grew progressively more hostile to White in the weeks and months following his backing of the governor in the 1834 campaign, primarily, the *Bee* said, because the job as sheriff which he coveted had gone to a foreign Frenchman.[13] His hostility led him to merciless attack upon White as a "weak and prejudiced governor" for favoring aliens over the native born, climaxing in a passionate protest against his giving the post of register of conveyances to an ex-captain in the French Lancers, who happened to be the son-in-law of Etienne Mazureau.[14]

Five days later, William de Buys, a creole Whig representative from New Orleans, offered the following resolution to the state house of representatives:

11. New Orleans *Bee*, February 3, 1835.
12. *Louisiana Advertiser*, March 19, 23, 31, 1835.
13. New Orleans *Bee*, March 13, April 4, 1835.
14. *Louisiana Advertiser*, March 27, 31, 1835.

Resolved by the house of representatives of the state of Louisiana, that this house in common with the great mass of people of this state, view with feelings of deep regret, mingled with mortified pride, the evident, unconquerable determination of the governor to appoint to office foreigners who have been naturalized in preference to native born citizens of Louisiana, or of the United States, in opposition to the principles and true policy of our country, and contrary to the most urgent solicitations of those friends who by their patriotic and zealous efforts succeeded by a majority unexampled in any former elections, in elevating him to the distinguished station which he now occupies.[15]

Defeated eighteen to twelve, the resolution won widest support from representatives of American parishes, one of whom, the Democrat Robert Haile of West Feliciana, defended his vote with observations which placed White in particular odium: "I believe the Governor betrayed a want of American feeling in setting aside the claims of a meritorious and gallant officer in the last war, who lost an arm in the service of his country, while repelling the invader from this very soil—and these claims were set aside for the purpose of selecting a foreigner who came at a gloomy period of our history with arms in his hands, ready to lay waste the land."[16]

Despite the *Bee's* repeated protests that of ninety appointments made by White only eight or nine had gone to naturalized citizens, the offensive particulars of the instances involving Mazureau's son-in-law and the one-armed veteran of 1815 stirred up a storm of resentment against the governor. Adding to his problems, White apparently persisted in peculiarities of behavior which led Alexander Porter to comment to a friend that "I suppose White is as you say eccentric & perhaps does not live as many people may think he ought, but so long as he discharges his public duties well, these are matters that I do not think the Public should be angry with him for."[17]

But the public obviously thought appointments to be very much a part of his public duties. William H. Christy presided over a mass meeting at Banks's Arcade in New Orleans on the night after the defeat of the de Buys resolution, where speech after speech denounced the malevolent foreign

15. *Louisiana House Journal,* 1835, p. 133.

16. St. Francisville *Phoenix,* April ?, 1835 (mutilated copy).

17. New Orleans *Bee,* April 6, 1835; Alexander Porter to J. Burton Harrison, March 8, 1835, in Harrison Papers, LC.

influence and those who would install it in places of power. The *Bee* ridiculed the gathering as made up of disappointed office seekers and claimed that not a single creole had been in attendance, an assertion given some credibility by yet another mass meeting on April 13, at which prominent creole spokesmen denounced what now had come to be called "Native Americanism."[18]

The volcanic force with which the antiforeigner crusade erupted in the state and the almost immediate disappearance of White as a pivotal figure in the furor which it produced would seem to indicate that his appointments to office had simply triggered a movement waiting to happen. It fed on the long-standing ethnic rivalries in the state which had pitted creole against American and both against the foreign French, growing ever stronger as great numbers of Irish and German immigrants flooded into New Orleans in the 1830s. No particular political party gave it birth, though it first began to evidence its formalization into the Native American movement with the activities of Jacksonians like Christy and Dr. James McFarlane. Attacks by Martin Gordon and his faction upon Alexander Porter's supposed Irish influence over White in the gubernatorial campaign of 1834 certainly gave it impetus, and though Gordon never formally joined the Native American movement, even as late as October 1835 he and other Democratic stalwarts persisted in challenging Porter's citizenship, with no result except receipt of a polite note from the clever Irishman stating that he would refrain from questioning theirs.[19]

The issue of the status of the foreign born in the life of the community touched a broad range of concerns among Louisianians, involving worry about economic competition from immigrants anxious to find employment at whatever level of pay, fears of diminished cultural identity or political influence, and simple primitive hostility to unfamiliar mores and lifestyles. The volatility of this combination of emotional reactions presented to ambitious political adventurers irresistible opportunities for demagoguery and exploitation, which the ferment surrounding White's appointments allowed them to put into play. William Christy, a Kentucky army veteran of the 1815 campaign forced from the service under a cloud of financial irregularites, seized upon the pervasive unrest to further his own political career, obviously hoping to ride it to an increased prominence which might even-

18. New Orleans *Bee*, April 4, 6, 13, 1835; New Orleans *Courier*, April 8, 1835.
19. Alexander Porter to Martin Gordon, *et al.*, October 12, 1835, in Jackson Papers, LC.

tually link him to the rising fortunes of his relative, Richard M. Johnson, nominated in May 1835 to be the Democratic vice-presidential running mate of Martin Van Buren in the coming election of 1836.[20] Although many in the creole community shared the public resentment of White's appointment policies, demonstrated by de Buys's attack in the legislature, they reacted with experienced caution to efforts by Christy and others to enlist them in a broad campaign against the immigrant. Christy himself had never been a particular friend of theirs, and his association with John Gibson and James H. Caldwell, the American sector entrepreneur, fueled their suspicion that the Native American movement did indeed include them among its targets. They noted, as well, that the de Buys resolution in the house had received its major support from American parish representatives like Haile of West Feliciana. General Jean B. Plauché, beloved creole veteran of the 1815 campaign, warned his compatriots of the dangers in Christy's appeals, and Bernard Marigny adopted much the same position in a successful run for the state house of representatives against the nativist McFarlane in May 1835.[21]

The rich ethnic mixture of its population and the centrality of its position as the capital of the state made New Orleans the obvious battle ground in the strident conflict set off by the nativist crusade. In the summer of 1835 Caldwell launched the city's *True American* newspaper, placed John Gibson in its editorial chair, and raised the pitch of the antiforeigner campaign to ever higher levels. The new sheet became the mouthpiece of the Louisiana Native American Association, which Gibson claimed to have founded on July 28, 1835, and immediately began to flood the city and state with inflammatory nativist propaganda which confirmed the creole community in its conviction that they too would be lumped together with foreign French, Irish, and Germans as intruders outside the mystical fellowship of original Americans.[22] They understood all too well how easy it would be for old foes to point out that the great majority of creoles had at birth been just as foreign to the United States as the most recently arrived French ex-lancer, Irish drayman, or German butcher.

20. *United States* v. *William Christy* (Case #2541), in *Conspicuous Cases in the United States District Court of Louisiana;* Listing of Public Debtors (1868), in RG 206, Records of the Solicitor of the Treasury, NA; William Christy to Martin Van Buren, September 24, 1836, in Van Buren Papers, LC.

21. *Louisiana Courier*, April 8, May 16, 1835; New Orleans *Bee*, May 2, 18, 1835.

22. New Orleans *True American*, August 15, 1835.

Caldwell's sponsorship of the movement provided one of its most bizarre features, for he had no claim to American origins at all, having been born in Manchester, England. First known in New Orleans as the owner and manager of the Camp Street Theatre, by 1835 he ranked as the major developer of the bustling American quarter, prominent as the founder and president of the new city gas works and impresario of the magnificent St. Charles Street Theatre scheduled to open in November of that year. A Jacksonian in his politics, he had won the hatred and fear of the creole protectors of the city's old quarter, who now saw in his nativist program yet another device by which he meant to despoil them of all influence in *their* native land just as he had brought ruin to their beloved Théâtre d'Orléans.[23] Christy, for the moment, yielded leadership to Caldwell and Gibson and denied that he held membership in their association, apparently out of fear that any more prominent role would damage the vice-presidential prospects of his relative Richard M. Johnson and lose what he hoped would be Democratic party support in his quest for the governorship in 1838. Whatever his formal membership status might have been, he made no effort to hide his obvious nativist sentiments.[24]

The patriotic celebration of July 4, 1835, provided clear evidence of just how easily the community's always smoldering ethnic differences could be set aflame again. The committee organizing the event chose the new Presbyterian church on Lafayette Square as the site for ceremonies to be held at the termination of the day's parade, bypassing the traditional Catholic cathedral and Place d'Armes, a shift which the creole population took as a sign that they had no legitimate part in an American ritual. The Louisiana Legion and the Orleans Guards refused to march beyond Canal Street, and the Catholic clergy stayed away from the parade altogether. Gibson poured out his wrath upon them all in the *True American*, to be answered in the French columns of the *Bee* with the plaint, "Puritans! Do you wish then to set ablaze a religious war in the state of Louisiana?"[25]

A few weeks later on August 30 the Louisiana Legion, composed largely of naturalized Frenchmen, moved to suppress violence at a meeting of hun-

23. For an overview of Caldwell's theatrical history, see Paul S. Hostetler, "James H. Caldwell: Theatre Manager" (Ph.D. dissertation, Lousiana State University, 1964); for his role as nemesis of the Gallic council, New Orleans *Bee*, November 14, 1834, July 23, August 1, December 12, 1835; *Louisiana Courier*, March 15, 1834.

24. New Orleans *Bee*, August 1, 3, 1835.

25. *Ibid.*, July 7, 8, 1835.

dreds of persons gathered in the Faubourg St. Mary's Lafayette Square to protest the teaching of mechanical skills to slaves and free persons of color but actually, according to the *Bee*, to propose prohibiting the hiring of any foreign-born or nonwhite citizens so long as natives lacked employment. Although the Legion's performance won praise even from Caldwell, the editor of the *Louisiana Advertiser* published a few days later a series of crude jokes ridiculing the militia unit's competence and commenting disparagingly on the national origins of its members. Outraged Legionnaires and their sympathizers stormed the *Advertiser*'s offices, destroyed the premises, smashed its type, sent the editor fleeing from the city, and attempted to lynch the paper's owner, who escaped their wrath only by the intervention of Prieur and Mazureau.[26]

Through the last months of 1835 and into the early weeks of 1836, eruptions of anger over foreigners continued to plague the community. Each day, Gibson waged relentless war upon the immigrant newcomers in the *True American*, reviling them as the chief tools of demagogues who made every election a "saturnalium" of debauchery, where whiskey flowed and men died by the knife or the "shelalah." In New Orleans, he complained, foreign-born editors used the columns of the *Bee*, the *Courier*, the *Louisiana Advertiser*, and the *Daily News* to denigrate American institutions and political processes, an evil which the Native American Association particularly aimed to destroy. Christy added to the tension in November 1835 by beginning publication of his own newspaper, the New Orleans *Post*, protesting anew his nonalliance with the nativist organization but still appearing to the creole community as a stalking horse for Caldwell and Gibson.[27] In January 1836 the *True American* brought out the Louisiana Native American Association's pamphlet, *Address to the Public Authorities of the United States*, calling for a twenty-one-year residency requirement for naturalization and denouncing foreigners already in their midst for having "come to feed at our prosperous tables." No foreigner, they claimed, could ever throw off his attachment to Europe or resist voting for one of his kind against the most worthy native candidate.[28] As a counterforce, the Louisiana Loyal American Association organized at Davis's Ball Room on Feb-

26. *Ibid.*, September 4, 7, 1835; *Louisiana Courier*, September 1, 3, 1835.

27. New Orleans *True American*, August 3, 5, 11, 13, 14, 15, 1835; New Orleans *Post*, November 29, 1835.

28. *Address to the Public Authorities of the United States. By the Louisiana Native American Association* (New Orleans, 1836).

ruary 11; its president, Gilbert Leonard of Plaquemines, dismissed the nativists as "persons, tired of their insignificance, disappointed in their ambition, opposed to a government to the administration of which they were not called," a clear reference to the movement's origins in the dispute over White's appointments. The *Bee* feared that this move would only stir up additional bitterness and lead to possible bloodshed, but saw nothing in the rising controversy to dispute its earlier contention that the overriding impulse driving the Native American cause remained "anti-Louisianaise."[29]

Whatever the validity of that judgment, the continuous flaying of the city's emotions by these recurrent outbreaks of ethnic intolerance inevitably intensified old quarrels between the original and the newer sections of the metropolis. As far back as the 1820s, various spokesmen for the Faubourg Ste. Marie had protested what they considered to be the neglect visited upon their section by a city council dominated by Gallic aldermen, even to the point of several times proposing a division of the city into separate municipalities.[30] The protests continued year in and year out, centering in 1835 on claims that every cross street from Canal to Esplanade had been paved in the Old Quarter while only two or three had been improved in St. Mary. Caldwell and his associates charged the council as well with trying to concentrate the city's new gas lights in the favored part of town after deliberately stalling the entire project out of animosity for its promoter.[31]

The sectional dispute, fittingly enough, came to climax out of the impact on the city of the great Mississippi, the source of its wealth and eminence as the commercial mart of the American west. As the river curved around the crescent bend on which the metropolis rested, its current bounced off the west bank and coursed back to the eastern shore where it broke into two parts, one continuing downstream, the other flowing upriver in front of the American suburb, where it deposited the silt forming the batture which had enriched Edward Livingston. By 1834 the continuing buildup of that extension of the river bank left the wharves originally constructed to service the steamboats of the western trade farther and far-

29. New Orleans *Bee*, August 5, 1835, February 10, 12, 13, 1836.

30. New Orleans *Argus*, September 26, 1826; New Orleans *Emporium*, December 10, 1832.

31. New Orleans *Union*, November 13, 1835; New Orleans *Bee*, December 14, 1835; *Louisiana Advertiser*, February 28, 1835.

ther from the water's edge, threatening to choke off the thriving commerce responsible for the upper faubourg's remarkable growth and prosperity. The anguished cries from St. Mary merchants pleading with the city council to provide funds to extend the wharves beyond the batture's outer limit went unheeded, the French aldermen insistent on some other arrangement which might extend the steamboat traffic deeper into the original old quarter. Even a proposal in late 1835 by Samuel J. Peters, Caldwell's rival in promoting the American quarter, to arrange for financing the project through funds loaned to the council by St. Mary commercial houses met with a similar rebuff, leading the usually pro-Gallic *Bee* to condemn the city's refusal to act with the observation that "the upper faubourg consider themselves neglected in the distribution of the corporation revenues and we are left few arguments and fewer facts to undeceive them." Adding to the charges and countercharges of prejudice and discrimination, creole protagonists berated the state legislature for what they perceived as American hostility to Bernard Marigny's Citizens Bank. It had been created after a bitter legislative battle in 1833, its capitalization of $12 million the largest of any state-chartered bank in the nation, but that very size made it impossible to raise the funds necessary to begin its operation without some kind of state guarantee of its bonds. Proposals to grant that aid tied up the legislature for years before winning approval in 1836, much of the debate reflecting the same ethnic division so prevalent in the wider community, as evidenced by John Gibson's charge that all Citizens Bank supporters lived below Canal Street.[32]

The disputes over street paving, gas lighting, extension of the St. Mary wharf system, and support of the Citizens Bank would almost certainly have occurred had the Native American Association never been heard of in Louisiana, but the leading roles taken by Caldwell and McFarlane in the city council debates inevitably linked those issues to the angry passions unloosed by the nativist movement, giving them a divisive force comparable to that which had produced the near civil war of the mid-1820s.

Through all of 1835 and the early months of 1836, the city agonized in a welter of ethnic hatred and dispute. Weary of the endless angry exchanges,

32. *Louisiana Advertiser*, February 12, 21, 28, March 7, July 15, 1834; New Orleans *Bee*, February 13, 1834, September 30, October 20, 1835; *Louisiana Acts*, 1833, pp. 124–36, 1836, pp. 15–35, 103–105; *Louisiana House Journal*, 1836, pp. 103–105; *Louisiana Senate Journal*, 1836, pp. 22–27.

alarmed at the increasingly violent tone of the confrontations, and resentful of the intrusion into the quarrel by notoriously anti–New Orleans legislators like Senator Larry H. Moore of the Florida district, both sides early in 1836 accepted the proposal offered in the house of representatives by J. B. Labatut of New Orleans to divide the city into three semiautonomous municipalities, the First comprising the original city, the Second including St. Mary and the other upper faubourgs, and the Third made up of the Faubourg Marigny below the Esplanade. No one could question the Gallic credentials of Labatut, who had once horsewhipped John Gibson on the streets of New Orleans, and only Bernard Marigny and four other ultra-French representatives held out against the arrangement. The longstanding Old Quarter resistance apparently crumbled before a growing awareness that the continuing growth and wealth of the American section in a very short time would in any case have allowed it to wrest control of the whole city from its traditional French leadership.[33] This tripartite city structure, unique in the American scene, provided each municipality its individual council and presiding officer, with authority over internal financial, economic, and domestic affairs, but retained a single mayor, police force, and a general council to legislate functions which cut across municipality lines, such as regulation of drays and hacks. The novel system would last until 1852, when New Orleans once again returned to unified control. While it eventually ameliorated the bitterness of the decades-old feud between the opposing original and new sections of the city, the compromise did not end it. But it did in a sense close the once open question of who was to rule in New Orleans. The creoles had clearly lost.

The apparent easing of the strains of that particular conflict did not restore the city and state to a relaxed peace and comfort, steeped as they were in other concerns laden with even greater cause for fear and alarm. Governor White gave voice to the widespread apprehensions of his fellow citizens when he reported to the legislature on January 4, 1836, that "In the full career of peace and prosperity, a feverish excitement has come upon the country." Its origins could be traced back to the massive blow to the South's sense of security dealt by the rising force of antislavery sentiment in the North, dramatically articulated in 1829 by the publication of *David Walker's Appeal*, an essay by a North Carolina free man of color writing from Boston, which called upon blacks to rise in rebellion against their

33. New Orleans *Bee*, January 7, 16, 1836; *Louisiana House Journal*, 1836, p. 79.

masters. The appearance of William Lloyd Garrison's *Liberator* in 1831, followed a few months later by the bloody insurrection of Nat Turner in Virginia and the success of Garrison and Arthur and Lewis Tappan in organizing the New England Anti-Slavery Society and the American Antislavery Society in 1833 plunged the South into a paroxysm of fear that the horrors of slave rebellion threatened them everywhere and at every moment.

The hysteria peaked in Louisiana in late 1835, with reports from all parts of the state detailing acts of violence by slaves, describing incitements to insurrection by a gang of white men headed by John A. Murrell, and complaining of distribution of abolitionist literature through the United States mails. In the single month of August a shotgun blast fired by his bondsmen killed a Dr. Solange in Franklin, and reports spread through the southwestern parishes of an insurrection set for Christmas; vigilantes hanged two white men in St. Helena for preaching to slaves and one of Murrell's band in Clinton for stirring up rebellion; authorities announced the crushing of a detected slave conspiracy in Baton Rouge; and the *Opelousas Gazette* claimed to have knowledge of fifteen hundred rifles sent to New Orleans to arm the blacks. From St. Francisville, Rachel O'Connor's letters to her kin in New Iberia reveal the kind of frenzy sweeping through the state: "The country is full of Murrel's men, and I fear they may yet do harm. . . . The white men are taken up on all occasions. They have one in jail that they expect to hang, which is more merciful than is common, for they generally whip them nearly to death. They call it Lintch's law, giving them from two to three hundred lashes, and then let them go with orders to be out of the state in eight hours." James M. Bradford, editor of the *Louisiana Journal* (St. Francisville), confirmed this general collapse of legal due process in the Floridas, explaining to Francis P. Blair, "Our committees are still organized, and proceed extrajudicially, whenever necessary. If any abolitionist, or the agent of an abolitionist should be detected here, he will be led to immediate execution."[34] In New Orleans, Christy on August 10 presided over a meeting called to "counteract the pernicious effects of the

---

34. St. Francisville *Phoenix*, August 1, 1835; *Louisiana Courier*, August 19, 25, 1835; New Orleans *True American*, August 6, 12, 13, 1835; William Taylor Palfrey to John Palfrey, August 12, 1835, in Palfrey Family Papers, HU; Rankin Rogers to Maria Rogers, August 23, 1835, in Hudson Tabor Papers, LSU; Rachel O'Connor to A. T. Conrad, August 24, 1835, O'Connor to Frances S. Weeks, September 7, 1835, in David Weeks Collection, LSU; James M. Bradford to Francis P. Blair, August 25, 1835, in Blair-Lee Papers, PU.

measures now being taken by the abolitionist societies of the eastern and northern states to disseminate their notorious doctrines," but effective action stalled when his supporters tried to pass a resolution calling upon the state to contribute $500,000 to mount a defense against the antislavery attack. Randall Hunt, a young lawyer at the beginning of his long career in Louisiana, denounced the proposal as a device to raise a slush fund for Christy's 1838 gubernatorial bid, and protested further that he would have nothing to do with a campaign of generalized hatred against the North. Entangled with the nativist movement in this fashion, the resolution failed, and the meeting accomplished nothing.[35]

But it did precipitate a round of reactions to the supposed threat of abolitionist terrorism. The city council met on August 14 in closed session, from which it issued a circular to be distributed throughout the state warning of impending dangers and how to counteract them. Gibson in the *True American* rushed to the defense of Christy, denounced foreigners as engaged in a plot to undo the work of those opposed to the abolitionist fanatics, and summoned his readers to constant vigilance with the warning that "Danger is at your doors—let no syren voice lull you to procrastination!"[36]

The tumult occasioned by the nativist meeting on August 30 to protest the training of slaves and free persons of color in the mechanical trades and the attack upon the *Louisiana Advertiser* which followed it convinced many in the city that the disturbance had actually been fomented to cover an impending assault by antislavery forces. Groups of citizen companies organized to defend the community against attack, German and Swiss units prominent among them, obviously hoping to dispel something of the rampant nativist hatred engulfing them. The city remained literally on the verge of panic for several days, and when on September 5 new rumors spread of an uprising threatened for that evening, hundreds of armed men streamed to Lafayette Square to meet the foe, only to find everything in perfect order. By October 6, Peters, as president of the Louisiana Constitutional and Anti-Fanatical Society, announced that a thorough search had found no abolitionists or antislavery sympathizers in the city and that the community could safely relax. But henceforth no night meetings of slaves or free persons of color, common occurrences only a month previously,

35. *Louisiana Courier*, August 11, 1835; New Orleans *Bee*, August 12, 1835.

36. *Louisiana Courier*, August 13, 1835; New Orleans *Bee*, August 15, 1835; New Orleans *True American*, August 13, 15, 20, 1835.

were to be tolerated. Despite Peters's reassurances, apprehensions remained high well into the new year. Discovery of a planned slave rebellion in Jackson on December 24 threw the town into panic, resulting in the hanging of two blacks, and in New Orleans on January 10, 1836, Sunday services at the Methodist Church ended in confusion when interrupted by "some persons who apparently feared that evil would result from the presence of negroes in the assembly."[37]

Deepening of public concern soon resulted throughout the state in major strictures upon the activities of slaves and free persons of color, measures totally at odds with the generally permissive attitudes long traditional in the community. In Ascension Parish new controls prohibited the one-time customary visits by slaves to Donaldsonville and banned the Sunday gatherings which they had so enjoyed.[38] In New Orleans the press began to emphasize what it called the baleful influence of the liberties enjoyed by free persons of color upon impressionable slaves who might be led into rebellion by their example. Incidents of violence committed by free men of color upon tavern keepers, reports of rioting by them on the city's new transit buses, and fear that the free colored community harbored insurrectionists and incendiaries gradually intensified willingness to impose harsher limits on their prerogatives and activities, a tendency which would grow ever stronger as anxieties over abolitionism mounted.[39] Even the notoriously popular quadroon balls became the focus of suspicion and concern. In November 1835 acting mayor John Culbertson called upon the city council to consider stricter regulation of the gatherings, and when it gave little attention to his request, he returned a week later with renewed demands for action. "I know from positive information," he claimed, "that these meetings are the sink of the most dissolute class of women, and that the spectacle of their abominations is constantly offered to the public gaze." Moreover, he stipulated, they "bring with them unprincipled men who have been expelled from other states, and who find here, in consequence of the disguise they are allowed to assume, and the protection of these females, every opportunity of following their swindling career." The editor of the *Bee*, checking on the mayor's account, visited the Washington Ball

37. *Louisiana Courier*, September 5, 1835; New Orleans *Bee*, September 7, October 6, 1835; New Orleans *Observer*, January 2, 16, 1836.

38. New Orleans *Courier*, August 15, 1835.

39. New Orleans *Bee*, September 30, 1835, July 2, 1836.

Room on St. Philip Street one Saturday night and came away with the report that while everything had been decorous at the affair, "two thirds at least of the females present were white women." Not even the specter of possible quadroon sanctuary for slave insurrectionists could turn the council against an institution so cherished by the city's male population, and despite Culbertson's pleas to end these "schools of immorality," the balls continued as before.[40]

Some observers did, indeed, remain relatively unconvinced of any impending danger from rebellious bondsmen. In Opelousas, Henry Adams Bullard put on a brave face at the very height of the anxieties gripping the state, writing his old friend Amos Lawrence to congratulate him on a recent Boston antiabolitionist meeting:

> But, after all, what have we to fear? What can the African head (I speak phrenologically) do against the Saxon? The negro has neither courage nor revengeful feelings nor power of combination. With fifty armed whites I can overcome five thousand with another Tappan at their head. There is not one in a hundred that can be excited against the whites. They cannot act in concert. Generally speaking the negroes are kind-hearted—even affectionate towards their master and his family. They feel their dependant condition and have no ambition. In sickness they are provided for—in old age they have a home. At the same time, you cannot be half as sensible as I am how great a moral and political evil slavery is—because you do not see all its influences on the characters & habits & feelings of the whites.[41]

Governor White voiced no such optimism, preferring instead to present to the legislature in early 1836 visions of an almost apocalyptic future. He decried "a class of persons in the northern states [who] have arrogated to themselves the province of interference in the domestic affairs of the south." Like Bullard he saw slavery as a benign system where "there is now peace and happiness" based on "the obligation of service on the one hand, accompanied by the reciprocal obligation of protection and support, as well in the weakness of infancy as in the decrepitude of age." But these northern "infuriate zealots," he charged, "would sow discontent and insubordina-

40. *Ibid.*, November 21, 28, 30, 1835.

41. Henry Adams Bullard to Amos Lawrence, September 24, 1835, in Amos Lawrence Papers, MHS.

tion. If successful in their machinations they would kindle the flame of ser-
vile war, deluge the land in blood, and cause the extermination of their
hapless deluded victims." He accompanied his message with seized copies
of antislavery literature being sent into the state through the federal mails
and ended with the graphic warning that abolitionists were even then
"lighting the torch and presenting the knife to the hand of the assassin."[42]

A house committee responded to the governor's message with a report
that proclaimed slavery to be "a natural and inherent principle of social
life, which has universally prevailed from the foundation of social order to
the present time . . . consistent with morality and the Christian religion,"
invoking both the Old Testament and the words of Jesus to substantiate its
claims. It called upon the North to bridle its "fanatics," cautioning that "if
we must hope in vain, and may the Great God of Heaven avert it, then *we
must and we will adopt such measures as may be deemed necessary to protect
ourselves.*" Without such restraint, the report concluded, "a dissolution of
the union must be inevitable." The resolutions won approval of both the
house and senate, reinforced by house authorization for the governor to
purchase arms for protection of the community and for raising companies
of volunteers to guard against insurrection.[43]

In stark contrast to this atmosphere of gloom and apprehension, the
state enjoyed a basically sound economic health in the first two years of
White's administration, highlighted by a remarkable expansion in banking
and real-estate investment in the metropolitan center of New Orleans. A
jump in the value of its cotton production from $10,590,000 in 1834 to
$12,260,000 in 1836 helped ease the drop in that of the sugar crop from
$6,000,000 to $4,200,000 in the same period, while income from commerce increased from $3,757,000 to $4,352,000.[44] The chartering of seven
new institutions, largely designed to underwrite the construction of the
famed St. Charles and St. Louis Hotels, provide gas lighting for the capital,
and expand the operations of the city's street car line to Carrollton,
boosted the state's banking capital by an additional $16 million to

42. *Louisiana House Journal*, 1836, pp. 2–3.

43. Ibid., 36–37, 50, 52.

44. James L. Watkins, *King Cotton: A Historical and Statistical Review, 1790–1908* (New
York, 1908), 190–200; Lewis C. Gray, *History of Agriculture in the Southern United States to
1860* (2 vols.; Washington, D.C., 1933), II, 1027, 1033–34; Green, *Finance and Economic Development in the Old South*, 197.

$57,500,000, which the *Bee* acclaimed as surpassing that of any other state in the nation.[45] This rise in available capital encouraged investors to borrow from banks to purchase federal lands, paid for in state bank notes which the government allowed to remain on deposit in local institutions, thus increasing the capital available for even more land purchase loans. From 1823 through 1835, federal land sales in the state amounted to $11,003,000; in the single year of 1836 they brought in $10,990,000. To pay their bank debts, speculators inflated the price of property which they held for sale, skyrocketing values all over the state and stimulating what quickly became a spiraling land boom.[46] In New Orleans even day laborers and mechanics bought up swamp lands between the city and Lake Pontchartrain at $150 a square, the speculative fever becoming so pervasive that the business season which usually ended in June continued apace well into the fall. "Business in New Orleans is amazing this year," one observer noted, marveling at the sight of sales offices "entirely covered with plans," but being French he also remarked sadly that most of the activity centered in the "higher quarter where all the Americans are. . . . In the low quarter, all is pretty solid, but hopelessly slow."[47]

The building boom sparked by the improvement banks quickened the economy of the whole community, intensifying the already existent scarcity of skilled labor in the city, where even workers with below-average competence might earn as much as five dollars a day, a wage scale perhaps the highest in the nation. "No man need be idle in New Orleans who is inclined to work," the editor of the *Union* observed, "and none need be poor who are willing to put aside a portion of their gains."[48]

Even in the midst of this burst of prosperity, Governor White continued to find himself immersed in controversy which made his life miserable. With complaints about his appointments policy still being voiced, he had

45. Green, *Finance and Economic Development in the Old South*, 22–23; New Orleans *Bee*, March 17, July 31, 1835.

46. Caldwell, *A Banking History of Louisiana*, 58; Green, *Finance and Economic Development in the Old South*, 53; *Congressional Debates*, 24th Cong., 1st Sess., 4366.

47. New Orleans *True American*, August 27, 1836; Ferdinand de Feriet to Jacine de Feriet, May 13, August 26, 1836, in Feriet Family Papers, TU.

48. New Orleans *True American*, October 12, 1835; New Orleans *Union*, October 16, 1835. The labor shortage became so acute in 1836 that several newspapers had to suspend publication because, as one of them reported, "there are no workers in the city." See *Le Franc Parleur* (New Orleans), April 7, 1836.

at one and the same time to push for enlistments in the state's quota of militia companies to fight in the Florida Seminole wars which held little interest for Louisianians and to interdict the raising of volunteers to help Texas wage its war of independence against Mexico, in a community which had strong and intimate ties to that neighboring settlement. His executive proclamation of November 13, 1835, citing the federal law banning recruitment of troops to be used against a friendly nation met with widespread condemnation, which became even more strident with publication of a letter by William Christy in the *Bee* of April 23, 1836, demanding that he issue commissions for Louisianians to head a brigade to strengthen General Edmund Pendleton Gaines's troops along the Louisiana-Texas frontier. When the governor demurred, again stipulating that he could act only in response to a request from the federal government, Christy declared him to be derelict in his duty and General Ripley condemned him on the floor of the national House of Representatives. When the war department eventually sanctioned Gaines's request for assistance, White did authorize the dispatch of ten companies of mounted volunteers to the Texas border, but his earlier resistance still rankled among his critics.[49]

He might have found some solace, at least, in the knowledge that others shared his discomfort, for things had not gone well for the Whigs as a whole after their sweeping victories in 1834. An opening came in early 1836 to win back the United States Senate seat lost the year before, occasioned by Charles Gayarré's resignation because of poor health which had reduced him, he said, to the status of a "living skeleton."[50] But the ineffectiveness and creole apathy which had immobilized the party in the 1835 choice still persisted, and despite a Whig majority in the legislature Robert Carter Nicholas, a Terrebonne Democrat, won the position in a close election over Alexander Barrow of West Feliciana.[51] That no creole had contested the seat against the Virginian Nicholas and the Tennessean Barrow astonished observers in other parts of the country, to the disappointment of Whigs and the delight of Democrats. A fellow Virginian wrote to tell J. Burton Harrison in New Orleans that he had "recd. in due time yours announcing the election of Mr. Nicholas to the Senate. We were prepared for

49. New Orleans *Bee*, April 28, 1836; *Congressional Debates*, 24th Cong., 1st Sess., 3523.

50. Charles Gayarré to John Dimitry, May 25, 1891, in John Minor Wisdom Collection, TU.

51. *Louisiana Senate Journal*, 1836, p. 10.

defeat in Mississippi, but your Legislature certainly took us by surprise—from them we expected some sort of a Whig-creole. . . . This divides the Senate equally 24 to 24, and little Mattie has the game in his own hands." But William C. Rives at the same time was congratulating little Mattie "most cordially on the accession to the Republican phalanx in the Senate which Louisiana & Mississippi have just given us. We may now hope, I trust, to see better times in that *august* body."[52]

The tide of public opinion seemed supportive of Jackson's policies in other matters as well. Some still grumbled about the removal of the deposits and destruction of the Bank of the United States, but with the economy booming this seemed of small consequence. The deep attachment to France felt by so many Louisianians made the president's demand that the French honor spoliation indemnities arising from depredations on American commerce during the Napoleonic wars something of a problem for the administration's friends in the state, but one that yielded to fundamental American patriotism. The New Orleans *Franc Parleur* did indeed rage against Jackson and Livingston for supposedly insulting the proud French and claimed that Americans actually feared their onetime European allies, but the *Courier* and *Bee* adopted a much more conciliatory tone. They regretted the hostile demeanor of the eastern press toward France and printed innumerable letters from concerned readers deploring the possibility of Louisianians being asked to shed French blood, but in final judgment they came down squarely in support of Jackson's position. The president's traditional enemies at the *Commercial Bulletin* and the *Mercantile Advertiser* backed him as well, with only the choleric John Gibson at the *True American* blowing hot and cold on the issue. Even he finally gave grudging support to the president, still insisting nonetheless that he was an ignorant old man bungling his way through a dangerous crisis. John Catron, chief justice of the Tennessee Supreme Court, observed on an 1836 visit to New Orleans that the "French business excites a deep interest here, among the trading class, but the stand taken by the Presdt. is approved by a large majority even in the City, much averse as they are to a war. The country is strong for the measures of the Administration." So the answer to the query

---

52. W. W. Nowell to J. Burton Harrison, February 26, 1836, in Harrison Papers, LC; W. C. Rives to Martin Van Buren, January 29, 1836, in Van Buren Papers, LC.

put to J. Burton Harrison by W. W. Nowell, "Would yr. French population be loyal in the event of War?" seemed to be a very decided "Yes."[53]

On the obverse side, the national Whigs offered little to boost their fortunes in the state. Hoping to promote the protective tariff program so central to his American System, Clay in the early 1830s had pushed through Congress several bills to distribute among the states federal funds derived from the sale of public lands, the accumulation of which made higher import duties to raise revenue unnecessary. But the West bridled at the proposed allocation of the moneys based on population, thinking it preferential to the older eastern communities, and Jackson had struck down the measures with a series of vetoes. The *Bee* assailed the attempt as "the mad project of Mr. Clay," and Gayarré claimed shortly after taking his seat in the Senate that Louisiana owed as much to Jackson for killing the land bills as for his victory at the Battle of New Orleans, belittling the Kentuckian as a "skillful politician" playing to the "cupidity" of northern states. "For my part," he said, "I had rather see the public lands of Louisiana which were so unjustly extorted from our convention in 1812, deeply buried in the bosom of the ocean than wrested from the hands of our fellow citizens, to be made the spoils of party ambition and held out as a splendid bauble to purchase the votes of the old states at the expense of the weaker confederates."[54] A year later the *Bee* repeated the same argument, insisting that if New York could claim part of the land sale revenues Louisiana should have an equal right to a share of the import tolls collected at that great eastern port.[55]

But the Louisiana Democrats faced troubles of their own in 1835 and 1836 despite these signs of public approval on such specific issues. Their humiliating defeat in the gubernatorial and congressional elections of 1834 gave them little cause for optimism in the approaching legislative and presidential contests, their party ranks dispirited and shaken not only by recent

53. New Orleans *Bee*, July 28, 1831, March 5, 6, 13, 19, December 25, 1835; New Orleans *Courier*, June 12, 15, 1835; New Orleans *Commercial Bulletin*, November 14, 1835; New Orleans *Mercantile Advertiser*, May 22, 1834; *Louisiana Advertiser*, March 26, 1834, December 27, 1834; John Catron to Andrew J. Donelson, February 11, 1836, in Donelson Papers, LC; W. W. Nowell to J. Burton Harrison, December 24, 1834, in Harrison Papers, LC.

54. Robert V. Remini, *Andrew Jackson and the Course of American Democracy, 1833–1845* (New York, 1984), 318–19, 321; *Louisiana Courier*, January 28, 1835.

55. New Orleans *Bee*, April 15, 1836.

failure but equally as much by collapse of the Gordon White House clique, a major force in their earlier efforts. The United States Senate's rejection of Gordon's reappointment to the New Orleans collectorship in June 1834 removed him from the position of authority in the city's commercial community which had so enhanced his political clout, and though he remained active in Democratic circles and received a new federal appointment as agent for construction of the branch mint of the United States at New Orleans in April 1835, he had obviously lost his once dominant role in party affairs.[56]

At first, little seemed to have changed at the custom house. James Breedlove succeeded Gordon as collector, largely through the old incumbent's influence with the president, who had also intervened personally to make Martin Gordon, Jr., naval officer of the port.[57] But those new appointments gave evidence of the crumbling of the old order. The position filled by young Gordon had previously been held by Peter K. Wagner, once the chief publicist for the egalitarian and moral claims of the reform Democracy but now disgraced as a public defaulter and peculator. As early as 1832 his accounts had shown a delinquency of more than three thousand dollars, but the appallingly ineffective system of supervision of public moneys in place at the time allowed this to go uncorrected, and his appointment had been renewed in 1834. By September 1835 a new examination of his accounts showed that he had simply stopped making returns altogether in 1832, swelling his delinquency to some twelve thousand dollars. When called upon for an explanation by the senior Gordon, one of the guarantors of his surety bond, he packed up his belongings at the office, left, and never returned.[58] Despite assurances to the president that they stood firm in their

56. *Ibid.*, April 17, 1835.

57. Endorsement, Martin Gordon to Andrew Jackson, October 8, 1835, Miscellaneous Letters Received, in RG 56, GRDT, NA.

58. *United States* v. *Peter K. Wagner*, in Records of the United States Eastern District Court of Louisiana, Case #3666 (1836), FRC.; Martin Gordon to Andrew Jackson, October 2, 1835, Collectors of Customs Applications, Louisiana (Gordon file), in RG 56, GRDT, NA; Joseph Anderson to Virgil Maxey, September 2, 1835, Letters Received from the First Comptroller, 1820–1839, in RG 206, Records of the Solicitor of the Treasury, NA; Andrew Jackson to Levi Woodbury, January 5, 1835, Martin Gordon to Woodbury, January 25, 1835, Gordon to Jackson, October 8, 1835, Miscellaneous Letters Received, in RG 56, GRDT, NA.

commitment to honor their obligation to the government as endorsers of his two-thousand-dollar surety bond, both Gordons eventually refused to fulfill those promises, ignored a federal court judgment against them, and as late as 1868 remained on the treasury books as public debtors.[59]

The later history of the Gordons only further diminished their political influence. Despite his notorious 1833 attacks upon the Union Bank as a den of Andrew Jackson's enemies, the old collector soon after leaving office joined that institution's board of directors and began to speak for it in communications with friends in Washington. He also quickly became enmeshed in financial difficulties of his own as agent of the federal mint, not clearing an 1836 delinquency of some seventy thousand dollars in his accounts until 1841.[60] Young Gordon left the custom house in 1836 to become cashier of the Union Bank, finally to be discharged from that position in 1839 when fifty thousand dollars disappeared from funds supposedly transferred by him to branch offices in the country parishes. He claimed to have bundled the money in plain packets, which he had then dropped into ordinary mail receptacles, taking no receipts and registering no bill numbers.[61] Reflecting the decline of the Gordons in the esteem of Democratic party loyalists, Browse Trist, once one of their greatest admirers, observed to his brother Nicholas in 1837, "By the bye, I think the Gordons but little cut to the Jackson cloth. They are true skinflints, who dream of nothing but ways to grab up and to horde." But Jackson continued to defend them to the last, endorsing a letter recommending Gordon's reappointment to the

59. Virgil Maxey to P. K. Lawrence, April 8, 1837, Letters on Debts and Suits, 1821–1869, Clerk's Returns, 1821–1929 (1838), General Index of Public Debtors, 1820–1868 (1868), in RG 206, Records of the Solicitor of the Treasury, NA; Martin Gordon to Andrew Jackson, October 2, 1835, Collectors of Customs Applications, Louisiana (Gordon file), in RG 56, GRDT, NA; *United States v. Martin Gordon, Sr., and Martin Gordon, Jr.,* in Records of the United States District Court of Louisiana, Case #4363 (1838), FRC.

60. Martin Gordon to Andrew Jackson, August 22, 1835, April 8, 1836, Letters from Banks, Levi Woodbury to Martin Gordon, October 22, 1835, Letters to Banks, all in RG 56, GRDT, NA; audits 72,293 (December 28, 1836) and 81,124 (February 17, 1841), Miscellaneous Treasury Accounts of the General Accounting Office, First Auditor's Reports, in RG 217, Records of the United States General Accounting Office, NA.

61. Martin Gordon, Jr., to Andrew Jackson, March 22, 1836, Collectors of Customs Applications, Louisiana (Gordon file), in RG 56, GRDT, NA; Hore B. Trist to Nicholas P. Trist, April 18, 1839, Trist Papers, LC.

collectorship in 1845 with the notation, "Mr. Gordon Senr. deserves all that Doctor McFarlane says of him."[62]

In the midst of this climate of hysterical fear and paranoia, disarray in traditional Whig areas of support, and widening splits in Democratic leadership, the state prepared for the presidential and congressional elections of 1836. Democrats met in Baltimore on May 20, 1835, and there nominated Martin Van Buren of New York and Richard Mentor Johnson of Kentucky for the presidency and vice-presidency of the United States. The choice of Van Buren had long been ordained as the clear wish of Andrew Jackson, but the vice-presidential nomination created major problems with significant overtones of impending difficulties in the approaching campaign. If the selection had been left to Van Buren, he almost certainly would have picked William C. Rives of Virginia, the favorite of the party's southern bloc, hoping to revitalize the New York–Virginia axis so productively crafted years before by Jefferson and Madison. But the western wing of the party preferred Johnson, whose chief credential seemed to be his claim to have killed the Indian chief Tecumseh at the Battle of the Thames during the War of 1812. Even some among the westerners found it difficult to accept his nomination, scandalized by his notorious connection to a Negro mistress who had borne his daughters and supposedly demanded equality with whites. But Jackson's coolness toward Rives and Van Buren's reluctant recognition that a western running mate might be needed to balance the ticket ended the Virginian's chances, and Johnson prevailed.[63] The Whigs held no convention, convinced that their best chance of success lay in fragmenting the electoral college vote among a scattering of candidates chosen to appeal to areas in which they had particular strength, thus forcing the election into the House of Representatives where they hoped to prevail. In due course Daniel Webster represented the party in New England, William Henry Harrison in the West, and Hugh Lawson White in the South, though White, a longtime associate and crony of Jackson, insisted that he

---

62. Hore B. Trist to Nicholas P. Trist, May 14, 1833, March 30, 1837, in Trist Papers, UNC; James McFarlane to Andrew Jackson, January 7, 1845, Collectors of Customs Applications, Louisiana (Gordon file), in RG 56, GRDT, NA.

63. John Catron to Andrew Jackson, March 31, 1835, Jackson Papers, LC; Remini, *Andrew Jackson and the Course of American Democracy*, 255–56; John Niven, *Martin Van Buren* (New York, 1983), 377, 395–96; H. A. Garland to William C. Rives, May 29, 1835, W. B. Slaughter to Rives, May 28, 1835, in Rives Papers, LC.

had not broken with the president on any issue except that of his successor and refused to call himself a Whig until 1839.[64]

Compared to the excitement and dramatics of the presidential and gubernatorial elections of 1832 and 1834, the campaign of 1836 in Louisiana proved tame indeed. None of the candidates possessed the personal magnetism or ties to the state which had made Jackson and Clay such formidable figures, and both parties found themselves uncertain and tentative in their awareness of disunity and conflict in their ranks. From the beginning of the canvass Webster and Harrison had so little claim on southern support that the race in Louisiana clearly came down to one between Van Buren and White, but even that narrowing of the field did little to clarify the stakes of competition. Most confusing of all, the campaign concentrated on a major theme actually not truly reflective of the real concerns of the two parties. Spokesmen for both sides agreed that the question of slavery and abolition held undisputed primacy in the interest of Louisianians as the election approached, obviously the result of the near hysteria which had swept the state since late 1835.[65] Political strategists accordingly seized on that popular obsession as the one issue most capable of destroying their opponent if they could identify him as likely to upset the racial status quo in the nation. Slavery thus became for the first time a pivotal question in a presidential campaign, but not in the form of a truly distinguishing point of conflict, because no side would claim championship of an antislavery position. In short, the greatest part of the ensuing campaign oratory aimed at painting one's opponent as in some way dangerous to the South's peculiar institution even though the real basis of opposition very likely rested in the candidate's personality and perceived overall lack of atunement to the state's way of life.[66]

In such a context, only the fact of his having been anointed by Jackson gave Van Buren much of a chance against White. His identity with eastern seaboard interests, his role in the passage of the Tariff of Abominations, and his supposed engineering of the expulsion of John C. Calhoun from Jacksonian ranks, all made him especially suspect to many southern Democrats. In addition, his dominance in the New York political machine

64. Powell Moore, "The Revolt Against Jackson in Tennessee, 1835–1836," *JSH*, II (1936), 335–39.

65. *Congressional Debates*, 1836, p. 1978.

66. New Orleans *Bee*, June 22, 1835.

known as the Albany Regency cast him in the role of just the kind of political professional Jacksonians had so contemned back in the party's formative years of 1824 to 1828, and his personal lifestyle seemed hardly consonant with southern and western values. His status as heir apparent to Jackson offended many as smacking of royalist overtones, and though he worked diligently to ease southern fears that he might indeed harbor abolitionist sentiments, the constraints imposed on him by the significant antislavery contingent in his New York constituency made him always vulnerable on that issue. Many Louisianians, therefore, found themselves in agreement with Davy Crockett's assessment that "Van Buren is as opposite to General Jackson as dung is to a diamond," even heretofore faithful followers of the General feeling more comfortable with the familiar southern presence of Tennessee's Hugh Lawson White. Richard M. Johnson, for his part, brought little distinction to the Democratic ticket, Whig partisans having for years ridiculed him with the chant, "Rumsey dumsey, Colonel Johnson killed Tecumseh," as they delighted in taunting Christy with the charge that his heroic relative had been shot in the buttocks at the Battle of the Thames.[67]

White accordingly made serious inroads into traditional Jacksonian strength in Louisiana, but he carried as well several burdens which hobbled his progress. In the first place, many could not forgive what they considered his renegade betrayal of Jackson in entering the field against Van Buren, and if the New Yorker suffered because of his part in the Tariff of Abominations sleight of hand, White had to explain away a long and vigorous opposition to the sugar tariff so critical to the Louisiana economy, as well as support for Clay's various land bills and Jackson's nullification proclamation, removal of the deposits, and veto of the Bank of the United States. George Waggaman publicly denounced White's tariff record and openly declared he would go for Van Buren in his stead. Van Buren, moreover, seemed to many clearly White's superior in talents and political skill, the Tennessean being judged by some as "the weakest man in the Senate." Although White's unassailable status as a southern slaveholder made it impossible for Democrats to charge him with abolitionist tendencies, they nonetheless managed to find a way to turn the antislavery scare against him. They did

67. *Louisiana Advertiser*, July 27, 1835; David Crockett, *The Life of Martin Van Buren* (Philadelphia, 1836), 13; New Orleans *Mercantile Advertiser*, May 17, 1834; New Orleans *Whig*, September 25, 1834.

so by cultivating the suspicion that the Whigs meant to use him as a device to steal the election in much the same way John Quincy Adams had despoiled Andrew Jackson of the White House in 1825. White, they claimed, had been brought forth to drain traditional pro-Jackson votes away from Van Buren in the South and Southwest, with all Whigs chosen as electors bound then to cast a combined vote behind their most successful candidate, assuring him either outright victory or place in a House of Representatives choice. This almost certainly would be William Henry Harrison, whose imputed abolitionist views and strong ties to the anti-Masonic party made him especially unacceptable in Louisiana.[68]

The ensuing campaign found the Louisiana Jacksonians wracked by internal party strife once again, with Breedlove proving to be almost as divisive in the collectorship as his predecessor. He precipitated no great Jacksonian split comparable to the Gordon-Slidell schism of 1833, but he cut himself off from such longtime champions of the Democratic cause as the *Courier* and the *Bee*, giving the custom-house printing contracts to relative newcomers like the New Orleans *Daily News* and, if his critics could be believed, even favoring that bitter foe of the president, John Gibson at the *True American*. Understandably, the *Bee* and the *Courier* denounced him passionately, in vitriolic language reminiscent of Gordon's assaults upon the party's "traitors" in years past, fittingly enough, given that the old collector had now broken openly with Breedlove despite having been chiefly responsible for his appointment.[69]

Unlike Gordon, Breedlove seemed relatively uninterested in wielding any particular political control over his Democratic colleagues, apparently more concerned with reaping financial gain from his pivotal position in the commercial community. His past history as a merchant in Tennessee, Kentucky, and New Orleans, marked by at least two bankruptcies prior to his appointment, may have made him more than usually responsive to opportunities for self-enrichment, suggested at least by a record studded with

68. John M. Niles to Gideon Welles, January 27, 1836, in Gideon Welles Papers, LC; W. W. Nowell to J. Burton Harrison, July 21, 1836, in Harrison Papers, LC; New Orleans *True American*, October 31, 1836; *Louisiana Advertiser*, July 27, 1836; New Orleans *Bee*, June 20, August 26, 1835, July 15, 17, August 5, 1836; *Louisiana Courier*, October 15, 1836.

69. New Orleans *Bee*, June 25, 26, 27, 29, July 2, August 7, November 10, 1835; Martin Gordon to Levi Woodbury, March 22, 1835, Collectors of Customs Applications, Louisiana (Thomas Kennedy file), in RG 56, GRDT, NA.

324 • Louisiana in the Age of Jackson

charges of exploitation of his office for profit.[70] These may well have been nothing more than commonplace attacks by political enemies, and he at least seems to have kept on the right side of the treasury auditors, Secretary Woodbury in 1839 affirming the currency of his accounts.[71] But there could be no denying the turmoil he generated among Democratic party faithfuls. His refusal to follow instructions to deposit federal funds impartially in both deposit banks in New Orleans raised letters of protest to the treasury from William G. Hewes of the Commercial Bank and resulted in repeated scoldings from Secretary Woodbury.[72] Obviously smarting from Breedlove's refusal to give it a share of custom-house printing, the *Bee* angrily charged him with disloyalty to the administration, claiming that he had "unequivocally given his personal and official support to the opposition party . . . in order to aid the whigs and nullifiers" while "wallowing in the luxuries and consequentialities of his office." Breedlove's response was to ban the *Bee* from any access to the books or notices at the custom house.[73]

But as the campaign wore on it became increasingly clear that others beside Breedlove in the traditional Democratic fold had little enthusiasm for the Van Buren–Johnson ticket. Late in 1835 Joseph Walker, a major Democratic figure in Rapides Parish, confided to Senator Gayarré his fears that the party might be too sanguine as to Van Buren's election. "The prejudice against northern men is such," he wrote, "I fear it will be impossible to overcome it; our enemies take advantage of this state of things & under the pretense of supporting Judge White they are producing a division in our ranks that must in the end prove ruinous to us." No longer held together by the annealing force of Andrew Jackson's personal candidacy, even previ-

70. New Orleans *Bee*, June 29, 1835; Charges Against Custom House Officers, 1833–1841 (Breedlove file), William McCullough to Levi Woodbury, May 23, June 7, 1838, Herman Schroeder to Thomas Ewing, May 30, 1841, Miscellaneous Letters Received, in RG 56, GRDT, NA; Hore Browse Trist to Nicholas Trist, January 4, 1840, in Trist Papers, LC.

71. Woodbury endorsement on John B. Watts to Levi Woodbury, July 24, 1839, Miscellaneous Letters Received, in RG 56, GRDT, NA.

72. Levi Woodbury to William G. Hewes, August 27, 1834, January 12, February 19, 1835, Letters to Banks, William G. Hewes to Levi Woodbury, February 24, 1835, Letters from Banks, Levi Woodbury to James Breedlove, February 16, 1835, Letters to Collectors of Customs, all in RG 56, GRDT, NA; William G. Hewes to Levi Woodbury, January 13, 1835, in Woodbury Papers, LC.

73. New Orleans *Bee*, June 25, 26, 27, 29, July 2, 1835.

ously committed Jacksonians felt the inclination to support the southern slaveholder rather than the New Yorker, whatever his party affiliation. Despite his close ties to Jackson, it took Browse Trist until June 1836 to break free of that impulse, telling his brother "that I have by reflecting on the subject convinced myself, that the policy of the south is to unite with V. B. & his party, of which I was not sure before." In what ordinarily constituted the stronghold of Louisiana Jacksonianism, James M. Bradford, publisher of the influential *Louisiana Journal* (St. Francisville), warned Frank Blair that support of Van Buren out of respect for the president's wishes might easily be shattered. The large faction of Carolinians and Tennesseans in the Florida population, he wrote, felt strongly attached to Hugh Lawson White, "and if he is treated with tenderness, these men can be secured to the Baltimore nomination. But the slightest attack on the Judge would excite the sympathy of this population, and a large and determined vote in this section of the state would be given to him. To guard against this is the difficult task before us."[74]

The virulence of the slavery question made that assignment increasingly complicated. Fear of the abolitionists tended to sweep all other considerations aside, leading the New Orleans *Union* late in 1835 to propose abandonment of all party loyalties in furtherance of a united southern stand in defense of its beleaguered institution. "It is indeed time," the *Union* argued, "for every slaveholding state to avoid pledging herself to the support of any candidate for the Presidency, untill one true position is ascertained, and untill the accurate force of our enemies and their design are fully understood. The interest of the south have arrived at that crisis, *there must be but one party.* Our interests are the same, the same ties, feelings, and sentiments which bind the inhabitants of our state together at this time, should connect every slave holding state of the Union." Whatever else might be said for that proposal, clearly its implementation would spell doom for a Van Buren candidacy.[75]

The Whigs moved quickly to exploit this and other weaknesses in the Democratic position. J. Burton Harrison, newly ensconced in early 1836 as editor of the *Louisiana Advertiser* and secure in his impeccable Virginia lin-

74. Joseph Walker to Charles Gayarré, November 15, 1835, in Gayarré Collection, LSU; H. B. Trist to Nicholas Trist, June 1, 1836, in Trist Papers, UNC; James M. Bradford to Francis P. Blair, August 25, 1835, in Blair-Lee Papers, PU.

75. New Orleans *Union*, October 17, 1836.

eage, hit upon a particularly compelling appeal to wavering Jacksonians. The Democratic party, Harrison maintained, had degenerated from its early great commitments and allowed New York influence to divert it to an offensive search for selfish gain. What he proposed in effect was a return to the republicanism of 1824 in precisely the same way that Andrew Jackson in that year had called for a rededication to the values of 1798 and 1800. "The principles of the men of 1824 are virtually banished from power," he proclaimed, subverted by those "eleventh hour Jacksonians," the men of the Albany Regency. Hugh Lawson White alone now represented what Jackson had originally stood for, he argued, not forgetting to point to White's Irish heritage as yet another claim upon the Gaelic readership of the *Advertiser*. How, he asked, could sons of Erin who remembered the pristine virtues and strengths of the first Jackson crusade align themselves with a crypto-abolitionist, "an ambitious Hollander, whose veins are filled with the fish-blood of the nation of the Orange King William," and what "rustic democrat can have any fondness for Van Buren, who is pronounced by Englishmen the most exact courtier ever seen at the Court of St. James—a mere lavender dandy." A vote for White, he concluded, actually would do honor to Andrew Jackson, whose original principles he meant to reaffirm; it would be given to a "primitive democrat . . . a man who holds *our* feelings, *our* opinions, *our* faith."[76]

This skillful move to seduce Jacksonians to the White camp did not stop the Whigs from attempting to hold their traditional supporters true to the cause by exploiting old familiar charges against their Democratic foes. While Harrison extolled the virtues of White's version of Jacksonianism, Gibson's *True American*, the *Mercantile Advertiser*, and the *Commercial Bulletin* returned to the crimes which longtime opponents of the General ascribed to him as King Andrew I, tyrant of the veto, revisiting time and again the evils and distress attributed to the removal of the deposits and the destruction of the Bank of the United States. Whig exploitation of all these Democratic vulnerabilities peaked shortly before election day in a giant rally at the Merchants Exchange in New Orleans on October 26 which deliberately rejected identification as a Whig gathering by labeling itself the "Great Anti–Van Buren" meeting. The participants adopted sweeping resolutions:

76. These *Louisiana Advertiser* citations are taken from clippings in the Francis Harrison collection at the University of Virginia, dated June 29, July 25, July 28, August 25, 30, 1836.

They behold with uneasiness the rapid growth in the United States of a disposition to regard the President as the only true and complete representative of the people, and thus (under the pretended cover of the sovereignty of the people) to consider all duty to our country as embraced in a conformity to the wishes of the President. . . . They have witnessed the too successful introduction of the tone and habit of *Absolutism* into the executive chair, which had hitherto been the modest seat of secondary, responsible power.

They have witnessed an entire revolution in the former policy of the Government, introduced and maintained by the dominion of the veto, actual or apprehended.

They have witnessed the plain manifestation of a disposition on the part of a great portion of their countrymen to accept, as the successor of the present Executive a person whose prominent recommendation to them consists in his being the recognized favorite of the President.[77]

"A party combination is made to pervade the land," the resolutions declared, "governed by a discipline most emphatically described as 'the New York tactics,' which proscribe the exercise of individual opinion, denounces as the worst of crimes the departure of any member from party dictation, deadens the instinct of liberty, and seems almost to lose sight of the love of country in the love of party." More than anything else, the statement insisted, there must be a national commitment to the principle that "the honor and welfare of the republic rèside, above all other things, in the jealous keeping of elections free from executive dictation," making it clear that "sycophancy to the President is not the path to the succession." Labeling Van Buren as totally unacceptable to slave states because of his problack sentiments and as a "spoilsman" bereft of any talent save "cunning," the assemblage gave its rousing endorsement to Hugh Lawson White, a foe to "executive dictation and caucus combination . . . a primitive Democrat [around] whom the South and Southwest have rallied," ending with the ringing assurance that "We cannot go wrong in adhering to our Southern brethren."[78]

Even with evidence all around them of how potent this kind of appeal to original Jacksonianism and southern patriotism could be, Democrats seemed unable to bring their party together to save Van Buren's candidacy. More than Breedlove's disruptive policies kept them divided. Christy's na-

77. New Orleans *True American*, October 27, 1836.
78. *Ibid.*

tivist attachments cost his New Orleans *Post* much of its patronage, forcing a close-down in February 1836, although it did manage a resurrection a week or so later.[79] Some additional support came with the shift of the *Union* to the administration cause in May, but the oldest and most influential of the traditional Jackson presses in the capital proved relatively less aggressive than in the past. Once the vigorous and powerful voice of the party in earlier campaigns, the *Bee* remained officially uncommitted to the Van Buren–Johnson ticket until March 12, 1836, when it begrudgingly announced for the Democratic candidates but continued to protest being denied administration printing contracts which had gone instead to "a paper now supporting Judge White." Its disaffection from the party leadership continued to grow, until on April 16 it announced that "The *Bee* was formerly the gazette of a party, a class, a district; it is now adapted for families and merchants," and its pro-Democrat enthusiasm remained decidedly restrained. Henry P. Leonard, editor of the English side of the paper and once a committed champion of the Jackson cause, grew increasingly critical of the administration, faulted Ripley's performance in Congress, and even called for the election of the Whig A. B. Roman to the governorship in 1838. By late June he had left the *Bee* to launch the new and politically independent New Orleans *Standard*.[80]

Resurgence of old bitterness dividing the ethnic sections of the city also prevented any headway in ameliorating intraparty strife. The early cordiality attending adoption of the tripartite municipality structure of the metropolis had quickly broken down in acrimonious dispute over division of the city's assets and liabilities, focused, as one might guess, principally upon distribution of funds to be derived from exploitation of the batture fronting the First and Second municipalities.[81] The *Bee* threw itself into the fray with passionate defense of the prerogatives of the old quarter, going so far as to insist that the entire New Orleans delegation to be chosen in the July elections be comprised of none but Louisianaise. That proposal enraged the New Orleans *Post, Union,* and *Bulletin,* whose editors asked the pointed question as to what distinguished this kind of selectivity from the Native

79. New Orleans *Bee*, February 21, 27, 1836.

80. *Ibid.*, April 6, 16, 26, May 7, June 6, 18, 1836; New Orleans *Standard*, October 10, 1836; New Orleans *Commercial Bulletin*, June 13, 1836; H. P. Leonard to Levi Woodbury, February 2, 1836, in Woodbury Papers, LC.

81. New Orleans *True American*, October 10, 13, 1836.

Americanism so decried by the creole press. The battle raged for weeks, so engrossing the attention of the city that the presidential campaign went almost unnoticed in comparison. In the meantime, old wounds had been reopened, and the *Bee's* wonted Democratic fervor continued to be sorely missed in its preoccupation with the always dominant ethnic antagonisms. It added further to unrest in Democratic ranks by carrying on an incessant feud with St. Romes at the *Courier*, reflective of the antiforeign French sentiments of its proprietors, the creole Jerome Bayon and his family.[82] Equally offended by Breedlove's lack of patronage, the *Courier* remained steadfast in its loyalty to Jackson and his handpicked nominee for the succession, but it too lagged in pronouncing its official support of Van Buren and Johnson until late July 1836.[83]

Not until the very eve of the election did the Democrats begin to show any evidence of revived enthusiasm for the campaign. Louis M. Booth, Leonard's successor at the *Bee*, finally returned the old champion to its previous level of advocacy with emphasis on what would prove to be the central theme of the Democratic attack upon their opponents. "All who know anything about the abolitionists know them, almost to a man, to be Whigs and violently opposed to the administration," he claimed, further arguing that White's inability to win support outside a few southern states meant that the Whigs had in effect abandoned him. The White candidacy, in his view, simply played to the Whig intention of gathering all their support eventually behind William Henry Harrison, in effect using the Tennessean as a decoy. "If we must be disgraced by being driven after the triumphal car of an arch enemy," he proclaimed, "let it be done in the light of day, our arms unshackled, our eyes unbandaged. . . . Hang out the real banner of Harrison and Granger—let us see the Genuine *Abolition Flag!*"[84]

On October 3 Booth launched the New Orleans *Daily Evening Times* to boost the capital's proadministration publications, yielding his place at the older journal to Robert J. Ker, who had been such an ardent Jackson spokesman on the paper back in the turbulent 1834 gubernatorial election. As late as August 8 Booth had warned that the Democrats were "without leaders or organization, without committees of correspondence and those signs of preparation usually exhibited on the eve of an important election,"

82. New Orleans *Bee*, October 7, 1836.
83. *Louisiana Courier*, July 21, 1836.
84. New Orleans *Bee*, August 19, 1836.

and Ker sounded the alarm again on October 21. In oblique reference to Breedlove and other administration officeholders who had long been charged with pro-White sentiments, he continued by cautioning against "the very persons who now repress any system of organization, and rely forsooth on their personal influence and political aggrandizement." "Republicans," he exhorted the faithful, "be not found sleeping; for ye have wily antagonists and dangerous friends."[85]

Jackson's issuance of the Specie Circular on July 11, 1836, requiring all public land purchases after August 15 to be paid in gold or silver except by actual settlers, raised the inevitable Whig protest that the president had again displayed his fondness for executive usurpation of power. The measure greatly increased the premium on specie, already in short supply in New Orleans banking institutions because of curtailment in the usual imports of hard money from Mexico occasioned by the Texas revolution, and the Whig press rejoiced in yet another opportunity to curse the stupidity of an administration which had killed the Bank of the United States. But Jackson's defenders dismissed the criticism as the noise of "Panic Makers" and dismissed the stringency as a temporary inconvenience.[86] As had been true throughout the campaign, emphasis on the abolitionist threat dominated the proceedings of the only major rally held by the administration forces in the state. At the meeting in New Orleans on October 22 no issues other than slavery received even minimal attention, and the acceptance of Booth's earlier version of the real Whig threat resulted in White going totally unmentioned as Harrison received the full censure and condemnation of the gathering, despite having no organized backing of any sort anywhere in the state. Meanwhile, the congressional elections went essentially unnoticed.[87]

The results of the November elections gave eloquent testimony to the immobilizing power of the uncertainty and confusion of identities which had marked the campaign. Even the validity of the supposed excitement over the slavery issue is brought into question by the miserable turnout of the electorate across the state, many eligible voters apparently unwilling to

85. *Ibid.*, August 8, October 3, 21, 1836.

86. G. Burke to Levi Woodbury, July 27, 1836, Letters from Banks, in RG 56, GRDT, NA; New Orleans *Commercial Bulletin*, September 27, 1836; New Orleans *Bee*, October 12, 14, 15, 1836; *Louisiana Courier*, October 18, 1836.

87. *Louisiana Courier*, October 22, 24, 1836.

vote for either of the two candidates, puzzled and affronted by the contradictions and questionable associations surrounding each of them. To an astonishing degree, as well, the election simply failed to impress much of the
public as having any great importance in any event. St. John the Baptist
Parish reported only four votes, all in the Democratic column, the judge
there confessing that he had been unaware that an election was being
held.[88]

Van Buren carried the state by a slim margin of 259 votes out of 7,425
cast, the total ballots less than three-fourths of those counted in the gubernatorial election two years earlier and only 39 percent of those to be polled
in 1840. White bested Van Buren by a mere ten votes in New Orleans,
where voter turnout fell below that recorded in the July legislative canvass,
when less than half of those eligible had voted. Whig strength concentrated in the American commercial sector of the Second Municipality, not
sufficient to overcome the loyalist Van Buren vote in the two Gallic districts. Outside the city White did best in the southwestern sugar country,
polling heavily in St. Landry, St. Martin, St. Mary, and Lafourche Parishes
despite his anti–sugar tariff record, but doing almost as well in American
cotton regions like Avoyelles, Concordia, Natchitoches, and Rapides. The
Democrats won several coast parishes such as St. Charles, Iberville,
Plaquemines, and Ascension, whose demography and economy differed little from that of the areas in which White polled his highest vote. In the
end, only the constancy of the Florida region saved the state for Van Buren,
the size of his majorities in St. Helena, East and West Feliciana, St. Tammany, East Baton Rouge, and Washington Parishes giving him his slender
margin of victory. The concurrent congressional races also confirmed the
status quo, all three incumbents being returned practically without opposition.[89] Nothing in the distribution of the presidential vote suggests any determining ethnic, economic, or regional basis for the election's outcome,
hardly surprising in a campaign seemingly centered on the primary issue of
slavery but actually dominated by individual reaction to the place of Andrew Jackson in the life of the republic. Perhaps the failure of the campaign
to spark any wider public attention reflected recognition that the truly
dominant character at its core could neither be voted for or against except

88. *Ibid.*, November 12, 1836.

89. New Orleans *Bee*, November 11, 1836; Donald B. Dodd and Wynelle S. Dodd,
comps., *Historical Statistics of the South, 1790–1970* (University, Ala., 1973), 486.

by proxy. With his usual insight, the General's first major biographer, James Parton, best sums up the reality of this strange phenomenon of 1836: "The election of Mr. Van Buren to the presidency was as much the act of General Jackson, as though the constitution had conferred upon him the power to appoint his successor."[90]

90. Parton, *Life of Andrew Jackson*, III, 595.

Epilogue

As Andrew Jackson lay dying in June 1845, the young American artist George P. A. Healy arrived at the Hermitage to paint the ex-president, postponing for the moment an appointment to do the same for Henry Clay. When finally he made a belated appearance at Ashland, Clay studied him and observed, "I see that you, like all who approached that man, were fascinated by him."[1] The Kentuckian had good cause to appreciate the magnetic hold of Jackson on the imagination of the American people, but in truth he enjoyed a similar place in the esteem of his countrymen, even if it failed to bring him to the same position of power.

These two commanding figures dominated the Age of Jackson in Louisiana, each tied to the state by a variety of relationships which placed them at the center of the young community's coming of age politically after the emptiness of decades of colonial dependence on France, Spain, and Britain. The world into which the United States moved after the War of 1812 seemed energized by the glorious victory of Jackson at Chalmette, eager to exploit previously unimagined opportunities opened by new technologies of rail and steamboat locomotion, expanding industry, and the richness of a virgin land to the west waiting to be settled. Old restraints of a deferential political and economic order could no longer contain the aspirations of a population eager to make the most of this new experience of rapid change, and Jackson and Clay were seized upon as champions to lead the way.

1. George P. A. Healy, *Reminiscences of a Portrait Painter* (Chicago, 1894), 144, 149.

Andrew Jackson's vision of the American future had little to do with abstract ideological principle, except in its unanalytical devotion to a primitive kind of republicanism seen as regnant in the days of the founding fathers. In large part it held to a Jeffersonian belief that government should be limited in scope—let people alone and allow them to make their way by individual effort—while Clay looked more to a Hamiltonian state as a positive engine for growth and development through programs such as his American System of internal improvements, tariffs, and a national bank.

But considerations of this sort actually had little to do with how Louisiana approached national political questions in the 1820s and 1830s. Because of its history the state had no commitments to the nascent political factions formed around Thomas Jefferson and Alexander Hamilton, except as these might be imported by newcomers to the scene, and much of the public discourse and many of the national figures famed in other regions remained remote and foreign to the great mass of its citizens until well after the Purchase. At the height of the 1824 presidential campaign, for example, some Ascension Parish residents told Browse Trist that they would not vote for Adams because he had allowed his levee to break and flood their lands, thinking the candidate to be their neighbor, Ned Adams.[2] But the personalities, services, and local ties of Andrew Jackson and Henry Clay made them almost as familiar to most Louisianians as Ned Adams was to his Ascension Parish colleagues, with a hold on their affections or a place in their disdain which transcended abstract political concerns. Inevitably, politics being what it is, the state's citizens found themselves immersed in party propaganda dealing with issues like nullification, the Bank of the United States, and internal improvements, but seldom did these questions really divide them except as causes championed by one or the other of the great national heros. Still in a basically frontier stage of growth, Louisiana possessed little of the stability or maturity which might have allowed for a more theoretical approach to economic and political problems. Its society responded primarily to immediate personal attachments, for individual advantage and advancement dominated the concerns of the great mass of its people. From 1824 to 1836, therefore, Louisianians divided into two camps, each committed with almost fanatical dedication to the fortunes of their competing champions. Clay's strength always rested primarily in the

2. H. B. Trist to Nicholas P. Trist, May 12, 1828, in Trist Papers, LC.

French-speaking element of the population, grounded in the influence of his son-in-law, Martin Duralde, but profiting as well from the antagonism which many Louisianians still harbored against Jackson because of his treatment of them during the British invasion. To his good fortune, as well, his protariff position especially pleased the sugar parishes in which the French population predominated. Around the Tennessean gathered a host of old friends from past relationships and all those eternally grateful for his deliverance of their loved ones from the British threat, among them a portion of the Gallic population sufficient to prevent the Clay-Jackson split from duplicating the ethnic divide in the community. In short, for most Louisianians, Jackson and Clay became the pivots around which their concerns in national politics revolved.

In local politics, however, the state split along lines which had little relationship to either of the two national protagonists, and attempts to unify national and state political identities in Louisiana always foundered on the persistent issue of ethnic division. Louisianians insisted on relating to national issues according to their personal attachments to Jackson or Clay, but in their state campaigns national party identifications went largely ignored as Gallic and American loyalties prevailed. Recognizing the danger to their cultural survival if they faltered, the French community proved better able to cut across these Clay-Jackson lines, making it thoroughly logical to send Derbigny to the governorship in July of 1828, give the state to Jackson in November, and then vote Roman into the governor's chair in 1830. To outsiders this seemed inexplicable. To Louisianians the matter seemed simple enough—they found no inconsistency in a man's being devoted to Jackson but opposed to a Florida Jacksonian as governor.

One naturally had to argue about something in politics, but all of the oratory raging around aristocracy versus mechanics and the supposed evils of the Bank or the tariff always seemed in Louisiana to be more the product of loyalty to the official stand of Jackson or Clay than of independent political analysis. Nor did political groupings reflect any significant divisions along class or economic lines. The "egalitarian" Wagner could never find any political faction of mechanics in New Orleans and proved to be a public defaulter; the loudest critics of the Bank, such as Martin Gordon, Maunsel White, James Caldwell, and Bernard Marigny, stood at the forefront of banking activity in the state; despite Jacksonian assaults upon "monopoly" and "privelege," Democrats like Gordon and John Holland headed the most notorious monopoly in the state, the Orleans Navigation Company, while others such as James Caldwell and William G. Hewes controlled public services like the New Orleans gaslight and waterworks utilities; and few Whig merchants, factors, and financiers could rival the wealth and commercial clout of Jacksonians like Maunsel White and J. B. Plauché.

The presidential and gubernatorial campaigns of 1832 and 1834 reflected this dominance of Jackson-Clay identity and ethnic discord with particular emphasis. Following them, party alignments entered a period of confusion and indecision, for no longer did the magic of a Jackson or Clay candidacy divide the state into conflicting groups rallying behind their names. Even party nomenclature signaled this shift in orientation. Prior to 1834 there had been some adoption in Louisiana of the labels "National Republican" and "Democratic Republican" in reference to the Clay and Jackson camps, but these had been so rare that to use them today in speaking of that period is really to distort the contemporary political reality. For men of that time in Louisiana thought and spoke of themselves primarily as Jacksonians or Clayites. By 1834, however, the Whig party had been created by the Kentuckian to overcome the weakness of a political position dependent on his personal leadership, and in Louisiana the name gradually became adopted to identify what had once been simply the partisans of Henry Clay. For their part, Jacksonians had begun to identify themselves as Democrats at the party's national convention in 1832, probably to tie their following more closely to the always controversial Martin Van Buren. After 1834, in effect, time and events forced Jacksonians and Clayites to move away from the identities which had dominated the previous decade.

But in one instance, at least, the old personalism continued to maintain its sway. The 1836 election in Louisiana might well stand as a metaphor of Andrew Jackson's place in the political history of the state. For all the noise about abolitionist threats and regional concerns could not cover over the dominant issue in that campaign, which really had to do with whether Andrew Jackson would be vindicated or rejected in his selection of a successor. Even in the disruption of Democratic unity flowing from the divisiveness of his choice, Jackson's spell continued to work and his imprimatur proved sufficient to carry Van Buren to victory, a triumph more reflective of his will and personality than of anything said or done by the official candidates. Once again the state remained true to the Hero of New Orleans.

Appendix: On the Term *Creole*

The literature on the meaning of *creole* is both voluminous and contentious. Key to an understanding of the difficulties surrounding the term's usage lies in recognition that language represents a consensus of those who speak it and in awareness that confusion generally springs from failure to understand the difference between two distinct questions: how is the term generally understood in a particular community of today, and how was it used in a clearly defined area during a specified period of the past. The present work does not contest the right of members of any group to decide, like Humpty-Dumpty, that a word shall mean just what they choose it to mean; it only challenges any attempt to impose such selective current meaning on the community of pre–Civil War Louisiana. This, regrettably, is precisely what the defenders of the creole myth attempt to do.

Edward Laroque Tinker, a scholar of considerable if sometimes questionable learning, for many years presumed to speak *ex cathedra* in his insistence that when "the noun Creole is used, it can mean only one thing and that is a pure white person born of European parents in Spanish or French colonies."[1] A native New Yorker, Tinker perhaps failed to recognize that a strict application of his definition would strip creole identity from all Louisianians born after 1803, excluding even such as Charles E. A. Gayarré. The Louisiana protagonists of the creole mythology, therefore, while still embracing the "pure white" criterion, found it necessary to adopt a usage widening the application of the term to those descended from colonial stock.

1. Edward L. Tinker, *Toucatou* (New York, 1928), 8.

Thus a typical study of the 1930s could state: "*Créole* . . . a person of pure white race born in colonial Louisiana of French or Spanish parentage; also applied to descendants of the foregoing."[2]

This dictate has been so consistently advanced by Louisiana authors and historians that authorities in a broad range of disciplines generally accept it without question. The eminent student of cultural relations between the United States and France, Howard Mumford Jones, for a single example, has written that "a Creole is properly a member of the French-speaking portion of the ruling class in Louisiana whether of Spanish or French descent or both. He is never an Acadian."[3]

The degree to which this thesis has been embraced in Louisiana is demonstrated in a 1939 poll of a cross section of those identifying themselves as creole, all of whom insisted upon the white Latin definition, with almost complete agreement that members of the group comprised the rich and cultured leaders in every phase of New Orleans life before the Civil War.[4] Significantly, no one at a meeting of the Louisiana Historical Society in October 1915 found anything strange or amusing in the adoption of a motion to the effect that the "definition of 'creole' as stated by Prof. [Alcée] Fortier be the correct one." Professor Fortier's explication, it need hardly be added, stressed the white Latin ancestry so central to the mythic credo.[5]

It is difficult to see how this distortion could continue to persist through the pages of Fortier, Grace King, and a host of others down to and including a steady stream of current writers on Louisiana history, folklore, and lifestyles. How can the exclusionary definition disregard such newspaper notices as these, for example, which clearly refute a pure white connotation of the term in antebellum Louisiana: Joseph Veillon advertises to sell "three fine negro slaves, creoles"; Mrs. Plantevignes, "being about to depart for France, desires to sell the following servants, all creoles of this city"; "Wanted to purchase, a seamstress who can also wash and iron . . . she must be a creole or acclimated"; W. H. Overton advertises for sale his plantation

2. Simone de la Souchère Deléry and Gladys Anne Renshaw, *France d'Amérique* (New York, 1933), 184.

3. Howard Mumford Jones, *America and French Culture, 1750–1848* (Chapel Hill, N.C., 1947), 115.

4. Ben Avis Adams, "A Study of the Indexes of Assimilation of the Creole People in New Orleans" (M.A. thesis, Tulane University, 1939).

5. *PLHS*, VIII (1915), 54.

near Alexandria, "with or without Fifty Prime Negroes, principally creoles"; Isaac McCoy offers for sale "the Negress Louise, a creole"; Mossy et
Alpuente advise that on Monday, April 26, 1824, "sera vendu à la bourse
d'Elkins . . . Léon, negre àgé de 19 ans, créole."[6] Illustrative of the complete
irrelevance of race or status in determination of creole identity, the New
Orleans Bee in an 1850 article praised the artistic skills of Eugene Warburg,
a local sculptor, identifying him as "a young Creole of our city," the son of
Jewish Daniel Warburg and Marie Rose, a Cuban negro slave.[7] Referring to
a particularly attractive woman who had caught his fancy in the 1840s,
Judge E. H. Durrell noted that "She is a Creole, and, perhaps I need not
add, a quarteronne."[8] Even as late as 1868, George Rose reported that "I
had always been under the impression that the word Creole was intended
to express a person of mixed blood, but have been informed that such is not
the case; for that, in Louisiana, a Creole only means native American,
whether the descendant of colored or white parents."[9]

The official records of the state are equally unambiguous. The transcript
of a slave trial during the Spanish colonial regime clearly identifies one
group of bondsmen as creoles, and in 1812 the state legislative act incorpo-
rating the militia corps of free men of color directed that it be composed of
those "chosen from among the Creoles, and from among such as shall have
paid a State tax."[10] Finally, an early typical legal deposition notes: "To be
known by everyone who sees this letter that I Don Juan Bautista Poeyfarre,
neighbor of this City, grant that I have really sold to Don Pedro Bailly, free
mulatto of this neighborhood a piece of land of my own. . . . P[edro] Bailly
Senior being sworn . . . deposeth . . . that he is a creole of this Country."[11]

In a strange kind of alliance, defenders of the claim that creole always
connotes whiteness frequently join protagonists of nonwhite segments of
the antebellum native population in employing the term creole of color to

6. Louisiana Courier, June 11, 24, 1828; Louisiana Advertiser, November 12, 1823, January 20, April 6, 26, 1824.

7. New Orleans Bee, December 13, 1850.

8. [Durrell], New Orleans as I Found It, 29.

9. George Rose, The Great Country; or, Impressions of America (London, 1868), 194.

10. Gerald L. St. Martin and Mathé Allain, "A Slave Trial in Colonial Natchitoches,"
Louisiana History, XXVII (1987), 58, 76; Louisiana Acts, 1812, p. 72.

11. Morgan v. Livingston (1818), Louisiana State Supreme Court Archives, Earl K. Long
Library, University of New Orleans.

provide a kind of compromise phraseology in this semantic dispute. Despite its seeming linkage to valid terms like *free person of color, free man of color,* and *free woman of color,* the phrase actually has no historical validity, being essentially unknown to the antebellum period. It reflects instead the shaping power of the white racial dogma of the post–Civil War era.[12]

As for the Latin requirement, the evidence is again overwhelming. *Norman's New Orleans and Environs,* published in 1845, says: Creoles are those "who are born here . . . without reference to the birth place of their parents."[13] Oakey Hall tells us, "understand, good reader, that Creole is a word signifying 'native,' and applies to all kinds of men and things indigenous to New Orleans,"[14] and Harriet Martineau, "Creole means *native.* French and American creoles are natives of French and American extraction."[15] The equally observant J. H. Ingraham instructed his readers: "The term *Creole* will be used throughout the work in its simple Louisiana acceptance, *viz.,* as the synonym of *native.* . . . The children of northern parents, if born in Louisiana, are 'Creoles.'"[16] An 1839 note in the *Bee,* which prided itself on its attachment to the Gallic community of the city, observed that "A Kentuckian is a Creole of Kentucky and a Yankee a Creole of New England . . . and an Irishman of Ireland. . . . A Creole is a native of the state or country where he or she may have been born."[17] In reference to a recently elected member of the state legislature, the New Orleans *Picayune* in 1844 described Gilbert Leonard as "a native of New Orleans and the son of creole parents. In his blood, however, there is an admixture, and no bad one either; his paternal grandfather being an Irishman, and his grandmother on the same side, a native of Italy."[18]

Senator Josiah Stoddard Johnston, ruminating on the ethnic quarrels of

12. The need to provide a narrower identification within the creole group did allow occasional variations from this general rule, as when Governor Claiborne was warned that "certain Creoles of color in the City of New Orleans" were plotting to return Louisiana to Spain. See Carter, ed., *Territory of Orleans,* 575.

13. *Norman's New Orleans,* 73.

14. Oakey Hall, *The Manhattaner in New Orleans* (New York, 1851), 17.

15. Martineau, *Retrospect,* II, 136.

16. [Joseph H. Ingraham], *The Quadroone; or, St. Michael's Day* (2 vols.; New York, 1841), I, ix.

17. New Orleans *Bee,* May 19, 1839.

18. New Orleans *Times-Picayune,* September 6, 1844.

his day, reported that he "would be very happy to do away with the distinction [between Anglo-American and Gallic Louisianians]. But this cannot be done, until our children all become creoles of Louisiana."[19] Governor Paul O. Hébert, unquestionably accepted by his contemporaries as both creole and Cajun, once declared that he "was born in 1818 in the parish of Iberville—both my parents were creole born—my mother of American extraction—being a Hamilton."[20] During the debates at the constitutional convention of 1845, the "two leading candidates for governor," William de Buys and Isaac Johnson, Florida champion of the Anglo-American Democrats, were both described as creoles.[21] Johnson had long claimed creole identity, once telling Edward Douglass White, "I am a creole. . . . I had considered myself a creole in the ordinary acceptance of the term," by which he clearly meant native born.[22] In the same 1845 convention proceedings James F. Brent of Rapides, completely identified with Anglo-American political and cultural dominance, told his colleagues: "I am a native of Louisiana, but I would be the last one to secure a monopoly for creoles."[23] Timothy Flint, author of several works on early Louisiana, himself a Massachusetts Yankee, referred in this manner to his Louisiana-born son: "Mrs. Johnston will have seen my rustic son. He is a very good lad, & only wants a few months of teaching, under her eye and example, to make a tolerable concern, for a creole."[24] The New Orleans *Mercantile Advertiser* referred in 1833 to John B. Dawson, incorrectly but unambiguously, as a "creole of Louisiana . . . a native of the parish in which he resides, the District of Florida,"[25] though Dawson was in no way allied to the Latin element in the state. Commenting on his election to Congress in 1844, Isaac Morse, born in New Iberia of non-Latin parents, advised a friend: "In the lower parishes . . . they ran the Creole question into me . . . quoique créole, je n'étais pas

19. Josiah S. Johnston to Isaac L. Baker, December 24, 1823, in Johnston Papers, HSP.

20. Paul O. Hébert to John F. H. Claiborne, December 7, 1852, in Claiborne Collection, MSA.

21. Robert J. Ker, comp., *Debates in the Convention of Louisiana* [1845] (New Orleans, 1845), 87.

22. New Orleans *Mercantile Advertiser*, July 1, 1834.

23. Ker, comp., *Debates in the Convention of Louisiana*, 9.

24. Timothy Flint to Josiah S. Johnston, November 21, 1827, in Johnston Papers, HSP.

25. Quoted in New Orleans *Bee*, September 2, 1833.

aussi bon créole que Bordelon,"[26] and a report describing the pupils at Mme. Sidonie de la Houssaye's female academy in Franklin in 1851 speaks of French creoles and English creoles.[27]

It should be noted, conversely, that the claim in some accounts that creole identity attached to the foreign born of long residence and Gallic ancestry or others who became assimilated into the traditional Latin culture is without merit.[28] Although Edward Douglass White had been raised since infancy in the Gallic area of the state and spoke French as well as he did English, he was never allowed creole status, having been born in Nashville. Nor were Pierre Soulé, Pierre Rost, Etienne Mazureau, Joseph Roffignac, and Pierre Derbigny, all French born, or Louis Moreau Lislet, Louise Davezac Livingston, or John Davis, all immigrants from St. Domingue, ever admitted to Louisiana creole ranks, despite their long and intimate identity with the Gallic community of the state.

For some reason, modern students of Acadian culture insist on denying historic creole status to members of that distinctive portion of the Louisiana community. The Acadian migrants to Louisiana in the eighteenth century did not settle in an area totally without inhabitants, and the earlier French and Spanish settlers who had preceded them have no trouble in gaining acceptance as legitimate creoles. But with the Acadians it is a different story. The compiler of a dictionary of the Cajun language maintains, "In Louisiana the term Creole applies to both the Spaniards and the French whose ancestors came to Louisiana directly from Europe. The Cajuns, whose ancestors came from Acadia, are obviously not Louisiana Creoles."[29] Another account advises that when Frederick Law Olmsted's *Cotton Kingdom* refers to creoles in the Attakapas-Opelousas region of the 1850s, one should "read Cajuns; Olmsted was confused in his terminology."[30]

But clearly the confusion lies elsewhere than with Olmsted. Thomas Curry wrote Josiah Johnston during the 1832 congressional campaign that

26. Isaac Morse to William Nicholls, August 2, 1844, in Nicholls Family Papers, TU.

27. Franklin *Planters' Banner*, January 9, 1851.

28. Virginia Dominguez, *White by Definition* (New Brunswick, N.J., 1986), 102–103; Liliane Crété, *Daily Life in Louisiana, 1815–1830* (Baton Rouge, 1979), 69.

29. Jules O. Daigle, *A Dictionary of the Cajun Language* (Ann Arbor, 1984), xi.

30. James H. Dormon, *The People Called Cajuns: An Introduction to an Ethnohistory* (Lafayette, La., 1983), 48.

their fellow Clay supporter, Henry Adams Bullard, was certain to defeat the "Potent Creole"—the Acadian Alexander Mouton.[31] Edmund Vaughn Davis praised Mouton to Levi Woodbury as a "high-soul'd creole,"[32] and an 1842 newspaper clipping in the University of Southwestern Louisiana Mouton Collection labels the Acadian candidate "the Creole of the Prairies." An undated *Red River Republican* (Alexandria) clipping in the Emma Gardner Mouton Scrapbook in the Hill Library of Louisiana State University describes Mouton as "a creole of the state," and B. F. Linton in inviting Charles Gayarré to address the Democrats of Lafayette, St. Martin, and St. Mary Parishes in 1843 advised him that "the population of the above mentioned parishes is composed principally of Creoles."[33] Significantly, it was not as an Acadian but as a creole that Mouton was described to the delegates of the 1845 constitutional convention, and in commenting on the gubernatorial election of 1842, Henry Johnson blamed his defeat by Mouton on "the creole question."[34] It should be noted, as well, that in reporting on political matters the antebellum press regularly included the Acadian areas in their enumeration of "creole parishes."[35]

Perhaps the strongest refutation of the mythic tradition is found in a letter to the editor of the *Louisiana Courier* of October 28, 1831:

"Creole."—A most singular, and we think preposterous and absurd definition of this word, is contained in the *Emporium* of Wednesday last; namely, that none are creoles but such as are born of *European parents*. I have always been called, and so consider myself, a *creole*, notwithstanding my father and my father's father were called creoles. . . . [The word is one by which] we have ever been distinguished from those who have emigrated to the state . . . [and designates] such as have been born in the country, whether white, yellow or black, whether the children of French, Spanish, English or Dutch, or of any other nation.

31. Thomas Curry to Josiah S. Johnston, May 6, 1832, in Johnston Papers, HSP.
32. Edmund Vaughn Davis to Levi Woodbury, September 25, 1836, in Woodbury Papers, LC.
33. B. F. Linton to Charles Gayarré, September 28, 1843, in Gayarré Collection, LSU.
34. Ker, comp., *Debates in the Convention of Louisiana*, 87; Henry Johnson to William Johnson, July 18, 1842, in William Johnson Collection, MSA.
35. *Louisiana Advertiser*, July 27, 1827, March 7, 1834.

Bibliography

Manuscript Collections

Alderman Library, University of Virginia
    Harrison, Francis. Collection.
Dupré Library, University of Southwestern Louisiana
    Mouton, Alexander. Collection.
Firestone Library, Princeton University
    Blair-Lee Papers.
    Livingston, Edward. Papers.
Hill Memorial Library, Louisiana State University
    Butler, Thomas. Papers.
    Gayarré, Charles E. A. Collection.
    Hamilton, William S. Papers.
    Hennen-Jennings Papers.
    Mouton, Emma Gardner. Scrapbook.
    Neubling, Max. Letter Book.
    Palfrey, William. Papers.
    Tabor, Hudson. Papers.
    Taliaferro, James G. Papers.
    Weeks, David. Papers.
Historical Society of Pennsylvania
    Gratz, Simon. Collection.
    Johnston, Josiah Stoddard. Papers.
    Lewis-Neilsen Papers.
    Poinsett, Joel. Papers.
Houghton Library, Harvard University
    Palfrey Family. Papers.

Howard-Tilton Memorial Library, Tulane University
    Feriet Family. Papers.
    Nicholls Family. Papers.
    Slidell, John. Letter Book.
    Wisdom, John Minor. Collection.
King Library, University of Kentucky
    Clay, Henry. Papers.
Library of Congress
    Biddle, Nicholas. Papers.
    Blair-Rives Papers.
    Clay, Henry. Papers.
    Clay, Thomas. Papers.
    Donelson, Andrew Jackson. Papers.
    Harrison, J. Burton. Papers.
    Jackson, Andrew. Papers.
    Jefferson, Thomas. Papers.
    Personal Miscellaneous Papers.
    Polk, James K. Papers.
    Rives, William C. Papers.
    Trist, Nicholas P. Papers.
    Van Buren, Martin. Papers.
    Welles, Gideon. Papers.
    Woodbury, Levi. Papers.
Massachusetts Historical Society
    Everett, Alexander. Papers.
    Everett, Edward. Papers.
    Lawrence, A. A. Papers.
    Lawrence, Amos. Papers.
    Miscellaneous Papers.
    Otis, Harrison Gray. Papers.
Mississippi State Archives
    Claiborne, John F. H. Collection.
    Johnson, William. Collection.
Museum of the City of New York
    Livingston, Robert R. Papers.
New-York Historical Society
    Livingston, Robert R. Papers.
New York Public Library
    Lewis, William B. Papers.

Miscellaneous Papers.
Monroe, James. Papers.
Verplanck, Gulian C. Papers.
Southern Historical Collection, University of North Carolina
Hampton, Wade. Papers.
Trist, Nicholas P. Papers.
Tennessee Historical Society
Overton, John. Papers.

Public Records

Federal Records Center, Fort Worth, Texas
Records of the United States Eastern District Court of Louisiana
Edward Livingston v. *Benjamin Story*, Case #3380 (1834)
United States v. *Martin Gordon, Sr., and Martin Gordon, Jr.*, Case #4363 (1838)
United States v. *Peter K. Wagner*, Case #3666 (1836)
United States v. *Daniel T. Walden*, Case #2670 (1829)
Earl K. Long Library, University of New Orleans
Records of the Supreme Court of the State of Louisiana
United States Census, 1830 (National Archives Microform M19)
National Archives
Record Group 56, General Records of the Department of the Treasury
Charges Against Custom House Officers, 1833–1841
Collector's Letter Books of Correspondence Received, New Orleans, 1830
Collectors of Customs Applications, Louisiana
Letters from Banks
Letters to Banks
Letters from Collectors
Letters to Collectors
Miscellaneous Letters Received
Record Group 59, General Records of the Department of State
Letters of Application and Recommendation During the Administration of John Quincy Adams, 1825–1829
Letters of Application and Recommendation During the Administration of Andrew Jackson, 1829–1837
Letters of Application and Recommendation During the Administrations of Martin Van Buren, William Henry Harrison, and John Tyler, 1837–1845
Miscellaneous Letters Received, Secretary of State

Record Group 206, Records of the Solicitor of the Treasury
    Clerk's Returns, 1821–1929 (1838)
    General Index of Public Debtors, 1820–1868 (1868)
    Letters on Debts and Suits, 1821–1869
    Letters Received from the First Comptroller, 1820–1838
Record Group 217, Records of the United States General Accounting Office
    Miscellaneous Treasury Accounts of the General Accounting Office, First
        Auditor's Reports
Parish of Orleans Conveyance Office
    Record Book 1

Government Publications

American State Papers: Documents, Legislative and Executive of the Congress of the
    United States. Washington, D.C., 1832–1861.
Biographical Directory of the American Congress, 1774–1927. Washington, D.C.,
    1928.
Bullard, Henry A., and Thomas Curry, eds. A New Digest of the Statute Laws of the
    State of Louisiana. New Orleans, 1842.
Carter, Clarence, ed. The Territory of Orleans. Washington, D.C., 1948. Vol. IX of
    Carter, ed., The Territorial Papers of the United States. 26 vols. Washington, D.C.,
    1934–1962.
Compendium of the Enumeration of the Inhabitants and Statistics of the United States.
    Sixth Census. Washington, D.C., 1841.
Conspicuous Cases in the United States District Court of Louisiana. Compiled by the
    Survey of Federal Archives in Louisiana. 10 vols. New Orleans, 1940.
Debates and Proceedings in the Congress of the United States. Washington, D.C.,
    1824–1837.
Ker, Robert J., comp. Debates in the Convention of Louisiana [1845]. New Orleans,
    1845.
Louisiana Acts, 1820–1836.
Louisiana House Journal, 1820–1836.
Louisiana Senate Journal, 1820–1836.
"Memorial and Resolutions of Tradesmen and Others of New Orleans." Senate
    Documents, 23rd Cong., 1st Sess, No. 188.
"Memorial of New Orleans Citizens." Senate Documents, 23rd Cong, 1st Sess.,
    No. 187.
"Memorial of the Bank of Orleans for the Rechartering of the Bank of the United
    States." House Executive Documents, 22nd Cong., 1st Sess., No. 184.

"Memorial of the New Orleans Canal and Banking Company for Renewal of the Charter of the Bank of the United States." *Senate Documents*, 22nd Cong., 1st Sess., No. 108.

"Memorial of the President and Directors of the Louisiana State Bank for the Re-chartering of the Bank of the United States." *House Executive Documents*, 22nd Cong., 1st Sess., No. 153.

Moreau Lislet, Louis, ed. *A General Digest of the Acts of the Legislature of Louisiana Passed from the Year 1804 to 1827, Inclusive*. 2 vols. New Orleans, 1828.

Statistical Abstract, Fifth Census. Washington, D.C., 1831.

Statistical View of the Population of the United States from 1790 to 1830, Inclusive. Washington, D.C., 1835.

Other Printed Sources

Dart, B. W., ed. *Constitutions of the State of Louisiana and Selected Federal Laws*. Indianapolis, 1932.

Dodd, Donald B., and Wynelle S. Dodd. *Historical Statistics of the South*. University, Ala., 1973.

Livingston v. Cornell, 2 Martin (O.S.), 281–96.

Livingston v. Orleans Navigation Company, 3 Martin (O.S.), 309.

Livingston v. Story, 11 Peters, 351.

Story v. Livingston, 13 Peters, 351.

United States v. Louise Livingston et al., 11 Howard, 662.

United States v. The Mayor, Aldermen, and Citizens of the Cities of Philadelphia and New Orleans, 11 Howard, 609.

Newspapers and Periodicals

Alexandria, La.
  Alexandria Louisiana Messenger and Alexandria Advertiser, 1826
  Louisiana Herald, 1823–1825
Baltimore, Md.
  Niles' Register, 1820–1837
Baton Rouge, La.
  Gazette, 1824–1835
Charleston, S.C.
  Southern Agriculturist, 1828
Donaldsonville, La.
  La Fourche Gazette, 1826
  Louisiana State Gazette and Creole

Franklin, La.
    Planters' Banner, 1851
Monroe, La.
    Washita Gazette, 1825
Natchitoches, La.
    Courier, 1825–1827
New Orleans, La.
    L'Ami des Lois, 1820–1824
    Argus, 1824–1834
    Bee, 1830–1837
    Commercial Bulletin, 1835, 1836
    Daily Picayune, 1883
    Daily True Delta, 1853
    Emporium, 1832
    Le Franc Parleur, 1836
    Louisiana Advertiser, 1823–1836
    Louisiana Courier, 1820–1836
    Louisiana Gazette, 1820–1826
    Mercantile Advertiser, 1825–1834
    Merchants' Daily News, 1834
    Observer, 1835–1836
    Post, 1835
    Standard, 1836
    True American, 1835–1836
    Union, 1834–1836
    Whig, 1834
New York, N.Y.
    Hunt's Merchants' Magazine, 1851
St. Francisville, La.
    Asylum and Feliciana Advertiser, 1821–1825
    Crisis, 1828
    Florida Gazette, 1829
    Louisiana Journal, 1825–1826
    Phoenix, 1833, 1835
St. Martinville, La.
    Attakapas Gazette, 1830
Washington, D.C.
    Globe, 1834–1835
    United States Telegraph, 1833–1834

Published Correspondence

Adams, Henry, ed. *The Writings of Albert Gallatin*. 3 vols. Philadelphia, 1879.

Barck, Dorothy C., ed. *Letters from John Pintard to His Daughter*. 4 vols. New York, 1940.

Barker, Eugene, ed. *The Austin Papers. Annual Report of the American Historical Association for 1919*, Vol. II. Washington, D.C., 1924.

Bassett, John Spencer, ed. *The Correspondence of Andrew Jackson*. 6 vols. Washington, D.C., 1927–1935.

Brown, Everett S. "Letters from Louisiana, 1813–1814." *Mississippi Valley Historical Review*, XI (1924), 570–79.

Colton, Calvin, ed. *The Private Correspondence of Henry Clay*. New York, 1856.

Rowland, Dunbar, ed. *The Official Letter Books of W. C. C. Claiborne, 1801–1816*. 6 vols. Jackson, Miss., 1917.

Memoirs, Reminiscences, and Contemporary Accounts

Adams, Charles F., ed. *Memoirs of John Quincy Adams*. 12 vols. Philadelphia, 1874–1877.

"Andrew Jackson and Judge D. A. Hall (Report of the Committee of the Louisiana Senate, 1843)." New Orleans, 1843.

Benton, Thomas Hart. *Thirty Years' View*. 2 vols. New York, 1854.

Binns, John. *Recollections of the Life of John Binns*. Philadelphia, 1854.

Bullard, Henry A. "A Discourse on the Life, Character, and Writings of the Hon. François-Xavier Martin, LLD." *Louisiana Historical Quarterly*, XIX (1936), 45–69.

Clapp, Theodore. *Autobiographical Sketches and Recollections During a Thirty-five Years' Residence in New Orleans*. Boston, 1857.

Crockett, David. *The Life of Martin Van Buren*. Philadelphia, 1836.

Dart, Henry P., ed. "The Autobiography of Charles Gayarré." *Louisiana Historical Quarterly*, XII (1929), 9–27.

Davezac, Auguste. "Fragments of Unpublished Reminiscences of Edward Livingston." *United States Magazine and Democratic Review*, VIII (1840), 366–84.

Dufour, Cyprien. "Local Sketches." *Louisiana Historical Quarterly*, XIV (1931), 208–34, 393–497, 533–48.

Ellet, Elizabeth F. *Court Circles of the Republic*. New York, 1869.

Fitzpatrick, John C., ed. *The Autobiography of Martin Van Buren. Annual Report of the American Historical Association for the Year 1918*, Vol. II. Washington, D.C., 1920.

Foote, Henry S. *The Bench and Bar of South and Southwest*. St. Louis, 1876.

Gayarré, Charles E. "The New Orleans Bench and Bar in 1823." In *The Louisiana Book*, edited by Thomas McCaleb. New Orleans, 1894.

Hall, Oakey. *The Manhattaner in New Orleans*. New York, 1851.

Hamilton, James A. *Reminiscences*. New York, 1869.

Ivy, W. H. "The Late Henry A. Bullard." *De Bow's Review*, XII (1852), 50–56.

Lundy, Benjamin. *The Life, Travels, and Opinions of Benjamin Lundy*. Philadelphia, 1847.

Marigny, Bernard. "Reflections on the Campaign of General Andrew Jackson in Louisiana in 1814 and '15." *Louisiana Historical Quarterly*, VI (1923), 61–85.

"Memoir of the Honorable Henry A. Bullard, LLD." *Louisiana Historical Quarterly*, XIX (1936), 17–20.

Nolte, Vincent. *Fifty Years in Both Hemispheres*. New York, 1854.

Pearse, James. *Narratives of the Life of James Pearse*. Rutland, 1825.

"Report of the Committee of Inquiry of the Military Measures Executed Against the Legislature of Louisiana, Dec. 28, 1814." *Louisiana Historical Quarterly*, IX (1926), 223–80.

Sargent, Nathan. *Public Men and Events*. 2 vols. Philadelphia, 1875.

Sparks, W. H. *The Memories of Fifty Years*. Philadelphia, 1870.

Spear, Thomas J. *Ancient and Modern New Orleans*. New Orleans, 1879.

Weed, Harriet A., ed. *Autobiography of Thurlow Weed*. 2 vols. Boston, 1883.

Whitaker, John S. *Sketches of Life and Character in Louisiana*. New Orleans, 1847.

Wikoff, Henry. *Reminiscences of an Idler*. New York, 1880.

Winston, James, ed. "A Faithful Picture of the Political Situation in New Orleans at the Close of the Last and the Beginning of the Present Year, 1807." *Louisiana Historical Quarterly*, XI (1928), 359–433.

Descriptive and Travel Accounts

Alexander, J. E. *Transatlantic Sketches*. 2 vols. London, 1833.

Berquin-Duvallon. *Vue de la Colonie Espagnole du Mississippi*. Paris, 1803.

Bossu, Jean B. *Nouveaux Voyages aux Indes Occidentales*. Paris, 1802.

Brackenridge, H. M. *Views of Louisiana*. Pittsburgh, 1814.

Buckingham, James S. *The Slave States of America*. 2 vols. London, 1842.

Bullock, W. "Sketch of a Journey Through the Western States of North America." In *Early Western Travels*, XIX, edited by Reuben G. Thwaites. 32 vols. Cleveland, 1904–1907.

Conder, Joseph, ed. *The Modern Traveler*. 30 vols. London, 1830.

Daubeny, Charles. *Journal of a Tour Through the United States and in Canada, Made During the Years 1837–1838*. Oxford, 1843.

de Montlezun, Baron. *Voyage Fait dans les Années 1816 et 1817 de New Yorck à la Nouvelle-Orléans*. 2 vols. Paris, 1818.

Didimus, Henry [Edward Durrell]. *New Orleans as I Found It*. New York, 1845.

Evans, Estwick. "A Pedestrious Tour of Four Thousand Miles Through the Western States and Territories During the Winter and Spring of 1818." In *Early Western Travels*, VIII, edited by Reuben G. Thwaites. 32 vols. Cleveland, 1904–1907.

Fearon, Henry B. *A Narrative of a Journey of Five-Thousand Miles Through the Eastern and Western States of America*. London, 1819.

Ferrall, S. A. *A Ramble of Six Thousand Miles Through the United States of America*. London, 1832.

Flint, Timothy. *The History and Geography of the Mississippi Valley*. 2 vols. Philadelphia, 1832.

————. *Recollections of the Last Ten Years*. Boston, 1826.

Forstall, Edmund J. *The Agricultural Productions of Louisiana*. New Orleans, 1845.

Hall, Basil. *Travels in North America in the Years 1827–1828*. 2 vols. Philadelphia, 1829.

Hall, Margaret. *The Aristocratic Journey*. New York, 1931.

Hamilton, Thomas. *Men and Manners in America*. 2 vols. Philadelphia, 1833.

Heustis, Jabez W. *Physical Observations and Medical Tracts and Researches on the Topography and Diseases of Louisiana*. New York, 1817.

[Ingraham, Joseph H.]. *The Quadroone; or, St. Michael's Day*. 2 vols. New York, 1841.

————. *The Southwest. By a Yankee*. 2 vols. New York, 1835.

Keller, Herbert A., ed. "A Journey Through the South in 1836: Diary of James D. Davidson." *Journal of Southern History*, I (1935), 345–77.

Latrobe, B. H. *The Journal of Latrobe*. New York, 1905.

Levasseur, A. *Lafayette en Amérique, en 1824 et 1825*. 2 vols. Paris, 1829.

Martineau, Harriet. *Retrospect of Western Travel*. 3 vols. London, 1838.

————. *Society in America*. 2 vols. Paris, 1837.

Mémoires sur la Louisiane et la Nouvelle-Orléans. Paris, 1804.

Murat, Achille. *America and the Americans*. New York, 1849.

Murray, Charles A. *Travels in North America During the Years 1834, 1835, and 1836*. 2 vols. London, 1839.

Parker, A. A. *Trip to the West and Texas*. Concord, 1836.

Pierson, G. W. "Alexis de Tocqueville in New Orleans." *Franco-American Review*, I (1936), 25–42.

Pittman, Philip. *The Present State of the European Settlements on the Mississippi*. Cleveland, 1906.

Power, Tyrone. *Impressions of America*. 2 vols. Philadelphia, 1836.

Prichard, Walter, Fred Kniffin, and Clair Brown. "Southern Louisiana and Southern Alabama in 1819: The Journal of James Leander Cathcart." *Louisiana Historical Quarterly*, XXVII (1945), 735–921.

Robin, C. C. *Voyages dans l'Intérieur de la Louisiane*. 3 vols. Paris, 1807.

Rose, George. *The Great Country; or, Impressions of America*. London, 1868.

Royall, Anne. *Letters from Alabama*. Washington, D.C., 1830.

———. *Mrs. Royall's Southern Tour; or, Second Series of the Black Book*. 3 vols. Washington, D.C., 1830.

Saxe-Weimar Eisenach, Bernard. *Travels Through North America During the Years 1825 and 1826*. 2 vols. Philadelphia, 1828.

Stoddard, Amos. *Sketches, Historical and Descriptive, of Louisiana*. Philadelphia, 1812.

Stuart, James. *Three Years in North America*. 3 vols. Edinburgh, 1833.

Tasistro, Louis F. *Random Shots and Southern Breezes*. 2 vols. New York, 1842.

Trollope, Frances. *Domestic Manners of the Americans*. 2 vols. New York, 1894.

Warden, David B. *A Statistical, Political, and Historical Account of the United States of North America*. 3 vols. Edinburgh, 1819.

Directories and Annuals

Coleman, William. *Historical Sketch Book and Guide to New Orleans*. New Orleans, 1885.

Gibson's Guide and Directory. New Orleans, 1838.

Jewell's Crescent City Illustrated. New Orleans, 1874.

Norman, Benjamin. *Norman's New Orleans and Environs*. New Orleans, 1845.

Pamphlets

Barton, Edward H. *A Discourse on Temperance*. New Orleans, 1837.

———. *Introductory Lecture on the Climate and Salubrity of New Orleans*. New Orleans, 1835.

Halphen, Michel. *Mémoire sur le Cholera-morbus qui a Regne à la Nouvelle-Orléans en 1832*. Paris, 1833.

Letter of Mr. J. S. Johnston, of Louisiana, to a Gentleman in New York; In Reply to an Article on the Expediency of Reducing the Duty on Sugar. N.p., n.d.

A Letter to Edward Livingston, Esquire, Delegate from Louisiana to General Congress at Washington City, on the Subject of the Speech Delivered by Him, at Washington, at the Late Celebration of the Anniversary of the 8th of January, 1815. Natchez, Miss., 1828.

Livingston, Edward. *An Answer to Mr. Jefferson's Justification of His Conduct in the Case of the New Orleans Batture*. Philadelphia, 1813.

Rémarques Sur la Culture de la Canne à Sucre, à la Louisiane, et Sur la Diminution des Droits Sur les Sucres Etrangers. New Orleans, 1831.

[Rodriguez, Joseph]. *Défense Fulminante contre la Violation des Droits du Peuples*. New Orleans, 1827.

Secondary Sources

Abernethy, T. P. "The Early Development of Commerce and Banking in Tennessee." *Mississippi Valley Historical Review*, XIV (1927), 311–25.

Adams, Ben Avis. "A Study of the Indexes of Assimilation of the Creole People in New Orleans." M.A. thesis, Tulane University, 1939.

Baudier, Roger. *The Catholic Church in Louisiana*. New Orleans, 1939.

———. "The Creoles of Old New Orleans." Typescript, Tulane University, n.d.

Bettersworth, John K. "Protestant Beginnings in New Orleans." *Louisiana Historical Quarterly*, XXI (1938), 823–45.

Bispham, Clarence W. "Fray Antonio de Sedella." *Louisiana Historical Quarterly*, II (1919), 24–37.

Bonham, M. L. "A Conversation with the Granddaughters of General Philemon Thomas." *Proceedings of the Historical Society of East and West Baton Rouge*, I (1917), 48–49.

Bonquois, Dora. "The Career of Henry Adams Bullard, Louisiana Jurist, Legislator, and Educator." *Louisiana Historical Quarterly*, XXIII (1940), 999–1106.

Bretz, Julian P. "Early Land Communication with the Lower Mississippi Valley." *Mississippi Valley Historical Review*, XIII (1926), 3–29.

Burns, Francis P. "The Graviers and the Faubourg Ste. Marie." *Louisiana Historical Quarterly*, XXII (1939), 385–427.

Butler, Louise. "West Feliciana: A Glimpse of Its History." *Louisiana Historical Quarterly*, VII (1924), 90–120.

Caldwell, Stephen. *A Banking History of Louisiana*. Baton Rouge, 1935.

Caulfield, Ruby. *The French Literature of Louisiana*. New York, 1929.

Christian, John T. *A History of the Baptists of Louisiana*. Shreveport, 1923.

Corning, Charles R. "Eleazar Wheelock Ripley." Typescript, Louisiana State Museum, n.d.

Craig, Charles R. "John Slidell, Louisiana Politico, 1793–1847." M.A. thesis, Tulane University, 1948.

Crété, Liliane. *Daily Life in Louisiana, 1815–1830*. Baton Rouge, 1979.

Cunningham, Noble. *The Jeffersonian Republicans: The Formation of Party Organization, 1789–1801*. Chapel Hill, N.C., 1957.

Daigle, Jules O. *A Dictionary of the Cajun Language*. Ann Arbor, Mich., 1984.

Dart, Henry P. "The History of the Supreme Court of Louisiana." *Louisiana Historical Quarterly*, IV (1921), 14–71.

Dart, William K. "The Justices of the Supreme Court." *Louisiana Historical Quarterly*, IV (1921), 113–24.

Deléry, Simone de la Souchère, and Gladys Anne Renshaw. *France d'Amérique*. New York, 1933.

Deutsch, Eberhard P. "Jury Trials Under the Federal Rules and the Louisiana Practice." *Louisiana Law Review*, III (1941), 422–26.

Dominguez, Virginia. *White by Definition*. New Brunswick, N.J., 1986.

Dorfman, Joseph. "The Jackson Wage-Earner Thesis." *American Historical Review*, LIV (1949), 296–314.

Dormon, James H. *The People Called Cajuns: An Introduction to an Ethnohistory*. Lafayette, La., 1983.

Eriksson, Erik M. "Official Newspaper Organs and Jackson's Re-election, 1832." *Tennessee Magazine of History*, IX (1925), 37–56.

————. "Official Newspaper Organs and the Campaign of 1828." *Tennessee Magazine of History*, VIII (1924), 231–47.

Ficklen, John R. "Judge Gayarré's Histories of Louisiana." *Publications of the Louisiana Historical Society*, III (1905), Pt. IV, 14–20.

Flory, Ira, Jr. "Edward Livingston's Place in Louisiana Law." *Louisiana Historical Quarterly*, XIX (1936), 328–89.

Franklin, Mitchell. "Concerning the Historic Importance of Edward Livingston." *Tulane Law Review*, XI (1937), 163–212.

Freeman, Arthur. "The Early Career of Pierre Soulé." *Louisiana Historical Quarterly*, XXV (1942), 971–1127.

Gayarré, Charles E. "Historical Sketch of Pierre and Jean Lafitte." *Magazine of American History*, X (1883), 284–98.

————. *History of Louisiana*. 4 vols. New Orleans, 1885.

Goner, Samuel B. "Louisiana Law: Its Development in the First Quarter-Century of American Rule." *Louisiana Law Review*, VIII (1947), 350–82.

Gray, Lewis C. *History of Agriculture in the Southern United States to 1860*. 2 vols. Washington, D.C., 1933.

Green, Fletcher M. "Democracy in the Old South." *Journal of Southern History*, XII (1946), 3–23.

Green, George D. *Finance and Economic Development in the Old South: Louisiana Banking, 1804–1861*. Stanford, 1972.

Hardin, J. Fair. "The First Great Western River Captain." *Louisiana Historical Quarterly*, X (1927), 25–67.

Hart, W. O. "The Bible in Louisiana a Century Ago." *Publications of the Louisiana Historical Society*, IX (1916), 56–71.

Hatcher, William B. *Edward Livingston*. Baton Rouge, 1940.

Hunt, Carleton. "Life and Service of Edward Livingston." Louisiana Bar Association *Proceedings* (1903), 7–50.

Hunt, Charles H. *The Life of Edward Livingston*. New York, 1864.

Hunt, Louise Livingston. *Memoire of Mrs. Edward Livingston*. New York, 1886.

Ireland, Gordon. "Louisiana's Legal System Reappraised." *Tulane Law Review*, XI (1937), 585–98.

James, Marquis. *The Life of Andrew Jackson*. New York, 1940.

Jones, Howard Mumford. *America and French Culture, 1750–1848*. Chapel Hill, N.C., 1947.

Kernion, George C. H. "Samuel Jarvis Peters, The Man Who Made New Orleans of Today and Became a National Personality." *Publications of the Louisiana Historical Society*, VII (1913), 62–96.

Koch, Julie. "Origins of New England Protestantism in New Orleans." *South Atlantic Quarterly*, XXIX (1930), 60–76.

Lomask, Milton. *Aaron Burr: The Years from Princeton to Vice-President, 1756–1805*. New York, 1979.

Lynch, William O. *Fifty Years of Party Warfare*. Indianapolis, 1931.

McCutcheon, Robert P. "Libraries in New Orleans, 1771–1833." *Louisiana Historical Quarterly*, XX (1937), 151–58.

Malone, Dumas. *Jefferson the President: First Term, 1801–1805*. Boston, 1970.

Martin, François-Xavier. *History of Louisiana*. New Orleans, 1828.

Meyers, Marvin. "The Jacksonian Persuasion." *American Quarterly*, V (1953), 3–15.

Meynier, A., Jr. *Louisiana Biographies*. New Orleans, 1882.

Mitchell, Henry A. "The Development of New Orleans as a Wholesale Trading Center." *Louisiana Historical Quarterly*, XXVII (1944), 933–63.

Moore, Powell. "The Revolt Against Jackson in Tennessee, 1835–1836." *Journal of Southern History*, II (1936), 335–39.

Nettels, Curtis B. "The Mississippi Valley and the Federal Judiciary, 1807–1837." *Mississippi Valley Historical Review*, XII (1925), 202–26.

Noble, Stuart G. "Governor Claiborne and the Public School System of the Territorial Government of Louisiana." *Louisiana Historical Quarterly*, XI (1928), 535–52.

Parkhurst, Helen. "Don Pedro Favrot, a Creole Pepys." *Louisiana Historical Quarterly*, XXVIII (1945), 679–734.

Parton, James. *The Life of Andrew Jackson*. 3 vols. New York, 1860.

Pessen, Edward. *Jacksonian America: Society, Personality, and Politics.* Homewood, Ill., 1978.

Pfaff, Caroline S. "Henry Miller Shreve." *Louisiana Historical Quarterly,* X (1927), 192–240.

Posey, Walter B. "The Advance of Methodism into the Lower Southwest." *Journal of Southern History,* II (1936), 439–52.

Pound, Roscoe. *The Formative Era of American Law.* Boston, 1938.

Prichard, Walter, ed. "Some Interesting Glimpses of Louisiana a Century Ago." *Louisiana Historical Quarterly,* XXIV (1941), 35–49.

Ramke, Diedrich. "Edward Douglas[s] White, Sr., Governor of Louisiana, 1835–1839." *Louisiana Historical Quarterly,* XIX (1936), 273–427.

Remini, Robert V. *Andrew Jackson and the Course of American Democracy, 1833–1845.* New York, 1984.

Richardson, F. D. "The Teche Country Fifty Years Ago." *Southern Bivouac,* n.s., I (1885), 593–98.

Riley, Martin Luther "The Development of Education in Louisiana Prior to Statehood." *Louisiana Historical Quarterly,* XIX (1936), 595–634.

Robertson, Francis. "The Will of General Philemon Thomas." *Proceedings of the Historical Society of East and West Baton Rouge* (1917), 26–30.

Robinson, Elrie. *Early Feliciana Politics.* St. Francisville, La., 1936.

St. Martin, Gerald L., and Mathé Allain. "A Slave Trial in Colonial Natchitoches." *Louisiana History,* XXVII (1987), 57–91.

Schlesinger, Arthur M., Jr. *The Age of Jackson.* Boston, 1945.

Shugg, Roger W. "Suffrage and Representation in Antebellum Louisiana." *Louisiana Historical Quarterly,* XIX (1936), 390–406.

Skipwith, Henry. *East Feliciana, Past and Present.* New Orleans, 1892.

Smith, Culver H. "Propaganda Technique in the Jackson Campaign of 1828." *East Tennessee Historical Society's Publications,* VI (1934), 44–66.

Smither, Nellie. "A History of the English Theatre at New Orleans, 1806–1842." *Louisiana Historical Quarterly,* XXVIII (1945), 84–276.

Souvay, Charles L. "DuBourg and the Biblical Society." *St. Louis Catholic Historical Review,* II (1920), 18–25.

Stahl, Annie. "The Free Negro in Ante-bellum Louisiana." *Louisiana Historical Quarterly,* XXV (1942), 301–96.

Stephenson, Wendell H. *Alexander Porter, Whig Planter of Old Louisiana.* Baton Rouge, 1934.

Swisher, Carl B. *Roger B. Taney.* New York, 1935.

Taylor, Georgia F. "The Early History of the Episcopal Church in New Orleans, 1805–1840." *Louisiana Historical Quarterly,* XXII (1939), 84–276.

Tinker, Edward L. *The Palingenesis of Craps.* New York, 1933.

———. *Toucatou*. New York, 1928.

Tregle, Joseph G., Jr. "Another Look at Shugg's Louisiana." *Louisiana History*, XVII (1976), 245–81.

———. "Creoles and Americans." In *Creole New Orleans*, edited by Arnold Hirsch and Joseph Logsdon. Baton Rouge, 1992.

———. "Louisiana and the Tariff, 1816–1846." *Louisiana Historical Quarterly*, XXV (1942), 24–148.

Trufant, S. A. "Review of Banking in New Orleans, 1830–1840." *Publications of the Louisiana Historical Society*, IX (1917), 25–40.

Turner, Frederick J. *Rise of the New West*. New York, 1906; rpr., 1962.

Van Deusen, Glyndon. *The Life of Henry Clay*. Boston, 1937.

Walker, Alexander. *Jackson and New Orleans*. New York, 1856.

Waring, George E., and George W. Cable. *The History and Present Condition of New Orleans*. Washington, D.C., 1881.

Watkins, James L. *King Cotton: A Historical and Statistical Review, 1798–1908*. New York, 1908.

Way, R. B. "The Commerce of the Lower Mississippi in the Period 1830–1860." *Mississippi Valley Historical Association Proceedings*, X (1918), 57–68.

Wecter, Dixon. *The Saga of American Society*. New York, 1937.

Wellborn, Alfred T. "The Relations Between New Orleans and Latin America, 1810–1824." *Louisiana Historical Quarterly*, XXII (1939), 710–94.

Wigmore, John H. "Louisiana: The Story of Its Legal System." *Southern Law Quarterly*, I (1916), 1–15.

Wilkinson, James. *Wilkinson, Soldier and Pioneer*. New Orleans, 1935.

Winston, James E. "Notes on the Economic History of New Orleans, 1803–1836." *Mississippi Valley Historical Review*, XI (1924), 200–26.

Wood, Minter. "Life in New Orleans in the Spanish Period." *Louisiana Historical Quarterly*, XXII (1939), 42–709.

Zacharie, James S. "New Orleans—Its Old Streets and Places." *Publications of the Louisiana Historical Society*, II (1902), Pt. III, 45–88.

Index

Adams, John Quincy: political reaction to, in early Louisiana, 143, 153; in 1824 presidential election, 155, 161, 163, 164–65, 171–72; beginning of presidency of, 174–75; Livingston's relation to, 176–80; opposition to, in Florida parishes, 183; charged with revival of Federalist policies, 189–90, 194–95; accused of antislavery views, 197–99; defeated by Jackson, 208–27

Adams-Onis Treaty, 139, 143

Address to the Public Authorities of the United States, 305

Albany Regency, 322, 326

Allain, Valerien, 178

"American" ethnic faction: migration of, to Louisiana, 26; characteristics of, 31; creole reaction to, 31–32, 84–86, 89–90; its critical assessment of creole culture, 86–89; charges of, against "foreign faction," 91–92; dominance of, in some parishes, 39–41; and national officeholding, 70–71

Ancienne population, 23, 25, 26, 27, 80, 109, 114, 144

Baker, Isaac L., 99–100, 134, 136, 142, 147, 148, 154, 163, 171, 177, 186, 212, 216, 225, 242

Balize, 1–2

Banking, 18, 97, 259, 313–14

Bank of Louisiana, 137

Bank of the United States: importance of New Orleans branch, 18, 258; as central issue in 1832 campaign, 258–63; its role in 1834 financial stringencies, 285–87; mentioned, 193, 196

Barrow, Alexander, 247, 256, 266, 267, 315

Batture controversies, 121–22, 237–38, 306–307, 328–29

Bayon, Jerome, 295, 329

Beardslee, James, 94, 154, 185

Beauvais, Arnaud, 90, 102, 239, 240, 244, 250, 299

Benton, Thomas Hart, 190, 285

Biddle, Nicholas, 258, 261–62, 277, 286

Bissett, George, 155

Blair, Francis P., 260, 261, 272–73, 279–80, 281, 283, 292, 297, 309, 325

Booth, Louis M., 329

Bossier, Placide, 165, 241

Bouligny, Dominique, 116, 167, 175, 212–13, 231–32, 265

Bowie, Jim, 32

Bowman, Elisha, 49

Bradford, Fielding, 175, 186

Bradford, James M., 154, 181, 184, 309, 325

Breedlove, James W., 259, 318, 323–24, 330

Brent, James F., 341

Brent, William Leigh: characterized, 100; on Davezac, 125; defeats Johnston, 105, 146; on Tariff of 1824, p. 158; reelected to Congress, 162; supports Livingston for U.S. Senate, 168; casts Louisiana vote for Adams in 1824 election, 170–72; attacks Jackson, 213; loses congressional seat, 213–14, 224; mentioned, 155, 177, 181, 188, 191, 220

Broussard, Michel, 98

Brown, James, 143, 144, 145, 151

Brownson, John, 177, 213

Bry, Henry, 105

Buisson, Benjamin, 95

Burr, Aaron, 106, 118, 120, 124, 235

Butler, Thomas, 106–107, 135–36, 150–51, 153, 213, 219, 221, 224, 225, 230, 247

Cable, George Washington, 54

Cajuns, 38–39

Caldwell, James H., 29–30, 85, 299, 303–306, 335

Calhoun, John C., 129, 142, 144, 248–49, 255–56, 321

Call, R. K., 218

Canal Carondelet, 6, 168, 196

Carleton, Henry, 125–26, 177, 200, 241, 249, 252–53, 270

Carter, Robert M., 269

Catron, John, 316

Chew, Beverly, 232, 234

Cholera, 263–64

Christy, William, 301–305, 309–10, 315, 322, 327–28

Citizens Bank, 286, 307

Claiborne, William C. C., 55, 82, 112, 120, 122, 124

Clapp, Rev. Theodore, 50

Clay, Henry: ties of, to Johnston, 105; family connections of, 115, 143; support for, in Louisiana, 143, 145; 1824 presidential candidacy of, 154–56, 159, 161, 163–65; appointed secretary of state, 171; "corrupt bargain" charges against, 172, 213; heads anti-Livingston campaign, 179; death of, rumored, 220; masterminds 1830 Louisiana gubernatorial election, 240, 244; eroding of political position of, 253–54; defeat of, by Jackson, 263–64; pushes sale of federal lands, 317; place of, in Louisiana history, 334–36; quoted, 69, 211, 333; mentioned, 99, 175, 168–69, 200

Clay, John, 143, 165

Clinton, De Witt, 146

Clinton, George, 118

Coffin hand bills, 220

Collège d'Orléans, 44–45, 87, 123, 146

Commercial Bank, 281, 324

Compromise Tariff of 1833, pp. 267, 291, 300

Congressional districts, 61

Consolidated Association of Planters, 97

Constitution of 1812: as instrument of Gallic control, 55; structure of, 55–61; as issue in gubernatorial election, 287–90; calls for revision of, 287, 299

Cotten, Godwin B., 186

Crawford, William H., 144, 155–56, 161, 163, 165

Creole: in Louisiana mythology, 23–24; antebellum meaning of term, 25–26, 337–43

Creoles: characteristics of society of, 27–30, 70; attitude of, toward Americans and foreign French, 31–32, 80–87; in rural population, 37–39, 41; reaction of, to Louisiana Purchase, 54–55, 80, 84; and constitution of 1812, pp. 55–57, 61, 64; and Jackson, 142; and Clay, 143; fears of, of Native Americanism, 300, 303–304, 306

Crockett, Davy, 322

Cruzat, Manuel, 154–55, 175, 179, 233

Culbertson, John, 311

Cuvillier, Pierre A., 92–93

Daubeny, Charles, 50–51
Davezac, Auguste, 123–25, 132, 133, 148, 151, 160, 161–62, 168, 177, 179, 185, 200, 209, 210, 221, 236
Davidson, Richard, 243
David Walker's Appeal, 308
Davis, Edmund Vaughn, 343
Davis, John, 29, 342
Dawson, John B.: characterized, 108–109; ties to Jackson, 135, 154; nullification sympathies of, 256, 258, 280; complaints of, about Jackson, 234–35; loses bid for U.S. Senate seat, 247–48; Jacksonian candidate for governorship, 277–78, 284, 287, 295; mentioned, 225
de Armas, C. G., 160
de Buys, William, 300, 341
Declouet, Neuville, 70, 98
Derbigny, Pierre, 32, 112, 116, 213, 221, 222, 224, 238
Desha, Gen. Robert, 214
Donelson, Andrew Jackson, 125, 134, 171
Dow, Lorenzo, 48
Duhy, C. W., 171, 286, 289, 291
Duncan, Abner, 134, 136, 154
Duponceau, Peter S., 296
Dupré, Jacques, 239
Dupuy, Antoine, 179, 233
Duralde, Martin: as son-in-law of Clay, 70, 115, 143, 147, 148, 156, 159, 335; role in 1825 U.S. Senate race, 168; in 1826 congressional elections, 178–82; in 1828 presidential campaign, 225, 227; in 1830 gubernatorial election, 240–41, 244; and 1832 presidential campaign, 254; loss of influence of, 298; mentioned, 175, 299

Eaton, John, 124, 172, 235, 248, 256
Eaton, Peggy, 248
Education, 43–45
Elkin, Harvey, 259
Erwin, John, 143

Eustis, George, 161, 178, 227
Everett, Alexander, 102
Everett, Edward, 142, 211, 220, 254

Federal lands, 139–41, 314
Felicianas, 4, 10
Fenno, Capt. Edward, 93
Florida Bill, 90–91
Florida parishes, 10, 40, 49, 55–56, 64, 68, 89, 90–91, 140, 183, 234–35, 309, 325, 331
Foreign-born in Louisiana, 33–34, 65, 300–306
Foreign French: as third faction in Louisiana population, 26; origins and characteristics of, 32–33
Foucher, Peter E., 179
Free persons of color, 35–37, 41, 310–12
Fusilier, Agricole, 70, 98

Gaines, Edmund Pendleton, 315
Gallatin, Albert, 52, 118
Garland, Rice, 293
Garrison, William Lloyd, 309
Gayarré, Charles E. A., 45–46, 110, 293, 298, 315, 317, 324, 337, 343
Germans in Louisiana, 33
Gibson, John, 187, 191, 214, 220, 227, 254, 299, 300, 303–305, 306, 307, 316, 323, 326
Girod, Nicholas, 32
Gordon, Martin: characterized, 130; as leader of Louisiana Jacksonians, 134, 216, 222, 234, 249, 255, 291; as president of Orleans Navigation Company, 178, 196, 231, 286; appointed collector of customs at New Orleans, 233; clashes of, with Hamilton, 235; attempts of, at patronage expansion, 236; in 1830 gubernatorial campaign, 241–44; attacks Slidell, 269–76; backs Dawson in gubernatorial campaign, 277–81, 284–95; and pet banks selections, 276–77, 281–84; reappointment of as collec-

tor rejected, 292; challenges Porter's citizenship, 302; appointed agent for U.S. mint, 318; defaults on security bond, 318–19; affiliation of, with Union Bank, 319; mentioned, 212, 253, 259, 335
Green, Duff, 101, 297
Grima, Bartholomew, 30, 95–96, 160
Grima, Felix, 222–23
Grymes, John R., 120, 127–28, 132, 136, 151, 154, 160, 179, 223, 233, 260
Guidry, Louis, 98
Gurley, Henry H.: characterized, 108; as congressional incumbent, 162; in 1825 U.S. Senate election, 168; in 1824–25 presidential election, 169–72; in congressional elections, 178–79, 213, 224; attempts to win compensation for slaves, 198; resigns congressional seat, 245; mentioned, 212, 250

Hagan, John, 259
Haile, Robert, 242, 248, 301, 303
Hall, Dominick, 122, 132, 214
Hamilton, James A., 225, 238n36
Hamilton, William S.: characterized, 109; anti-Federalist principles of, 145; opposes Gurley in congressional election, 178–79; champions strict construction of Constitution, 183; in 1828 presidential election, 225; and Gordon, 235; defeated in gubernatorial election, 241–44
Haralson, Archibald, 186, 229–30, 247
Harper, Samuel H., 233, 238, 259
Harrison, J. Burton, 317, 325–26
Harrison, William Henry, 320–21, 329–30
Hayne, A. P., 218
Healy, George P. A., 333
Henderson, Stephen, 187
Hennen, Alfred, 126, 135–36, 226
Hewes, William G., 259, 281–82, 286, 324
Hiriart, Sebastian, 102, 178, 272
Holland, John H., 129, 281, 284, 293, 335

Holy Alliance, 91–92, 149
Hughes, Gen. John, 105
Hunt, Randall, 310

Ingersoll, Charles J., 259
Ingham, Samuel D., 236, 246, 250, 268

Jackson, Andrew: ambivalence toward, among Louisianians, 82; his impression upon New Orleanians in 1814–1815, pp. 131–33; network of friends in Louisiana, 133–36; identification of, with interests of the state, 142; antagonism toward, 142–43; in 1824 presidential campaign, 146–48, 154–64; wins some of state's electoral votes, 164–65; loses to Adams in House vote, 170–73; launched as candidate in 1828 presidential campaign, 184–87; equivocal position of, on tariff, 158, 191–92; character of, attacked, 199–200, 213–15, 220; campaign junket of, 215–19; carries Louisiana in presidential elections, 227–28, 263–64; opposition of, to nullification, 256–57; and Second Bank of the United States, 258–63; Nullification Proclamation of, 265; becomes embroiled in Gordon-Slidell party split, 271–76; supports Van Buren, 320; issues Specie Circular, 330; as critical factor in 1836 presidential election, 331–32; Healy's portrait of, 333; position of, in early Louisiana politics, 333–36
Jackson, Rachel, 132, 249
Jefferson, Thomas, 55, 81, 118, 120, 121, 122, 158, 183, 188, 195
Johnson, Henry: eases militia controversy tensions, 95–96; characterized, 103; on Auguste Davezac, 125; elected governor, 150–53; suspected role in Adams presidential victory, 164; in 1828 congressional election, 221–22; in 1829 Senate election, 231–32; elected to

Congress, 293; on the "creole question," 343
Johnson, Isaac, 108
Judiciary Act of 1807, p. 138

Ker, David C., 232, 233
Ker, Robert J., 291, 329

Labatut, J. B., 160, 259, 272, 308
Lacoste, Gen. Pierre, 93, 179, 215
Lafayette, Marie-Joseph, Marquis de, 8, 95
Laidlaw, Peter, 259
Lakanal, Joseph, 45
Land claims, 139–41
Landry, Trasimond, 272
Larche, Francis, 198
Larned, Sylvester, 49–50
Lawrence, Amos, 104, 106, 298, 312
Lee, Henry, 225
Leonard, Gilbert, 306, 340
Leonard, Henry P., 328
Lewis, Joshua, 186
Lewis, William B., 215–16, 273, 281, 283
Lewis, William D., 282
Linton, B. F., 244, 343
Linton, John, 163
Livingston, Edward: establishes first Episcopal church in New Orleans, 49; and federal jury legislation, 85; connection of, to the Trists, 103; characterized, 116–17; New York political career of, 118; dismissed from federal attorney post, 119; physical appearance of, 119; launches new career in Louisiana, 120–21; and batture controversy, 121–22; alliance of, with creole faction, 122; family life of, 122–23; recognizes political promise of Jackson, 131–32; elected to Congress, 146, 162; loses bids for U.S. Senate seat, 151, 167, 168–69; supports Jackson in House presidential election, 170; reelection of, to House, 175–76; patronage activities of, 177, 236–37,

253; loses House seat to White, 213, 221–22, 224; elected to U.S. Senate (1829), 230–32; declines appointment as minister to France, 237; clears debt to United States, 237–38; appointed secretary of state, 252; attempts to save Bank of the United States, 259–60; pens Jackson's Nullification Proclamation, 265; allies with Gordon against Slidell, 270–71; mentioned, 133, 198, 214, 316
Lockett, Henry, 253, 259
Louaillier, Louis, 199
Louisiana, state of: early routes into, 2, 3, 6; geographic regions of, 2–11, 50–52; banking in, 18, 97, 259, 313–14; "creole myth" in, 23–24, 337–43; gambling in, 21–22; as colony of France and Spain, 27–28; rural population of, 37–41; ethnic conflict in, 31–33, 79–96; education in, 27, 43–45; intellectual climate of, 29, 45–46; migration of Americans to, 26–27, 31, 81; free persons of color and slaves in, 34–37; religion in, 46–50; transportation in, 50–51; reaction of, to Louisiana Purchase, 54–55; constitutional structure of, 55–78; ethnic issue in politics of, 55, 57, 59, 61, 62, 64, 66–67, 68–69, 70, 72; distribution of suffrage in, 56, 63–65; court system of, 58; local government in, 58–59; political areas of, 62; election procedures in, 73–78; political patronage in, 75; political campaigning in, 74–77; dualistic nature of its politics, 79–80, 239, 244–45, 335; cultural tensions in, 81–96; legal system of, 84–85; city-state conflict in, 96–97; political leaders of, 98–130; personal ties of, to Jackson, 132–36; post–War of 1812 conditions in, 136–42; popularity of Clay in, 143; in pre-1824 national politics, 144; in 1824 presidential election, 146–48, 154–61, 163–73; and 1824 gubernatorial election, 149–53;

congressional elections of 1826 in, 177–82; 1828 presidential election in, 184–200, 208–11, 213–21, 225–28; beginning of organized political parties in, 209–10; 1828 gubernatorial and congressional elections in, 211–13, 221–25; 1830 gubernatorial election in, 239–44; 1830 congressional elections in, 245; 1831 Senate elections in, 252–53; response of, to the tariff and nullification controversy, 249–53, 255–57, 265–68; and Second Bank of the United States, 258–63, 285–87; 1832 congressional elections in, 263; cholera epidemic of 1832 in, 263–64; 1832 presidential election in, 253–64; 1834 gubernatorial election in, 277, 284–95; 1833 Senate election in, 279–80, 282–83; and "pet banks," 276–77, 281–82; and constitutional revision, 287–90; 1834 congressional elections in, 293; Native Americanism in, 300–306; reaction of, to antislavery movement, 308–13; 1836 Senate election in, 315–16; and French spoliation claims, 316–17; 1836 presidential election in, 320–32

Louisiana Constitutional and Anti-Fanatical Society, 310
Louisiana Legion, 92–95, 176, 304–305
Louisiana Loyal American Association, 305
Louisiana Native American Association, 303, 305
Louisiana Purchase, 80, 140
Louvet, Edouard, 186

Macarty, Augustin, 142
McConnell, E. A., 252
McFarlane, James S., 233, 263, 269
McKaraher, James, 166–67, 169–71, 173, 174, 175
McLane, Louis, 273, 274, 276, 283
Marigny, Bernard: defines American section of New Orleans, 15; reputed lack of education of, 27; antagonism of, to American newcomers, 83, 89, 90, 113; characterized, 113–14; in 1824 gubernatorial campaign, 149, 151–53; as early Jackson supporter, 161, 167, 168; in 1826 congressional campaign, 179; in 1828 gubernatorial campaign, 212–13, 219, 221, 224; and Jackson's 1828 junket to New Orleans, 217, 219; in 1830 gubernatorial campaign, 239–40; and Citizens Bank, 286–87, 307; in 1834 gubernatorial campaign, 293; as foe of Native Americanism, 303; opposes division of New Orleans into municipalities, 308

Martin, François-Xavier, 32, 45, 111, 150
Martin, Valery, 98
Masonry, 198, 253
Maurian, Charles, 161
Mazureau, Etienne: as leader of foreign French, 92; characterized, 109–10; disdain of, for Jackson, 142–43; supports Livingston for Congress, 146; backs Clay in 1824 presidential election, 148; in 1824 gubernatorial election, 148, 151–52; resigns as attorney general, 151; supports Livingston for U.S. Senate, 153; in 1828 congressional and presidential elections, 209, 223; in 1834 gubernatorial election, 292; mentioned, 161, 162, 300, 305, 342
Mead, Joel K., 155
Mechanics and Traders Bank, 277, 281
Mercier, J. J., 161
Metoyer, Benjamin, 241
Militia controversies, 92–96
Moore, Larry H., 308
Moreau Lislet, Louis, 32, 90–91, 93, 110–11, 116
Morse, Isaac, 341–42
Morse, Nathan, 210, 259
Murat, Achille, 29
Murrell, John A., 309

Native American Association, 303, 305
Native American movement, 300–306
New Orleans: approaches to, in early
    1800s, 1–6; description of, 11–22; subdi-
    visions of, 12–16; as export center, 16–
    18; as financial center, 18; intellectual
    climate of, 29, 45–46; theaters in, 29–
    30; foreign-born population of, 32–34;
    slaves and free persons of color in, 34–
    37; governmental structure of, 59;
    restraints on legislative representation
    of, 63, 66–69; as nerve center of Louisi-
    ana politics, 71–72; ethnic strife in, 88–
    91; attacks on position of, as state capi-
    tal, 89; militia controversies in, 92–
    96; clash of, with rural parishes, 96;
    political leaders of, 109–30; Jackson's
    activities in, 131–33, 214–19; cholera
    epidemic of 1832 in, 263–64; 1832 may-
    oralty campaign in, 278, 280–81, 284;
    as center of Native Americanism, 303–
    306; revival of ethnic tensions in, 306–
    308; division of, into municipalities,
    308; abolitionist fears in, 308–12
Nicholas, Robert Carter, 315
Nicholson, John, 233, 273, 276, 278, 282
Nolte, Vincent, 124, 218–19
Nowell, W. W., 317
Nullification controversy, 249–52, 255–58,
    265–68
Nullification Proclamation, 265

Oakey, S. W., 259, 286
Ogden, F. B., 219
Olivier, Charles, 70
Orleans Guards, 304
Orleans Navigation Company, 178, 196,
    231, 286
Overton, Walter H.: characterized, 103–
    104; connections of, to Jackson, 135;
    antagonism of, toward Livingston, 154,
    169; elected to Congress, 213, 221, 224;
    as 1830 gubernatorial candidate, 241–

44; retires from Congress, 245; loses
    enthusiasm for Jackson, 256; criticizes
    Jackson's Bank policy, 259; joins opposi-
    tion to Gordon, 278; makes bid for U.S.
    Senate seat, 279–83; mentioned, 177,
    212, 284, 338

Parton, James, 332
Peire, H. D., 273, 278
Penrice, John, 185
Peters, Samuel J., 307, 311
Pew, Thomas J., 187, 226, 254
Peychaud, Anathole, 219
Plauché, Jean B., 133, 135, 160, 259, 272,
    286, 303, 336
Poindexter, George, 283
Porter, Alexander: characterized, 98–99;
    seeks federal court appointment, 177;
    advises White, 221; supports Jackson's
    Nullification Proclamation, 265; suc-
    ceeds Johnston in U.S. Senate, 280,
    282; attacked as alien influence behind
    White, 289, 291, 302; quoted, 103, 107,
    108, 162, 176, 177, 211, 225, 226, 239,
    250, 254, 255, 257, 264, 301; men-
    tioned, 50, 97, 101, 143, 163, 220, 231,
    297
Preston, Isaac: characterized, 126;
    appointed attorney general, 151; cam-
    paigns for Jackson, 157, 160, 226;
    appointed register of land office, 233;
    breaks with Gordon's clique, 243, 268;
    mentioned, 135, 136, 232, 259
Prieur, Denis: characterized, 114–15;
    elected mayor of New Orleans, 219,
    245, 284; controls polls in 1828 Jackson
    victory, 226–27; and Jacksonian city
    patronage, 236; backed for governorship
    by anti-Gordon faction, 278–79, 280–
    81; collapse of candidacy of, 284; men-
    tioned, 241, 299, 305
Protestantism, 48–50, 86
Public lands, 139–41

Randall, David, 244

Richardson, R. D., 95, 154, 161, 166, 175, 184

Ripley, Eleazar: characterized, 129–30; arranges acquisition of *Louisiana Advertiser*, 185; in 1828 Jackson presidential campaign, 195, 210, 219, 226; backs Livingston for U.S. Senate seat, 231; joins Gordon's attempt to lure Hamilton from state, 235; 1830 bid of, for congressional seat, 245; posits Jacksonian anti-aristocracy program, 251; backs Dawson for governor, 277; elected to Congress, 293; attacks White, 315; mentioned, 160, 232, 246, 263, 328

Rives, William C., 237, 316, 320

Robertson, Thomas B.: elected governor, 83; administration of, 84, 89–96, 149; characterized, 107–108; vetoes usury bill, 136; criticizes federal neglect of Louisiana, 137, 141; aggravates ethnic discord in state, 151; as U.S. district judge, 176–77; mentioned, 134, 144, 155, 186

Robeson, William L., 95–96, 135, 188–89, 210, 233, 242, 243, 268, 273–74, 275–76, 278

Rodriguez, Joseph, 89

Roffignac, Joseph, 32

Roman, Andre B., 43, 102, 240, 241, 243, 244, 252–53, 266, 268, 298, 328

Rost, Pierre, 245, 342

Rousseau, Jean-Jacques, 160

Royall, Anne, 115, 116, 130, 236

St. Bernard Parish, 38

Saul, Joseph, 259

Saunders, Lafayette, 135, 136, 144, 213, 222, 224, 234, 245

Schlesinger, Arthur M., Jr., 193

Scott, Charles T., 213, 219

Sedella, Père Antoine de, 47–48, 198, 217

Shreve, Henry, 120–21

Sibley, John, 124, 165, 200

Skipwith, Fulwar, 107, 134

Slavery, 34–36, 41, 81, 191, 198, 308–13, 321, 323, 325, 329–30

Slidell, John: characterized, 128; on slavery and the sugar industry, 191; in 1828 presidential election, 210, 218, 223; appointed U.S. attorney, 233; assists Livingston, 238; break of, with Martin Gordon, 269–70; contests for party leadership with Gordon, 270–76, 277–79, 282, 284

Smith, Alexander, 269

Soulé, Pierre, 112, 292, 342

Specie Circular, 330

Spotts, Samuel, 243, 259, 268–69, 273–74, 276, 278, 284

Sugar industry, 159, 191–92, 250–51, 267–68, 290–91

Taney, Roger B., 259, 274, 281–84

Tappan, Arthur, 309

Tappan, Lewis, 309

Tariff controversies, 158–59, 190–92, 250–51, 252–53, 257–58, 266–68, 291, 300

Territorial Act of 1804, p. 84

Théâtre d'Orléans, 29, 304

Thibodaux, Henry S., 100–101, 181, 212, 220, 150

Thibodaux (La.), 7

Thomas, Philemon, 105–106, 150–51, 168, 211–12, 224, 245, 263

Trist, Hore B., 102, 123, 145, 223, 286, 294, 319, 325

Trist, Nicholas, 102, 123–24, 145, 208, 223, 319

Turner, Nat, 309

Union Bank, 281–82, 319

Urquhart, Thomas, 161, 209

Van Buren, Martin: as Jackson's secretary of state, 237; rivalry of, with Calhoun, 248, 255; role in Slidell-Gordon feud, 271–72, 275–76; chosen by Jackson as his successor, 320; weakness of, as candidate, 321–22, 324–25; attacked, 325–27; carries Louisiana in 1836 election, 331; mentioned, 163, 225, 303

Villeré, Jacques: first creole governor of Louisiana, 27; favors ethnic harmony, 82; attacked for pro-American policies, 114; in 1824 gubernatorial campaign, 149, 151–53

Waggaman, George, 253, 298, 322

Wagner, Peter K.: as pro-Jackson newspaper editor, 154, 185–86, 218, 229; anti-tariff stand of, 192; castigates social aristocracy, 195, 218, 260; in 1828 congressional elections, 222; as Gordon ally, 232, 268; appointed naval officer, 233; in 1830 gubernatorial campaign, 242; association of, with Dawson, 277; attacks Overton, 279–80; as public defaulter, 318

Walden, Daniel T., 238

Walker, Joseph, 283, 293, 324

Washington Globe, 76, 260–61, 273, 280, 285, 297

Webster, Daniel, 104, 128, 286, 320

Weed, Thurlow, 163–65

White, Edward Douglass: characterized, 101; quoted on 1828 presidential campaign, 208–209; defeats Livingston for Congress, 213, 221, 223–24; reelected, 245, 263; enters 1834 gubernatorial race, 277, 278, 284; attacked by Jacksonians, 287, 289–91; elected governor, 293; his appraisal of his administration, 296; beginning of his term in office, 297, 313–14; protests against his appointments, 300–302; disruption of his administration, 302–308; fans antislavery hysteria, 308–13; response of, to Texas Revolution and Seminole wars, 314–15

White, Hugh Lawson, 320–22, 324–26, 331

White, James, 101

White, Maunsel, 135, 142, 246, 261, 272, 286, 335

Wilkinson, James, 120

Willis, Joseph, 48

Withers, W. C., 160, 259

Woodbury, Levi, 324, 343

Woodrooff, Clark, 135